POWER, POSTCOLONIALISM AND INTERNATIONAL RELATIONS

Reading race, gender and class

Edited by
Geeta Chowdhry and Sheila Nair

London and New York

First published 2004
by Routledge
2 Park Square, Milton Park, Abingdon, Oxon, OX14 4RN

Simultaneously published in the USA and Canada
by Routledge
270 Madison Ave, New York NY 10016

Routledge is an imprint of the Taylor & Francis Group

Transferred to Digital Printing 2005

Typeset in Garamond by Taylor & Francis Books Ltd

British Library Cataloguing in Publication Data
A catalogue record for this book is available from the British Library

Library of Congress Cataloging in Publication Data
Power, postcolonialism and international relations: reading race, gender and
class / edited by Geeta Chowdhry and Sheila Nair.
p. cm.
Includes bibliographical references and index.
1. Postcolonialism. 2. Power (Social sciences) 3. International relations.
I. Chowdhry, Geeta, 1956— II. Nair, Sheila, 1959—
JV51 .P69 2002
327.1'01—dc21   2001051064

ISBN 0-415-32936-1 (pbk)
ISBN 0-415-27160-6 (hbk)

CONTENTS

CONTENTS

CONTRIBUTORS

Anna M. Agathangelou is the director of Global Change Institute, Nicosia, Cyprus and teaches at the University of Houston Clear-Lake. Some of her publications include: "Desire Industries: Sex Trafficking, UN Peacekeeping, and the Neo-Liberal World Order" with L.H.M. Ling The Brown Journal of World Affairs, Vol. X (1), Summer and Fall/2003 and "Gender, Race, Militarization, and Economic Restructuring in Former Yugoslavia and the U.S. Mexico Border" in Women and Globalization edited by Delia D. Aguilar and Anne E. Lascamana, Humanity Press, 2003.

Dibyesh Anand is currently completing his PhD at the University of Bristol. His thesis topic is "World politics, sovereignty and representation: the 'Tibet question' and the West". His publications include *Voices of Difference: Tibet and the Tibetan Diaspora* (Proceedings of the International Association for Tibetan Studies, Leiden University, Netherlands, 2001) and "(Re)Imagining nationalism: identity and representation in the Tibetan diaspora in South Asia" (*Contemporary South Asia*, 2000). His research interests include critical international relations theories, identity politics and Tibet.

J. Marshall Beier is Assistant Professor of Political Science at McMaster University. Recent publications include "Of cupboards and shelves: imperialism, objectification, and the fixing of parameters on Native North Americans in popular culture", in James N. Brown and Patricia M. Sant (eds) *Indigeneity: Constructions and Re/Presentations* (Nova Science Publishers, 1999) and, with Ann Denholm Crosby, "Harnessing change for continuity: the play of political and economic forces behind the Ottawa Process", in Maxwell A. Cameron, Robert Lawson, and Brian Tomlin (eds) *To Walk Without Fear: The Global Movement to Ban Landmines* (Oxford University Press, 1998).

Shampa Biswas is Assistant Professor of Politics at Whitman College. Her teaching and research interests include international relations, religious nationalisms, gender and Third World politics. She has presented papers on "Religious claims to identity: the shifting meanings of 'secularism' and 'nation'", "Globalization and postcoloniality" and "Gender, citizenship and identities". She has also published articles on Globalization and Indian nuclearization.

Geeta Chowdhry is Professor of Political Science at Northern Arizona University where she was also the Director of Women's Studies. Her teaching and research interests include political economy of development, gender and development, South Asia, postcolonial theory and international relations. Recent publications include "Communalism, nationalism and gender: the rise of the Bharatiya Janata Party (BJP) and the Hindu right in India", in Sita Ranchod-Nilsson and Mary Ann Tetreault (eds) *Gender, Nation and Nationalism: Feminist Approaches to Contemporary Debates* (Routledge, 2000) and "Engendering Development, Racing Women's Studies: core issues in teaching gender and development", in Mary Lay *et al.* (eds) *Encompassing Gender* (Feminist Press, 2002).

Siba N. Grovogui is Associate Professor of Political Science at Johns Hopkins University and is the author of *Sovereigns, Quasi Sovereigns, and Africans : Race and Self-Determination in International Law* (University of Minnesota Press, 1996), and several articles in books and journals in the field of international law, African studies, and international relations.

L.H.M. Ling is Senior Lecturer at the Institute of Social Studies in The Hague. She is the author of *Conquest and Desire: Postcolonial Learning between Asia and the West* (Macmillan, 2000), and she has published articles in *Asian Survey, Democratization, International Studies Quarterly, Journal of Peace Research, positions: east asia cultures critique, Review of International Political Economy, Review of Politics*, and *Women's Studies Quarterly*. Her research examines issues of democratization, hegemony, globalization, and subjectivity in international relations.

Sankaran Krishna is Professor of Political Science at the University of Hawai'i–Manoa where he was also Director of the Center for South Asian Studies. He is the author of *Postcolonial Insecurities : India, Sri Lanka, and the Question of Nationhood* (University of Minnesota Press, 1999), and he has published widely in international relations.

Sheila Nair is Associate Professor of Political Science at Northern Arizona University, USA. She is also Associate Fellow with the Institute of Malaysian and International Studies (IKMAS), National University of Malaysia. Her research and teaching interests include international relations, postcolonial theory, social movements, nationalisms, Southeast

Asia, and international political economy. Her most recent publications include "Human rights sovereignty and the East Timor question" in *Global Society* (2000) and "Colonial others and nationalist politics in Malaysia" in *Akademika* (January 1999).

Randolph B. Persaud is Associate Professor at the School of International Service, American University. His research and teaching interests include race and global politics, foreign policy analysis, international relations and political economy. He is the author of *Counter-Hegemony and Foreign Policy: The Dialectics of Marginalized and Global Forces in Jamaica*. His recent articles include "Marcus Garvey and the re-envisioning of sovereignty" in T. Shaw and K. Dunn (eds) *Africa's Challenge to International Relations Theory* (Macmillan, forthcoming).

ACKNOWLEDGEMENTS

This book is the result of a collaborative intellectual and political endeavor. As editors, we were keen to advance a postcolonial volume that not only contributed to the ongoing debates in international relations, but that was also reflective of our concerns with social justice and a progressive politics.

While the ideas for this book were shaped during intense and lively discussions between us, our collaboration with the other contributors to this project was critical to the final outcome accomplished in this volume. A workshop on this book was held during the International Studies Association Meeting in Los Angeles, California, in March of 2000. We are very grateful to the ISA Workshop Grants Committee for providing a grant in 2000–1, which enabled us to bring contributors together and helped get this project beyond the editors' abstract discussions.

We owe a special thanks to various friends, colleagues, and graduate students who helped us bring this project to fruition through either their moral support or direct assistance, and oftentimes both. We mention a few of them here and extend our heartfelt thanks to all. At Northern Arizona University (NAU) especially Sanjam Ahluwalia, Sara Aleman, Alex Alvarez, Mark Beeman, David Camacho, Jeff Ferrell, Sanjay Joshi, Sheryl Lutjens, Mary Ann Steger, and Neil Websdale provided collegiality, humor and a good working environment. We are very grateful for the kindness of many good friends in India, North America and Malaysia. Sheila is especially indebted to Sumit Mandal for his unwavering support and solidarity during the course of this project.

We thank Sumit for directing us to the Langston Hughes poem excerpted in the introduction, and Jessica Urban for the Martin Espada verse.

Edythe Weeks, Jessica Urban, and Krisztina Pongratz assisted in preparing various parts of the bibliography. Jessica Urban did excellent work in the final editing stages of this project and clearly went beyond the call of duty in carrying out her responsibilities. Louella Holter also provided valuable editing assistance and helped produce the final typescript. We thank Stephen Wright, Chair of the Department of Political Science, and Joseph

Boles, Director of Women's Studies, who gave us encouragement and support, particularly in the provision of student assistance.

If it were not for Craig Fowlie's interest and enthusiasm early in the project, and quick turnaround on the proposal we sent to Routledge, we would not be at this stage. We thank him for his support and other members of the Routledge staff including Heidi Bagtazo, Grace McInnes, and Alfred Symons for seeing us through. We are grateful for the anonymous reviewers' comments and constructive suggestions. Needless to say, the editors are responsible for any shortcomings or limitations of this volume.

The editors are also grateful to each other for the friendship and camaraderie which resulted in this endeavor, and the indulgences we permitted ourselves including sushi at Sakura's, which contributed in no small way to our well-being during this project.

This book would not have been possible without the love and support of our families who were critical to the timely completion of this project, even if they did not fully understand our preoccupation with the volume. Geeta is deeply grateful to many people whose ideas, love, and caring have guided her through the years: her father Jai Narain who taught her the value of knowledge, caring, and justice and whose memory still guides her, her mother Tripti Devi who taught her courage, the virtue of struggle, and the value of an education, her partner Mark Beeman whose intellectual companionship, emotional support, and humor have always made the difficult times easier, and her son Jai who has been a source of joy and always a link with reality. His appreciation for books, travel, adventure, and justice at a young age has made it all worthwhile. Meera, Ajay and Priya Shankar; Sudha, Ajay, Raghav and Pranav Sarin; A.K, Suneeti, Vishal and Udai Singh; Maxine and William Beeman have provided home, love, intellectual support and endless distractions for Geeta through many projects.

Sheila is indebted to her family, especially her parents Bhaskaran and Madhavi, who have provided unconditional love, supported her choices, and shown her the importance of staying grounded. As first-generation Malaysian Indians their narratives of migration, colonization, the occupation, and struggle have had a powerful impact on her own life. Mani and Rajan Pillai, Shyama Nair, Shobha Nair and David Wong, Ramesh Nair and Ng Sai Yeang, Reshmi Rajan, Karine Nair Wong, Jenna Nair and the most recent addition Jeevan Nair, have in their own exemplary and loving ways contributed to this project. From the first Malaysian generation to the third, her family is a wonderful reminder of how postcoloniality is constantly being mediated in the home and the world.

This volume is dedicated to our families.

Geeta Chowdhry and Sheila Nair
Flagstaff, Arizona
July 2001

1

INTRODUCTION

Power in a postcolonial world: race, gender, and class in international relations

Geeta Chowdhry and Sheila Nair

The past has been a mint
Of blood and sorrow.
That must not be
True of tomorrow.
　　　(Langston Hughes)

We have to imagine the possibility of a more just world before
the world may become more just.
　　　　　　　　　　　　　　(Martin Espada)

This book comes out of our concerns with the relative neglect of questions concerning inequality and justice in the field of international relations (IR).[1] With the ascendance of a neo-liberal paradigm, one that shapes not only the field but also international and national politics and policy, we find an increasing dissimulation around questions concerning equity, poverty, and powerlessness. With the end of the cold war, global infatuation with neo-liberal economics has intensified the peripheralization of the South along economic, political, social, and cultural lines. The facile notion that we have reached the "end of ideology" obscures the workings of power in a global capitalist political economy, and disguises its cultural and ideological under-pinnings. It further elides the racialized, gendered, and class processes that underwrite global hierarchies. Conventional IR with its focus on great power politics and security, read narrowly, naturalizes these hierarchies and thus reproduces the status quo. The theoretical insights generated by post-colonial studies offer a different vantage point than conventional IR from which to explore these concerns in international relations.

Despite its significance in other fields, such as literary studies, anthro-pology, and cultural studies, postcolonial theory has only recently made its presence felt in the field of IR. Its entry into the field, however, signifies to us an important theoretical shift in IR, albeit one that has not been accorded sufficient attention by the discipline. The significance of the postcolonial move in IR, which draws from already existing critical literatures such as Marxism, postmodernism, and feminism, is its attention to the imbrication of race, class, and gender with power. Such an attentiveness leads to different kinds of questions in the literature and constitutes an effort to generate an alternative critique of global power hierarchies and relations.

In this volume we are not only cognizant of some of the concerns generated in the wider postcolonial literature, but we are equally, if not more consciously, engaged by the need to advance alternative postcolonial readings of international relations. We believe that the strength and complexity of this volume rests not on a single reading or interpretation, but rather on a multiplicity of interpretations, voices, and struggles evident across different chapters. However, the volume as a whole collectively grapples with some of the concerns noted above including questions pertaining to the ways in which race, gender, and class relations on a global and national scale were, and continue to be, critical to the production of power in IR.

In assuming a postcolonial approach to the study of IR we are attentive like many critical IR scholars – postmodernists, Marxists, and feminists – to the margins of the discipline and the marginalized, but we also believe that a postcolonial approach adds a distinctive voice and critique. While conventional IR obscures the racialized, gendered, and class bases of power, and in fact as suggested earlier naturalizes these divisions, critical IR problematizes these sources and workings of power. However, the latter is less able or willing, with a few exceptions, to address the intersections of race, class, and gender in the construction of power asymmetries. Further, this genre of critical IR does not adequately engage the cultural politics of the colonial past and postcolonial present, a politics that accompanies the contestations surrounding global hierarchy. Postcolonial theory adds significantly to the critical IR literature by assisting in the interrogation of such a politics and addressing the ways in which historical processes are implicated in its production.

Like much of postcolonial scholarship, we begin with the premise that imperialism constitutes a critical historical juncture in which postcolonial national identities are constructed in opposition to European ones, and come to be understood as Europe's "others"; the imperialist project thus shapes the postcolonial world and the West. In addition, the wider postcolonial literature addresses important concerns such as the impact of colonial practices on the production and representation of identities, the relationship between global capital and power, and the relevance of race, gender, and class for understanding domination and resistance. We propose in this volume to explore these issues and their significance for re-reading IR. Specifically, the contributors to this volume address the ways in which contemporary Western discourses on human rights, gender, security, trade, global capitalism, and immigration, for example, have been constructed and represented, and the significance of such constructions for international politics. The articulation of power on a global scale can only be fully understood, as we suggest in this volume, by being more attentive to the imperialist juncture, the intersections of race, class, and gender relations within and across national boundaries, and the construction and subversion of those boundaries.

Situating power in international relations

The study of power in international relations has been central to the organization and production of knowledge in the discipline. Power in mainstream, particularly realist and neo-realist, IR scholarship is closely bound up with notions of the state, sovereignty, anarchy, and order. These notions are intimately linked, for realists, to the concept of power, whose workings are seen as integral to the ordering and functioning of IR. We consider the structuring of anarchy, order, and state sovereignty, and their relationship to the production of power, to be central analytic concerns in IR theory. By exploring the explanations of power found in the major schools of thought in IR including realism and neo-realism, neo-liberal institutionalism, Marxism, feminism, and postmodernism, we better situate postcolonial contributions to the study of power.

In this section we make three claims about how power is situated in international relations. First, we argue that mainstream IR is premised on an understanding of power that privileges hierarchy, "rationality," and a predominantly Eurocentric worldview, thus mystifying the ways in which states and the international system are anchored in social relations. Second, although critical IR interrogates many of the assumptions of conventional IR, it nevertheless fails, with some exceptions, to systematically address some of the erasures of the latter such as the intersectionality of race, class, and gender in the production of power in IR. Third, while feminist IR challenges the gendered assumptions of both mainstream and critical IR, it generally neglects to address the relationship of gender to (neo)imperialism and race. We begin with an exploration of power in mainstream IR, followed by discussion of critical and feminist approaches to power.

Power and conventional IR

Power has been the foundation of international relations scholarship, particularly realist scholarship, whose treatment of power is exemplified in the classical realism of Hans Morgenthau. Morgenthau introduces his realist text, *Politics Among Nations*, with the following:

> International politics, like all politics, is a struggle for power. Whatever the ultimate aims of international politics, power is always the immediate aim. Statesmen and peoples may ultimately seek freedom, security, prosperity, or power itself. They may define

their goals in terms of a religious, philosophic, economic, or social ideal. They may hope that this ideal will materialize through its own inner force, through divine intervention, or through the natural development of human affairs. But whenever they strive to realize their goal by means of international politics, they do so by striving for power.

(Morgenthau 1950: 13)

Morgenthau further argues that by power "we mean man's control over the minds and actions of other men" (Morgenthau 1950: 13). This understanding of power may be ascribed to realists' adherence to Hobbesian assumptions concerning the "state of nature," and the proclivity of human beings to pursue their self-interest. In contrast, neo-realist thought highlights the anarchical state system and the way it structures international politics (Waltz 1959, 1979; Gilpin 1975, 1981; Krasner 1978). Neo-realism, or structural realism, attempts to

systematize Realism ... on the basis of a "third image" perspective. This form of realism does not rest on the presumed iniquity of the human race – original sin in one form or another – but on the nature of world politics as an anarchic realm.

(Keohane 1993: 192)

Further, for Waltz, the anarchic state system determines state behavior and international outcomes; "structures are defined by not all of the actors that flourish within them but by the major ones" (Waltz 1979: 93), and power is understood "in terms of distribution of (state) capabilities" (Waltz 1979: 192).

Both realism and neo-realism focus on anarchy and the rational, self-interested actor as key assumptions in their analyses of power relations in IR. However, as others have argued, it is hierarchy, not anarchy, and a Eurocentric understanding of rationality that is privileged and reproduced in both realist and neo-realist renderings of power in IR. Further, power through realist lenses appears disaggregated (military, economic, and political power are seldom examined relationally), instrumental, and as an end in itself. In this view power is also a property of states measured in terms of capabilities and resources, emerging from the interactions of states in an anarchic international system. The weak structuralist, universalist, rationalist, and masculinist underpinnings of realism have already been critiqued elsewhere (e.g., Wendt 1987; Tickner 1988; Walker 1989). In addition, as this volume shows, realism pays no attention to the ways in which power is constituted and produced, or the role of history, ideology, and culture in shaping state power or practices in international relations. Marshall Beier challenges realism's originary myths, arguing that they are based on problematic assumptions concerning traditional worldviews and lifeways of indigenous peoples in the Americas. He argues, in this volume, that to the extent that realist IR excludes such knowledges and lifeways, in deference to anarchy and the "Hobbesian impulse," it cannot be separated from the invalidation and subjugation of indigenous peoples. Consequently, it is clear from Beier's analysis that realist understandings of power are founded on certain erasures of history and memory that privilege a Eurocentric self. It further renders anarchy as a universal condition when it is obvious that notions of anarchy garnered from European accounts of encounters with indigenous peoples have reinforced racialized and gendered ideologies of imperialism and colonization.

Given the problematic assumptions regarding power and anarchy, we argue that it is necessary to situate IR in reference to its historical, political, economic, and social context. As Rosenberg suggests the (international relations) "discipline *begins* by rejecting any working conception of the social world as a totality" (1994: 94). The domestic/international or the internal/external dichotomies evident in realist thought reify the state and the international system and make invisible the social world invoked by Rosenberg.[2] The hegemonic sway of realist thought within the discipline, which rejects the necessity or possibility for taking the social constitution of states as a starting point for analysis, is in his view seriously flawed. However, this neglect is not only a problem in realist thought, as it has also shaped and influenced neo-liberal formulations of state power. For example, despite his neo-liberal institutionalist credentials, Robert Keohane invokes the realist view in *After Hegemony*. Keohane writes that the case for international institutions, which help realize "common interests in world politics," is made not by

> smuggling in cosmopolitan preferences under the rubric of "world welfare" or "global interests," but by relying on realist assumptions that states are egoistic, rational actors operating on the basis of their own conceptions of self-interest. Institutions are necessary, even on these restrictive premises, in order to achieve *state* purposes.
>
> (1984: 245)

In the neo-liberal view the state is no less predisposed toward power accumulation but it finds it in its own self-interest to create cooperative arrangements and international institutions or regimes that systematize and make more predictable inter-state relations in various "issue areas" (Keohane and Nye 1989). In an economically interdependent world of multiple actors, including non-state actors, states remain central to the analysis of power. Although cooperation among states is itself a desired goal for neo-liberals, cooperation in the long run secures power, wealth, and stability in international relations. Thus both neo-liberals and neo-realists subscribe to the view that power and wealth are "linked in international relations through the activities of independent actors, the most important of which are states, not subordinated to a worldwide governmental hierarchy" (Keohane 1984: 18).

These understandings of power relations render invisible or inconsequential the racialized, gendered, and class nature of power in IR. We argue, therefore, that state power and sovereignty are not only embedded in the structures, cultures, and social relations of local and nationally organized communities, but are also always grounded and mediated on a transnational scale. It is only once we begin to problematize the understanding of power evident in realist and neo-liberal approaches that we may come to better grasp how key relations of power are elided in these models. In heeding the "sociological imagination" in IR, which Rosenberg invokes,[3] we would need an alternative research agenda, one that attends to the socially, culturally, and politically constituted forms of power on a national and global scale. In recent years, confronted by the radical implications of new forms of political and social organizations, which potentially challenge state power, IR theorists have begun moving beyond analysis of the "spatial container" called the state.[4] The emergence of new social, religious, cultural, and nationalist movements on a transnational scale suggests that a conventional understanding of power, anarchy and order, security, and sovereignty is limiting. A growing literature on global civil societies, transnational movements and networks, and international organization attempts to resolve these ambiguities only to raise other questions about the construction and negotiation of boundaries in international relations (Sikkink 1993; Thiele 1993). Yet, this literature not only leaves unanswered, but also fails to pose, important questions about the production and mediation of power in IR. The emergence of critical IR scholarship in the form of Marxist, feminist, and postmodern scholarship has meant a closer interrogation of the power *problematique* in IR, but these critical schools of thought have done so in quite different ways and with different implications. We explore below some of the major contributions of this literature to rethinking power in order to show how and why postcolonial IR theory might differ from these other more established critical perspectives in the discipline.

Power in critical IR

Postmodern and Marxist IR

In Marxist theories of international relations, power is a characteristic feature of the workings of a capitalist world economy and is both a cause and consequence of the unequal relations between rich and poor, developed and underdeveloped, or metropolitan center and periphery. Where realists view these asymmetries as an inevitable outcome of states' political survival under anarchy, Marxists look upon these asymmetries as historically produced and indicative of capitalism's expansionist tendencies and inherent contradictions. Classical Marxists view imperialism as a necessary condition for capitalist development but they do not problematize the cultural representations that sustain the unequal relations of power between the colonizer and the colonized. Indeed, Marx's writings on India reflect orientalist assumptions and imagery as indicated in the following passage:

> we must not forget that these idyllic village communities, inoffensive though they may appear, had always been the solid foundation of Oriental despotism, that they restrained the human mind within the smallest possible compass, making it the unresisting tool of superstition, enslaving it beneath traditional rules, depriving it of all grandeur and historical energies ... We must not forget that this undignified, stagnatory, and vegetative life, that this passive sort of existence ... rendered murder itself a religious rite in Hindostan.
>
> (Marx 1978: 658)

Neo-Marxists, in contrast to classical Marxists, view the development and expansion of European capitalism as dependent on the "underdevelopment" and "peripheralization" of the Third World and the structuring of a capitalist world economy (e.g. Baran 1957; Frank 1967; Amin 1974; Wallerstein 1976).[5] This scholarship addresses how and why the present global distribution of wealth has mostly served to perpetuate already existing differences between and among different sectors and regions of the global economy. Power is thus seen to be rooted in unequal ownership and exchange relations, uneven development, and the extension of domination and control over the many by a privileged few. However, neo-Marxists, with some exceptions like Wallerstein (1991), generally do not address the cultural underpinnings of imperialist and neo-imperialist relations.

Gramscian scholars address some of the limitations of the dependency and world-systems literatures by examining ideological and cultural hegemony and the ways in which it sustains the economic and political ordering of IR. The consensual and ideological dimension of power is central to the Gramscians' critique of IR; ideological hegemony combines with direct domination to better secure the power of the capitalist bloc. Significantly, Gramscian IR's emphasis on the structural power of capital challenges the realist treatment of the "autonomy" of the political and its related arguments concerning the role of power politics (Cox 1983, 1995; Gill 1993; Rupert 1995). For neo-Gramscians like Cox and Gill a capitalist world order has been brought about by the conjunction of certain social forces, states and ideas, and structures unequal power relations in the world economy. In addition, Gill has argued that neo-liberal formulations view economic forces "as beyond or above politics and [they] form the basic structures of an interdependent world" (Gill 1997: 211). Furthermore, neo-liberalism's version of globalization invokes a notion of what the political economist Susan Strange called "business civilization," which far from being free of political and ideological reasoning is actually anchored in a particular history and discourse, and ultimately is used to "justify and legitimate forms of class domination" on a global scale (Gill 1997: 211).

While Gramscian approaches enable us to consider how and why power is embedded in social relations and provide a far more useful notion of hegemony as consensually produced domination, they are less able to address questions concerning race and gender and how these are imbricated with class and power. For example, Agathangelou in this volume critiques Gramscian IR for its inability to address the sexualized and racialized dimensions of globalization. Using the flow of sex and domestic workers within peripheral economies as a case in point, Agathangelou demonstrates why it is important to foreground a postcolonial feminist critique for a better understanding of these relations.

From a different critical angle postmodern IR "denaturalizes" the concepts of anarchy, sovereignty, order, and power.[6] Challenging the epistemological foundations of mainstream IR, postmodern scholars explore the production of knowledge in IR by deploying an "intertextual strategy" to understand "how one theory comes to stand above and silence other theories," "the intimate relationship between textual practices and politics," the construction of modernity in IR and how modernity in turn structures IR, and the links between the "antihistorist practice of logocentrism [and] the political question of sovereignty" (Der Derian 1989: 6; Shapiro 1989: 13; Ashley 1989: 264). Postmodern IR is not only situated in opposition to mainstream realist and neo-liberal thought but also distinguishes itself from other forms of critical theorizing such as Marxism. The shift from "Marx to Nietzsche" (George 1989), strongly influenced by the poststructuralism and postmodernism of Foucault, Derrida and Lyotard, has enabled postmodern IR to chart a different research agenda, one that deconstructs taken-for-granted knowledge in the field. Postmodernism's premise that all "discourses are thus essentially contestable" and its "respect for ambiguity" (Krishna 1993: 387) open the way for challenges to metanarratives in IR. Thus, postmodern arguments about the nature of power in IR, attentive to the "micropolitics of power," have decentered the subject of realist IR, the state, and refuted key realist claims about sovereignty and anarchy among other concepts. This move enables postmodern IR to argue that power is dispersed and cannot be clearly located, and that all forms of essentialist critique are suspect. However, we agree with Krishna that "even works embarking from professedly critical postmodern and poststructural perspectives often replicate the Eurocentric ecumene of 'world' politics." These perspectives "seem to contain little recognition that a totalizing critique of all forms of essentialism and identity politics might play out very differently for people situated outside putative mainstreams" (Krishna 1999: xxix).

Hence, power is never clearly locatable in the disembodied spaces of this postmodern realm; it is both everywhere and nowhere in such a representation of international relations, and may lead to further disempowerment of the already marginalized in IR. The implications of this position for understanding race, gender, and class are addressed elsewhere in this volume.

Power and feminist IR

Feminist approaches have taken to task IR scholarship for rendering gender and women invisible. Although there are important distinctions among the various feminisms, we address what may be broadly termed "post-positivist" feminist contributions to the debate on power, focusing specifically on the arguments advanced by IR feminists (e.g., Elshtain 1987; Enloe 1990; Peterson 1992a; Peterson and Runyan 1993; Sylvester 1994). One of the key contributions of feminist thought has been to draw attention to the necessity for a "deconstruction of gender-biased knowledge claims" and the "reconstruction of gender-sensitive theory" (Peterson 1992a: 6). Spike Peterson has pointed out that this has allowed feminist IR to unsettle the gendered foundations of mainstream thought and to introduce gender into the analysis of key constructs in IR such as the state and sovereignty. Feminist IR also shows how and to what effect mainstream and also non-feminist critical IR theory has ignored gender hierarchy. While this problem is more explicitly associated with the masculinist assumptions of realist and neo-liberal IR, it is also something that eludes those theorizing from a Marxist or Gramscian perspective. Feminists point out that theories of structural violence pay little attention to "male violence against women" and gendered power and domination (Peterson 1992a: 15). Postmodern feminist Christine Sylvester points to the marginalization of feminist voices in the third debate, between the positivists and the post-positivists, where feminists are represented "without giving one among us voice(s), interpretation(s), writing(s), word(s), brush and canvas" (1994: 150). In the feminist view, it is imperative that IR theory give women voice, and take seriously the feminist critique of the gendered sources of security, war, militarism, peacekeeping, pact making, and the organization of labor, among other concerns.

While feminists have contributed much to revisioning IR theory, they seem more hesitant to confront directly the exclusion of race in IR, and its implications for the excercise of power. For example, in *Global Voices* (Rosenau 1993), which was an attempt by critical scholars including feminists to engage diverse voices in IR, the cast of characters include "Junior US or Foreign Scholar," "Western Feminist (Westfem)," and "Her Third World Alter Ego/Identity (Tsitsi)." However, these are all represented by white male and female critical scholars. There is no effort to include Third World scholars from the academy in this conversation.[7] Further, in this "dialogue" Christine Sylvester in her role as Westfem calls for recognizing difference, and suggests that the authors "entertain another woman's voice in the dialogue, one whose context is different–similar–hyphenating to mine," i.e. a Third World feminist from Zimbabwe called Tsitsi (Sylvester in Rosenau 1993: 28). However, Sylvester claims the identity of Tsitsi as her own and proceeds to speak on behalf of the Third World (feminist) other. The contradictions of this move are apparent particularly in light of her own claims concerning the ways in which even critical IR male scholars represent feminists without "giving one among us voice(s)." The problem of representation remains unresolved in the Rosenau volume and points to the role of "the West as interlocutor" even in critical IR.

We recognize the efforts of some feminists to foreground the similarities between feminist claims and the claims of other marginalized groups (for example Mies 1986; Peterson 1992a; Pettman 1996). For example Peterson has argued that in addressing the "empirical adequacy of knowledge claims," feminists, along with "theorists of other marginalized groups – e.g. colonized populations, racial and ethnic minorities, the underclass," challenge elite (male) knowledge that distorts understanding of social relations (Peterson 1992a: 11). Despite these exceptions, a discernible First World feminist voice has emerged in the IR literature, one that glosses over or elides the concerns and engagements of postcolonial feminists. The practical implications of this elision were evident in the differences that emerged in encounters between First World and Third World feminists at international women's conferences marking the United Nations Decade for Women (Desai 1999). A postcolonial approach, which foregrounds the erasures surrounding race and representation, resistance and agency, and the imbrication of race, gender, and class with imperialism and capitalism, is explored more systematically below.

Postcolonial theory and international relations

In this section we explore the relevance of postcolonial theory for power in international relations. We begin by addressing the debates around the term postcolonial, uncovering the different meanings of the term and exploring the genealogy of postcolonial discourse to better situate our volume in this literature. Drawing from this analysis we develop several critical themes that we see as central to a postcolonial understanding of power in IR. These include representation and cultural politics, resistance and agency, and the intersections of race, gender, and class.

What's in a name?

"Postcolonial" is a contested term, one that has evoked much admiration, controversy, and skepticism in academia. Emerging from a "variety of disciplines and theories," postcolonial studies has "enabled a complex interdisciplinary dialogue within the humanities" (Gandhi 1998: 3). However, its interdisciplinary origins have also confounded the development of a uniform understanding of the field (Gandhi 1998). Controversies over terminology and the meaning of postcolonial, and its political implications, have engaged both supporters and critics of postcolonial studies. As Stuart Hall points out, the questions of "When was 'the post-colonial'?" and "What should be included and excluded from its frame?" operate in "a contested space," and have "become the bearer of such powerful unconscious investments – a sign of desire for some, and equally for others, a signifier of danger" (Hall 1996: 242).

The first major controversy addresses the question of what the term post-colonial signifies.[8] Some critics of postcolonial theory argue that the term postcolonial suggests the demise of colonialism, rather than its continuing presence. They argue that postcolonial is more acceptable in the Western academy because it is politically more ambiguous and less confrontational than terms like imperialism, neo-colonialism, and Third World (Shohat 1992; Aidoo 1991). According to Shohat, postcolonial

> carries with it the implication that colonialism is now a matter of the past, undermining colonialisms' economic, political, and cultural deformative-traces in the present. The "post-colonial" inadvertently glosses over the fact that global hegemony even in the post-cold war era, persists in forms other than overt colonial rule.
>
> (Shohat 1992: 105)

Defenders of postcolonialism, however, argue that these criticisms are unfounded because they misrepresent the usage of the term and its meanings in postcolonial studies. Shome suggests that the term postcolonial

> enables us to conceive of complex shifts brought about by decolonization(s). While on the one hand, it does not go so far as to claim that there is a complete rupture from some of the earlier colonial relations in this phase, on the other hand it does claim ... that there is a lot new about the complex political, economic, cultural relations and conjunctures of the contemporary times.
>
> (Shome 1998: 206)

We agree with Shome and others that the postcolonial does not signify the end of colonialism, but rather that it accurately reflects both the continuity and persistence of colonizing practices, as well as the critical limits and possibilities it has engendered in the present historical moment. Hence the postcolonial has relevance for the study of IR because it provides insight into the ways in which the imperial juncture is implicated in the construction of contemporary relations of power, hierarchy, and domination.

A second and related controversy focuses on the spatial, geographical, and historical markers of the postcolonial. Where and "when exactly ... does the 'postcolonial' begin?" (Shohat 1992: 103). If postcolonial is taken to imply colonialism and its current consequences, then are the United States, Australia, New Zealand, and South Africa postcolonial in the way that India, Ghana, and Mexico are (Alva 1995; Shohat 1992; Pratt 1992; Frankenberg and Mani 1993)? We think this question mires us in debates that are not very productive. We believe that a reflective engagement with the experience of colonization and its power to shape past and current realities at the local, national, and global level is far more useful and constructive. In this volume we are concerned with postcoloniality as it is implicated in a variety of "colonizing" practices that structure power relations globally, and resistance to those practices. Our volume thus includes analyses of immigration and security discourses in the United States, colonization of indigenous lifeways among the Lakota in North America, and the internationalization of sex and domestic workers in Greece, Cyprus, and Turkey, along with other more conventional postcolonial "sites" of inquiry such as child labor in India and human rights in Burma.

The genealogy of postcolonial discourse

Although the term postcolonial has acquired much currency since the publication of Edward Said's *Orientalism* (1978), the work of forerunners like Albert Memmi (1965) and Frantz Fanon (1965, 1967) among others has also influenced the field.[9] These intellectual debts notwithstanding, *Orientalism* provides a critical and foundational point of entry into the field (Moore-Gilbert 1997). Said's celebrated and controversial critique of European imperialism illuminates how the concepts of knowledge and power relate to the imperial enterprise in the "Orient."[10] According to Said, orientalism is based on the "ontological and epistemological distinction made between the 'Orient' and (most of the time) 'the Occident'" (Said 1978: 2). This promotes a "relationship of power and domination" which "puts the Westerner in a whole series of possible relationships with the Orient without ever losing him the relative upper hand" (Said 1978: 7). Thus the idea of Western racial and cultural superiority over "oriental backwardness," promoted through Western academic, philosophical, and other cultural expressions, is seen as central to the promotion and protection of European imperialist ventures. By focusing on the political production of knowledge, and the dialectical relationship between knowledge production about the non-Western world and Western colonial ventures, Said has demonstrated the centrality of racialized knowledge in the spread and maintenance of imperialism.

12

Said's work draws on both Foucault and Gramsci, with different implications for postcolonial theory. He utilizes Michel Foucault's notion of discourse to "identify orientalism ... the enormously systematic discipline by which European culture was able to manage – and even produce – the Orient politically, sociologically, militarily, ideologically, scientifically, and imaginatively during the post-Enlightenment period" (Said 1978: 3). Said has also grounded his work in Gramsci, by drawing attention to the imbrication of colonial ideology with capital, and resistance and opposition to these structures of domination (Said 1994: 249, 267). However, unlike classical Marxism's alleged economic determinism, Gramscian Said emphasizes the dialectic of culture and imperialism. In other words, although postcolonial theory rejects the universalizing assumptions of nineteenth-century Marxian structuralism with its emphasis on rationality and linear development, it utilizes a Gramscian focus on the relationship between ideology and material domination, together with a Foucauldian analysis of power and knowledge.[11]

The subaltern studies group has also influenced postcolonial theory, and its contributions are consistent with the Gramscian emphasis highlighted above. Edited for the most part under the leadership of Ranajit Guha, subaltern studies was written to challenge the elitist nature of Indian historiography and to provide an alternative subaltern perspective (Prakash 1992). Influenced by Gramsci, the critical gaze of subaltern studies is not intended to "unmask dominant discourses but to explore their fault-lines in order to provide different accounts, to describe histories revealed in the cracks of the colonial archeology of knowledge" (Prakash 1992: 10).[12] Thus much of postcolonial theory critiques the "projection of the west as history" (Prakash 1994: 1475), and challenges the epistemic, ideological, and political authority of Western and elite knowledge.

Despite the focus on race and the imperial juncture in early postcolonial critiques, little attention has been paid to the question of gender. In critiquing the neglect of gender in postcolonial theory, and the lack of sustained attention to race and imperialism, particularly in mainstream and some strands of postmodern and Marxist feminist theory, postcolonial feminists make gender and race central to their analyses (Spivak 1986, 1987; Mohanty 1991a). Confronting the simplified and homogenized constructions of Third World women, Mohanty attempts two major tasks: deconstructing hegemonic Western feminist knowledge about Third World women, and reconstructing locally grounded knowledge and strategies (1991a: 51). She thus draws our attention to the "simultaneity of oppressions," and grounds "feminist politics in the histories of racism and imperialism" (Mohanty 1991a: 10). Spivak is equally critical of Western hegemonic knowledge and suggests that Western feminism, despite its critique of androcentricity, is grounded in the "imperialist vision of redemption" (Spivak 1986, 1987). For instance, according to Moore-Gilbert, Spivak sees Western feminisms, influenced by the "liberal humanist vision" and the anti-humanism of Foucault and Gilles Deleuze as embodying a vision, similar to "imperialist narratives, promising redemption to the colonized subject" (1997: 76–7). Postcolonial feminists are thus skeptical of notions of global sisterhood that are premised on the universality of shared or similar oppressions, and seek to contextualize feminist struggles and critiques in specific historical, geographical, and cultural sites (Mohanty 1991a). By identifying its key referents, this brief genealogy of postcolonial studies assists in situating a postcolonial approach to international relations.

Central themes of the volume

Although there have been some important efforts to relate postcolonial theory to the study of world politics (e.g., Krishna 1993, 1999; Darby and Paolini 1994; Darby 1997b, 1998; Grovogui 1996; Ling 2001a), its impact on IR until recently has been minimal. Consistent with the complex genealogy of postcolonial studies, these contributions, however, draw our attention to the variety of ways in which IR is informed by postcolonial theory. Darby and Paolini (1994), for example, discuss three "overlapping but nevertheless distinct movements" in postcolonial scholarship that are useful to the study of IR. The first movement, originating in the study of Third World fiction, interrogates representational practices in the service of colonialism, where colonialism signifies "a continuing set of practices that are seen to prescribe relations between the West and the Third World beyond the independence of the former colonies" (Darby and Paolini 1994: 375). A focus on the projects of "resistance and recovery," highlighted in the works of Memmi and Fanon among others, constitutes the second movement. The third movement in postcolonial studies, the "one world" movement according to Gandhi, engages with the "postcolonial desire for extra- or post-national solidarities and consider(s) concepts and terms such as 'hybridity' and 'diaspora' which have come to characterize mixed or global-ized culture" (Gandhi 1998: 123).

While these movements are useful in mapping the broader terrain of postcolonial theory, they do not show how the intersections of race, gender, and class, and the imbrication of culture and capital, are relevant for the study of IR. Darby and Paolini also point to three key areas where IR and postcolonial studies can converse: power and representation, modernity, and emotional commitment and radicalism (Darby and Paolini 1994: 384). Once again, they neglect to say how inattention to race, gender, and class inequalities has structured conversations in these areas. While Darby and Paolini are eager to have bridge-building conversations between postcolonial theory and IR, and we think this is a good idea, it is impossible to have these conversations without explicitly acknowledging these structural inequalities. We think the task before us is not so much building bridges, but rather one of uncovering the traces of empire and history, and recovering memory in the hierarchical construction of the discipline and its objects of inquiry. In this volume we call attention to the widely circulated material and cultural practices, legacies of the colonial encounter, that continue to shape international relations. We interrogate the exercise of power in global, national, and local spaces by foregrounding these categories and relationships.

The book is structured around the following major themes, which we see as central to a postcolonial analysis of IR. Although these themes are not addressed consistently by all of the contributors to this volume, each chapter highlights at least one of them:

- the power of representation
- the intersections of race and gender
- global capitalism, class, and postcoloniality
- recovery, resistance and agency

The power of representation

International relations might have largely ignored the question of representation were it not for some of the extra-disciplinary forays from the field evident predominantly in the work of postmodern, critical constructivist, and feminist scholars (see for example Der Derian and Shapiro 1989; Weldes *et al.* 1999; Doty 1996b; Sylvester 1994). These scholars have drawn attention to the contingent nature of discourse and the power of discursive constructions in naturalizing a whole host of "givens" in IR. For example, in a recent effort to explore "cultural processes through which insecurities of states and communities ... are produced, reproduced, and transformed," Weldes *et al.* foreground the role of culture and representation in IR (Weldes *et al.* 1999: 2). In doing so they have challenged received notions of security, sovereignty, and identity and brought to our attention the significance of representation in understanding IR. We find this critique useful, particularly the chapters by Muppidi (1999) and Niva (1999), which address postcoloniality and insecurity. However, aside from these exceptions *Cultures of Insecurity* (Weldes *et al.* 1999) does not significantly engage the interrelated themes that concern this volume.

The arguments about representation advanced here derive from the work of postcolonial scholars like Said, Mohanty, and Spivak among others, who have emphasized the "relationship between Western representation and knowledge on the one hand, and Western material and political power on the other" (Moore-Gilbert 1997: 34), and how these are underwritten by constructions of race, class, and gender. This scholarship reveals how pseudo-scientific racist and gendered constructions of the other, which we discuss more systematically in the next section, inscribe the cultural authority and dominance of the West under colonial rule and in the postcolonial present (e.g., Mudimbe 1988; McClintock 1995). Dichotomous representations of the West and East, self and other, which essentialize identity and difference (Moore-Gilbert 1997: 39), are critical to the maintenance of Western hegemony. Thus unveiling practices of power in IR requires at the very least an engagement with the problem of representation, and its racialized and gendered implications.

In a recent work that notes the significance of representation for power, John Beverly has suggested that some representations "have cognitive authority or can secure hegemony" and others "do not have the authority or are not hegemonic" (1999: 1). We argue that mainstream IR has cognitive authority, and a hegemonic and disciplining effect on global politics. It has not only ignored the question of representation, but has also assumed that mainstream IR's language is universal and unproblematic, giving it the authority to speak for and about others. In a useful reminder about the practical impact of representational power, Beverly has quoted Spivak's injunction that "representation is not only a matter of *speaking about* but also of *speaking for*. That is it concerns politics and hegemony (and the limits of politics and hegemony)" (Beverly 1999: 3). In applying some of the insights concerning representation and power generated in postcolonial scholarship to the study of international relations we hope to highlight the complex ways in which postcolonial others have been constructed, and discursively mapped and managed. We argue further that the disciplinary boundaries of conventional IR and its grand narrative, rooted in Western humanist notions of universality and rationality, have been maintained by the exclusion of certain "others." Such an exclusion implies a particular way of speaking and writing about those others that renders them marginal, insignificant, and invisible. We thus explore several specific sites where power is enacted in and through the representation of postcolonial others, and is manifested in relations of domination and subordination, hegemony and resistance on a global scale.

The different essays in this anthology show how dominant, Western representations of internal and external others emerge in immigration and security discourses, the sexualization and racialization of female migrant labor, child labor, and human rights, globalized notions of masculinity, secularism and its evil twin "religious fundamentalism," and presumptions about conflict and the state of nature in IR. For example, Biswas notes in this volume that the response in the West to the global Islamic resurgence is "framed by a 'reactive epistomology' – explaining religious nationalisms as some form of reactions to modernity – an epistomology that both presupposes and reproduces a troublesome and problematic Western secularism/Eastern fundamentalism ontology." Such an epistomology is also grounded in broader claims to history and heir to a Western grand narrative of progress and reason. The nexus between power and knowledge that postcolonialism borrows from poststructuralist thought by way of Foucault is further revealed in the production of the binary which Biswas addresses here.

Uncovering the sources and meaning of the "orientalist anxieties" generated among international relations scholars and analysts by the resurgence of Islam, Biswas shows how dominant understandings and representations of "modernization" and the "nation-state *form*" foster and reproduce hierarchy. Elsewhere in the volume, Chowdhry and Nair note that the construction of a liberal human rights discourse privileges particular representations and engenders certain erasures about Third World others. Human rights violations in Third World "sites" become the central focus of liberal critiques. However, these critiques ignore Western complicity in the production of these abuses. Significantly, Nair suggests that a liberal discourse constructs a particular human rights imaginary within which "Burma" as a cultural and postcolonial space of repression is continually reproduced, for example, in US policy discourses. Such a reproduction not only carries implications for addressing human rights abuses in Burma, but also presents certain analytic problems when viewed through a postcolonial lens.

In the following section we explore further the ways in which race and gender are implicated in these representations. We believe that to meaningfully engage in a debate about power in IR the intimate links between representation, power, race, and gender need to be uncovered.

Race and gender

By invoking race and gender in international relations we are not seeking to assert a fixed evidentiary status to them; rather we are suggesting that their meanings derive from their specific locations and histories, as is evident throughout this volume. Although there is little disagreement that the imperialist project was sustained through force and material exploitation, postcolonial theorists posit that the dehumanization and degradation of the racialized colonial subject, what Aime Cesaire has called "thingification," was critical to the efficacy of colonization. The colonial discourse on race thus forced postcolonial intellectuals to retheorize the class basis of domination. For example, Frantz Fanon in *The Wretched of the Earth* argued that "in the colonies ... you are rich because you are white, you are white because you are rich. This is why Marxist analysis should always be slightly stretched every time we have to do {sic} with the colonial problem" (Fanon in Loomba 1998: 22).[13] In this volume we hope to demonstrate that the stretching of Marxism and critical IR to better accommodate the historical interpellation of race, gender, and class is necessary for a more nuanced understanding of world politics.

As noted earlier, scholarship on imperialism and colonization has contributed significantly to understanding class and the role of capital in international relations (see next section).[14] However, it has very little to say about the relationship of race and gender to the imperialist project and the politics of power in postcolonial societies. There are some exceptions to this general neglect of race in the literature. For example, the work of Doty (1996b), Hunt (1987), and DeConde (1992) has illustrated the relevance of constructions of race and ethnicity for imperialism and US foreign policy. Both Hunt and Doty explore racial hierarchies and their ideological significance for the production of US national identity. Hunt has demonstrated through a critical analysis of cartoons and writings in popular magazines and newspapers in the United States how racialized understandings of Native Americans, Latin Americans, Asians, and Africans inform US national interest, immigration policy, and security discourse. In an equally compelling contribution to the literature, Campbell (1994) has analyzed representations of Japan and the Japanese in US foreign policy, and why "the Japanese threat" enables a particular formulation of US national identity. He explores the construction of US and Japanese cultural identity and difference through the lens of postmodernism, and while racial representations inform his analysis, he curiously does not theorize the "inscribing" of a racialized "world order." He does, however, bring gender much more explicitly into the analysis, by showing how the "performative constitution of gender and the body is analogous to the performative constitution of the state" (Campbell 1994: 149). This omission in Campbell's analysis reflects the neglect of race in much of critical IR and its failure to engage postcolonial scholarship. Although Said's *Orientalism* was published in 1978 and is seen as foundational to the literature on culture and representation, it surprisingly does not merit mention in Campbell's work.

Drawing from the work of postcolonial scholars like Said (1978) and Mudimbe (1988) we bring to the fore race as a major theme in this volume, particularly as it relates to constructions of North–South hierarchies, postcolonial and national identities, and immigration and security discourses (see, for example, Persaud in this volume). In addition, the postcolonial literature on gender, including works by Spivak and Mohanty, offers important insights on how gendered and racialized representations are insinuated into international relations. We argue that the concepts privileged in mainstream IR, such as anarchy, are grounded in racialized and gendered assumptions, although IR theory invokes anarchy as a universal condition (see Beier in this volume).

One of the pivotal features of the contemporary economic, political, and cultural dominance by the West of the Third World is the construction of race, which was formalized under colonial rule. Colonial discourse was structured by the nature and form of colonial interaction with pre-colonial societies; this discourse inevitably constructed Europeans as intellectually and morally superior and its others as backward and inferior. Consider, for example, the statement of Ernest Renan, the French historian and philologist:

> All those who have been in the East, or in Africa are struck by the way in which the mind of the true believer is fatally limited, by

the species of the iron circle that surrounds his head, rendering it
absolutely closed to knowledge.

(Ashcroft and Ahluwalia 1999: 58)

Other colonial discourses distinguished between the "barbarous infidels"
of the East and the "savages" of Africa and the Americas, suggesting that in
the former the excesses of too much civilization had led to decadence visible
in the greed of insatiable appetites, despotism, and power, whereas in the
latter the lack of civilization had led to a savage primitivism (Loomba
1998). Asians, Africans, and Native Americans were regarded as inferior to
whites, and colonization was deemed necessary for the establishment of a
modern white moral order, that is the project of *mission civilisatrice*.

Aided by the morphological classifications of race by colonial anthropologists, and the consequent construction of inferior and superior races, colonial
discourse legitimized its travesties by referencing race and its accompanying
characteristics. Scientific and anthropological discourses of the eighteenth
and nineteenth centuries posited that races were biologically constituted and
that the biological characteristics of people, evident in the size of the
cranium and brain, the width of their forehead, i.e. their race, determined
their capacity to be civilized, criminal, intelligent, and sexual beings (Gould
1981). These discourses classified white Europeans as endowed with higher
civilizational attributes than Asians, Africans, and Native Americans, and
constructed whiteness as inherently superior. Scientific and anthropological
racism thus calcified a global hierarchy that serviced the needs of empire,
which continues to influence contemporary global politics and the policies
of a hegemonic twentieth-century power like the United States. As Persaud
explains in his chapter on "Situating race in international relations," US
immigration policy has been shaped by deeply embedded notions of racial,
cultural, and civilizational superiority. He argues that "the control of
borders" along racial lines has been critical in the production and consolidation of a US national identity that privileges whiteness.

The focus on race has been complemented by attention to gender in postcolonial feminist scholarship. It draws attention to how the racialized
hierarchy of Europe and its others was often also a gender hierarchy in which
Asians, Africans, and indigenous Americans were feminized in contrast to a
masculinized European identity. Once again science was used to justify this
comparison:

> it was claimed that women's low brain weight and deficient brain
> structures were analogous to those of the lower races, and their inferior
> intellectualities explained on this basis. Women, it was observed,
> shared with Negroes a narrow, child like and delicate skull, so
> different from the more robust and rounded heads characteristic of

males of 'superior' races ... In short, lower races represented the 'female'
type of the human species, and females the 'lower race' of gender.
(Stepan quoted in Loomba 1998: 160–1)

Ironically, a hypermasculinity was also attributed to colonized men in
which they were constructed as oppressors of colonized women and the
mission of the colonial state was to save "these female victims." For example,
Lord Cromer, key representative of the British Empire in Egypt, raged
against the institution of veiling and used it as the *raison d'être* for the civilizing mission of the empire (Ahmed 1992). Interestingly, Cromer was once
the head of the anti-suffragist league in Britain. The cynical appropriation of
feminist themes in the service of empire meant the politicization of cultural
practices such as veiling, leading to its symbolic significance in the cultural
politics of revivalist Islamic movements (Ahmed 1992; Fanon 1965). The
memory and specter of empire, it is clear, continues to haunt world politics.
    A related problem is also the role that Western women played in the
imperialist project. For instance, women philanthropists from the West
often set out to liberate the Third World woman from "oppressive cultural
practices" (Mayo 1927).[15] Consequently, cultural symbols like the veil, seen
as signs of oppression of Third World women, have become nodal points
around which contemporary critiques of the "Orient," in particular Islam,
have revolved. In contrast, the veil has also been used as a symbol of resistance by some Muslim women and by Islamic social movements in their
reassertion of cultural identity.[16] While culture has been increasingly relevant to the study of IR as demonstrated in theses about the "clash of
civilizations," the "new cold war," and "fundamentalist Islam" (Huntington
1996; Juergensmeyer 1996), this scholarship treats culture as fixed and
immutable, rather than as a construction grounded in power relations and
emerging out of historical encounters. Mainstream IR scholars fail to contextualize culture or cultural practices and neglect their links to imperialism
and contemporary regimes of modernization. These understandings in IR are
premised on the separate historical evolution of West and non-West,
whereas we argue that these are mutually constitutive histories with implications for contemporary cultural discourses and practices of secularism,
nationalism, and identity politics (see, for example, Anand, Biswas, and
Krishna in this volume).
    Race and gender have also been central to the construction of nation and
national identity. According to Paul Gilroy "the ideologies of Englishness
and Britishness" are premised on the co-production and reproduction of race
and nation in Britain. Gilroy asks: "How long is enough to become a
genuine Brit?" Arguments that focus on originary myths "effectively deny
that blacks can share a significant social identity with their white neighbors
who in contrast to more recent arrivals inhabit ... 'rooted settlements' articulated by lived and formed identities" (1993, quoted in Lazarus 1999: 65).[17]

Nation and national identity have been complicated by colonial and post-colonial flows of people and culture making it impossible, as Gilroy demonstrates, to frame a civilizational discourse premised on racial exclusivity (see Krishna in this volume).

In international relations, scholars like Manzo (1996) have shown how race figures in the construction of nation, while others have drawn our attention to its gendered bases (Ranchod-Nilsson and Tetreault 2000; Peterson 1992a; Yuval-Davis 1993). This literature illuminates the racialized and gendered underpinnings of nations and nationalisms in IR, and reveals the influence of critical feminist and race theory. For example, Yuval-Davis argues that the control of female sexuality plays a critical role in maintaining the racial and national purity of the nation. Official constraints and proscriptions against racial intermixing are imposed to ensure racial purity, as demonstrated in past injunctions against intermarriage between whites and non-whites in the United States. The racialized female body therefore becomes the site of competing imperialist, nationalist, and feminist claims with different implications for power and politics in IR (see Nair and Biswas this volume). We take seriously these insights and emphasize the role that both race and gender play in constituting relations of power, domination, and resistance in world politics.

Global capitalism, class, and postcoloniality

International relations has only recently begun to address the question of representation, identity formation, and culture as evidenced by recent boundary-challenging postmodern, critical constructivist, Gramscian, and feminist work. Marxist and neo-Marxist, including Gramscian, writings in particular are concerned with issues of imperialism, colonization, and neo-colonial relations, but they rarely foreground the interconnections between the material, discursive and cultural. We not only emphasize the imperialist juncture and its formative power, but we also explicitly address the interconnections between culture, discourse, and material practices in constructing North–South relations. For example, Ling, in this volume, analyzes the gendered and cultural dimensions of Asia's financial crisis by exploring what she calls the "triple move" of the West's liberal international order which "reflects an openly calculated coordination of institutional interests to sustain Western capitalist hegemony in the global economy." Agathangelou, Chowdhry, and Nair in this volume also attend to the material and cultural dimensions of global hegemony. We thus address the criticism leveled at postcolonial scholarship by critics like Arif Dirlik (1997) and Aijaz Ahmad (1992) who have accused it of a "culturalism."

Both Ahmad and Dirlik in trenchant arguments against postcolonial scholarship have posited that postcolonial theorists have abandoned the classical Marxist concerns with material inequalities between the First and

Third Worlds, replacing them with Foucauldian and poststructuralist preoccupations with discursive truth regimes and representation. Dirlik has asserted that postcolonial scholars are guilty of a "culturalism" and the post-foundational and poststructuralist focus on Eurocentrism leads postcolonial scholars to deny the "foundational status" of capitalism for the spread and maintenance of European power. He writes:

> The denial to capitalism of "foundational" status is also revealing of a culturalism in the postcolonial argument that has important ideological consequences. This involves the issue of Eurocentrism. Without capitalism as the foundation for European power and the motive force for its globalization, Eurocentrism would have been just another ethnocentrism (comparable to any other ethnocentrism from the Chinese and the Indian to the most trivial tribal solipsism). An exclusive focus on Eurocentrism as a cultural or ideological problem, which blurs the power relationships that dynamized it and endowed it with hegemonic persuasiveness, fails to explain why this particular ethnocentrism was able to define modern global history, and itself as the universal aspiration and end of that history, in contrast to the regionalism or localism of other ethnocentrisms.
>
> (Dirlik 1997: 515–16)

Ahmad and Dirlik's arguments hinge on the assumption, also supported by Shohat (1992) and McClintock (1992), that the privileged and "prominent position" of postcolonial theorists in Western academia directs their gaze away from the material anxieties and deprivations that result from the global expansion of capitalism. According to Dirlik, as the concern of post-colonial intellectuals with disrupting the "archeology of knowledge enshrined in the west" (Prakash 1992: 14) "acquires respectability and gains admission in US academic institutions," it obscures "the condition of pessimism" that characterizes postcoloniality in the Third World (Dirlik 1997: 513).[18] Thus the genealogy of postcolonial theory and the location of postcolonial theorists, for Dirlik and Ahmad, leads to the neglect of traditional Marxist concerns and a focus on poststructuralist and anti-foundationalist issues.

Although some postcolonial scholarship is guilty of the culturalism noted above, we claim that these criticisms are misplaced and indeed are based largely on a misreading of the origins and concerns of postcolonial writing. As discussed in the earlier section on genealogy, Marx and Gramsci have clearly influenced the thinking of postcolonial scholarship reflected in the work of subaltern scholars among others; the latter have critiqued the Eurocentrism of Marx and provided a postcolonial corrective. While a few postcolonial scholars argue that "Marxist discourse is really at one with

22

liberal discourse within the circumambient episteme of modernity," others like Ranajit Guha suggest that a Marxist critique of capitalism "possesses a clear externality to the bourgeois 'universe of dominance'" (Lazarus 1999: 127, 132). Despite this difference, postcolonial scholars generally agree that the foundationalist and universalist assumptions of Marxism need to be rejected to further a genuinely non-Eurocentric history.[19] Illuminating this point, Gyan Prakash argues that postcolonial theory rejects "Eurocentric Marxism" with its focus only on the narrative of class which assumes that, in India for example, the "caste system, patriarchy, ethnic oppression, Hindu–Muslim conflicts ... [are] forms assumed by the former (Prakash 1997: 496)." Postcolonial theory recognizes that while class does not subsume other forms of stratification it seriously molds the relations of power in India and often underwrites caste, ethnicity, communalism, and gender. Thus the rejection of the economic determinism of Marx in which capitalism functions independent of the cultural manifestations of power is not tantamount to dismissing capitalism (or class) as a "disposable fiction"; rather, the "historicization of the Eurocentrism in nineteenth-century Marxism enables us to understand the collusion of capitalism and colonialism and to undo the effect of that collusion's imperative to interpret Third World histories [only] in terms of capital's logic" (Prakash 1997: 497). Dipesh Chakrabarty has also echoed Prakash's analysis of Marxism by pointing out that

> (un)like in the Paris of the poststructuralists, there was never any question in Delhi, Calcutta or Madras of a wholesale rejection of Marx's thought. Foucault's scathing remark ... may have its point, but it never resonated with us with anything like the energy that anti-Marxism displays in the writings of some postmodernists.
>
> (quoted in Lazarus 1999: 123)

Commenting on the relationship between culturalism and materialism, Teresa L. Ebert has suggested that there are two "fundamentally different ways of understanding" postcoloniality. The first mode, which she argues is more prevalent, Foucauldian, and culturalist, demonstrates the links between power and regimes of knowledge, and "foregrounds the problems of representation." The second mode, which foregrounds "the international division of labor and poses the problem of the economics of untruth in the relations of the metropolitan and periphery" does not dispense with issues of representation; rather it suggests that the politics of representation cannot be understood separate from the political economy of labor (Ebert 1995: 204–5). We are attentive to both modes throughout this volume; whereas some chapters more explicitly emphasize the role of global capital, it is implied or assumed in other chapters. This is consistent with Hall's injunction that "certain articulations of this order are in fact either implicitly assumed or silently at work in the underpinning assumptions of almost all the post-colonial critical work" (Hall 1996: 258). We see the modes discussed by Ebert as overlapping rather than distinct moves, as evident in many of the contributions to this volume. A good example of this overlap is the chapter by Sankaran Krishna which relates identity politics in postcolonial Guyana to the "fractured inheritance" of colonial rule, and the political economy of the plantation. Through the figure of West Indian cricketer Shivnaraine Chanderpaul, Krishna "attempts to map out the multiple and dynamic trajectories of national identity" in Guyana, and shows the imbrication of class, ethnicity, race, and gender with imperialism in the contemporary production of Afro-Guyanese and Guyanese-Indian politics.

Other chapters in this volume directly address the impact of the political economy of globalization, and more explicitly reflects Ebert's second mode. Agathangelou, for example, discusses the "lower circuits of capital" inhabited by sex and domestic workers. She distinguishes these lower circuits, which are characterized by "tourism, reproduction, and activities such as food preparation, janitorial/custodial jobs, and the sex trade," from the "upper circuits of capital" relations which focus on trade, financial markets, and capital flows. By being attentive to the production of these lower circuits of capital, Agathangelou exposes the serious limitations of neoliberal international political economy (IPE), and also draws our attention to the gendered "silences and invisibilities" evident in Marxist IPE. Elsewhere in this volume, Chowdhry explores the framing of global and national debates surrounding child labor in the carpet industry in India. She argues that the global discourse surrounding child labor draws from a liberal human rights critique and obfuscates the workings of global and national capital regimes. The imbrication of the discursive and the material in these works further illuminates the necessity for a postcolonial re-reading of international relations and political economy.

Resistance and agency

With the possible exception of some feminist IR it is unclear whether and how the critical IR literature approaches the question of resistance and agency.[20] The literature on global civil society, social movements, and transnational advocacy networks has more recently engaged questions concerning transnational mobilization on gender, the environment, and human rights, among other issues, and has made a significant contribution to the IR literature (Keck and Sikkink 1998; Lipschutz and Mayer 1996; Risse et al. 1999). Although this work does explore agency and is useful in theorizing transnational activism and its impact on sovereignty claims, it does not directly address our concerns about resistance, or representation, and more significantly it elides the workings of global capital. We find the postcolonial literature more helpful in addressing these concerns.

24

As noted earlier, postcolonial theory has been accused of merely "deconstructing" knowledge, of failing to locate its critique and analysis in the material histories of the oppressed, and of being seduced by French "high theory" at the expense of indigenous literatures.[21] However, as discussed in the previous section, its intellectual debt to postmodernism and poststructuralism notwithstanding, postcolonial theory is attentive to these material histories, and in fact relates these histories to the question of resistance and agency. In this section we explore various forms of resistance and agency in relation to power and IR by drawing on the insights of postcolonial scholarship. Hence, the significance of colonizing practices, counter-narratives, and struggles, and the marginalized's "recovery of self," that is, forms of resistance and agency, constitute the main focus of our analysis.

From the view of many postcolonial scholars uncovering oppressions, and ultimately shifting one's gaze toward the colonizing practices of Europe and the United States, constitutes a form of resistance.[22] In addition, a postcolonial critique of power in IR must also move beyond the deconstruction of knowledge. Such a move entails, according to Said, "the political necessity of taking a stand, of *strategically essentializing* a position from the perspective of those who were and are victimized and continue to suffer in various ways from an unequal, capitalist, patriarchal, and neocolonial world order" (Krishna 1993: 389). While addressing representation is critical to understanding the power–knowledge nexus in IR, the "postmodernist suspicion of subjectivity and agency" disenables political action. This is particularly a problem for those who, as Krishna points out, are not so advantaged by their placement in late capitalism's international hierarchy (1993: 388). We also see the postmodernist aversion to "taking a stand" as a form of disempowerment wherein the deconstruction of Western forms of power–knowledge have made alternative sources of identity and resistance difficult, if not impossible, to envision within the same discursive space. These arguments surfacing in Krishna's critique are clearly reflective of concerns in postcolonial studies around the gnawing question of subjectivity even as the "death of the subject" is proclaimed in postmodernism. However, even as some postcolonial scholars aver that the question of subjectivity, which is part of a larger debate in postcolonial studies on commitment to "universalism, metanarrative, social emancipation, revolution" (Lazarus 1999: 9), is best dealt with by sticking to efforts to resist such essentialisms, others like Said and Spivak have argued otherwise. According to Lazarus, Said has explained the differences between postmodernism and postcolonialism on the question of resistance and agency thus:

> Yet whereas postmodernism, in one of its most programmatic statements (by Jean-François Lyotard), stresses the disappearance of the grand narratives of emancipation and enlightenment, the emphasis

behind much of the work done by the first generation of post-colonial artists and scholars is exactly the opposite: the grand narratives remain, even though their implementation and realization are at present in abeyance, deferred, or circumvented.

(Lazarus 1999: 10)

The point here is that postcolonialism opens up possibilities for resisting dominant discourses of representation and power by framing its own "counter-narratives." Thus Grovogui, in this volume, addresses the context "in which the production of international knowledge occurs" and the locations from which postcolonial theorists challenge the hegemonic narrative. Analyzing and responding to the charges leveled by contemporary critical Western scholars and thinkers such as Hopkins and Todorov against postcolonial scholarship, Grovogui explores African postcolonial criticism embodied in the Rassemblement Democratique Africain (RDA) in the aftermath of World War II, and draws out its counter-narratives and implications.

Postcolonial writings vary in their approach and understanding of resistance and agency, ranging from the early works of anti-colonial thinkers such as Fanon and Memmi, the later subaltern historiography of scholars like Chakrabarty (1992), Guha (1982), and Prakash (1997), to postcolonial thinkers like Spivak (1988) and Bhabha (1995).[23] In the case of the former, resistance and agency are conceptualized as "recovery," specifically the "recovery of self" (Fanon 1965, 1967; Memmi 1965; Nandy 1983). Such a recovery entails political struggle and liberation from colonial rule, and the search for, and realization of, cultural identity, an identity that has been systematically degraded and denied by the colonizers. However, anti-colonial and postcolonial writers have also been suspicious of nationalism's potential hegemony and the exclusions that it engenders (Fanon 1965: 148–205; Chatterjee 1993: 13). In particular, the subaltern school, whose project is to foreground and make visible the voices, histories, locations, struggles, and movements of the marginalized, has challenged nationalism's exclusions and addressed its complicities with capital.[24]

The attempted recovery of the subaltern voice raises the question of whether the oppressed and marginalized can actually have a voice, or as Spivak put it, "Can the subaltern speak?" (1988). Her answer in the negative has triggered an important debate in the field, pitting those like Spivak who caution against the construction of a romanticized, authentic subaltern against others who argue that it is possible and necessary to articulate resistance and agency (Parry 1994; Chancy 1997; Loomba 1998).[25] We agree with Loomba, who has pointed out that this disagreement presents us with a difficult and unnecessary choice; it is far more desirable that we pay attention to the recovery of voice, and simultaneously engage questions concerning the politics of "subaltern silence" (1998: 239).

We locate subalternity by being attentive to the modalities of power, domination, and resistance in IR, paying particular attention to the multiple ways in which racialized, gendered, and classed hierarchies reproduce these modalities. This volume offers counter-narratives, that not only address questions of representation in international relations, but also acknowledge the spaces for recovery, resistance, and agency. In exploring Lakota cosmological beliefs, Beier challenges the assumptions of realist IR, or what he refers to as the IR "orthodoxy." Beier attempts to show why listening to native voices, without mythologizing or essentializing native identity, not only offers us a critique of conventional IR theory, but helps frame an alternative discourse that contradicts realist claims concerning survival, anarchy, and conflict as constitutive of international relations. He argues that an interrogation of the archaeological evidence yields not only an account of the aboriginal condition of the Lakota, which is quite different from those put forth by the anthropological and historiographical orthodoxies, but also an alternative conception and practice of political order that is equally at odds with that which is held to by the orthodoxy of international relations.

While recovery of voice and the framing of counter-narratives enable us to understand resistance and agency, other forms of resistance such as mimicry and hybridity are equally significant. According to Homi Bhabha, identity is destabilized through a

> strategy of disavowal ... where the trace of what is disavowed is not repressed but repeated as something different – a mutation, a hybrid. It is such a partial and double force that is more than the mimetic but less than the symbolic, that disturbs the visibility of the colonial presence and makes the recognition of its authority problematic.
>
> (Bhabha 1995: 34)[26]

Ling extends Bhabha's concept of mimicry by distinguishing between its "formal" and "substantive" forms in her analysis of the Asian crisis in this volume. While formal mimicry is imitative, substantive mimicry is hybrid and "articulates an internally developed ideology" that is more destabilizing to global power arrangements. Ling claims that both "types of mimicry destabilize self-other relations, but the hegemonic self's response to them differs markedly. Formal mimicry invites amusement, tolerance, even encouragement. (After all, imitation is the highest form of flattery.) But substantive mimicry provokes a punitive, disciplinary reaction." She argues that the West tolerated Asia's miracle growth "so long as it remained formal mimicry" and Asian capitalism never threatened Western liberal capitalist hegemony. However, once "a distinctive Asian capitalism," an instance of substantive mimicry, emerged in the 1980s and challenged the established Western order, punitive actions followed.

Anand, in this volume, explores how Tibetans appropriate "the hege-monic language of sovereignty, autonomy, and nationalism to make their case" for an independent state. In addition, he demonstrates that the Tibetan diaspora navigates its claims within the multiple discourses that surround Tibetan-ness, such as that of *"exotica Tibet."* Concerned about the possibilities for transformation and resistance Agathangelou assesses the potential for workers' struggles to bring about change in the desire economies of Cyprus, Greece, and Turkey. She suggests that such struggles ultimately confront the transnationalization of capital and its gendered effects through the building of solidarities and alliances across gender, race and class. In addition, Chowdhry and Nair address similar concerns in their chapters.

We suggest that to properly confront the metanarratives of conventional IR, the historical production of hierarchy must be not only problematized and challenged, but resisted through a strategic rewriting of IR, which we attempt to do in this volume. For us the relationship between an academic enterprise, which may be implied in the "rewriting of IR," and a politics of resistance "out there" is dialectical – one informs the other. This relationship is also productive of certain kinds of tensions, such as the dangers of "nativism," valorization of subalternity, and the "safety" of the academic narrative or its distance from the "practical" everyday politics of marginality and resistance. We are cognizant of these tensions, but we hope with some humility that this project will assist in addressing some of the exclusions and marginalizations of contemporary world politics.

Organization of the volume

The chapters in this volume address one or more of the main themes discussed above. While all of the authors situate themselves at the intersec-tions of postcolonial studies and IR and are committed to an interdisciplinary effort, their thematic emphases in these chapters vary. The next three chapters in the volume foreground race even as they address its intersection with gender and class. These chapters also highlight representa-tional strategies enabled by and enabling colonizing practices. Grovogui in Chapter 2 addresses the criticisms leveled by A.G. Hopkins and Tzvetan Todorov against postcolonial scholarship that dismisses the latter's methods as reductionist and misguided. He argues that their arguments reflect mistaken views of the postcolonial intellectual and political traditions. Focusing on the relationship between the French left and Coulibaly, Hama, and other West African politicians during the period of decolonization in West Africa, Grovogui proposes that it was not the method, but rather the politics of decolonization that influenced the latter's denunciation of the French postcolonial imaginary. He thus refutes Hopkins and Todorov's accusations of "reverse ethnography" and "cultural relativism" against post-colonial scholarship. In Chapter 3, Persaud assesses the impact of race on IR by focusing on security and immigration. Using the United States as an example, he argues that race has operated as a powerful social force in the construction of security. Persaud analyzes "civilizational security" and "civilizational hegemony," particularly in reference to immigration, as discourses that construct and map difference within a racialized, global politics. In Chapter 4, Beier proceeds from a concern with the near complete neglect of aboriginal peoples by scholars working in the field of IR; this neglect stems in part from conventional IR scholars' attachment to Hobbesian notions of the state of nature. The chapter shows how these attachments make invisible the question of race and gender in IR. Evidence for this is provided by examining the histories and experiences of indigenous peoples like the Lakota. By doing an alternative historiography, one that is also attentive to the racialized and gendered (ongoing) colonization of the Lakota, the chapter shows the necessity for an alternative cosmology of IR.

The next two chapters by Ling and Agathangelou highlight gender and draw out its implications for race, class, and global capital relations. In addition, Ling more systematically addresses the politics of representation and Agathangelou questions of resistance and agency. In Chapter 5, Ling reveals how and why a racialized hypermasculinity facilitates the globalization process in reference to the Asian financial crisis. Weaving a postcolonial perspective with constructivist IR, the chapter uncovers the "triple move" by the Western liberal international order to sustain Western capitalist hegemony. This move, Ling argues, entails the (re)feminization of Asia, the (re)masculinization of Western capital, and the (re)hegemonization of domestic and international relations "mimicking cold war power politics." In Chapter 6, Agathangelou "explores the silences accompanying female sex and domestic labor migration in discourses of IR and mainstream perspectives on globalization." She examines the "movement of sexual labor within the peripheries" and demonstrates that race, ethnicity, and nationality are crucial elements in this desire economy. She attempts to show how IR and the international political economy would look different if desire economies and the sex trade were taken seriously as integral to globalization.

The following three chapters address the politics of nation and nationalism, religion and cultural identity, and its transnational dimensions. Krishna, in Chapter 7, examines the issue of national identity in postcolonial societies by focusing on a West Indian cricketer named Shivnaraine Chanderpaul from Guyana. Through this figure, who is Guyanese-Indian, the author attempts to map the multiple and dynamic trajectories of national identity in a postcolonial setting where multiple ethnic identities come into play. Guyana's population is about 50 per cent "East Indian" and 38 per cent African origin. Krishna asks, "How does one adjudicate between ethnic fragments that emerge as a legacy of the period of imperialism and battle over entitlements in a post-colonial national order?" This chapter marks an effort to think about the contentious issues involved in such an adjudication. Biswas, in Chapter 8, begins by problematizing Western secular discourse and its orientalist-racialized assumptions. Focusing on the resurgence of religious nationalism in world politics, her chapter exposes the Christian cultural core of Western secularism. She examines the "Rushdie affair" in Britain to show how the presence of religious minorities in the West unsettles the claims of Western secularism. By exploring the racial and cultural core of Western secularism, Biswas also sheds new light on the resurgence of religious movements such as Hindu and Islamic nationalism, and their imbrication in the global project of modernity.

In Chapter 9, Anand seeks to engage the questions of Tibetan diasporic transnational identity, and its struggle for nationhood, and argues that such an interrogation tests the limits of current postcolonial theorizing. He delineates some of the many dynamics of Tibetan identity and explores how it is shaped by multiple narratives, bringing to the surface tensions that play performative and constitutive functions in imagining Tibet as a nation. One of the tensions addressed in the chapter is Tibet's location as a postcolonial entity, but in rela-tion to a hegemonic regional power, China, and a larger international order dominated by the West. He suggests that even serious works on Tibet often use contrasting images to begin with – a Shangri-la on the verge of extinction and a semi-colony whose culture has been destroyed by the Chinese (and by the process of modernization). This pessimistic scenario ignores the creative potential of Tibetans to adjust and survive in a changing world.

The last two chapters in the volume address the global human rights discourse in reference to child labor and Burma, by drawing out the racial-ized and gendered representations of the "other" implicit in this discourse. Further, the two chapters situate this critique in reference to the politics of global capital. Chowdhry in Chapter 10 interrogates liberal human rights discourses and the cultural relativist response to child labor, and examines the ways in which both are imbricated in the "conjuncture of global capital." She argues that the voices of children who labor are lost in these discourses. A postcolonial retrieval of these narratives provides agency to these children, and offers a more complex understanding of the relationship between child labor, international trade, and IR. In Chapter 11, Nair explores Burma's representation in the dominant liberal human rights discourse and attempts to uncover the erasures that accompany such a repre-sentation. Problematizing the discursive power and authority of liberal human rights scholarship and policymakers, particularly in the United States, the chapter suggests that an alternative postcolonial re-reading of the Burma human rights problematic reveals the gendered and orientalized structure of human rights discourse, and its class underpinnings.

Notes

1   We subsume the study of international political economy under the broad rubric of IR.

2 Rosenberg's assessment and critique of the methodological and ontological three-step "levels of analysis" framework is instructive. He points out how, in adopting such a framework, IR theorists like Kenneth Waltz create an artificial separation between spheres of action while calling for them to be "integrated" into a more holistic frame of reference. And yet, "once the basic method of levels of analysis has been accepted, the problem of how to construct that frame cannot help but appear in the false terms of how to reassemble the misshapen fragments" (1994: 96).

3 *The Sociological Imagination* by C. Wright Mills (1959) is pertinent to Rosenberg's critique of IR.

4 Walker refers to the state as a "spatial container" in IR theory, an image that is incapable of supporting "a plausible analysis of historical transformation in any context" (Walker 1992: 126–7).

5 For a synthesis of the dependency literature see Chilcote (1974).

6 Despite the nuances between poststructuralism and postmodernism we use them interchangeably in reference to this scholarship in IR.

7 In justifying the "far from complete" nature of this cast Rosenau has claimed that "space limitations" precluded the inclusion of "Third World analysts, rigorous quantifiers, and political economists ... the most conspicuous silences" in the volume (Rosenau 1993: x).

8 There is also a debate over the use of the hyphenated "post-colonial" and the unhyphenated "postcolonial". For supporters of the former, it serves "as a decisive temporal marker of the decolonizing process." Others prefer the non-hyphenated, or unbroken "postcolonial" because it more accurately reflects the continuity and persistence of the consequences of colonialism (Gandhi 1998).

9 Said has acknowledged his debt to these writers and thinkers in *Culture and Imperialism* (1994).

10 The Orient analyzed by Edward Said is not what is popularly understood as the Orient, i.e. Far East Asia; rather it is the Middle East or Near East, and India.

11 Said's reliance on both Foucault and Gramsci, and by extension poststructuralism and Marxism, is reflected in postcolonial scholarship and may explain some of the critical tensions evident in postcolonial work.

12 Ranajit Guha, one of the main architects of subaltern studies, argues that the use of Gramscian analysis poses serious problems for subaltern scholars. According to Guha, the Gramscian use of ideology and hegemony privileges colonial discourse, giving very little or no agency to the subaltern, defeating the very purpose of subaltern scholarship. Others consider Gramsci central to understanding the subaltern voice. It remains doubtful whether the autonomous positions of the subaltern can ever be "discovered" since the concept of subalternity, as enunciated by Gramsci in *Prison Notebooks*, "signifies the impossibility of autonomy" (Prakash 1992: 9). This position is echoed in Spivak's "Can the subaltern speak?" (Spivak 1988).

13 For the extended passage see Fanon (1965: 40).

14 For a survey of Marxist approaches to imperialism see Brewer (1989). Also see Chilcote (1999).

15 For example Annette Ackroyd's passage to India more than a hundred years ago exemplifies the efforts of Western feminists to save their Eastern sisters. The construction of Indian women by Ackroyd whose "Victorian sensibilities are offended by her Indian benefactor's wife" is interesting to note:

> She sat like a savage who had never heard of dignity or modesty – her back to her husband, veil pulled over her face – altogether a painful exhibition –

31

the conduct of a petted foolish child it seemed to me, as I watched her playing with her rings and jewels.

(quoted in Ware 1996: 152)

16 For a discussion of resistance, women, and veiling see Abu-Lughod (1986), Ahmed (1992), Hoodfar (1997).

17 Gilroy is responding to Raymond Williams's comments on "rooted settlements" of the Welsh in the formation of British national identity, in contrast to the place of recent immigrants in Britain.

18 However, Stuart Hall has dismissed this argument by suggesting that it resonates with the "whiff of politically correct grapeshot" and affords an "unwelcome glimpse" into the "ins and outs of American Academia" (Hall 1996: 243).

19 Neil Lazarus has argued that Prakash, Chakrabarty, and Chatterjee are anti-foundationalist and hence more influenced by Foucault than others like Guha of the subaltern school. According to him Gyan Prakash's suggestions for writing "post-Orientalist histories" equally implicates national, Marxist, and orientalist histories in furthering the project of a universalist modernity. While critical of the representations of India present in orientalist histories, both national and Marxist histories ironically "replicate Orientalist reason" in their "own ideologically and institutionally determined procedures and protocols" (Lazarus 1999: 122). For Prakash, nationalist historians' allegiance to the nation-state, which was based on and fostered an image of an undivided, albeit sovereign India, engendered certain erasures. In doing so it replicated the orientalism of colonial history. Marxist historiography, for Prakash, with its focus on class and capitalist history, is also foundationalist and Eurocentric. Its "vision cannot but reproduce the very hegemonic structures that it finds ideologically unjust in most cases and occludes the histories that lie outside of the themes that are privileged in history" (Prakash quoted in Lazarus 1999: 124).

20 James Scott's *Weapons of the Weak* (1985) has influenced the literature on peasant resistance and is relevant to our concerns about resistance and agency. The literature on global civil society, social movements, and transnational advocacy networks, which has more recently engaged questions concerning transnational mobilization on gender, the environment, and human rights, does address agency but from a different vantage point than we do in this volume.

21 This is reflective of Darby and Paolini's analysis of the third movement in post-colonial studies, which they suggest is pervaded by postmodernism, unlike the first move which engages "the fiction of excolonial countries" (Darby and Paolini 1994: 375).

22 Ania Loomba points out that critics of Edward Said have accused him of concentrating "too much on imperialist discourses and their positioning of colonial peoples" at the expense of agency. But as she further notes, other scholars see Said's project as inspiring or coinciding with "widespread attempts to 'write histories from below' or 'recover' the experiences of those who have been hitherto 'hidden from history'" (1998: 232).

23 Spivak has been a key contributor to, and feminist critic of, the subaltern school. See especially her arguments in "Can the subaltern speak?" (1988).

24 See the extensive literature on subaltern studies in volumes I–X of *Subaltern Studies*.

25 See Loomba's succinct discussion of this debate (1998: 231–45).

26 Our reading of Bhabha's contribution to understanding resistance and agency is different from Darby and Paolini's interpretation. They place him in the third movement, which they argue "is less sanguine about any prospect of recovery" (Darby and Paolini 1994: 377).

2

POSTCOLONIAL CRITICISM

International reality and modes of inquiry

Siba N. Grovogui

Since 1945, the idea of postcoloniality, or fostering international existence beyond colonialism, has stimulated the reflections of the vast majority of intellectuals worldwide and practitioners of international relations, particularly those of the former colonial empires. It has also galvanized the plurality of debates at the United Nations and associated institutions and fora. Yet Western scholars, a part of this debate, have remained oblivious to this international shift and also to the so-called postcolonial theorists who examine it.[1] Indeed, although postcolonial interventions have frequently found their ways into the academy and its professional journals, only a few scholars have fully appreciated the modes of inquiry and ontological discourses associated with postcolonial criticisms. As a result, the representations of "international reality" and "international existence" have remained grounded in Western institutional and discursive practices so as to reflect and affirm parochial structures of power, interest, and identity.

Such attachments become problematic when they are accompanied by explicit attempts to preserve the authority of the West as sole legislator of international norms and values, to foster ontological discourses that question the legitimacy of the "non-West" as enactors of international morality, and to cast doubts on non-Western modes of hermeneutics, ethnography, and historiography. Unfortunately, an increasing number of Western theorists have compounded their neglect of the complexity of international existence with an explicit advocacy of non-engagement with postcolonial critique (Todorov 1993; Hopkins 1997). They suggest that the non-adherence of postcolonial critics to disciplinary and institutional norms leads to normative ambiguity.

This concern is tied up with the charges that the methods of postcolonial critics are likely to lead to the breakdown of productive exchanges within the academy because postcolonial criticisms are emotional, subjective, and irrational responses. According to Hopkins and Todorov, such responses undermine the attainment of universal or transcendental values that can be attained only through an understanding of the purpose of empirical inquiry and an empirical social theory of cross-cultural relations and global politics

(Todorov 1993; Hopkins 1997). The present essay focuses on the arguments that (1) the methods of postcolonial theorists are non-normative and nonsensical in that they allow for a conflation of judgments of fact and judgments of value; (2) postcolonial critics are uninterested in the free exchange of ideas and good-faith communication; and (3) Western intell-ectuals exclusively possess the cultural "dispositifs" for cross-cultural interlocutions and translations that promote a convergence of values across cultures and regions.

Political philosophers and cultural historians are not alone in doubting whether postcolonial intellectuals can contribute to the production of inter-national knowledge. But the peremptory dismissals of the substance of postcolonial criticisms – particularly the ideological, political, and ethical questions arising from postcoloniality – are troubling. It is equally puzzling that many international scholars and others are loath to confront the historicity of their disciplines – in the present case, "international knowl-edge" – and, as such, to re-imagine these disciplines in terms of alternative methodologies, ethics, and politics. In this conjunction, the broader point of this chapter is whether Western methodologies (claiming universality) can be imposed upon postcolonial interventions without undermining the *telos* of postcolonial criticism itself.

I address these issues in the context of post-World War II debates over the restructuring of the global order. I refer particularly to Franco-African contestations over the nature of the postcolonial order, its values and norms in particular. The chapter highlights the context in which the production of international knowledge occurs, and the loci from which postcolonial theo-rists make their counterpoints to disciplinary and other authoritative verities. In the aftermath of World War II, the governing or establishment French left urged African intellectuals, on the one hand, to recognize the commonality of the human condition and the demonstrable truths of French canonical texts and, on the other hand, to reject political radicalism and disruptive discursive forms such as sarcasm and parody. This appeal set the context for a system of norms based on fixed standards according to which French elites envisaged engaging the formerly colonized on the future of the French empire and the postcolonial order. The appeal itself carried political weight because it was also leveled by progressive French parties and individ-uals who both maintained political ties with African organizations and professed a commitment to postcolonial reforms (Biondi and Morin 1992: 243–341). They included the socialist party, the republican democratic socialist union (USDR), and nearly a third of the leadership of the popular republican movement (MRP) and non-official French associations. Together, these groups formed a left-leaning coalition that governed France under the short-lived Fourth Republic. This political left is the precursor to the vast majority of today's left-leaning French parties, groups, and associations (Becker 1998).

Between 1946 and 1950, both the accusation of non-conformity and the related political repression befell the Rassemblement Democratique Africain, or RDA, the single largest political organization in the French colonial empire to be represented in the three postwar legislative bodies of the Fourth Republic: the National Assembly, the Assembly of the French Union, and the Council of the Republic. Among RDA spokesmen, Ouezzin Coulibaly, the RDA's political director, Gabriel d'Arboussier, its general secretary, and Boubou Hama, its unofficial historian and sage, self-consciously opposed the "neocolonial agenda" charted by the governing political left. On this and other accounts the African deputies were accused by French officials of antagonism toward French traditions and ill-will toward meaningful and constructive dialogue between France and its colonies. According to the first charge, the African leaders favored relativistic arguments and parochial propositions over universalism and the collective good. In the second instance, French authorities accused their African critics of indulgence in sarcasm and a "communist fad." Critically, these accusations served to purge the RDA of its most eloquent representatives and to eliminate any space for constructive postcolonial criticism of French proposals for colonial reform. I suggest that this Franco-African contest and its outcomes provide an allegory for today's debates over the desirability, merits, and consequences of postcolonial criticism. These resonate well with contemporary reactions to postcolonial criticism in the social sciences and humanities generally, and international relations theory in particular.

Fables of warfare and reverse ethnography

The positions expressed by Hopkins and Todorov as conditions of cross-cultural and cross-regional exchanges contain a fundamental paradox. They simultaneously express a commitment to intellectual, cultural, and political exchanges between Western intellectuals and others, on the one hand, and claim a privileged knowledge of the necessary normative parameters for both such an engagement and the collective good, on the other. Their justifications for such a paradox are clear. A cultural historian of the British empire, Hopkins has faulted postcolonial cultural criticism for the breakdown of cross-cultural exchanges within the academy in the interest of a more complete understanding of modernization and globalization. To this end, Hopkins has amalgamated postcolonial criticisms under the cloak of cultural and subaltern studies and stigmatized them as derelict, overzealous, and simplistic. He is perturbed by the tendency of postcolonialists to posit a "stereotype of the European master narrative" and to project this said totalizing enterprise "on to an identikit picture of subject peoples, referred to as the Other, in order to demonstrate that many Europeans held racist views" (Hopkins 1997: 14). As cultural criticism, Hopkins has argued, this kind of discussion gives a bad name to the word and worlds of culture. They are driven by "the dictates of postmodernism" in the service of contemporary issues such as minority rights (Hopkins 1997: 13). Likewise, Hopkins has maintained, postcolonial critics do injustice to history by mobilizing only a few ideas in the interest of nation-building. Significantly, these critics have misguidedly omitted "the role played by the British empire" in laying the foundation of a global, fully integrated, universal order for the benefit of all humanity (Hopkins 1997: 30–42). In sum, he has expressed regret that postcolonial analyses have not contributed much to the necessary dialogue that must occur in the present era of globalization.

Hopkins's theses are themselves founded upon the erroneous perception of the uniformity and function of postcolonial criticism. Specifically, Hopkins postulates that postcolonial criticism originates in the fields of literary criticism and cultural studies among South Asian critics of the British empire. As Mignolo has eloquently argued, it would be mystifying indeed to claim that postcolonial theories emerge exclusively from the legacies of a particular colonial trajectory or are "postulated as monological and theoretical models to describe the particularities and diversity of colonial experiences" (Mignolo 1995: ix). In actuality, postcolonial discourses reflect the diversity of colonial histories, their linguistic and scientific reasoning, and the loci of enunciations of theorists and/or critics (Mignolo 1995: ix). Indeed, the legacies of colonialism manifest themselves today according to different colonial trajectories, their modes of administration, and the extent of participation of the subject populations in the political economy and the production of knowledge. Significantly, the degree and sphere of participation of colonial populations in the production of knowledge affected both the accounts or memories of empire and their related modes of inquiry.

Like Hopkins, Todorov too is inattentive to the diversity of postcolonial intellectual traditions when he posits a mistaken trend among the "inhabitants of the former colonies" to associate French humanism with colonialism (1993: 88). He is bothered by postcolonialist generalizations about Europe and by their lack of commitment to humanist universalism. In this latter regard, Todorov associates the methods and approaches of postcolonial authors with those of French anti-humanists. Accordingly, for him postcolonial critics indulge in ethnographic and cultural relativism that often veers into ethically questionable politics. This move from anti-humanists to postcolonial critics obliterates significant divergences and complementarities of the divergent and contradictory ethical stands of postcolonialism. While postcolonial criticism of the South Asian subaltern variety may have originated in cultural studies, postcolonial criticism in the French empire does not. Here postcolonial criticisms originate from a longstanding anticolonialism that owes its character to its ambivalence toward Enlightenment ideas, associated modes of inquiry, and the political project of colonial *assimilation* (Mudimbe 1992: 95–117). As I will show, contrary to Todorov's assertions, the anti- and postcolonial criticisms of post-Enlightenment

French ideologies were textured by the familiarity of colonial populations with metropolitan individuals and associations as well as by an intimate knowledge of colonial practices.

It is therefore surprising that Todorov should join Hopkins in dismissing postcolonial critics for their reductionism and non-conformity to disciplinary norms of inquiry. Both are alarmed by the dependence of postcolonial critics on historical revisionism, deconstruction, postmodernism, and anti-humanism. They have rejected as misguided the postcolonial views of Western scientific and cultural practices, particularly in regard to their connections to the "colonial project." They are also irked by the insistence of postcolonial critics on a link between colonialism, global material inequities, and social malaises, on the one hand, and humanism and modernity in their multiple instantiations, on the other.

Hopkins and Todorov relate their comments directly to disciplinary norms and the constitution of knowledge as well as to methodologies, ethics, and politics of inquiry. Their comments on the methods and modes of inquiry of postcolonial critics are particularly elucidating. In regard to the methods and modes of inquiry recently espoused by postcolonial critics, Todorov (1993) particularly rejects the principle, ontological claims, and pedagogic values of an ethnography of the West by the formerly colonized, what he calls *reverse ethnography*. Todorov is particularly contemptuous of the attempt by postcolonial critics to "particularize" Europe in its modernity. By his accounts, reverse ethnography is not only reductionist and revisionist, it leads to the breakdown of cross-regional exchange and the quest for universal values. Presumably, the objectionable approach is grounded in parochial preoccupations and not in any scientific rationale. As such reverse ethnography only undermines cross-cultural dialogue and the collective capacity for global communication (Todorov 1993: xiii). In short, Todorov argues that reverse ethnography and other postcolonialist modes of inquiry do not lend themselves to legitimate and productive engagements. He is convinced that the formerly colonized have not shown a capacity as analysts and readers to separate themselves from their objects: Western societies and texts. Consistently, postcolonialist modes of inquiry do not lend themselves to legitimate and productive engagements.

In contrast to his views on *reverse ethnography*, Todorov infers the possibility and superior ontological standing of *ethnographic distancing*. Specifically, he argues that the outcome of the former "will not be very different from that achieved by Europeans when they *detach* themselves methodologically from their own society" (Todorov 1993: 88). In so arguing, Todorov assumes that Western theorists possess the sufficient methodological designs to reach objectivity by metaphysically removing themselves from the ontological grounds through which their societies have imposed coherence on social knowledge and its representations. On this ground, he is able to propose Western modes of inquiry as the proper means to social knowledge.

It is telling that Todorov and Hopkins offer Western discursive rules, norms, and sensibilities as the proper context for global exchanges. Hopkins' reasons are based on his contempt for the "postmodernist chic" of postcolonial criticism. He also impugns the pre-discursive motivations and competencies of postcolonial critics. The attribution of postmodernist chic is intended to convey the impression of the ephemerality and baselessness of all forms of postcolonial criticism. This impression is itself based on a not-so oblique assumption of the incompetence of postcolonial critics or their deviance from disciplinary norms (Hopkins 1997: 10–16). Like Hopkins, Todorov insists that non-Western critics abandon their wayward ways and necessarily adapt their modes of inquiry to the epistemological and ontological fields charted by Western canons and intellectuals. Specifically, he protests that speech acts favored by postcolonial critics have negative consequences on communication across boundaries. In his eyes, such speech acts promote a "textual warfare" against Western canons and arise from the critics' hostility toward the relevant texts, their authors, and their ideas. Accordingly, the ironist, satirist, and parodist would be uninterested in the truth dimensions of their critiqued "texts" and, in fact, would frequently obscure their meanings (Todorov 1993: xv).

This equivalence of disagreeable postcolonial utterances and speech acts such as sarcasm with "textual warfare," unfounded skepticism, or postmodernist chic needs investigation to establish the validity of the related claim that postcolonial modes of inquiry and rhetorical proclivities cause the breakdown of dialogue globally, across regions and cultures. The *Oxford English Dictionary* (1971) defines sarcasm as a "sharp, bitter, and cutting expression or remark; a bitter gibe or taunt" intended to make false pretenses conspicuous. In this sense, sarcasm has much affinity with irony (p. 2639). Sarcasm is believed to be unsuited to sustained composition, although it figures prominently in debates as retort. Its effects rest with the generalized context of the exchange and the language within which it is expressed rather than the formulation of speech (p. 2639). In contrast, satire is believed to be a higher rhetorical form, prose, or speech-act in which the author holds up prevailing follies or vices to ridicule (p. 2642). Unlike sarcasm, satire lends itself to a sustained composition and is generally recognized as a more serious form of denunciation. Satirists may choose their form for their intended effects. In the above instances, satire has much in common with irony and parody. They all lend themselves more easily to systematic prohibition than sarcasm.

One last and crucial difference between sarcasm and satire is that the former is not unambiguous. It retains a degree of ambiguity in regard to its object, which depends on the context of the exchange. This is to say that the effectivity of sarcasm depends equally upon the author's intentions and the listener's sensibilities. In other words, sarcasm is most effective when the listener succumbs to the author's intended effects or impressions.

This situation is not without paradoxes. The author of sarcasm may easily feign innocence when confronted by the listener. On the other hand, the listener (audience) may dismiss a sincere rejoinder on the grounds of sarcasm. The listener who feels victimized may concurrently repress the author of sarcasm and dismiss a sincere rejoinder on the ground of sarcasm, depending on their inclination, interest, and power. The charge of sarcasm, therefore, necessarily shifts attention away from the substance of the parties' competing positions or claims to their methods. It allows the accuser to dismiss even a sincere rejoinder and, depending on the relations of power, to reassert the self through the imposition of extra-discursive conditions as rules of engagement.

The postwar exchanges between RDA deputies and their French counterparts on the form of the postcolonial order is a case in point. It shows that the so-called parliamentary dialogue between the metropole and the colonized was set against the background of a paternalist French insistence that Africans conform to metropolitan cultural sensibilities. This expectation was not happenstance. It was a subterfuge designed to protect a political agenda by diverting the focus of debate away from African criticisms regarding the substance of the official French imaginary as well as African alternatives of the postcolonial order. This inattention to the particulars of RDA anticolonialism was more than ironic. First, it served no ethical or epistemological purposes but rather helped to squelch RDA members' desire for intellectual spaces within which to consider previously unexamined questions regarding identity, interest, and power. Second, in impugning the methods of African critics as baseless and ill-intended, French officials augured an era of political repression and the suppression of African rights in conjunction with the advancement of parochial French interests as transcendental collective good. In short, the postwar Franco-African parliamentary discussions demonstrate that any insistence on the propriety of speech acts and modes of inquiry must also examine the political context of the related exchanges if it is to sincerely cultivate dialogue and cross-boundary exchanges.

Postcoloniality and immanent critique in Francophone Africa

It would be hard to ascertain that French liberal sensibilities provided a suitable context for rationality and transparency and, consequently, goodwill and good faith negotiations with Africans. It would be harder even to prove that French suppression of anticolonial reflections flew solely from Africans' antipathy toward cross-boundary exchanges and related French texts and traditions. As I show below, the perception that RDA spokesmen indulged in sarcasm and that they opposed constructive Franco-African dialogue appears to be the result of French frustration. French officials were frustrated that the war and its outcome had placed them in a position where they were compelled to justify their colonial reform proposals to Africans.

Indeed, metropolitan elites were incensed by the skepticism of anticolonialists toward the metropolitan vision of the postcolonial order. The French administration was piqued that Africans were not sanguine about the prevailing French assumption that the necessary condition of postcolonial reform was the prior assimilation of the colonized and the conversion of African elites to the central tenets of post-Enlightenment rationalism, liberalism, and other derivative ideologies.

This frustration had its outward manifestations in the public political arena. Such was the case with the outrage over the tone of Daniel Ouezzin Coulibaly, the political director of the RDA, during one of his interventions in the French National Assembly. The full context of Coulibaly's arguments lies beyond the scope of this essay but the "long murmurs" and "protestations" that interrupted the delivery of the speech do not. It is particularly interesting that the ruling left coalitions joined the political right in denouncing the African's tone and sarcasm. This particular exchange between Coulibaly and a French parliamentarian is illustrative, however, of a larger problem between the African anticolonialists and even the most sympathetic of French anticolonialists:

Mr Ouezzin Coulibaly:	These words of Diderot come to mind: "There is one thing more odious than slavery: it is having slaves and calling them citizens."
Mr Pierre Montel:	And you tolerate this, Madame President? This is a scandal!
Mr Gabriel Lisette:	Are you renouncing Diderot, Mr Montel?
Madame President:	I could not possibly censure Diderot, Mr Montel.

(République Française 1949b: 5300)

As might be expected, Africans reacted positively to such exchanges. To them, the context of Coulibaly's revulsion was self-evident. They believed that the make-up and rules of debates in parliament undermined the base principles of democracy. Many also suspected that the French left had begun to move away from its wartime commitment to Africans. The Africans felt betrayed that French officials had undervalued their own war effort, particularly the extraordinary acts of African solidarity toward the colonial power when it was under Nazi occupation. Indeed, Africans acted on the basis of their self-perceived moral duties to the oppressed everywhere by consenting to disproportionate material burdens in support of the French resistance. Now, at the conclusion of the war, France and the Allied Powers demanded that Africans and other colonial populations accept marginalization and subordination instead of justice and solidarity. RDA members were disturbed that France had been fighting intermittent colonial wars since VE Day (8 May 1945), with the massacre of Algerian civilians in Setif. In these battles, French soldiers often fought against their old comrades from the colonies who had helped to defend them against Nazi Germany. What appeared to be sarcasm was in effect an appropriate response to French political cynicism and its subtending intellectual and ideological pretensions. These consisted of centuries of universalisms supported by hollow anthropological suppositions informed by rationalism, orientalism, and other forms of Eurocentrism.

A limited number of French intellectuals and political activists admired anticolonial assertiveness. Claude Gerard was among a handful of French elites who admired Coulibaly's talents and his evocation of French canonical teachings. A one-time French resistance leader, renowned journalist, and inductee of the French Légion d'Honneur, Gerard was an admirer and rumored lover of Coulibaly. Although on the political right, she joined many others on the left in finding in the oratory and political skills of RDA militants evidence of the success of the *mission civilisatrice*. In her never-completed biography of Coulibaly, Claude Gerard fondly remembers the oratory skills of the African parliamentarian and French reactions to it:

> [Ouezzin Coulibaly] expressed himself and wrote with remarkable ease. He possessed a singular style. The vehemence of his indignation [at postwar Western designs] and the power of his arguments were paralleled by a distinct style in evidence in his articles as well as his speeches and parliamentary interventions. These were peppered with *specks of humor and sarcasm as well as poetic notes and unpredictable but moving images* ... Regarding his interventions at the podium of the French National Assembly, there is one, more memorable than others, that Ouezzin made about the Atlantic Treaty. His exuberance provoked both indignation among colonialists and, of course, enthusiasm among RDA deputies and the left ... All present will forever remember that speech.
>
> (Gerard 1988; my translation and italics)

Coulibaly's oratory skills, his candor, and his grasp of Enlightenment ideas gained recognition among French elites regardless of their political affiliations. Yet, according to parliamentary records, many metropolitan elites disapproved of Coulibaly's prose and poetry (République Française 1949b: 5300). To anyone who shared the widespread aversion to anticolonial assertiveness, the above exchange confirmed the prevalence of sarcasm and other non-normative speech acts in postcolonial discourses. In fact, the political right generally dismissed the anticolonialist as ideologically misguided and a communist puppet. Reactions on the French political left to Coulibaly and his African colleagues were more shaded and complex. On the one hand, the communist party and others among the so-called extreme left showed understanding about African frustrations toward, and challenges to, the metropole. On the other hand, the establishment-left claimed to be bothered by what it perceived to be the sarcastic tone of RDA spokesmen and their irreverence toward French Enlightenment.

The French aversion to the methods of the anticolonialists in this context must be evaluated on two grounds. One is that French sensibilities are neither given, unique, timeless, natural, nor universal. This may explain why other Africans do not find the counterpoints made by Coulibaly and African anticolonialists to be sarcasm as French audiences do. The other reason for skepticism is that French intellectuals have historically adopted speech-acts and communicative practices as legitimate discursive techniques that are not inherently higher in form than African practices that appear sarcastic to the French. By this I do not mean just irony and parody, but also legitimate parliamentary practices. Finally, incidences of RDA sarcasm appear only occasionally in the public record, including parliamentary speeches or personal commentaries. In such cases, as shown below, French cynicism toward the bitter jibes of anticolonialists disguised French parochial interests as a universal good. In short, so-called African hostility and non-conformity was limited to exposing inconsistencies and flaws in the French imaginary of the postcolonial global order.

The ruling elites, it seems, were aggravated further by the strategic affinities between the RDA and the communist party. Although the RDA maintained parliamentary affiliations with non-communist parties as well, its association with the communist party was its Achilles' heel. Soon after France joined NATO, Vincent Auriol, then President of the Republic, Réné Pleven, President of the Council, and François Mitterrand, Minister of Overseas France, collectively enjoined Félix Houphouët-Boigny, President of the RDA, to disaffiliate his organization from the communist party and rid itself of radical elements in the interest of dialogue and cooperation with the metropole (Houphouët-Boigny 1952: 50–2). In so doing, the French establishment summarily halted the debate brought about by African deputies on the political configuration of the international order. The French administration also chose to censor the most eloquent of the outspoken anticolonialists, although the offensive speech acts did not violate French legislative rules of deliberations or transgress the allowable norms of civility in parliamentary debates. Irony, satire, and sarcasm have long been the staple of French parliamentary debates, which stress spirited political discussions over personal aesthetics or preferences.

Even if one were to grant the establishment-left that RDA members turned increasingly sarcastic, the charge in itself reveals nothing about the nature of the act. The pathos of the transgression and the reaction to it depends upon the discursive or political context of the speech act. In the politically and ideologically diverse context of the French Union, one would expect French rulers to be open to the possibility that the perceptions of propriety also hinge on cultural dispositions which are themselves subject to regional variations. Notably, as they accused African deputies of taunts and sarcasm, French deputies frequently transgressed regional African norms of civility according to which one never brazenly interrupts and walks out on an interlocutor. Both actions are familiar French parliamentary practices. Indeed, in certain West African cultural milieus, it is not an acceptable form for a wrongdoer or any person owing a moral debt to interrupt the person(s) that s/he recognizes to have aggrieved. In this light, French legislators who rejected colonialism for a postcolonial order implicitly conceded the anti-colonialist point that the defunct system offended human dignity. Thus, they owed a minimum degree of deference to African legislators and the former's consideration of the latter's views on the mechanisms for breaking with the past. Further, African deputies tolerated metropolitan parliamentary practices that were non-normative (in fact rude) according to the standards of their own traditions. Accordingly, it would be unacceptable behavior to lodge an accusation against an interlocutor without backing it up with substantive explanations bearing on the substance of the faulted speech-act(s). From these and other standpoints, countless West African deputies found certain body languages and French manners to be offensive and thus less acceptable than a crude but candid rejoinder.

It is not hard to imagine that whereas Africans were compelled to act in accordance with parliamentary decorum, the French government did not have to mind African sensibilities. But cultural sensibility and decorum were not the central point in French denunciations of Africans on sarcasm and radicalism. As I intimated above, the response of the French government was to censure the offensive Africans, not their behavior, and by this token to subvert the rules and principles of representative democracy. The metropolitan establishment applied political blackmail, repression, and bribery to undermine and later purge and tame the RDA to its liking. There is abundant evidence that French insistence on formality and propriety was part of a much larger political struggle where the end game for the metropole was to silence its African critics. One indicator is that the French accommodated a variety of anticolonial critics, including the *négritudistes*, who were equally critical of colonial rule and French policies (Mudimbe 1992: 95–117) and, as such, satirized and parodied official French invocations of humanist universalism (Kesteloot 1991: 15–89). The political determinant for tolerating the latter group was that it re-affirmed the authoritative French allocation of human faculties and associated hierarchies of values and subjectivity according to which the West possessed reason and science, while Africans had art and emotion. In short, French elites tolerated African critics who ultimately accepted the notion that the domains of science and reason were best left to the prerogatives of the colonizer (République Française, Centre des archives d'Outre-mer 1944: 1–2).

It may still be ascertained that the reactions of African deputies (or anti-colonialists) to the peculiar French legislative agenda were sarcastic. Yet it is hard to imagine that African "transgressions" caused the establishment-left to cast aside its self-professed passion for historical justice, or to end all forms of subjugation in favor of liberty. Rather, the basis of the official French reactions to RDA critics must be sought in extra-discursive structures of legitimacy, authority, power, and interest within the empire. The political gap between RDA and the French establishment centered on their differing views of what would constitute the proper interest and ethos of a Franco-African union. This gap was so great that no amount of African civility, good faith, and goodwill could have bridged it.

If Gerard is to be believed, the stakes of the debates were apparent to all parties involved but it is the sarcastic tone of the speech that retained the attention of the newspapers and politicians. Gerard's implicit argument is that French reaction to that speech had little to do with Coulibaly's prose. Coulibaly touched upon undeclared boundaries that protected substantive desires as well as material interests and the supremacist ideology that symbolically structured the constitutional debate over the French Union, uniting the metropole to the former colonies. RDA remarks generally ventured beyond the symbolic boundaries set by the French with respect to the role of the colonized within the French Union. This is to say that if they had any passion for historical justice, metropolitan governors subordinated this disposition to the more compelling desire to regain national grandeur as members of a reconstructed West and of the United Nations Security Council. These positions reinforced the claim of France as the inherent leader of the yet-to-be-defined Francophonie, a socio-political and cultural sphere for the French-speaking world. Indeed, French political elites had generally assumed that African legislators would defer to their French counterparts on the crucial matters of security, economy, education, and foreign policy (République Française, Centre des archives d'Outre-mer 1944: 1–15). Based on this expectation, the parliamentary metropolitan majority had questioned the right of the RDA to make pronouncements on such matters as the Atlantic Alliance.

It is in this latter sense that the perceptions of and reactions to sarcasm must be evaluated as dependent upon the sentiments (affect or antipathy) and interest of the judging party. It was a political subterfuge that metropolitan legislators insistently charged the anticolonialists of sarcasm. Such a charge obfuscated legitimate disagreements with the colonized by shifting the focus of the debate away from substantive African comments on actual policies to the personal style of individual African deputies. This deflective strategy muted all discussions about the essential objects of postwar reform – political community, economy, and international morality. Worse, it led to esoteric debates over African uses of recognizable humanist concepts or canonical adages in support of colonial claims against the French; hence, the uproar over Coulibaly's invocation of Diderot and metropolitan reservations on the teleology and forthrightness of African criticism. Even so, the patterns of French ill-will were evident. Whereas some

French legislators must have felt an antipathy toward Coulibaly's uses of Diderot (and other canonical texts), few could question his mastery and interpretations of French canons or accuse him and African deputies of lacking familiarity with French policies, their motivations, and their sources.

Dialogue, transparency, and goodwill

Postwar Franco-African exchanges had all the requisite elements for a rational debate, as envisaged by Todorov. In particular, the exchanges between the RDA and the French left took place within the context of a humanist proclamation of solidarity, cooperation, and dialogue. From French perspectives, this conviction coexisted with a paternalist insistence on African conformity with metropolitan cultural sensibilities and political agendas. Indeed, the French "civilizing mission" prepared Africans for a high degree of familiarity with canonical French texts. The primary aim of colonial education under French rule was to produce a category of colonial subject known as the *évolués* – or colonial subjects who were sufficiently imbued in French intellectual traditions, ethical sensibilities, political dispositions, and ideological preferences (République Française, Centre des archives d'Outre-mer 1949: 1–2). As a class, therefore, the colonized were expected to master Western cultures, traditions, and languages of politics for purposes of scholastic, professional, and political advancements within the empire.

The result was that Francophone Africans generally developed a great deal of sympathy for core Enlightenment and post-Enlightenment French ideologies and their core theses, if not principles. Educated to be *évolués*, they were expected to fully and competently assimilate French formulations of liberty, community, human rights, and solidarity, particularly the representations of these ideals by such historical French figures as Montaigne, Montesquieu, Rousseau, Diderot, and La Bruyère. In fact, by all indications, the Africans were also committed to these ideals of liberty, human rights, and solidarity as they had been shaped by wartime events. Even RDA critics and others who objected to the neocolonial imaginary of postwar French elites retained a great deal of sympathy for core postwar ideals if not principles. As shown earlier, Ouezzin Coulibaly best symbolized this paradox. He and other radical RDA members shared with their French counterparts linguistic and political cultures as well as iconic texts. Coulibaly graduated from colonial school as a *médecin africain*, a breed of physicians trained by the French to meet the estimated medical needs of Africans. Upon the completion of his training he became president of the alumni association of the graduates of William Ponty, his alma matter. He later turned politician and publisher. As his parliamentary interventions suggest, Coulibaly was a passionate moral philosopher, fond of quoting Diderot, Emile Zola, Molière, and Voltaire, and others. Indeed, he shared in the intellectual and artistic passion of the French left for radical (meaningful) political reform. Like his contemporary French left intellectuals, Coulibaly had declared his love and friendship for the oppressed and devoted much time to advocating reform of the moral order. He owed his own position to post-Enlightenment ideologies and, significantly, to the inter-war years entreaties between the progressive forces of the Front Populaire and Africans and, later, the collaboration among anti-Vichy forces and Africans. In addition, he was gifted with linguistic talents symbolized by his use of prose, poetry, and imagery.

Imbued with the ethos of post-Enlightenment ideologies, Coulibaly professed an interest in the quest for truth as well as a devotion to justice, peace, equality, and human solidarity. In this context, he related quite comfortably and intelligibly to the same canonical texts that inspired the French left. While in the Assembly of the Union, he maintained political affiliation with several metropolitan organizations with whom he conversed in French idioms of modernity and, as such, significantly contributed to reproducing the prevailing ideologies. It is not surprising, therefore, that a close African ally of Coulibaly, Gabriel d'Arboussier, would formulate the RDA's *raison d'être* as the restoration of the universal values of the international order in geopolitical spaces from which they had been suspended. He listed human rights, justice, liberty, democracy, free trade, free exchange, human solidarity, and interdependence as key universal values.

With few exceptions, French elites recognized the oratory skills and intellectual versatility of the key spokesmen of the RDA. Coulibaly's colleagues in the legislature also admired the legislative talents of African representatives as well as their mastery of procedures and rules. In these roles, African deputies established working relationships with metropolitan individuals and associations through informal ties and formal political affiliation with progressive French groups and parties. The Africans therefore acquired an intimate knowledge of the French intellectual and political landscape. Such ties cemented the overall process of African acculturation. The post-World War alliances emerged during the war as a result of African empathy for and solidarity with the metropole, which began with the Vichy surrender to Germany and Nazi occupation of France. Specifically, the vast majority of anticolonialists shared the aversion of the anti-Vichy French forces to Nazism and its racial policies, including antisemitism. This empathy drove Africans to actively support French resistance and related anti-Vichy and anti-Nazi networks. Upon victory, and at the 1944 Brazzaville Conference, the heirs to the anti-Vichy and anti-Nazi coalitions solemnly promised to extend political freedom and amity to colonial populations in recognition of the African war effort. This conference initiated the debate over a Franco-African union which the French formalized constitutionally as the French Union. The latter led to political affiliation (or *apparentement*) between the French left and the African heirs of wartime antiracist and anticolonialist mobilization. Specifically, the French communist party, the radical republicans, and several other non-communist progressive parties extended parliamentary affiliation or established working relationships with the RDA.

The tradition of *apparentement* was not the only source of African familiarity with French individuals, organizations, and traditions. While living in the metropole, Africans necessarily acquired French friends and adversaries with whom they interacted on a daily basis. This familiarity nurtured African appreciation for the intricacies of French traditions and politics, but it also provided the anticolonialists with personal knowledge of the contradictory aims of the postwar French political imaginary. This personal experience and knowledge formed the basis upon which the RDA came to judge French humanist propositions. In this sense, RDA comments were founded on prior knowledge. It was with cause (*en connaissance de cause*) that the anticolonialists reached their conclusion that the new French humanism consisted of parochial Western understandings of both subjectivity and interests and that this parochialism underlay the new global institutions – including norms, principles, and organizations – proposed by Western powers to the international community as a whole.

It is evident, therefore, that colonial education endowed Africans with the capacity to convey their views within translatable idioms to their French audience. However, many who have examined the trajectories of African intellectuals have conflated the latter's acculturation with a conversion of their will, interest, and desire with French ones. As decried by their French interlocutors, RDA members combined their mastery of French texts with "sarcastic taunts" and other methods of criticism spanning comparativism, hermeneutics, historiography, and ethnography. More often than not, Africans reacted to postwar French policies by contrasting their didactic references to humanist canons with their actual implementation and practical forms. These Africans also sought to particularize France within the Franco-African union, along with its moral and political imaginaries which stood against those of others. Boubou Hama specifically insisted on the need of the members of the Assembly of the French Union to recognize the particularity of the sovereign will of the French Republic in contrast with that of the legislature of the union of France and its colonies (République Française 1949a: 360). Hama also wished to ascertain that his French peers understood that what appears to the French elites as truth and objective reality may be perceived legitimately by others in the union as subjective French perceptions and not truth or objective reality in the context of the union: "What we want is truth, truth that ... will reflect the points of view of the French Union. What we want is that relative truth [founded upon an] objective reality which is also the subjective reality [of the Franco-African Union]" (République Française 1949a: 360). This truth, according to Hama, "must give room to different points of view" based on open and free contestations (République Française 1949a: 360). To Hama, as to Coulibaly and other RDA radicals, truth and reality were inseparable from their subjects' will, desire, and interests. Hama was of the opinion that the advent of a Franco-African union would usher in an objective reality, but this was a subjective kind of objective reality because the very institutions of the union would be founded upon "a point of synthesis that preserved the mutual interests" of French and Africans (République Française 1949a: 360).

Hama admitted the relativity of his own truth and position. In his view, the historic reality of the French Union arose from the institutional void created by the war. Wartime events had undermined Western reliance on rationalism and shattered the myth of the autonomy of reason. But this objective reality alone did not delineate the configuration of the new union, a successor reality to empire. The new union would be founded upon a "subjective reality," a reality nonetheless of consciousness and desire of multiple subjects, agents, and actors. Accordingly, the colonized called upon hegemonic Western powers to adhere to democratic pluralism not by virtue of reason or tradition alone, but also as a matter of unfulfilled historic claims and historical realizations of past shortcomings. It is also on these very subjective grounds that Hama implored the French establishment-left to allow Africans "to talk about [the objective reality of neocolonialism] and topics that are objectionable to [the French]" (République Française 1949a: 360). In short, Hama and other Africans were keenly aware that democracy does not inherently lead to transparency and openness. The kind of democracy envisaged by Africans would allow them to talk about those "subjective French realities" that form "the deeper reason that pushed" metropolitan legislators to "obstruct" open parliamentary debates and thus undermine an equitable postcolonial order. (I need not point out here that RDA critics anticipated today's postmodern conventions.)

By Hopkins's and Todorov's accounts, such commonalities should have led to a uniform understanding of the collective interest. RDA deputies should have had unrestricted, unconditional, and transparent exchanges with their French counterparts. After all, French elites and their RDA critics shared linguistic and discursive affinities. Yet to many Africans, while the French policy of African assimilation bore noted advantages for cross-empire discussions, it was also condescending and oppressive to Africans. As a result, the colonial experience undermined in the eyes of Africans the French humanist claims propounded by colonial education. Indeed, colonial education failed to impress upon the colonized that France possessed a unique capacity to generate universal art, culture, philosophy, and science. Many Africans also came to scorn French views that the "natives" did not possess any useful political languages or moral imaginaries. In a way, Coulibaly symbolized African disappointment and disillusion at the gap between Western canonical views of the human experience, transcendentalism, and ethical existence, on the one hand, and postwar Western policies, on the other. He and other RDA spokesmen were made to understand that their persuasive power depended upon their relation to a field of significations defined by French texts and traditions.

One result of African disillusionment was that anticolonialists ceased to accept the notion that France (the West) alone may be expected to generate positive global ethical matrixes and moral values for a postcolonial world order. Indeed, even as they continued to use the same idioms or vehicular languages, the RDA and the French left incorporated their differing interpretations of French canons into different visions of the moral order, international community, and international relations. The French views become apparent in the text. For now, it suffices to say that although a plurality aspired to modernization and globalization, they did so without necessarily espousing the corresponding Western imaginaries of community, liberty, rights, and justice. In short, the vast majority of African deputies ceased to uncritically embrace French humanist and rationalist propositions.

Familiarity, empathy, and contempt

Intellectual affinities and cultural commonalities do not necessarily lead to a convergence of interest among two unequal subjects. Nor do such commonalities guarantee goodwill and good faith. These faculties are to be demonstrated by exploring the substance and objects of the speaker's utterances as well as the *telos* of their adopted policies. Further, the behavior of RDA deputies must be explored according to the substance and objects of their utterances (anticolonialism and postcolonial reform) and an appreciation of the historical context of the utterances and the actual policies to which the speakers object. In contrast, the sensibilities of the metropolitan politico-intellectual establishment (the audience of RDA deputies) alone are not sole indicators of the intentions, empathy, or antipathy of RDA deputies. It remains that the exchanges between the RDA and their immediate interlocutors on the French left were mediated by a structural context and a subjective element.

The structural context was constituted by the colonial context of Franco-African disputes while the subjective element consisted of French ambivalence over the future of empire. RDA members maintained a legally and politically ambiguous status as elected legislators in metropolitan bodies and representatives of the colonized. As colonized, RDA legislators could not participate in the determination of the agendas for debate or subsequent rules of engagement between colonizers and colonized. In these instances, French deputies used their structural advantages over Africans to add weight to their own political positions. Consistently, the French assigned electoral colleges and apportioned parliamentary seats in the three chambers so as to ensure metropolitan numerical advantages over the colonized. These numerical discrepancies were particularly significant in the colonial context in which African deputies did not enjoy the same civil and political standing as their French counterparts. Indeed, although African deputies could freely venture their opinions in legislative chambers, they remained tied to metropolitan institutions and organizations by colonial bonds. These structural constraints imposed upon Africans had a greater impact on the flow of ideas across cultures and regions than any methods used by postcolonial critics. They shaped the ethical and ideological outlook of African deputies such that the postcolonial ethos was necessarily understood in the colonies in opposition to French policies.

The subjective dimension of the Franco-African debate evolved around both political and ideological motivations and intellectual transparency. As shown earlier, it was convenient for French elites to obscure the grounds for the profound distances that separated their visions of the postcolonial order from those of the colonized and, as in the case of the RDA, to attribute related disagreements to the unwillingness of the colonized to engage in trans-regional and cross-cultural dialogues. In such instances, French legislators and commentators frequently de-emphasized the intellectual diversity, ideals, and objectives of colonized constituencies in favor of a debate over language and conduct which the French would inevitably win, as they were simultaneously colonizers and enactors of the rules of engagement.

It is seldom acceptable to take the charge of nonconformity at its face value, especially when leveled by an interested party, and to assume a priori goodwill and transparent motive on the part of the complainant. But Todorov does so on the basis of the identity of the parties: the French (or Western origin) of the authors of the iconized texts and the postcolonial locus of the criticisms against them. Having taken these criticisms to denote hostility, Todorov is even more mistaken to attribute the related sentiment to the absence of familiarity with texts and lack of empathy for their authors. As much as it broods goodwill and transparency, familiarity also may generate contempt depending on context and experience. Again, during these Franco-African contestations, RDA critics reserved their strongest antipathy for the political structures and the extra-discursive norms through which the French establishment sought to delegitimize the positions advanced by the anticolonialists. This kind of contempt is neither hostility nor antipathy *sui generis*; it is a direct challenge or response to such ill-willed positions or ill-intended policies as proposed by the French in the guise of humanism, rationality, and universalism.

On the other hand, the RDA was not entirely averse to the central tenet of humanist universalism that ideas may transcend the context of their origin to apply to other situations and in other regions.[2] RDA members too espoused that view independently of their acquired French cultural traditions. Nonetheless, the RDA challenge to the French imaginary and its model of postcolonial reform underscored important points about the possibility of dialogue (or else "textual warfare"), empathy (or antipathy), and cultural exchange (or universal fundamentalism). One is that anticolonial criticism arose from prior knowledge and legitimate African concerns, however self-interested, about the constitutive interest and underlying ethos of any Franco-African union. It was, therefore, with cause (*en connaissance de cause*) that Coulibaly and his colleagues contested the arguments put forth by the metropole to justify its positions. Indeed, it was on the basis of prior knowledge that Africans concluded that the new French humanism consisted of parochial Western understandings of both subjectivity and interests and that this parochialism subtended the postcolonial and global institutions proposed by France and the West. It was also on the basis of their acquaintance with prior Western policies that RDA critics argued that the norms and principles subtending the new institutions and organizations – among them, the Bretton Woods financial institutions, the Marshall Plan, and the United Nations Organization – would formalize parochial interests as universal principles and the collective good.

It is significant that RDA critics contested the official French vision of the moral order but that they never cast doubts or impugned the legitimacy of the sovereign French will, desire, and interest. African critics were displeased that the institutions, norms, and organizations that concretized the French vision contradicted the progressivist French discourse of trans-communal relations, particularly in its insistence on open communications and fair exchanges. The Africans feared that so-called universal institutions would arbitrarily differentiate historically entangled identities of colonized and colonizers along the narrow axis of the West and the rest. The resulting moral order would embody the will and desire of a few powerful states and, as a result, legitimize colonial practices and rituals of power under new guises. It also appeared to RDA deputies that their French counterparts wished to achieve two contradictory objectives: one, to maintain their own particularity as endowers of reason and science and, two, to bolster this "provincialism" with universalist claims to justify the collective French will to grandeur and the related desire to hegemony and colonial interests. Humanism remained intertwined with the colonial project in this context and universalism served mostly to disguise parochial interests and to justify the extra-territoriality of related ethical and legal matrixes. These perceptions led Africans to the conclusion that Western policies and institutions did not deserve universal approval.

In sum, RDA critics saw no need to be exclusively deferential to French humanism (or, elsewhere, the manifest British imperial past). They did not fully accommodate French pretensions to a unique disposition to universalism. They likewise repudiated the ethnographic epistemology underlying this pretension, along with its categories and conclusions in regard to subjectivity, agency, and the moral order generally. Consistently, these Africans rejected the philosophical, doctrinal, and jurisprudential interpretations of canonical texts that often masked a continuing metropolitan desire and related will to maintain a hierarchical order. RDA critics also repudiated narrow understandings of humanism that were founded upon nefarious Eurocentric ideologies, including orientalism and various forms of rationalism.

Whether they constituted sarcasm or not, anticolonial taunts availed themselves, in this context, as an effective antidote to French (and Western) cynicism, itself signifying the absence of goodwill or interest in maintaining dialogue. On such occasions, RDA critics turned to sarcasm as an effective mode of rebuffing French cynicism. This cynicism was complemented by the skepticism of a significant segment of the French elite about Africans' capacity to bring to light any compelling moral questions regarding the postwar order other than those framed by the West. Rhetorical taunts, in this context, served as a *rappel á l'ordre*, or a call to order, that countered French tendencies toward self-aggrandizement. The "bitter gibe or taunt" signaled a motion of disagreement with the relevance or appropriateness of the implicated canonical texts, their interpretations, or the related ideologies and political actions. Thus, RDA taunts applied to particular objects: the universalist pretensions and underlying cynicism of postwar French humanist discourse.

Still, anticolonial criticism was productive intellectually and ideologically. Above all, it was constitutive of a discourse (or politics) of subjectivity based upon an ethos of equality and pluralism. RDA critics particularly sought to broaden the discursive spaces within which Africans and French conjointly elaborated on the ethical matrixes of the postcolonial order. Their initial understanding of the ethos of the international order proceeded from their examinations of the central categories of postwar institutions: the international community (as embodied by the United Nations, the French Union, and other international bodies); cultural exchanges through the UN Educational, Scientific and Cultural Organization (UNESCO) (as catalysis and cataloguer); human and collective rights (including the right to self-determination); and international duties and obligations (encapsulated by legally assigned roles to international organizations and individual member states). The latter were to be defined and articulated by the UN Economic and Social Council (for social and economic issues), the Security Council (for matters of war and peace), and the General Assembly (for the expression of the will and opinion of the general membership). In these regards, RDA critics imagined the emerging international order to produce multiple, complementary, and contestable notions of power, identity, and interest instantiated in international politics.

Conclusion

The reluctance to conceptualize or envisage postcoloniality in the field of international relations is a lost opportunity. First, such an absence undermines the intellectual claim and moral purchase of a discipline that aspires to understand international politics. This intellectual deficit pales, however, before the ethical implications of speaking for and acting upon a world that theorists and policymakers do not engage. I do not intend to make a claim here about the possibility of knowledge. Rather, I appeal to humility and prudence in a complex world. For instance, it is *not* ethically sufficient today to proclaim the advent of a near-universal order after the collapse of the Soviet Union in order to justify a Western enactment of international morality. One must also come to terms with the fact that the process of universalization has not been open to greater participation by the multiple constituencies of international society and that the ethos and teleology of the prevailing moral imaginary are not viewed by these multitudes as generally congruent with their own needs.

Hopkins and Todorov seem oblivious to such pragmatism when they summarily dismiss "reverse ethnography" and "cultural relativism." In their individual ways, they assume that there exists a universal order of knowledge and that the formerly colonized do not possess ethical, useful, and intellectually compelling political languages and moral imaginaries. This position singles out postcolonial critics to bear the burden of translation and moral learning in order to facilitate trans-boundary communication. In this light, the formerly colonized must adhere to master Western languages of politics and their canonical texts to access the related forms of knowledge. In contrast, they do not require that Western rationalists and humanists learn other languages or idioms as a matter of value. Their dismissive tones suggest that Western theorists are absolved of the obligation to familiarize themselves with native cultures and traditions. Such a task remains the province of specialists residing mostly in the academy, whose research agendas may or may not stress the standpoint of their subjects.

The events related in this essay suggest that decolonization offers an opportune moment to rethink international knowledge, to reflect on international reality in its complexity, and not just certain salient dimensions. This pursuit also means that the discipline must revisit its attitudes toward its own institutional practices and modes of inquiry. Postcolonial critics, like anticolonialists before them, do not necessarily dismiss the philosophical principle of ethnographic distancing and its associated modes of inquiry, cultural history, and reflexive philosophy. The postcolonialists simply expect the likes of Hopkins and Todorov to spell out the grounds upon which they defend cultural history and reflexive philosophy and to extend their methods and justifications to reverse ethnography. Indeed, cultural history and reflexive philosophy may be understood here as mirrors through which the West examines itself and its own conscience. However, the implied reflexivity of ethnographic distancing does not in itself guarantee transcendentalism, or transcultural communication and moral exchange. Nor are its methods and discourses uniquely redemptory, that is that they guarantee ethical outcomes in human interactions.

Reverse ethnography must not be viewed as a substitute for reflexivity, particularly one achieved through ethnographic distancing and vice versa. To its defenders, reverse ethnography is a fitting reply to Western self-understanding, particularly as it relates to its own anthropological and ethnographic ambition and knowledge of the other. In this light, reverse ethnography and postcolonial cultural criticism are windows through which the formerly colonized cast their gaze using available methodologies upon colonialism and its ontology, beyond self-professed intentions. This window allows the formerly colonized to shed light on certain moral questions bearing on the universal human condition that may fall outside the expressed concern of the former colonial powers. Significantly, as a window, reverse ethnography allows the formerly colonized to capture the West in its most unsuspecting and unauthorized moments and, through its modes of inquiry, to re-examine the claims made by the cultural historian and the reflexive philosopher. Again, the point here is not that one set of methods produces better results, but rather that each examines questions that are peculiar to their subjects' self-understanding and that, together, they illuminate international existence. Neither reverse ethnography nor ethnographic distancing leads inherently to goodwill in regard to trans-boundary (trans-cultural) communications. They merely enrich our moral dispositions – including empathy, identification, detachment, distancing, assimilation, syncretism – and enrich the quality of our judgment.

Like anticolonialism, today's postcolonial project provides a rich account of the context of universalism as well as alternatives to humanism and other relevant ideologies. The articulation of this project may not resonate with traditional Western discursive norms (or academic fields) but its aim is to create discursive spaces within which the formerly colonized hope to engage Western authors, texts, and policies in order to expand on the ethical and ontological boundaries of the prevailing political imaginary. Again, this is not to say that the methods of postcolonial criticism, including reverse ethnography, better serve truth and wisdom (and ultimately justice). Nor am I suggesting that humanists and rationalists cannot, through ethnographic distancing, arrive at an ethical position that may serve justice. I am suggesting, however, that neither epistemological principle nor related modes of inquiry are complete without the other. Indeed, international theory must assimilate the lessons of anticolonialism, however tentatively, in the interest of productive exchanges among the constituents of the moral order – that is if there is any interest in the expressed voices, wills, and desires of the formerly colonized.

Notes

1 These debates have involved *inter alia* realists against idealists, historians against behaviorialists, and positivists against constructivists.

2 As Mignolo has shown in a different context, many cultures around the world envisage the applicability of their beliefs, modes of inquiry, and values to other contexts and subjects through both attachment and comparative analysis (Mignolo 1995: vii–xxii).

3

SITUATING RACE IN INTERNATIONAL RELATIONS

The dialectics of civilizational security in
American immigration

Randolph B. Persaud

This chapter analyzes the ways in which the issue of immigration is seen as a security or civilizational threat to the United States. While the broadening of security studies has created room for discussions of immigration as a security matter, the focus has been generally limited to issues such as illegal entry and trafficking, and other matters pertaining to sovereignty, narrowly defined. But there is another dimension to this problem that needs to be explored, namely the cultural elements that inform nationhood. The demographic structures of western states have been undergoing notable changes, not the least on account of the substantial amounts of immigrants from former colonies, and more generally, the Third World. The presence of the new immigrants has caused considerable friction. Nativist anxieties have surfaced in practically all of the western states and groups dedicated to limiting entry and denying rights to those immigrants already present have increased significantly. There is substantial evidence of physical violence as well. The groundswell of opposition seems to be informed by some sense of the loss of nationhood by the nativists, and in many instances the immigrants are seen as a threat to the very existence of communities. In the case of the United States a good deal of the resentment against immigrants has been expressed in racial terms, and there are instances of explicit racist mobilization against the newcomers. These developments provide an interesting opportunity to explore the racialized dynamics at play in "defending the nation" against immigrants. To make more sense of what is happening in this regard, it is necessary to examine, on a broader scale, the presence of race in international relations.

The wider undertaking, therefore, is to make a contribution to a growing but still negligible literature on race in international relations.[1] The task is rather complicated because our understanding of both race and international relations has changed considerably over the past several years. In general, there has been a displacement of race as a morphological category, and of international relations as primarily concerned with questions of strategy. Analysis of race has been increasingly broadened to include problems of gender, identity, culture, ethnicity, class, and even nationalism. Some writers in fact insist that "[r]ace-ethnicity, gender, and class are interconnected, interdetermining historical processes, rather than separate systems" (Amott and Matthaei 1996: 13). The general direction of reconceptualizing race has been to put a lot more emphasis on its social construction (Malik 1996). The effect of this broadening of the concept of race is that problems once deemed outside the narrow band of international race relations are increasingly incorporated into its problematization. It is important to note that developments in theorizing race are not merely the result of intellectual practices divorced from lived history. Rather, civilizations and identities have emerged as nodal points for a re-racialization of global politics, as well as the cultural and political bases for resistance and counter-hegemonic struggles.[2]

As for the discipline of international relations, not only has it been expanded to include new areas of investigation, but there has been a corresponding modification of the theoretical field on account of a more comprehensive destabilization of global politics, as essentially concerned with great power conflict and the balance of power. Feminist scholars in particular have shown the ways in which both international relations and its study have been built as a complex of gendered practices (Whitworth 1989; Peterson and Runyan 1993; Grant and Newland 1991; Sylvester 1994). The insertion of gender into the problematics of IR, and the more general feminist "war of position" against the discipline's hitherto fixed universals,[3] have in fact helped in opening a point of entry for theorizing race and the imbrication of race and gender in global politics. But gender, like race, is not a homogeneous, universal category. Western feminist IR scholarship has therefore been articulated from a particular cultural perspective, and has itself been critiqued as a dimension of western hegemony (Mohanty 1997). These critiques have developed largely in the form of postcolonial theoretical practices and have emerged partly from an engagement with poststructuralism and postmodernism (Loomba 1998; Gandhi 1998). Much like the latter two, postcolonial critics have been carrying out a broad-based attack on essentialism, foundationalism, universal rationality, and the epistemological hegemony of the knowing subject. However, as noted in the introduction to this volume, some postcolonial scholars are concerned that a "totalizing critique of all forms of essentialism and identity politics" may reinforce dominant power hierarchies, and therefore emphasize the need for strategic essentialism (see also Krishna 1999). In addition, what gives the postcolonial intervention its distinctiveness is the attempt to show the ways in which the axial privileges of the West were in fact forged by and through the simultaneous constitution of economic, political, and cultural marginalization on a global scale. As many of these writers have noted, race has been a central articulating principle of that marginalization.

The social purpose of retheorizing global politics by accounting for race and culture, therefore, is not simply to add to the existing inventory of issue areas, but to construct an epistemological and ontological platform for an engagement with the hegemonic knowledges that have hitherto organized the world as a coherent movement of history (Fukuyama 1992: 60). The achievements of this Grand History have been accomplished by a well-trained silence on major components of histories, peoples, and civilizations, which if more systematically incorporated in the making of the world, would interrupt an entrenched historiography of progress. The absorption of a vast array of particular genetic histories into the teleological Grand History of modernization, progress, liberal democracy, hegemonic leadership, and market civilization, amounts to a disciplinary strategy of fixing a global regime of truth within the civilizational assumptions of western man (Gill 1995a). The objective here, however, is not to introduce an epistemology of victimization, or an ontology merely founded on marginalization, oppression, and subordination. The task rather, is one of practicing a sort of "discursive disturbance" through a critical pedagogy that disallows the bid for epistemic closure.[4] Knowledges are constitutive of the world as we know it. In this context Foucault's suggestion that the "essential political problem for the intellectual is not to criticize the ideological contents supposedly linked to science, or to ensure that his own scientific practice is accomplished by correct ideology, but that of ascertaining the possibility of constituting a new politics of truth" (Foucault 1972: 133) is entirely pertinent. One of the first things to do, therefore, is to understand the modalities of inclusion and the simultaneous repression of race in international relations, and how the product of this doubly constituted inclusion/exclusion has allowed the discipline to reproduce itself in the image of western man and the Great Powers.

The problem of inclusion/exclusion of race in IR is rather complicated. It is not so much a problem of quantity per se; the issue rather is the epistemological status of its *presence*. While generalizations can often be untenable, it is not problematic to suggest that an analysis of race in international relations functions at the margins of the discipline, and by so doing, figures in the authentication of other, supposedly legitimate structures, forces, and institutions that configure the terrain of the global. One way to demonstrate this is to refer to the widely accepted notion that the cold war was a period of relative stability, marked by the absence of war and by general predictability in the system. But as Bradley Klein has pointed out, "For the overwhelming majority of the world's peoples, global politics since World War II has been anything but peaceful" (Klein 1994: 15). The claim of stability in international relations during the cold war, therefore, is only possible if one actively forgets the millions of lives lost in the Third World during the same period. The relationship between the common-sense understanding of IR and those who structurally and institutionally control the knowledge of international affairs, in this instance, is staggering. What sense might we make of these practices of erasure?

Some thirty-one years ago Roy Preiswerk noted that "it is as legitimate and necessary today to study race as a distinct factor in international relations as it has been in the past to isolate other basic forces which determine the behavior of groups and result in conflict" (1970: 55). Preiswerk was to be disappointed, however, for as Roxanne Lynn Doty (1993) has found from her survey of five leading IR journals spread over some fifty years, only a handful of articles have been published on race and international relations. A look at some of the most widely used textbooks on international relations also reveals the *erasing practices* about the impact of race in global politics. This exclusion is not only symptomatic of acute (structural) peripheralization, but is constitutive of the supposedly legitimate boundaries of the discipline. Further, the academic and pedagogical practices of exclusion seem to mirror the more general retrenchment concerning the globally dispossessed who are preponderantly people of color (Cheru 1995). Whenever the latter are factored into the making of the global system, they are attached as threats to preexisting objects known as the global economy and inter-state system. The conditions of incorporation, therefore, apart from being "additive," are such that the West is reproduced as the privileged center around which the rest of the world rotates.[5] The defense and reproduction of the hegemonic axial system, however, has not been restricted to economic and military power, but includes supposed racial, cultural, and civilizational superiority. The control of borders through immigration policy has been and continues to be the official instrument used to achieve what I would like to call *civilizational sovereignty*.

The amorphous character of race in international relations

The amorphous presence of race in international relations might be traced to four sources. The first has to do with the genealogy of the discipline. International relations was founded largely in response to war and, as a result, the proper subjects of the field were defined largely in terms of war and peace.[6] The problems of war and peace, as Barry Buzan has pointed out, have crystallized into a subfield (after World War II), namely strategic studies, and this subfield according to Buzan has been privileged by the discipline as a whole – with the consequence that other significant entities have been ignored (Buzan 1991; Klein 1994). War studies did not necessarily have to ignore the problems of race, since a large number of wars were conducted along racial and cultural lines (Drinnon 1997; Horsman 1981; Dower 1986; Tinker 1977). For example, the expansion of European imperial power overseas, and particularly empire building, was largely justified on the basis of racial and cultural superiority. Tzvetan Todorov, for example,

has shown through his "exemplary history" the ways in which the subjugation and eventual annihilation of the indigenous populations of the
Americas were legitimated through pre-experiential notions of "spiritual
expansion" and conquest (Todorov 1984).

Wars were also racialized in the imperialist fight to beat back decolonization, and even some wars of liberation were explicitly racio-civilizational in
nature (Fanon 1965; Doty 1996b). Yet the discipline ignored these racialized dimensions of international relations. Part of the reason why was neatly
captured by P. Darby and A.J. Paolini:

> The root of the problem was that Asia, Africa, and other non-
> European territories were seen to be outside the civilized world. The
> European states acquired title and ruled in their own right. Hence,
> imperial relations were not international relations and they fell
> outside the proper concerns of the discipline. It was thus left to
> other fields of study to grapple with the processes that played such a
> large part in determining the future of the peoples, societies, and
> states that now constitute more than two-thirds of the world.
>
> (Darby and Paolini 1994: 380)

The second reason is directly related to the first. Given the overwhelming
stress on security and strategy, and given that states have a monopoly of
violence, the field has concentrated very much on state-to-state relations.
The latter itself was theoretically legitimized by the near hegemonic position of realism in the discipline up to only a few years ago. Realism's stress
on inter-state relations, however, does not in and of itself lead to the exclusion of race. The problem is less a matter of emphasis and more one of
ontology – the definitive objects of investigation that are deemed to be
capable of revealing relevant and useful knowledge. As Robert Cox put it:
'Ontology lies at the beginning of any enquiry. We cannot define a problem
in global politics without presupposing a certain basic structure consisting
of the significant kinds of entities involved and the form of significant relationships among them' (Cox 1992: 132).

For realist and neorealist theorists, states are containers of identities.
There is an assumption that national identity is a privileged site that absorbs
all other competing identity dynamics. As a result, the extra-national
elements that go into the production of an overdetermined identity configuration such as race, gender, ethnicity, and class, are subsumed under a
supposedly universal equivalent. The reconciliation of the multiplicity of
elements is in fact a conscious strategy in nation-state formation, since the
legitimacy of state power is directly related to domestic political support.
The end product of the interpellative process is a political subject represented
in purely national (if not nationalist) terms, viz., American, Canadian,
Indian, etc. Having secured identity *as* national identity, the state retrieves

its political subjects, that is its citizens, as resources in global competition. Given the definitive place of inter-state conflict in realist and neorealist problematizations, the state-produced notion of the domestic population as a single people whose identity is fixed in the national imaginary is accepted. The identity of citizens, therefore, is seen as mirroring the identity of the nation, which is assumed to have an essentialist essence. The internal differentiation of identities is thus displaced by the general category.

Third, because the principal focus in the field has been understanding and managing the balance of power (and the balance of terror), only the relations among the Great Powers have been considered valuable in making general statements in the field as a whole. The neglect of the discipline actually mirrors the level of neglect in policy. The balance of power preoccupation by the Great Powers has meant that even when race (and even genocide) is directly part of war, unless it upsets the global balance it is ignored altogether or incorporated only tangentially. To the extent that race has figured in theorizing global politics, therefore, it has done so in the form of what Foucault has called "subjugated knowledge" or "disqualified knowledge" (Foucault 1980: 78–84).

Finally, the East–West superpower conflict was as much an intellectual and ideological war (of position) as it was a geostrategic confrontation with the threat of nuclear annihilation. On account of this, a good deal of the literature on international relations during this period was suffused with ideology. As used here ideology refers not merely to justification, but also to a set of constitutive practices that defined the contents as well as the parameters of common sense. For policymakers in the West, race was given some attention because it pointed to a major weakness in liberal democracies, and there was concern that the denial of civil rights (especially in the United States) might give the Soviets ammunition in their ideological campaign against racism and colonialism.[7] The Soviets saw a natural front between themselves and the Third World against racism and neocolonialism, and despite the Non-Aligned Movement, as late as 1975, Cuba was pushing this thesis. Ironically, Robert Gardiner has also pointed out that the Chinese used racial arguments against the Russians in their attempt to gain influence in the Non-Aligned Movement (Gardiner 1968).

Theorizing race in international relations

Critical thinking about the extent to which race has been excluded from IR depends on (1) what is meant by international relations and, by implication, what literature is included in the inventory under appraisal, and (2) what is meant by race. In the first instance, if the discipline is reduced to inter-state relations, and particularly to war and peace, and foreign policy and diplomacy, the literature is indeed negligible and we are restricted to works by Dower (1986), Lauren (1996), Tinker (1977), Deconde (1992), and Shepherd and LeMelle (1970). A broader definition of the discipline however allows us to draw upon a much larger literature. In this sense the literature on imperialism, nationalism, comparative civilizations, colonialism, and some of the works on foreign policy, and immigration provide rich sources for race and what may be called global politics (see for example Doty 1996a, 1996b; Campbell 1994; Manzo 1996).

If in addition we see race as a contested social, cultural, and ideological problem, or more precisely as an element in social formations and intercivilizational relationships, a wider literature avails itself.[8] This other literature, which may be put in the category of the postcolonial movement, is primarily concerned with imperialism, orientalism, and culture (Darby and Paolini 1994: 379). Although international relations has not concerned itself with these subjects, Darby and Paolini are correct in suggesting that "a dialogue between the two discourses would be mutually provoking and therefore enriching" (1994: 372). This appropriation of the literature on postcolonialism both broadens and deepens the authoritative sources from which a rereading of international relations may be launched as involving a historically sedimented constellation of racialized practices (see for example Fanon 1965; Hall 1977; Said 1978).

It has already been mentioned that race should not be reduced to physical, biological, or morphological markers. Though stating what race is not is important in specifying what it is, a purely negative definition is not sufficient. At the same time, to be consistent with the theoretical problematic developed here, race cannot be defined as a self-enclosed entity with positive, foundational, or essentialist properties, since race as a pre-ideological and pre-political category is devoid of any inherent racialized meaning. In other words as a natural taxonomical category, race is essentially descriptive and "innocent." The racialization of race occurs in specific space and time, and under specific historical, political, socio-economic, and ideo-cultural conditions. While *longue durée* sedimentations of racialized histories and discourses may and do form part of the structural template of a society, the conditions and modalities of their retrieval very much depends on the conjunctural forces that occasion their being "woken up from the dead." Similarly, while short-term snippets of racial referencing may be present, they cannot have the generative capacity to structure enduring social relations. Put differently, race must be understood both synchronically and diachronically.

If the meaning of race cannot be apprehended at the *durée trop courte* or the *durée trop longue*, it is because such meaning is only constituted in the act of configuring determinate *historical structures* (Hexter 1979; Braudel 1980). This happens at the temporal level of conjunctures. As I have claimed elsewhere, in the making of such structures,

> race may shed old meanings, take on new ones, [may get] called
> upon to delineate inside from outside, [be] employed in the contes-

tation of what is good and evil, [be] combined with other cultural artifacts to produce identity and mark difference, become a nodal point of cultural or national unity, act as the fulcrum of political mobilization, serve as a principle of justifying valorized class inequality, economic exploitation and the division of labor, function as an explanatory concept in the development of civilizations [where discourses of the latter become activated], [be] used as "technology" to inscribe status, [be] drawn into movements of resistance, and last but not least, excluded from the knowledge infrastructure which shapes the intellectual "limits of the possible."

(Persaud 2001: xvii)

This does not mean that the meaning of race is what you make it. It is not a free-floating signifier. Rather, the process of racialization has multiple dimensions, and the way in which it actually becomes "real" cannot be understood outside of history. The reason is that race itself is only one element which is combined with other historically specific factors in social reproduction. As used here, "historically specific" requires an analysis of the following factors of race in the process of racialization – overdetermination (or multiplicity), relationality, contestability, mediation, articulation, and hegemony. The complex forms in which race expresses itself, therefore, might in fact displace the category of race per se. The question, then, becomes one of identity. Let us examine these conceptual categories at closer range.

First, race is always subjected to mediations. While biological markers such as skin color, hair texture, the shape of eyes, and so on, are significant, they do not themselves have any meaning; there is no logically necessary link between the morphological and the social, or between the latter and the political. A direct move from race at the level of the morphological to the social ignores the fact that the valorization of difference can be (and has been) fixed and stabilized around a plethora of signs of otherness. However, skin color is the most widely known and employed instrument of instantiating racial difference today, as Ania Loomba has pointed out (Loomba 1998: 121). Loomba has also noted that in different historical contexts, class belonging or other physical attributes have served the purpose of inscribing racial difference. This may be referred to as "attribute in dominance," meaning that in different conjunctures, different attributes, or mixes of attributes, may be used to racialize the common sense of the social formation in question. The history of antagonism against immigrants in the United States, for example, shows clearly that a racialized project of exclusion need not depend on the simplicity of physical markers to underwrite its articulatory cohesion. Irish immigrants from the mid nineteenth century through the early twentieth century, for example, were displaced from the inside (of America) not by color or physiognomy, but through behavioral attributes and the modality of their incorporation (Ignatiev 1995). More than that, the colonial production of the Irish by the British in the United Kingdom formed a sort of backdrop that fused with the structural location of the immigrants in the American economy, and thus allowed their marginalization based on racialized discourses.

Recent nativist discourses of exclusion have circulated around language and the "public charge," sovereignty (of the border), and demographic composition.[9] More recent immigrants from Africa and Haiti have been compartmentalized not necessarily on the basis of physical difference, but around discourses about the danger of the West being flooded by refugees. Without understanding the process of mediation there is considerable risk in assuming that race is nothing other than a self-evident fact, and that, based on this fact, there are corresponding forms of consciousness and actions.

Second, the fact that race is capable of mediation at the social level, as just described, is possible because the identity of agents is overdetermined and constituted through multiple practices. Particular elements of an identity may thus be appropriated in the symbolic construction of racialized otherness. Quite often, it is in the transition from the pre-social (i.e. morphological), to the social, that the identity of the agent becomes racialized. What the concept of over-determination allows us to understand, therefore, is how a particular fragment of the identity of an agent may be reified, objectified, isolated, and then deployed as the essential property of the agent and his or her culture. Central Americans and Mexicans in the United States have been marked off by language as much as by color. Being a native speaker of Spanish in the United States is almost tantamount to having a certificate of low status. The mix of factors here is important. Spanish in itself is not the problem for the nativists. We know this because Americans whose first language is English are perceived as having an asset if they speak Spanish. They are represented as worldly, cosmopolitan, educated, or even liberal. Parents in fact spend huge amounts of money to send their children to Spanish-speaking countries to acquire the "product." From a different angle, Indians who also have a native first language other than English (Hindi or other languages from the Indian subcontinent) are not subjected to the same marginalization, and this despite the greater dissimilarity between Indian languages and English, compared to Spanish and English. Instead of racial marginalization, Indians, like other Asians, are looked up to as a model minority population. Why? Because their *attribute in dominance* is constructed around science and technology. They are hi-tech Indians! In this discourse the language and skin color of Asians has been positioned as less significant than their presumed privileged conditions of entry into the labor market, and into the United States. Nevertheless these images of the model minority have not permanently diffused the animosity and violence toward these groups.

To further illustrate the mediated nature of race and the ways in which identity is overdetermined, let us return to the question of language and

Central Americans. While it is true that language, in this case Spanish, is like an albatross hovering over Latinos, that in itself needs to be clarified because the depth of overdetermination is quite spectacular. There is a real sense in which language and gender might fuse to produce the racialized identity of the Central American or Mexican. In the case of Central Americans, women preceded men in migration to the United States (Repak 1995).[10] The issue is not that they came first, but that they came to replace African American women as domestics. The Central American women, especially those living on the East Coast of the United States, assumed the already racialized occupation of child rearing and house cleaning. The most interesting thing here is that the job of the domestic itself was constructed in highly gendered and racialized terms before the Central American and more poor Third World women even arrived in the country. In this case the gendered and racialized structures of the social formation in general, combined with the valorization of these in the sector of domestic work, almost required poor (Central American) women (who are not white), as against say, a poor Argentinian male. The concept of overdetermination thus allows for an analysis of the complexity of identity formation.

It is especially important also from a point of view of counter-hegemonic struggle. Attempts that privilege class exploitation as the fount of consciousness and resistance tend to miss the fact that race and gender are actually generative in the structuration of the social division of labor (Mohanty 1997). The articulation of a project of liberation may therefore be conducted in terms of cultural liberation. Following Stuart Hall it is possible to posit that the race–class–color configuration is an overdetermined complexity.

> It does not help ... to depress some factors of this matrix, e.g. race/colour, class, in favour of others, e.g. culture, and then, analytically subsume the former into the latter, since it is precisely the generative specificity of each, plus the overdetermined complexity of the whole, which is the problem.
>
> (Hall 1977: 154)

The same has to be said of gender, since it is a basis on which some people understand the political. It might be the case that women are more inclined to radical politics because the negative consequences of gendered practices are felt more by them, but such a restricted view runs the risk of being gendered all over again.

Third, race and the identities that emerge from the processes of racialization may also be seen relationally – that is, the reality of race has to be understood in terms of its relational character. But relationality is not a set of fixed logics of confrontations as suggested in frontal opposition discourses. Rather, the relationality of identities is dependent upon a field of racialized discourses and has to be historicized. It is not sufficient to work with some general notion of us/them or we/they, as if the simple binary opposition of subject and object is capable of authoring identity and difference. The reason for this is twofold. As David Campbell has argued, "identity is a condition that has depth, is multilayered, possesses texture, and comprises many dimensions" (1992: 86). The complexity of identity, and its relationship with race, therefore, must be grounded in historical analysis. Also, consistent with Ernesto Laclau and Chantal Mouffe, the specificity of an identity is dependent upon the totality of the discursive formation rather than simple parts of it (1985: 105–14). According to these authors, "all identity is relational and all relations have a necessary character" (p. 106). To theorize the relationality of race we must see how race is activated and how it figures in the relational constitution of identity.

Fourth, what also needs to be theorized is the way in which race becomes activated from its pre-political/ideological status to being productive of identity. It is here we have to arrest how race figures in the making of an identity. Identities are, however, not self-contained attributes. Race is not something that in the process of its activation remains outside the principles of a new ideological formation. Quite the opposite. In the very act of racialization, racialized texts play a part in the making of the new ideological infrastructure. The reproduction of racialized social institutions are often indistinguishable from the reproduction of a racio-gendered common sense. The replacement of African American women by poor colored women from poor countries in the domestics industry, for instance, further consolidated colored people as the serving class, and at the same time, (colored) women as the appropriate people for that type of work.

The process of racialization, however, is not smooth, because the identity-constituting practices that attend racialization do not jump out from a fountain of already made, fully constituted instances that are simply emptied into the public sphere. Racialization is always specific to time and place and so the attempt to employ race in political or ideological mobilization has to be specific to a social formation, and involving specific sets of historically concrete agents. There is resistance, however, to acts of racialization, which puts limits on the extent to which the hegemonizing discourses can go. Resistance will actually help determine the limits to which the historical activation of race can go, not the least because it will affect the practices of articulation and the attendant discourses that emerge. What then are articulation and discourse?

Following Laclau and Mouffe, articulation means "any practice establishing a relation among elements such that their identity is modified as a result of the articulatory practice ... The structured totality resulting from the articulatory practice [is called a] discourse" (1985: 105). Articulatory practices operate through the construction of chains of equivalences such that pre-discursive elements are sutured into the discursive ensemble and are thereby transformed into moments. Put differently, the practice of articulation brings into relation (or combines) disparate and disconnected elements into a coherent system of signification. Elements of a discursive system, which previous to their discursive incorporation did not have logically necessary effects (i.e. they were floating signifiers), now assume a (valorized) and enabling position. According to Roxanne Doty:

> The discursive practices that construct a discourse include writing and speaking as well as practices often considered "behavioural." Discourses work towards closure, creating the effect of an inside that is clearly distinguishable from an outside, but ultimately fail to escape the irresoluble tension between interior and the exterior, the inside from the outside. It is here at the margins that the attempts to fix meaning, to institute closure, are often most evident.
>
> (Doty 1996a: 239)

Several historical studies have found convincing evidence of this. John Dower (1986) has pointed to anthropological studies that attempted to fix Japanese cruelty during WWII to toilet training; the lack of facial hair of the Japanese was also employed to construct them as children. Michael Hunt has demonstrated the ways in which American foreign policy practices produced Mexicans as "half-savages" and Latin America as a "black child" in order to subordinate them (Hunt 1987: 58–61). David Campbell has produced considerable evidence of the ways in which diseases and even "bad teeth" have been engaged in signifying danger to America; Doty has pointed to the fixing of US/Filipino and British/Kenyan imperial relationships as parent/child relations (Doty 1996b). It is immediately noticeable that the facticity of toilet training, facial hair, black child, bad teeth, or parent/child relations have absolutely no racialized meaning in themselves. It is only when these empirical elements are transformed into discursive moments, within a historically specific discursive formation, that they are able to inscribe identities. In the study of international relations the production of difference is central to nation-state formation, nationalism, and war fighting.

Fifth, and finally, the concept of hegemony needs elaboration because it is crucial in helping to understand both historical structures and the knowledges that function to preserve the social order. As Robert W. Cox put it, hegemony refers to a "structure of values and understandings about the nature of order that permeates a whole system of states and non-state entities. In a hegemonic order these values and understandings are relatively stable and unquestioned" (1992: 140). The said values are contingent upon the interpellative practices that manufacture ideational structures straddling the boundaries between myth and history. At its most strategic level, the making of a hegemonized imaginary involves systematic practices of erasure, ongoing drainage of historically embedded signs of epistemic disturbance and, simultaneously, the re-filling of these signs compatible with the authoritative rendition of national history. Louis Althusser wrote some time ago that the educational system is a major ideological apparatus employed in the organization of knowledges, for the purpose of social control. To that must be added the various signs and performances – monuments, memorials, flags, independence celebrations, holiday charity, beauty pageants, and so on. These institutions, signs, and performances are all implicated not only in bourgeois hegemony, but also in regimes of racial and patriarchal hegemony. These knowledge regimes shape the boundaries and contents of common sense and generate the standards of the social order, as well as the intellectual strategies for the rejection of competing and alternative interpretations that may threaten the privileges of the dominant groups of the extant order. Following Antonio Gramsci, hegemony may be seen as a complex cultural war of position.

> The overarching strategy is to rationalize contradiction, by transforming structural antagonisms into simple differences. Whereas the former might call into question the social order in its entirety and thus generate a "revolutionary" movement, the latter is well disposed to reconciliation within the boundaries of the existing social order.
>
> (Persaud 2001: 38)

Further, and as Foucault has suggested, hegemony is therefore a form of power that goes beyond the apparatuses of the state. Like Gramsci, Foucault's analysis of power allows an understanding of the way in which truth claims are produced, circulated, consolidated, legitimated, and reproduced in the social formation. Specifically, this capillary form of power is more concerned with how power is diffused outside juridical and repressive apparatuses. This is important in understanding the processes of racialization that are integral to the production of cultural hegemony. An analysis of US immigration policy reveals the ways in which this racial and cultural hegemony has actually operated in a specific social formation.

In what follows, concepts and categories developed are applied to an investigation of US immigration policy. This analysis demonstrates that racial and cultural identity have been critical to America's understanding of itself; racialization has impacted heavily on the management of the US border, and more specifically on the composition of the nation itself. At its broadest level immigration policy is one dimension of national security. The question is security against what, or in this instance against whom, and for what purpose? As the following analysis demonstrates, management of the border is fundamental to the production of national identity within the parameters of a hegemonized imaginary of civilizational security.

Immigration and civilizational security

On 19 November 1997 a man standing at a bus stop in Denver, Colorado, was shot to death. Though 25,000 people are murdered in the United States every year, this death had a meaning larger than the victim or the perpetrator. The victim, Oumar Dia, and the killer, Nathan Thill, did not know each other; November 19th was their first and only contact. But this is only partly true, for the unfamiliarity of the individuals notwithstanding, the two had encountered each other before – as peoples in a nation increasingly torn by the politics of belonging and citizenship. Dia died not as a result of something he had done, but because of the way he looked, his socio-economic position, and most of all the discursive space he occupied at a particular conjuncture of American (and world) history. He was a West African refugee, a signifier of threat to the cultural security of America. And how about Mr Thill? At 19 years old, he is part of a movement dedicated to the idea that whiteness is central to the preservation of America.[11] Thill did not by himself invent this nodal point of American racio-cultural supremacy; rather he is attached to a trace, a social force historically active in the structuration of American society. That social force is nativism. It is founded on a discourse of originary presence (perhaps best expressed in the sign "Founding Fathers") in which the Anglo-Saxon protestant pioneers, having claimed a historical right to the foundations of the nation, have to constantly defend it from (throngs of) new immigrants who supposedly threaten the material and cultural basis of the nation.

While murder may not be that common, racial violence against immigrants is neither parenthetical, nor new. Let us have a quick glance. Some five years ago, twenty-five immigrants seeking asylum in the United States were beaten up by guards in a New Jersey holding facility. "One immigrant testified that a guard grabbed his penis with pliers, while another said he was dragged by his beard. Several said guards pushed their heads into toilets, pummeled, kicked and stripped searched them" (Associated Press 1998). In 1994 seven US Marines from Camp Pendleton's Special Reaction Section 1 military police carried out a night-time raid in battle fatigues against a group of migrant workers. The migrants were dragged from their makeshift tents and beaten, one of them unconscious. Three of the Marines later pleaded guilty (San Diego Union Tribune 20 December 1997: A1). On 10 August 1999, Buford O. Furrow, a neo-Nazi white supremacist, burst into a Jewish community center "filled with children attending day care and a summer camp ... and sprayed the building with 70 bullets from a submachine gun" (Sanchez 1999: A1). Shortly after this, he shot to death Joseph Ileto, an immigrant from the Philippines. Furrow acknowledged that he shot Ileto for no other reason than that the man looked "non-white." Furrow is attached to the Phineas Priesthood, a group committed to "Aryan resistance."

Barely a month before this rampage, the United States was witness to a weekend of violence against minorities and immigrants in Illinois and

Indiana. In this instance, a 21-year-old devotee of the World Church of the Creator took the motto of the organization – RAHOWA (racial holy war) – to the streets and gunned down anyone with attributes of foreignness or, more broadly, otherness.

> The shootings ... began early Friday night in Chicago's West Rogers Park neighborhood, home to the largest concentration of Orthodox Jews in the city. In six separate incidents, the gunman ... shot six Orthodox Jewish men.
>
> From there, the gunman drove to the Chicago suburb of Skokie, where he fired seven shots at Ricky Byrdsong the black former coach at Northwestern University ... Byrdsong, 43, was struck once in the back and died later Friday night.
>
> The same night, in the Chicago suburb of Northbrook, the gunman shot at an Asian couple as their car passed his ... He next surfaced Saturday morning in Springfield, Ill., where he injured one black man, and that afternoon in Decatur, where authorities believe he wounded a black minister. Late that night, in Urbana, Ill., he shot at a group of six Asian University of Illinois students, wounding one.
>
> On Sunday, the gunman was in Bloomington, Ind., where he fired at a group leaving a Korean church. The gunfire killed Won-Joon Yoon, 26, a doctoral student.
>
> (Walsh 1999)

The gunman, Benjamin Smith, once told an Indiana University student newspaper that his feelings about race started when he observed "a large influx of Asians and Mexicans and blacks." Of significance was the fact that the shootings occurred on the 4th of July weekend, a time of celebration for the founding of America.

The United States has a particularly long history of such violence. But violence against the immigrants has to be understood in the larger context of managing global space. The treatment and representation of immigrants seems to be directly related to four factors: namely, the magnitude of infusion, the velocity of intake, the socio-economic mode of incorporation, and the source of immigration. These factors seem to have cross-national regularity as studies of the United States, Australia, Great Britain, Germany, France, and Canada have shown.[12] In the case of the United States, there is also sufficient evidence to posit that these factors are also valid at different temporal conjunctures. While the magnitude of infusion refers to the aggregate numbers of immigrants to the receiving country within a specified time, the velocity of intake refers to the rate at which immigrants are arriving. Both factors are necessary, but not sufficient to elicit racialized responses and racially driven policymaking. Combined with the first two factors are the mode of incorporation and the racial and cultural origins of the immigrants. If immigrants enter with a background of economic dispossession and are incorporated as cheap labor or domestics, or if they come as refugees, they are more likely to be racially ostracized and constructed as threats to the hegemonic community. And finally, the source of migration seems to be one of the most significant bases upon which "the evangelism of fear" is built.[13]

Wherever immigrants come from, though, they are subjected to a systematic reconditioning of what they should become. The official language for this is Americanization, a set of practices deeply implicated in a mixture of cultural nationalism.

The immigrant threat

Americanization is really the hegemonic socialization of the immigrant into the major assumptions, myths, institutions, and ideological orientations of the United States. At its broadest level Americanization is an attempt to securitize the nation from unwanted cultural influences. Americanization is an ongoing process; it is not a condition that is ever finally reached. Historically this process has involved the erasure of the identities of peoples from the world over with the exception of most western and northern Europeans. The late nineteenth and early twentieth centuries witnessed a major upward movement of immigrant arrivals to the United States. Invariably, the new immigrants were coming for much the same reason earlier immigrants had come. The new wave of immigrants offered up a new source of cheap labor in a period when the United States was about to enter into a period of manufacturing takeoff. This was the period when the groundwork for a whole new regime of accumulation would be put in place. These were not well-off people and the average immigrant arrived with $30.14. But not everybody was admitted. An analysis of who was rejected gives some indication of the supposed danger to the United States. In the period 1892–1910, 65.6 per cent of all rejections were based on "paupers or persons likely to become public charge" (US Government Immigration Commission 1911: vol. 41, 73). Another 12.9 per cent were turned back because they were "loathsome" or had "dangerous contagious disease," with an additional 2.8 per cent disallowed because they were put in the category "other physical or mental disease or defects." But the state agencies were not the only instruments of control. The response from civil society was far-reaching, as analysis of evidence from the 41-volume (1911) *Immigration Commission Report* shows. The general concern was that the new immigrants had been brought up in conditions that might mitigate their industrial, political, and cultural incorporation into America. And correspondingly, the task was how to drain or empty the immigrant from his or her previous cultural socialization, and make then available as ideal Americans.

Testimonies at the hearing gave a vivid picture of the perceived threat by the "lower classes" of Europe.

The delegation from New York state expressed its fear thus: "The idea of this nation is founded upon the belief that free and universal education of all its people will eventually produce a homogeneous race" (US Government Immigration Commission 1911: vol. 41, 254). Race as used in this context was constructed as a national identity referent, not as a morphological marker. The cultural nodal point of this identity was Britishness, and every step away from the latter was seen as a mark of degeneracy. The threat of the immigrant, and particularly his or her foreign language, was viewed with such seriousness that it was portrayed by the New York delegation as "a detriment to our fundamental institutions," if not to "democratic principles" (US Government Immigration Commission 1911). The dispersion of "group identity" is not new; in fact it has simply been "woken up from the dead." Witness, for example, the following excerpt from a 1915 speech by President Woodrow Wilson, "Address to newly naturalized American citizens," delivered in Philadelphia:

> You cannot dedicate yourself to America unless you become in every respect and with every purpose of your will thorough Americans. You cannot become thorough Americans if you think of yourselves as groups. America does not consist of groups. A man who thinks of himself as belonging to a particular national group in America has not yet become an American, *and the man who goes among you to trade upon your nationality is no worthy son* to live under the Stars and Stripes.
>
> (Scott 1918: 93, emphasis added)

Wilson's message was quite clear: those who retained an explicit language of their foreign past were unworthy, were threats to the cultural cohesion of America. The immigrant must engage in a long-term project of erasure, a project geared toward exorcising sign differences. The president's admonition of a group identity, however, was not as categorical as it seems. Rather it was more a matter of who in America might demonstrate collective identity, and for what purpose. One year after his Philadelphia speech to new immigrants, the president delivered a speech on Flag Day in Washington in which he called on Americans to work individually and collectively to ensure that the flag is honored. In his own words:

> Are you going yourselves, individually and collectively, to see to it that *no man is tolerated* who does not do honor to that flag? It is not a matter of force. It is not a matter, that is to say, of physical force. It is a matter of a greater force than that which is physical. It is a matter of spiritual force. It is to be achieved as we think, as we

purpose, as we believe, and when the world finally learns that America is indivisible then the world will learn how truly and profoundly great and powerful America is.

(Scott 1918: 215, emphasis added)

This exhortation to defend America from the foreign threat within, which was so powerful at the beginning of this century, has in fact resurfaced, and it has in fact been carried out with force. In the New Jersey beatings mentioned above, the immigrants, after being kicked and punched, were forced to repeat "America is number one." Dia's murder amounted to a public execution, a modern spectacle that valorizes the commitment of the nativist movement to defend whiteness in America.

The four factors (magnitude, rate, location, and source) that seem to elicit the racialization of immigration and the construction of the new agents as threats were all present at the beginning of this century. Depositions before the Immigration Commission clearly bring this out. In a statement on behalf of the Junior Order of United American Mechanics, a Rev. M.D. Lichliter engaged in an articulatory practice that combined a range of disparate elements into a coherent discourse of immanent and imminent danger. In part his testimony read:

This country has wonderful assimilating powers and can assimilate and distribute through its body politic a great army of worthy and industrious people and those of the high moral type. But it can not assimilate the mass of lower Europe and protect its high standard of morality and good order.

(US Government Immigration Commission 1911: vol. 41, 17)

And again:

It is clear to every observant citizen, it seems to me, when we take into consideration the vast hordes of undesirable aliens, approximating a million a year, that are coming to us, that something will happen; in fact, something has happened. The moral fiber of the nation has been weakened and its very life-blood vitiated by the influx of this tide of oriental scum.

(US Government Immigration Commission 1911: vol. 41, 17)

The reverend's deposition cannot be understood as mere stereotype, or even xenophobia. To reduce the testimony to these categories, as is often done, misses the productive capacity of these statements – that is to say, the way in which they functioned to inscribe the identity of America as a moral space, a space of industrious people, and a space of European and more especially, Nordic superiority. The logic of the testimony was that there was already a fully made America, built by a previous stock of people, who must now take on the further responsibility of protecting it from civilizational decomposition. Lichliter, in fact, did not leave us with doubts. In his own words, "It was from ... Aryan blood that immigration came previous to 1875. They did not come because they were assisted by others, ... they came because they wanted to be free" (US Government Immigration Commission 1911: vol. 41, 16). Industry, solid character, good values, purity, morality – these were attributes fixed onto the Aryan pioneers. But how do these attributes figure in the making of America, or more specifically the identity of the nation and its founding people? The answer lies in the process of othering which secures this iconic ideal of America. The discursive strategy that defines the conditions of emergence for this iconic America is founded upon the racialization of the identities of the newcomers.

Here is the reverend again:

> The country is not the same. It is being destroyed by the new comers. The illiterate, the unclean, morally and physically, the un-American, the criminally inclined, yea, the lower classes of aliens from the dangerous portions of our municipalities, and are becoming a menace to our institutions.
> (US Government Immigration Commission 1911: vol. 41, 18)

Thus the attributes that were imputed to the identity of the nation were not sufficient to consolidate the hegemonized America. For the latter to be produced and made available, relations of difference had to be specified. Racialized otherness served this purpose. This racialized identity/difference relation in the early part of this century, however, was not written *tabula rasa*. The United States already had a deep structure of racialized consciousness, framed as it were through 300 years of racial oppression and cultural dehumanization. The portrayal of African Americans and indigenous Indians as internal dangers, based on a morphological otherness, had long been inscribed in the hegemonic common sense. What was necessary in the late nineteenth and early twentieth centuries *vis-à-vis* immigrants was an activation and refiguration of the cultural symbols that had hitherto accomplished the task of drawing boundaries. There were also some adjustments to be made. While some elements of morphological otherness were preserved, especially with regard to Asian immigrants (from Japan, China, and India), the massive infusion of unwanted skin-white immigrants required new discursive stratagems. Whiteness itself had to be reinvented, but not from scratch. The real task was how to use the historical template of morphological otherness as a backdrop for the framing of some who were skin-white as dangerous to America. The testimony of a New Orleans author and banker, a Mr James Dinkins, was symptomatic of both the challenge and the immense flexibility of discursivity.

We do not need statistics to show the injurious effects of pauper immigrants upon our people. Even our negroes are injured by contact with them, which has at this time almost destroyed the civilizing influences of our people in efforts to improve the negro. I can safely say that 90 percent of the immigrants coming to this section are unable to read or write in any language and 95 percent of them are thieves and anarchists. They come here like cattle in crowded stock cars, with hatred for every form of government or social restriction, and they transfer that hatred to our Government and to our high class of people.

(US Government Immigration Commission 1911: vol. 41, 135)

It is important to understand that while the hostility toward new immigrants at the turn of this century was civilizational, it does not exclude economic factors. The new immigrants for one thing provided a major source of cheap labor, and because of the modality of incorporation in the industrial system (i.e. extreme dependency), they were not well given to immediate unionism. The immigrants then lowered the price of industrial labor, and this had far-reaching consequences for the new system of industrial and production relations that were developing at the time. The point is that the new Fordist industrial system was actually consolidated through a simultaneous process of Americanization, such that the social conditions for the reproduction of the new system of social relations were to be found at once in the home and in the factory. Mark Rupert's analysis of the rise of Fordism in the United States shows clearly the ways in which the new American was made in the image of the production practices at the Ford Motor Company (Rupert 1995). Thus the task of the sociological department at Ford was not simply to educate or Americanize the immigrants, who made up 70 per cent of the Ford labor force. At this point the notions of individualism, which the new immigrants are inculcated in, becomes key. Individualism was actually employed by the training department to push the new labor away from unionism. Things started to happen. First, the new immigrant was seen as threatening to American unionized labor, in terms of both institutional development and wages. Second, the new immigrants were treated harshly precisely because they became a major weapon for employers. Witness the following from the Junior Order of United American Mechanics:

In eight times out of ten an immigrant on reaching this country has a job waiting for him, even if there is no job for an American. Scores of instances have come under my own observation of such gross injustice done American workmen in the interest of an alien.

(US Government Immigration Commission 1911: vol. 41, 19)

The construction of the non-Nordic immigrant as a civilizational danger was in fact in full force since the 1880s, and as the numbers increased and the source began to change even more, the nativist movement in the country initiated a period of intense cultural and political contestation. The sense of threat was powerful enough, and the social forces arrayed against the new immigrants sufficiently determined, that soon the border began to be secured.

In 1882 the United States imposed its first restrictions on immigration when Congress passed the Chinese Exclusion Act, which prohibited Chinese immigration. This act marked the post-slavery beginning of the American experiment with immigration policy as a strategy of managing the racial composition of society. Continuing in this trend in the early 1900s, state and local governments in the western United States passed discriminatory laws against Japanese immigrants. For example, in 1906 the School Board of San Francisco segregated the schools, sending Asians to special schools and thus instituting a sense of cultural quarantine. The political mobilization against Japanese immigration was so powerful that President T. Roosevelt negotiated the Gentlemen's Agreement of 1907, which restricted immigration from that country.

Between 1901 and 1908, 8.8 million immigrants entered the United States. To offset this rise, and given the severe resistance to sustained high numbers after World War I, the United States implemented immigration quotas for the first time in 1921. These quotas limited immigration from Asia and placed a quota of 3 per cent on each nationality. Even after this legislation, many eastern and southern Europeans migrated, causing Congress to cut the quota to 2 per cent in the National Origins Act of 1924. In this act Congress combined a number of restrictions, including literacy requirements, classes of inadmissible aliens, and deportation regulations. In effect, the National Origins Act allowed for more northern and western Europeans to immigrate while restricting groups in southern and eastern Europe and Asia whose migration to the United States supposedly threatened the nation's cultural security. Consequently, Congress passed an additional act, the National Origins Plan of 1929, to ensure Nordic superiority by restricting the numbers of Jews, Italians, Irish, and Poles.

Contemporary nativism

The theme of Americanization has been revived in recent years. The 1997 immigration report, *Becoming an American: Immigration and Immigrant Policy*, actually put more emphasis on hegemonic socialization than the 1911 report. The report recommended "asserting the primacy of individual rights over the 'collective' rights that are paramount in many parts of the world." It noted that as long as the United States continues to emphasize the rights of individuals over those of groups, we need not fear that the diversity

76

brought by immigration will lead to ethnic division and disunity (Branigin 1997).

The factors that influenced the earlier movement are present again, this time with a distinctive focus on non-European migration. Thus in the period 1970–90, 9 million new immigrants arrived in the United States, and in the same period while the "US population grew by a fifth, the Asian American and Latino populations were at 385 per cent and 141 per cent respectively" (Feagin 1997: 78). The fear of civilizational decomposition, which disappeared from public discussion during the cold war years, has been dug up. Preserving a white national identity is fundamental to the nativist attitudes again, except that now the terrain of exclusion has moved from the broader discourses of kind to more specific articulations of threat.

In the current conjuncture language has become one of the nodal points of constructing difference and securing identity. The words of Senator Robert C. Byrd (Democrat, West Virginia) during a 1992 floor debate are indicative of the new articulation of threat to America:

> I pick up the telephone and call the local garage ... I can't understand the person on the other side of the line. I'm not sure he can understand me. They're all over the place, and they don't speak English. We want more of this?
>
> (Tatalovich 1997: 78)

The type of remark made by the senator is not at all isolated; in fact there are a number of legally registered and even publicly respected organizations dedicated to fortifying America from the new dangers to whiteness. Well-funded organizations such as US English (with a membership of 620,000), Official English, and English First, have taken the lead against the new wave of immigrants who come mostly from Mexico, Central America, the Caribbean, and Asia. Much like the earlier nativism, the new episode has made its way into the federal political contestation. Thus during the 1996 general elections, Republican candidate Robert Dole openly called for the "return as a people to the original concept of what it means to be American" (Tatalovich 1997: 92). Pat Buchanan proposed putting up an electrical fence between the United States and Mexico. In 1986 California passed Proposition 63, making English the official language. Similar legislation has been passed in several states. Language, however, is not the only site of exclusion, and for that matter exclusion itself has to be understood in the larger context of managing demographic composition.

The fear of civilizational erosion is increasingly being expressed in terms of whites becoming a minority in the United States. This fear goes back to earlier racialized discourses of foreign "invasion." Concrete steps are currently being taken to manage racial and cultural hegemony of white

America. Thus two types of legislation are currently proposed to restrict who may give birth to citizens: (1) laws that prohibit certain immigrants from using reproductive health services and (2) the elimination of automatic citizenship to US-born children of undocumented aliens. These recommendations require constitutional amendment (Amendment 14). They are designed to control numbers but also send a powerful message about who is worthy "of adding their children to the national community" (Roberts 1997: 215). The primary reasons given for restricting services and rights are that undocumented immigrants drain local services, are a burden on taxpayers, and often have higher fertility rates than the rest of the population. The demographic configuration of the nation is especially problematic. The American economy has been demanding cheap manual labor for the service sectors (restaurant, gas stations, security guards, maids, farm hands) and Mexicans and Central American have essentially filled these labor needs. Coming here to work, however, does not seem to be a sufficient basis to become a member of the community. The types of hard work the new immigrants have been engaging in has been disconnected from the discourses of industriousness as a mark of moral fiber and good character. Specifically, the new immigrant worker is expected to work, but not to produce children or aspire to citizenship. The new nativism targets 9 million children by the year 2010 for exclusion. Dorothy Roberts is thus absolutely correct when she argues that denying immigrants privileges of citizenship "is a way of maintaining an exclusive meaning of citizenship while continuing to exploit immigrants' economic contribution" (1997: 215). Roberts puts the racialized management of demographic composition in much wider terms:

> Policies that devalue dark-skinned immigrants by excluding their children from the community of citizens help to resolve the paradox of American immigration policy. The federal government has opened the nation's borders to immigrants, even facilitating the entry of illegals, in order to meet employers' demands for cheap labor. Yet, many white Americans see the resulting demographic shift as a threat to their sense of national identity.
>
> (Roberts 1997: 214)

The sense of threat and danger to America is actually intensifying as a tight labor market in the 1990s has been conducive to migrants from Mexico and Central America responding to the call of the market for labor. In February of this year signs at a right wing, anti-immigrants protest in Siler City, North Carolina (led by former KKK member David Duke), read "To Hell with the Wretched Refuse"; "Pollution of Our Population Is Stupid." The immigrant as a security threat to American civilization is again being articulated. One sign reading "Full," superimposed on a US map, was perhaps most indicative of what action needs to be taken. The issue again, as it has been so often in US history, is to seal the border and keep out the lower classes and races.

Conclusion

This chapter started out by arguing that race has had an amorphous career in the problematization of international relations, being both absent and present at the same time. To a considerable degree this double existence has been one of presence at the margins, but a presence that, nonetheless, has served to consolidate the monological authority of realism and its various intellectual byproducts. The realist paradigm has been breached over the past fifteen years or so, and the pillars upon which it has for so long grounded itself, state-centrism, externality, military power, and most of all, a universal assumption of egotistical rationality, have been gradually weakened. On account of the turn to theorizing non-state agents, the domestic realm, and the broadening of security, it is now possible to see the ways in which powerful cultural forces have been constitutive of the world as we know it.

Nation-states for too long have been represented as containers of identities without careful examination of the processes through which such identities have been manufactured, inscribed, hegemonized, and reproduced. The analysis of immigration provides an excellent basis to understand the multiple forces that operate at both the domestic and global levels to configure the identities. More than that, it speaks to the complexity of borders, both in the traditional sense of territorial space, but more powerfully in terms of the management of cultural citizenship.

Racial identity is one of the more significant elements in the production of cultural belonging. Unlike other elements which are merely constitutive of inside/outside, racialized practices, including racism, find their very leitmotiv in the production of hierarchies. Racial hierarchies, while not fixed, tend to be long-term in nature, and are at once structural and emotive. The structural dimension develops through historically embedded social relations, often tied to forms of wealth accumulation. Put differently, racial hierarchies cannot be separated from the ways in which social classes and gendered practices are developed. There is thus a structural recursivity among race, gender, and class, where the racial and gendered elements form part of the ideological system of legitimation. Changes in the race–class–gender articulation might very well allow a racialized group to evacuate the space of the inferior, as in the case of Chinese immigrants, or Irish and Jewish women in the United States. During the second half of the nineteenth century Chinese immigrants in California were treated as racially inferior beings, posing an Asiatic threat to America (Takaki 1993). These same Chinese a hundred years later are portrayed as model minorities.[14] Irish maids on the East Coast who during the mid to late nineteenth century were thought to be racially and culturally inferior, would also eventually graduate to the status of full whiteness by the end of the twentieth century. And Jewish women, once seen as natural candidates for sweat-shop jobs in the garment industry of New York, would leave that classification behind. Undoubtedly, class tells. However, the emotive dimension of race is more enduring, even if the status of economic success is achieved as, for example, in the case of model minority Asians. This came to the fore in California when Robert Page, an unemployed musician, stabbed Eddie Wu, in Novato, California. Page told police he was determined to kill a "Chinaman" on that day because "they got all the good jobs" (Rojas 1996: A13).

There seems to be a real sense in which national identity is a personal belonging of the dominant group. The national space is, accordingly, deemed private. Those who do not look or behave like the dominant population are viewed as trespassers who must be kept out, or sent back. If they stay on, their presence is circulated as an ongoing threat that must be contained in the name of national–civilizational security. And finally, in the very processes of containing the alien immigrants, the structural and emotive conditions required for the continued privileged citizenship of the dominant groups are generated. In the case of the United States, therefore, each new generation of aliens has inadvertently but dialogically contributed to the consolidation of the idea of America.

Acknowledgements

The author wishes to thank Geeta Chowdhry, Sheila Nair, Shampa Biswas, Mark Beeman, and Walter H. Persaud for their insightful comments on this chapter.

Notes

1 Some interest in race and international relations surfaced during the late 1960s and early 1970s. The civil rights movement in the United States and violent conflicts around decolonization influenced the initial writings. See for example Gardiner (1968), Issacs (1969), and Preiswerk (1970). About the same time a systematic attempt was made to conceptualize race in international relations and to develop a research agenda. See Shepherd and LeMelle (1970).

2 Writers such as Huntington (1996) and Sowell (1994) have contributed to a literature that explains conflict in terms of civilization and cultural (read racial) differences.

3 "Fixed universals" refers to the near permanent fixation of realist IR theory on questions of interest, power, and the state, as the bases of reliable knowledge. For a more general discussion see Persaud (2001).

4 The notion of "discursive disturbance" is borrowed from Bhabha (1985).

5 Roxanne Doty is specifically critical of simply adding race to international relations. Her own work marks a significant departure from much of the earlier literature.

6 "Proper subject" as used here means problems and issues that are considered the basis of relevant and reliable knowledge in the discipline of international relations.

7 In early 1947, the acting secretary of state for the United States, Dean Acheson, acknowledged that "the existence of discrimination against minority groups in this country has had an adverse effect on our relations with other countries" (DeConde 1992: 130). Deconde also pointed out that the Soviets made much of the fact that the United States had a hypocritical position of calling for free elections in Eastern Europe, while it deprived millions of blacks the right to vote (Deconde 1992: 131).

8 The conceptual differences between race as a physical–morphological and cultural–ideological concept is discussed with great insight by Roxanne Doty (1993).

9 For an excellent collection on the new nativism vis-à-vis the Latino population in the United States see Perea (1997).

10 For an excellent analysis of the presence of Central Americans in the United States see Repak (1995).

11 For a discussion of whiteness as a historical force see Lipsitz (1998).

12 The following works are particularly useful in bringing to light the factors that elicit hostility toward immigrants: Manzo (1996), Simmons (1996), Cornelius *et al.* (1994), Hamamoto and Torres (1997), and Jacobson (1998).

13 For more on the notion of "evangelism of fear," see Campbell (1992), chapter 2.

14 Thomas Sowell (1994) is an exponent of the model minority thesis.

4

BEYOND HEGEMONIC
STATE(MENT)S OF NATURE

Indigenous knowledge and non-state possibilities in international relations

J. Marshall Beier

Among the more enduring oversights and omissions of international relations is its near total neglect of Indigenous peoples.[1] In particular, the First Nations of the Americas, ensconced within advanced colonial states, have been accorded almost no attention.[2] Critical reflection upon the sources of this lapse gives rise to some important insights into the concealed commitments that underwrite mainstream international relations theory and exert considerable authority in defining and delimiting disciplinary problems, prospects, and possibilities. The origins of these conceptual predispositions and of the neglect of Indigenous peoples can be traced to the travelogues of the first Europeans in the Americas, the enduring influence of which in social contractarian thought recommends their treatment as foundational texts of the social sciences. This view highlights the relevance for international relations of challenges raised against the veracity of these formative ethnographical accounts inasmuch as such re-evaluations simultaneously call into serious question some of the most fundamental ontological commitments of orthodox international theory – commitments which have their conceptual origins in the travelogues. Significantly, the neglect of Indigenous peoples is inseparable from the not inconsiderable conceptual indebtedness of orthodox international theory to these earliest writings about the peoples of the Americas. To the extent that the accounts and claims contained therein are not sustainable in the face of challenges brought against them in critical anthropological literature and cannot be reconciled with autoethnographical accounts of the peoples whose lifeways they purport to document, then, realist-inspired international relations theory becomes identifiable as an advanced colonial practice for perpetuating the erasures they effect.

Following from this, the purpose of this chapter is threefold. First, it seeks to highlight how particular representations of Indigenous peoples – bound up with a litany of discursively gendered and racialized binary oppositions – have facilitated and legitimized European colonization of the Americas. The resulting accounts of Indigenous peoples, their histories, and their experiences have underwritten not only orthodox international relations theory, but the project of state-making and construction(s) of the modern Western "self" as well. A second aim, then, is to expose the indeterminacy of these accounts, in part by making room for autoethnographies as authentic and legitimate documentary sources. Such a move profoundly unsettles both orthodox ontological commitments and prevailing notions about whose voices may speak meaningfully in disciplinary international relations. Finally, the consequences of orthodox renderings of Indigenous peoples are considered in terms of the continued politico-ideational marginalization of Indigenous peoples in international relations and in the world that it helps to (re)produce – by precluding non-European/non-Westphalian possibilities of theory and practice, resistances that are contingent upon those very possibilities are simultaneously denied plausibility. And international relations itself is much the poorer for its consequent inability to (re)think the world in ways enabled only by these unimagined possibilities.

It might be argued that Indigenous peoples have never constituted a subject matter appropriate to the focus of the field inasmuch as none has ever been possessed of the principal preoccupation of its mainstream scholarship: the Westphalian state. But neither were the Ancient Greeks, so that one is left to wonder at the comparatively greater attention devoted to Thucydides' account of the Peloponnesian War and its alleged relevance to the study of contemporary international politics. We may also wonder what marks Indigenous American peoples' statelessness as very much different from that of the Palestinians or the Kurds, both of which groups have been spared the same degree of neglect. And lest the objection be raised that the politics of the Indigenous nations of the Americas have been specific to their places within the states in which they are spatially embedded and have not extended into the international realm, it is well to remember that the enactment of treaties has been a widely used instrument in relations between the First Nations and the colonial powers. Similarly, the presence of Indigenous peoples' representatives at the United Nations as recognized observers and under the auspices of the Working Group on Indigenous Peoples builds on a history of such involvements that began with attempts to gain standing at the League of Nations and, earlier still, with delegations to the royal courts of Europe.[3] Moreover, Indigenous nations have their own histories and traditions of socio-political organization and inter-national interactions, which predate the advent of the European settler state. How, then, do we account for the failure of international relations scholars to see them?

Phillip Darby and A.J. Paolini note that international relations was similarly inattentive to the rest of the non-European world during the era of direct colonialism (Darby and Paolini 1994: 380). Owing to the subsumption of the colonies into the various European empires, their external relations were not understood to be international. Not until they became intelligible to it by way of the proliferation of statehood in the mid-twentieth century could international relations engage the former colonies – and this suggests a great deal about the sources of the continued invisibility of peoples in places where decolonization has not occurred. Likely the most important determinants of international relations' neglect of Indigenous peoples, then, are hegemonic accounts of the possibilities for political order, in respect of which the state is treated as monopolistic. The ontological commitments of the theoretical orthodoxy of the field, chief among which is an abiding faith in a Hobbesian state of nature, foreclose the possibility of political community in the absence of state authority. Hence, not only are the Indigenous peoples of the Americas rendered invisible to the international relations orthodoxy, but it also becomes possible to characterize the settler states resident on their territories as *former* colonies, thereby mystifying the contemporary workings of advanced colonialism. In this sense, the undifferentiated idea of the state, making no distinction with respect to settler states, obscures even the obscurity that it creates. This construction turns principally on a prior acceptance of the Westphalian state as the only possible – or at least the only legitimate – expression of political order.

Although, as R.B.J. Walker points out, Hobbes's radical conception of the autonomy and equality of individuals in the state of nature – a condition that is fundamental to the emergence of anarchy – does not lend itself well to the unequal relations between states (Walker 1993: 93), the derivative idea of an international anarchy remains axiomatic to the theoretical orthodoxy of international relations. Scholarship situated in this tradition is in the same instant furnished with its unit of analysis, the state, and committed to a circumscribed conception of political community, once again the state. That these commitments undergird the theoretical edifices of the orthodoxy marks out, in turn, a very limited ontological terrain upon which to imagine security, sovereignty, community, and the metaphysics of the good life. Thus, with respect to one of these, Walker argues that "[s]ecurity cannot be understood, or reconceptualized, or reconstructed without paying attention to the constitutive account of the political that has made the prevailing accounts of security seem so plausible" (Walker 1997: 69). Imperiled in any contestation of the appropriateness of the state as the referent object of security, then, are deeply held commitments with regard to the possibilities of political order – possibilities that are presumed to begin and end with the state. Remarkably, this whole assemblage of convictions rests upon an unsubstantiated idea: the anarchical state of nature.

The Western philosophical origins of the order/anarchy dichotomy reside most famously with Hobbes and the other social contractarian theorists of the so-called Age of Enlightenment. But though they advanced and elaborated their ontological commitments with airs of certain knowledge and experience, most of these theorists had never seen the natural worlds so fundamental to their philosophies. Rather, they relied on accounts from travelogues authored by persons on the leading edge of the European empires' march into the rest of the world. This has led Peter Hulme and Ludmilla Jordanova to suggest that these lesser-known writings from the frontiers of European imperial expansion ought to be considered as Enlightenment texts. Following from this proposition, they have found the canons of social contractarian thought implicated in the imperialist project:

> Some of the principal works of writers like Hobbes, Locke, Rousseau, Ferguson, and Diderot draw on accounts of these travellers in ways both important for their status as key texts of the Enlightenment, and revealing of their implication with the whole process of European exploration and colonization of the non-European world.
>
> (Hulme and Jordanova 1990: 8)

Given this connection and the enduring influences of social contractarian thought, we should also regard the travel writings as foundational texts of the contemporary Western social sciences. Though we do not read these accounts directly in international relations, they insinuate themselves through underinterrogated ontological commitments of mainstream realist-inspired international theory, most conspicuously in hegemonic renderings of the state of nature.

Interestingly, many of the same assumptions that underpin the orthodoxy of international relations and its more fundamental political commitments may be found at the root of a number of orthodox anthropological and historiographical accounts about Indigenous peoples that cast their pre-Columbian condition in terms consistent with a Hobbesian state of nature. This shared commitment suggests the arbitrariness of the disciplinary division of knowledge which, coincidental with the racial ideologies of late nineteenth-century imperialism, marked out anthropology as a discrete sphere within which to construct discourses about those Others whom Eric Wolf (1997) has called "the people without history."[4] It is therefore instructive to consider some of these accounts and to assess both the integrity of the evidence upon which they rest and the extent to which they can or cannot be reconciled with the traditional worldviews and lifeways of the peoples to whom they ostensibly refer. Such an interdisciplinary approach has much to recommend it inasmuch as anthropologists and historians have been among the most attentive to those other foundational texts of the social sciences: travelogues. This makes it possible to challenge key ontological commitments of the orthodoxy of international theory at their points of conceptual origin.

In what follows, the idea that the aboriginal condition of Indigenous peoples is unproblematically apprehendable by way of reference to European accounts from the early contact period is challenged. Evidence of the distortive influences set forth by the arrival of Europeans in the Americas is briefly considered in reference to the Yanomami and Cherokee peoples. The evidentiary bases of several orthodox anthropological and historiographical accounts of the pre-Columbian warfare of the Lakota[5] people of the Northern Great Plains of North America are then assessed and shown to be reconcilable to a range of conclusions other than the Hobbesian-inspired ones of which they have been deemed supportive. Inasmuch as these same accounts and the hegemonic conceptions of order/anarchy with which they are mutually constitutive render Indigenous peoples invisible to the orthodoxy of international relations, their indeterminacy suggests that they should rightly be viewed as advanced colonial practices – all the more so when we consider that Lakota traditionalism's non-state articulations of a social world and political order are simultaneously invalidated by them.[6]

In more concrete terms, this might be little more than academic were it not for the fact that it is an existing community – not a historical curiosity – that is thus marginalized. It should be emphasized that Lakota traditionalism is by no means a reference to the past or to some contemporary conjuring in the ethnographic present. Lakota traditionalists make up a sizeable proportion of the *contemporary* Lakota nation and are characterized most fundamentally by their enduring fidelity to traditional cosmological commitments – a fidelity that has thus far survived the assimilationist practices of colonialism and is significant notwithstanding that some of its referents might turn out not to be wholly unaltered inheritances of pre-colonial times. A lingering legacy of colonialism is the particular fragmentation among many Indigenous peoples that tends to manifest most conspicuously in the cleavage between traditionalists and the more Westernized progressives.[7] The Lakota are certainly no exception in this regard and have, in fact, suffered some of the worst of the political violence that sometimes attends this division. Thus, while they are not representative of the whole of the Lakota people, the traditionalists do constitute a contemporary community that resides quite decidedly beyond the pale of orthodox international relations theory. And it is precisely the sort of wholesale invalidations of the cosmologically based worldview and lifeways of the traditionalists, in which orthodox international relations theorists are implicated, that constitute the ideational dimension of the advanced colonial domination to which they are subjected. These same conceptual predispositions (among which the Hobbesian impulse is prominent) seem to render traditional Lakota lifeways quite implausible and thereby privilege the (more) Westernized progressives.

But before proceeding, an important caveat must be advanced. In attempting to draw insights from a traditional Lakota worldview and lifeways, it is necessary to make certain cognitive leaps across epistemological boundaries and to take seriously culturally specific ways of knowing (see

Whitt 1995). There is an inherent danger in this that involves the possibility of succumbing to the pretension that one who has no lived experience rooted in Lakota culture can unproblematically appropriate the voice of a Lakota person. Accordingly, a sincere effort has been made herein to hear and to take seriously Lakota voices on their own terms. Still, notwithstanding this self-conscious resolve, none of what follows should rightly be regarded as anything more authoritative than a considered set of interpretations. Of course, there are good and well-established grounds upon which to argue that this should always be the case when one approaches a subject matter with which one does not share a thorough and intimate lived experience. Nevertheless, the point is particularly important to underscore in this instance, given the long history of spurious accounts of Indigenous people(s) that have issued from ostensible "authorities" and the nefarious political purposes to which they have sometimes been turned. Finally, it must be emphasized that, while the following analysis draws on a particular tradition that is distinctly Lakota, not all Lakota people would freely associate themselves with this tradition. There is value in what Gayatri Chakravorty Spivak has called "strategic essentialism"[8] – constructing for purposes of collective political action or analytical expediency an essentialized oppositional identity – and there is an element of this in the references to Lakota traditionalism that follow as, to be sure, there is bound to be in the presentations that traditionalists make of themselves.[9] But we must not lose sight of the fact that, like any other people, the Lakota nation is not monolithic and we must take care not to contribute to the vast store of existing essentialized caricatures of Indigenous North Americans, whether they evoke images of the ignoble or noble savage.

Following from this, a few words on the theoretical perspective that informs this chapter are also in order. The approach taken herein is postcolonial to the extent that it explicitly seeks to deprivilege hegemonic narratives and to hear voices marginalized in the colonial encounter, taking heed of the subjugated knowledges they bear. Mention of postcolonialism might, at first, seem out of place in reference to peoples not yet emancipated from advanced colonial domination. But postcolonialism is not a synonym for postindependence (Loomba 1998: 12–13). The "post" in postcolonial should not be taken to mean that colonialism is over; indeed, in the indelible marks it has left on peoples and on histories it will never truly be over, but will endure genealogically in the possibilities it has created and in those it has foreclosed (see Chowdhry and Nair, Chapter 1). And that is rather the point: if the "post" in postcolonial signals an "after," it is in reference to the *effects* of colonialism much more than colonialism itself. That is to say, the postcolonial is as relevant to contexts of continuing direct colonial domination as to the post-independence state; both contexts have been inscribed by colonialism and, though this experience does not define them by itself,[10] neither is it at all insignificant in that regard. As Ruth Frankenberg and Lata Mani

put it, the post "mark[s] spaces of ongoing contestation enabled by decolonization struggles both globally and locally" (Frankenberg and Mani 1993:
294).[11] Moreover, a central theme of this chapter is the proposition that
international relations is simultaneously subject and object of advanced colonialism. The postcolonial subject here is not only the Indigenous peoples
marginalized by the theoretical orthodoxy in international relations, but
international theory itself which has been both shaped and constrained – in
short, subjugated – through colonialism. That is, international theory too
has been deeply inscribed and conceptually bounded by the colonial experience in ways that have diminished its potential by artificially delimiting its
ruminations of the possible.

Representing Indigenous peoples: the imperialist juncture and state(ment)s of nature

Michael Dorris has observed that learning about and from Indigenous North
American cultures and histories is rather different from acquiring knowledge
in other fields because the researcher more than likely has already received
and internalized a huge amount of misinformation about Indigenous peoples,
which threatens to subvert inquiry from the outset (1987: 103). That is to
say, there is a great deal that must be unlearned before serious and productive
investigation can begin. This is perhaps nowhere better illustrated than in
the corpus of literature purporting to elucidate the functions and conduct of
warfare in pre-Columbian Indigenous societies. Despite the epistemological
predisposition on the part of some scholars working in anthropology, history,
and other disciplines to present their conclusions as matters of objective fact,
backed up by the (supposed) rigors of Western science, discerning the
aboriginal condition of Indigenous peoples is not at all a straightforward and
unproblematic undertaking. As Dorris has pointed out,

> [i]t depends on the imperfect evidence of archaeology; the barely-
> disguised, self-focused testimony of traders, missionaries, and
> soldiers, all of whom had their own axes to grind and viewed native
> peoples through a narrow scope; and, last and most suspect of all,
> common sense.
>
> (1987: 104)

Significantly, traditional Indigenous sources are seldom ever consulted,
their exclusion typically justified on the grounds that the oral literatures
characteristic of so many Indigenous societies are less reliable than written
forms. Consequently, the body of scholarship on the histories of Indigenous
peoples has been largely self-referential, continually reproducing whatever
errors of perception and assumption may derive, per Dorris's reproof, from
the application of a generally ethnocentric "common sense."

Convincingly demonstrating this point is an article by renowned military historian John Keegan (1996) that follows from his investigations into the history of warfare on the Northern Great Plains of North America, in which he seems not to have consulted, much less taken seriously, Indigenous sources. He does, however, appear to have relied quite heavily on a decidedly Western brand of common sense in his analysis of the putative facts of warfare on the Plains. Central to this widely accredited wisdom is the familiar Hobbesian impulse that, finding in the aboriginal condition nothing akin to the state as a means by which political order might be furnished, posits a perpetual state of war and insecurity in its stead. Here Keegan is in distinguished – if notorious – company: Hobbes himself maintained as evidence of the plausibility of his idea of the state of nature that "the savage people in many places of *America* ... live at this day in that brutish manner, as I said before" (Hobbes 1968: 187). While Keegan did not explicitly articulate this assumption, it is implicit in, for example, his assertion that the famed US General George Armstrong Custer and his 7th Cavalry were "wiped away in an outburst of native American ferocity" while their intended Lakota and Cheyenne victims are described as having been motivated less by the pressing need to defend their encampment from the attacking soldiers than by their own "ferocious emotions" (Keegan 1996: 41).

In this instance, Keegan seems unable to imagine that certain characteristics and conceptual commitments of the society of which he is a part and product may not be generalizable to the lived realities of the whole of humanity. Similarly, and perhaps partly in consequence of a prior assumption of unrestrained savagery, he ascribes an entrenched and pervasive individualism to the people of the Plains. Indeed, the Hobbesian overtones of his work are complemented by his characterization of the lifeways of the Plains people(s) as "rigorously masculine and individualistic" (Keegan 1996: 15). Keegan attempts to back up this position by reducing the Sun Dance – a protracted ceremony in which individuals undergo considerable personal suffering as a mode of self-sacrifice on behalf of the whole of their people and as a means by which to gain spiritual enlightenment – to a contest between participants motivated by nothing more than the selfish desire by each to "demonstrate in public his powers of endurance" (Keegan 1996: 15). According to Howard Harrod, "sun dances and other ritual processes provided occasions for individuals to endure the suffering that was requisite for religious experience" (1995: 26). Keegan, however, saw, as the only functional outcome of this most sacred of rituals, the participants' acquisition of "qualities of physical hardness, contempt for pain and privation, and disregard of danger to life that both disgusted and awed the white soldiers who fought them" (Keegan 1996: 15). In this racialized discursive construction – in opposition to "awed ... white soldiers" – he thus participated in the rendering of the Plains people(s) as unreal, constructing them at what might be termed the super-subhuman nexus.

It is immediately apparent that this, like so many orthodox representations of Indigenous peoples, is simultaneously highly gendered and racialized. In this regard, too, these accounts share discursive terrain with the orthodoxy of international relations – as J. Ann Tickner has reminded us, "nonwhites and tropical countries are often depicted as irrational, emotional, and unstable, characteristics that are also attributed to women" (Tickner 1992: 7). Indeed, the culture/nature dichotomy has always privileged the masculinized European self as against the exotic feminine other. And, as Spike Peterson (1992b) has so convincingly argued, this, in turn, has been inseparable from processes of state-making. As such, the advent of the settler state is the concrete expression of the parallel centrality of gendered and racialized discourses to advanced colonialism. However, it is important to point out that the discursive renderings of Indigenous peoples also evince a certain ambivalence in both regards; orthodox accounts of the aboriginal condition of Indigenous peoples are permeated with discourses of gender and race, but these discourses are oftentimes conflicted in themselves. In ways that seem more than coincidentally to befit particular colonial purposes, Indigenous people(s) are variously constructed as frighteningly masculine or piteously feminine, as supremely rational or hopelessly irrational, as coldly stoic or wildly emotional, as superhuman or subhuman. This highlights both the contingency of these varied discourses and the colonial purposes they serve(d). It also draws our attention to the important role of negative definition – as expressed through these dichotomies – in the construction of Western self-knowledges.[12]

Keegan is by no means alone in citing individualized motives as the basis of Indigenous peoples' warfare. Anthony McGinnis, for example, argues that "[i]n war, the tribe was important only insofar as it supported the individual warrior and his combat and in the fact that the tribe's noncombatants ... needed to be defended" (1990: 12). Emphasizing this point, he draws a comparison to a French officer, Pierre de la Verendrye, who was wounded at the Battle of Malplaquet in 1709:

> Fortunate enough to recover from his wounds, Verendrye returned home to Canada, having willingly shed his blood for God, King Louis XIV, and France, something the Indians of the northern plains would not have understood – sacrifice for an ideal or a leader rather than for oneself.
>
> (McGinnis 1990: 4)

Individuals in Plains societies, according to McGinnis, were prompted into warfare only in order to obtain wealth and glory for themselves (McGinnis 1990: x). Similarly, John C. Ewers identifies opportunities for individuals "to distinguish themselves" and the pursuit of "coveted war honors" as important determinants of warfare between Plains peoples (Ewers 1975: 401). The hyper-individualism in these accounts dehumanizes to the extent that it precludes all but the barest sketches of a social world; for lacking loyalties more profound than the satisfaction of their personal appetites, Indigenous people are thus rendered all the more frightening.[13]

But perhaps the most extreme position as regards the presumed individualized sources of aboriginal warfare was advanced by Napoleon A. Chagnon. His account of warfare among the Yanomami people of Amazonia finds biological determinants prominent among its sources. Central to his argument is the idea that Yanomami warfare, though sustained by a revenge complex wherein violence by one group begets reciprocal violence in kind from its erstwhile victims, is, at base, motivated both by competition over scarce material resources and by a supposed biological imperative on the part of males in kinship-based groups to secure, by means of violence if necessary, enhanced access to "reproductive resources" – i.e., women. According to Chagnon:

> It is to be expected that individuals (or groups of closely related individuals) will attempt to appropriate both material and reproductive resources from neighbors whenever the probable costs are less than the benefits. While conflicts thus initiated need not take violent forms, they might be expected to do so when violence on average advances individual interests. I do not assume that humans consciously strive to increase or maximize their inclusive fitness, but I do assume that humans strive for goals that their cultural traditions deem as valued and esteemed. In many societies, achieving cultural success appears to lead to biological (genetic) success.
>
> (Chagnon 1988: 985)[14]

This formulation clearly hints at what sociobiologists have termed the "selfish-gene" concept: the idea that certain social behaviors are, at least in part, biologically determined and that the resultant social outcomes are a determining factor in the evolutionary natural selection of species. Put another way, it presumes to "show that there are evolutionary 'optima' for behaviours such as aggression" (Van Der Dennen and Falger 1990: 15). But what may be most interesting about this argument from the point of view of someone who works primarily in the field of international relations are the similarities it shares, on several fronts, with realism. There is, of course, the obvious implication that human nature – or at least the nature of the "successful," in evolutionary terms – is as Hobbes imagined. And absent the state, it is individuals – more particularly, individual men – who are cast as the "rational gains maximizers," such that the possibility of political order is effectively precluded. Having thus found his subjects residing in a

Hobbesian state of nature, Chagnon, like Keegan, McGinnis, and Ewers, set about explaining the sources and conduct of their wars in terms consistent with this condition.[15]

If Chagnon is right and warfare in Amazonia is indeed in some significant measure a function of genetic fitness, then it would logically follow that the apparently warlike tendencies of the Yanomami can, with confidence, be mapped back onto their pre-Columbian ancestors. Furthermore, if this behavior is biologically determined, it must be specified as a general human characteristic. The imposition of Hobbes's Leviathan, then, would serve to explain why the conduct of the Yanomami is peculiar and not universal to the human condition. The political implications of such an inference are simultaneously abstract and immediate: in the abstract sense, it would seem to lend support to the notion of the state as the sole locus of political order; more immediately, it confers moral approbation upon the conquest of Indigenous peoples and the suppression of their traditional lifeways, if only (ostensibly) to save them from themselves. Indeed, as Jacques Lizot has pointed out, Brazilian newspapers supporting the interests of resource industries that have been accused of orchestrating genocide against the Yanomami in order to gain access to their lands have enthusiastically embraced Chagnon's writings (Lizot 1994: 845).[16]

Here again, the Hobbesian impulse is not anomalous. It is as readily invoked as a justification for past conquests as for those that are ongoing. Though he does not follow Chagnon onto the thin ice of socio-biology, Ewers (apparently oblivious to the sum and substance of Dorris's warning about the questionable reliability of early Euroamerican sources) has argued that "intertribal warfare was rife [on the Northern Plains] at the time these Indians first became known to whites" and that this "is evident in the writings of the pioneer explorers" (Ewers 1975: 399). And, although he acknowledges that there is scant evidence suggestive of large-scale battles, presumably with the aim of demonstrating that the possibility of large-scale exterminative warfare was not precluded, Ewers cites the example of an 1866 battle in which "the Piegan are reputed to have killed more than three hundred Crow and Gros Ventres" (Ewers 1975: 401). Nevertheless, inasmuch as raiding for horses was the principal form of warfare among Plains peoples, he submits that this is likely to have been the primary source of casualties (Ewers 1975: 402). With an apologist agenda beginning to show, he continues: "Nor is there reason to doubt that, during the historic period, many more Indians of this region were killed by other Indians in intertribal wars than by white soldiers or civilians in more fully documented Indian-white warfare" (ibid.). Having thus outlined the rudiments of a Hobbesian state of nature as extant on the Northern Plains at the earliest stages of European contact, Ewers makes what seems a thinly veiled attempt to rationalize the forced imposition of the Euroamerican Leviathan, proposing that

[h]ad each of the tribes of this region continued to stand alone, fighting all neighboring tribes, it is probable that many of the smaller tribes either would have been exterminated, or their few survivors would have been adopted into the larger tribes, thereby increasing the latter's military potential.

(Ewers 1975: 402)

Once more, then, the aboriginal condition has been presented as representative of a state of nature, constructed in decidedly Hobbesian terms. But what Ewers seems to miss is the possibility that the aboriginal condition of the peoples he has studied is not, in fact, known to him. In this too he keeps company with Keegan, McGinnis, and Chagnon.

De/re/construction: toward a space for subjugated narratives

Anthropologist Brian Ferguson raises a compelling challenge to the pretension of orthodox scholars to know the pre-Columbian lifeways of the Indigenous peoples of the Americas, regardless of whether their focus is on the conquered and colonized Plains peoples of North America or the as yet largely unsubdued Yanomami of Amazonia. Investigations by Ferguson in which he focused primarily on the Yanomami suggest that, contra the received wisdom of the Hobbesian impulse, "the most general cause of known warfare in Amazonia is Western contact" (Ferguson 1990: 237). Although he does not contend that warfare was unknown to pre-Columbian Amazonia, he does insist that, "[c]ontrary to Hobbes, the intrusion of the Leviathan of the European state did not suppress a 'war of all against all' among Native peoples of Amazonia, but instead fomented warfare" (Ferguson 1990: 238). "Ultimately," he continues, "wars have ended through pacification or extinction, but prior to that the general effect of contact has been just the opposite: to intensify or engender warfare" (Ferguson 1990: 239). Moreover, Ferguson holds this to be a general consequence of European imperialism virtually wherever it has confronted non-state societies, albeit with notable local variations arising from indigenous peculiarities (Ferguson 1992: 109).

Ferguson attributes this phenomenon to an array of influences that fall roughly into three broad categories (Ferguson 1990: 239). The first is concerned with the purposeful incitement or direction of Indigenous warfare by Europeans. As Ferguson notes, such practices were very common in the initial contact period and were manifest in a variety of forms. The most obvious and direct of these was the use of conquered or allied Indigenous peoples as "auxiliaries or impressed recruits" in European campaigns against unsubjugated peoples on the peripheries of the expanding colonies (Ferguson 1990: 239). In some cases, notably along the line of confrontation between the English and French colonies of northeastern North America, Indigenous peoples were unable to avoid becoming entangled in wars between the colonial powers themselves. Elsewhere, Europeans found it expedient to facilitate – generally by the provision of arms and other goods – warfare among contending groups lying beyond the reach of direct colonial authority. And Tom Holm notes that the militarization of Indigenous American peoples also served European interests as "a method of absorbing them into a larger imperial system" (Holm 1997: 462).[17] Ewers, however, rejects the idea that European contact incited warfare between Indigenous peoples in this way and, as evidence, points to the matter of the support that was given by Euroamericans to the Crow and Arikara in their struggles against the Lakota:

> To view the Crow and Arikara as "mercenaries" of the whites is to overlook the long history of Indian-Indian warfare in this region. The Crow, Arikara, and other tribes had been fighting the Sioux for generations before they received any effective aid from the whites. They still suffered from Sioux aggression during the 1860s and 1870s. Surely the history of Indian-white warfare on the northern Great Plains cannot be understood without an awareness of the history of intertribal warfare in this region.
>
> (Ewers 1975: 409–10)

While Ewers is right to point out that the colonial powers, by means of exploiting existing animosities between some peoples, frequently did not need to rely on coercion in enlisting the service of Indigenous recruits, in the end it was still these powers that enkindled enmity into open hostilities.[18]

A further impetus toward the deliberate and utilitarian incitement and direction of warfare between different Indigenous peoples was the European demand for slaves in the early stages of the colonization of the Americas. As Ferguson explains it:

> The initial European colonization of the New World was based on the coerced labor of Native peoples. Adult male captives were sought as field laborers, women and children as domestic servants. Royal decrees – which were often circumvented but which still had an impact – allowed two main avenues for enslaving Indians: taking captives in "just wars" against allegedly rebellious Natives or putative cannibals; and "ransoming" captives held by Indians from their own wars. It was the latter that became the routine source of slaves ... Slaving was encouraged by payments in European goods, but raiding was not entirely optional; people who did not produce captives were commonly taken as slaves themselves. Slave raiding

was often a constant danger even hundreds of miles from European settlements.

(Ferguson 1990: 240)

Wilma Dunaway draws our attention to similar conditions that had a profound effect upon the nature and extent of warfare as practiced by the Cherokee during the early period of contact in southeastern North America:

> Prior to the development of a profitable market for war captives, slaves remained only a by-product of conflicts waged primarily for vengeance. Cherokee clans frequently adopted prisoners of war to replace kinsmen who had died, or captives could be ransomed by the enemies. Once the traders began exchanging goods for war captives, the market value of the captured slaves intensified the frequency and extent of indigenous warfare.
>
> (Dunaway 1996: 462)

Thus, peoples who may never before have been enemies, or perhaps had never even come into direct contact with one another, developed enduring mutual malevolence.

Ferguson's second broad category is concerned with demographic pressures arising from European colonization and the influences they exerted on Indigenous warfare. The introduction of epidemic diseases against which Indigenous people had little or no immunity was, according to Ferguson, a source of increased hostility between groups when it led to charges of sorcery (Ferguson 1990: 241). In some instances, catastrophically high rates of mortality due to disease spurred raiding with the express purpose of acquiring captives to be integrated into the abductors' society as a means of population replenishment (Ferguson and Whitehead 1992: 9). Of greater consequence, however, were the migrations prompted by epidemics, slave raiding, and the ever-expanding colonies themselves. Migration forced direct contact between historically separated groups and increasingly brought them into conflict as refugees arrived in regions that were already well populated (Ferguson 1990: 242).

The third and final set of transformative influences identified by Ferguson is associated with the introduction of Western manufactures. Owing to the greater efficiency of steel tools and other Western goods, such as firearms, vis-à-vis their indigenous equivalents, European trade wares dramatically increased the war-making potential of many Indigenous peoples. These items thus became both objects and implements of war with the deleterious effect that warfare became a means by which to forcibly appropriate its instruments. This, in turn, made possible the expansion of warfare and the appropriation of still more of its instruments. It is almost certainly more

95

than mere coincidence, then, that Indigenous peoples who enjoyed ready access to these goods are frequently the same ones regarded as most warlike in Euroamerican ethnographies and historiographies. Jeffrey Blick, for example, notes that the gun-toting mounted warriors of the Plains owed their reputation as a warlike people largely to the historical accident of having been situated at the point at which the lines of trade in firearms supplied by the French in the northeast of the continent first intersected with the diffusion of horses introduced by the Spanish in the southwest. As Blick puts it:

> The combination of the gun and the horse ... enabled many tribes to expand their traditional ranges and to wage warfare in a much more efficient manner. What ultimately resulted was an unequal access to guns and horses. Tribes of the Great Plains proper were able to take advantage of the geographic continuity of the Plains and of the rapid diffusion of the horse and gun. Marginal tribes however, such as the Bannock and the "Digger" Indians of the Plateau and Great Basin, were forced to retreat into inhospitable regions to avoid the raids of their mounted predators, the Blackfoot, Piegan, Shoshone, etc.
>
> (Blick 1988: 666–7)

Thus, we see here the confluence of two broad sets of influences as the migratory pressures felt by the Plains peoples in the face of the advancing Euroamerican colonies, combined with their acquisition of horses and firearms, induced warfare with other Indigenous peoples, thereby setting in motion still more waves of migration with all of the disruptive effects which that entailed. It must be emphasized that Blick's position, like Ferguson's with respect to the Yanomami, is not that warfare was nonexistent on the Plains before the introduction of Western manufactures, but rather that the appearance of these items was typically accompanied or followed in short order by an increase in the frequency and intensity of warfare.

All of this makes Ewers's above-cited admonition to take into account the history of intertribal warfare on the Plains seem rather more problematic than it might at first appear. It also serves to underscore Dorris's suggestion that the early Euroamerican accounts of the aboriginal condition of Indigenous peoples may be unreliable – a point that he is not alone in making.[19] Ferguson echoed Dorris's concerns, arguing that the first accounts of contact with Indigenous peoples tended to come from "the most disruptive observers imaginable: raiders seeking slaves or mission 'converts'" (Ferguson 1990: 238). Moreover, he poses as a more general problem for anthropology itself the fact that the first literate observers are seldom present at the time of initial contact:

[E]thnology is built upon a paradox. Traditionally, it has sought the Pristine Non – non-Western, nonliterate, noncapitalist, nonstate. Yet the quality of our descriptions of other cultures is generally in direct proportion to the intensity of the Western presence. Literate observers usually arrive rather late in the encounter. The specter haunting anthropology is that culture patterns taken to be pristine may actually have been transformed by Western contact.

(Ferguson 1990: 238)

But, setting aside for the moment the issue of veracity and the question of timeliness, an even more serious problem from the point of view of anyone hoping to access the aboriginal condition of Indigenous peoples through the accounts of observers, whether contemporary or historical, is the fact that European influences have repeatedly preceded Europeans themselves, changing the lived realities of Indigenous peoples long before first contact. This problem effectively precludes reliance on the accounts of observers with respect to the "pristine" condition of aboriginal warfare: refugee migrations, almost by definition, precede the advance of colonial frontiers; following indigenous trade routes, manufactured goods can become commonplace in a given locale centuries before first contact; epidemic diseases are borne by refugee flows as well as along trade routes. By way of example, the winter counts of the peoples of the Northern Plains indicate a very high frequency of epidemics dating back to 1714, with the first recorded outbreak among the Oglala Lakota having taken place in 1780[20] – twenty-four years before they were first visited by the renowned Euroamerican explorers Meriwether Lewis and William Clark in 1804.

So, whether our focus is on the Yanomami of Amazonia, the Cherokee of southeastern North America, or the Lakota of the Northern Plains, accounts of the supposed aboriginal condition of Indigenous peoples that rely to any significant extent upon what was, or may yet be, empirically observable are highly suspect. How, then, should we proceed? Douglas Bamforth proposed that, if "ethnohistoric documentation of warfare tells us little about precontact circumstances," this leaves "archaeological data central to any understanding of post-contact changes in these circumstances" (Bamforth 1994: 97). Accordingly, he directs us to consider the evidence uncovered in the excavation of agriculturally based pre-Columbian settlement sites along the Missouri Trench in present-day North and South Dakota, with particular emphasis on one site at Crow Creek. As a control case, he also discusses the Larson site, an excavation of a large former Arikara community near the Missouri River that was occupied between 1750 and 1785, by which time the disruptive influences of the arrival of Europeans on the continent should certainly have been keenly felt. Bamforth notes that trenches and palisades were generally common features of all of these sites, though the extent of their overall development and completeness as well as the degree of attention paid to their maintenance varied across time (Bamforth 1994: 106). Bamforth, probably accurately, interprets these features as defensive fortifications. But this assumption, in part, leads him to another rather more tenuous one: namely that large-scale exterminative warfare was "endemic" on the Northern Plains even prior to the arrival of Europeans on the continent.

Bamforth bases this position primarily on evidence uncovered in the excavations of the Larson and Crow Creek sites. The latter town is estimated, according to Bamforth, to have been built sometime in the early part of the fourteenth century (Bamforth 1994: 106). It was at this site that a particularly grisly discovery was made in 1978: a mass grave in which were interred the skeletal remains of somewhere in the neighborhood of 500 people.[21] In addition to the fact of their having been buried together in a mass grave, the condition of the human remains at Crow Creek indicates that the inhabitants of the town almost certainly were the victims of a massacre. A very high frequency of depressed fractures to the skulls of the victims as well as other similar indications would seem to make at least this much irrefutable. Significantly, analysis of the skeletal remains yielded a further insight into the tragic situation of the victims: telltale signs in the condition of many of the long bones indicate that the townspeople had suffered from malnutrition at various points in their lives and many of them were malnourished at the time of the massacre (Bamforth 1994: 106–7). According to Larry Zimmerman and Lawrence Bradley,

> [a]ctive and organizing subperiostial hematomas along with the other bony alterations provide convincing evidence that nutritional deprivation had been present for some time prior to the deaths of these people and probably was rampant at the time of their demise.
>
> (Zimmerman and Bradley 1993: 218)

This, then, suggests a motive and context for the slaughter: forcible appropriation of foodstuffs during a famine. Bamforth compares this evidence to that found at the post-contact Larson site where a similar massacre took place approximately four and a half centuries later, likely in consequence, he argues, of the conflict created by mass migrations that were in turn a result of the same disruptive influences of European colonialism identified by Ferguson and Blick (Bamforth 1994: 101–2). And finding the same sorts of osteological evidence – with the exception that indications of malnutrition were not found at the Larson site – and similar fortifications at the two sites, he arrives at the conclusion that "precontact tribal warfare on the northern Great Plains resulted from indigenous cultural-ecological processes rather than from external influences" (Bamforth 1994: 109).

As noted above, Bamforth is probably right in regarding the ditches and palisades of the villages in the Missouri Trench as defensive fortifications.

Less clear, however, is the conclusion that these measures were undertaken in response to endemic large-scale warfare in the region as a feature of its various peoples' aboriginal condition. Yet this is precisely what Bamforth implies when he suggests that the construction of such defenses would have been a tremendous burden for such small populations (Bamforth 1994: 111). To be fair, he does acknowledge that "features which archaeologists interpret as fortifications could have primarily symbolic or ceremonial significance ... or ... could have served simply as warnings which by themselves dissuaded rival groups from resorting to all-out war" (Bamforth 1994: 105). Ewers, on the other hand, is considerably less cautious: "Surely the prehistoric villagers would not have taken elaborate steps to fortify their settlements had they not been endangered by enemies" (Ewers 1975: 399). And, "[w]hoever those enemies were," he continues, "we can be sure that they were other Indians" (Ewers 1975: 399). But can we, in fact, be so sure of all of this? What if the fortifications – if, indeed, they have been correctly interpreted as such – were inspired by a *fear* of attack rather than the experience of it? The very fact that, at least in the cases of the Larson and Crow Creek sites, they would seem to have been unequal to the purpose ascribed to them, suggests the possibility that they were designed in response to some lesser threat. In this regard, it is significant that the Northern Plains was noted for small-scale raiding between groups and, especially if archaeologists are correct in assessing periods of food shortage, sedentary agricultural communities, such as the one uncovered at Crow Creek, would have been likely targets of such incursions. Moreover, particularly if we accept Patricia Albers's suggestion that raiding, as a "mechanism for resolving short-term imbalances in the distribution of goods," was a way of maintaining symbiosis between groups (Albers 1993: 108), the complete destruction of a food-producing village would seem contrary to the interests of the raiders and, therefore, unlikely to have been a common enterprise. Some support for this view resides in Bamforth's own observation that the fortifications at Crow Creek had not always been well maintained, as well as in evidence that the village had grown beyond the confines of the encircling ditch which had itself been abandoned and converted to a refuse dump.[22] Of course, none of this is intended to suggest that any of these explanations necessarily represent more accurate portrayals of the reality of pre-Columbian existence on the Northern Plains than those proposed by Bamforth and Ewers. On the contrary, the point here is only to make clear that the archaeological evidence cannot speak to us as unproblematically as Ewers and, to a lesser degree, Bamforth would have us believe.

Bamforth's argument leaves room for a range of conclusions other than those at which he arrives. We may note, for instance, that while he is able to draw our attention to a number of sites along the Missouri Trench, just two bear evidence of large-scale exterminative warfare, and only one of these dates to pre-Columbian times. He does indicate two additional sites at which partially constructed settlements appear to have been abandoned before completion (Bamforth 1994: 105), but his interpretation of this as evidence that the would-be inhabitants had been driven off by force, though a plausible enough explanation, is hardly conclusive. Bamforth acknowledges that the data he examined are more suited to determining the scale of warfare than its frequency, even as he concedes that the fortification of settlements became more common after the arrival of Europeans (Bamforth 1994: 111).[23] One wonders, then, on what basis the Crow Creek massacre should be regarded as anything more than an aberration under conditions which, like the influences set forth from European colonization, were disruptive of the customary lifeways of the peoples concerned. Finally, Bamforth himself draws attention to evidence of famine at the time of the Crow Creek massacre as well as episodically in the years prior. Surely this must be regarded as an extreme circumstance which, though it may well have resulted in a massacre, is in no way indicative of a general trend. In fact, the evidence cited by Bamforth would seem to bespeak precisely the opposite inasmuch as the earlier periods of malnutrition that are also indicated did not result in a similarly catastrophic conflict.

Still, Bamforth and Ewers are not alone in drawing the conclusions they do from the archaeological record. Lawrence Keeley, for example, refers us to the evidence uncovered at the Crow Creek and Larson sites in the course of his direct rejection of Ferguson's thesis (Keeley 1996: 68–9). According to Keeley:

> From North America at least, archaeological evidence reveals precisely the same pattern recorded ethnographically for tribal peoples the world over of frequent deadly raids and occasional horrific massacres. This was an indigenous and "native" pattern long before contact with Europeans complicated the situation. When the sailing ship released them from their own continent, Europeans brought many new ills and evils to the non-Western world, but neither war nor its worst features were among these novelties.
>
> (Keeley 1996: 69)

Apart from his somewhat unfair treatment of Ferguson's argument,[24] Keeley lacks a reflexive sense of the ambiguity of the archaeological evidence he cites. And his is also perhaps the most direct example of a Hobbesian-inspired perspective on the aboriginal condition of Indigenous peoples. Concerned at what he regards as "pacified" renditions of the human past, Keeley's purpose is to discredit what is in his view their underlying "theoretical stance that amounts to a Rousseauian declaration of universal prehistoric peace" (Keeley 1996: 20). Accordingly, he appeals directly to Hobbes in support of his argument that, "[i]f anything, peace was a scarcer commodity for members of bands, tribes, and chiefdoms than for the average citizen of a civilized state" (Keeley 1996: 39). And in so doing, he furnishes a clear illustration of the shared ontological commitments underlying both orthodox interpretations of archaeological evidence and realist-inspired international relations theory.

If the archaeological evidence is rendered suspect in consequence of being susceptible to a variety of incompatible interpretations – and this certainly seems to be the case – then we are returned to our earlier problem of how to proceed. The answer proposed here is simply that the validity of an account of any aspect of the aboriginal condition of a given people must, to the extent possible, be judged also in light of the sociopolitical, cultural, and cosmological contexts of that people. This calls for a more broadly intertextual approach, admitting some of the very voices silenced by orthodox treatments. Therefore, while it has been useful to discuss the disruptive influences and effects of the arrival of the Leviathan in a more inclusive way, deliberating upon the shared – or at least similar – experiences of a number of Indigenous peoples throughout the Americas, it is appropriate to turn now to a more focused consideration of the Lakota people and to assess the degree to which various accounts of their warfare are or are not consistent with autoethnographical descriptions of a traditional Lakota worldview and lifeways. Interrogating the evidence in this manner, it will be argued, yields not only an account of the aboriginal condition of the Lakota which is quite different from those put forth by the anthropological and historiographical orthodoxies, but also an alternative conception and practice of political order that is equally at odds with that which is held to by the orthodoxy of international relations.

Listening to autoethnographical voices

Johannes Fabian has observed that, "[i]n ethnography as we know it, the Other is displayed, and therefore contained, as an object of representation; the Other's voice, demands, teachings are usually absent from our theorizing" (Fabian 1990: 771). In his study of military patterns on the Plains, Secoy begins by noting that his work is temporally constrained by "the period of the earliest adequate documentary sources for the area" (Secoy 1966: 1). Elsewhere, he notes that, "[a]nalysis of the Pre-gun–Pre-horse military technique pattern of [the Sioux] must of necessity be incomplete, since there is little factual material on the Sioux during this period" (Secoy 1966: 65). Secoy thus seems to share in the widespread reluctance, exhibited most especially by scholars wedded to positivist epistemological commitments, to consider the oral literatures of Indigenous peoples as viable documentary sources – a bias which, while reflecting the gender and race prejudices inherent in the culture/nature dichotomy, contributes to the exclusion of Indigenous knowledges and, by extension, of the voices of

Indigenous people as well. But, as Neta Crawford rightly points out, the objection that oral literatures are suspect for being impermanent and susceptible to being altered to reflect the subjective inclinations of their human repositories is not so sound as might be imagined:

> Written texts are handy because they are semipermanent. But written "primary" texts are no more omniscient than oral histories; in fact, they may be less so. Written texts usually are inscribed by individual authors who rarely give us a sense of how widely shared their interpretations are. Even if widely shared, the written history is necessarily incomplete and reflective of a particular set of concerns and biases. In contrast, given the process of preserving and transmitting oral history, we know that more than one author was involved in shaping the account, for the generation of oral history is a public event, subject to public scrutiny and correction.
>
> (Crawford 1994: 351)

Travelogues and the canons of Western philosophy are, to the orthodoxies of anthropology and international relations respectively, "primary" texts of the sort mentioned by Crawford. As much – if not more so – than oral literatures, they reflect many of our deepest and least interrogated assumptions about the world; they reflect, in short, the common sense(s) of the society of which they are part and product. The commitments bound up in them – like the Hobbesian notion of the state of nature – shape ideas, beliefs, and knowledges by delimiting the possible and denominating the unthinkable.

What this points to is the imperative of listening to voices whose own common sense(s) are radically different from our own. This performs two vital functions: it is a first tentative step toward the liberation of these marginalized voices from the obscurity imposed by hegemonic narratives and ideas; and it aids in exposing the indeterminacy of some of our own most fundamental "truths." Revelations of this sort, by denaturalizing hegemonic orders and ideas, aid in highlighting the vital contribution of the travelogues to the Enlightenment; much more than merely confirming key Enlightenment ideas, these accounts helped to constitute them by furnishing the negative definitions necessary for their full articulation. In unsettling the accounts of the travelogues we simultaneously destabilize the hierarchies generated by a host of discursively gendered and racialized dichotomies: order/anarchy, culture/nature, rational/irrational, civilized/savage, to name but a few. But even as we acknowledge the transformative potential of Indigenous autoethnographies,[25] we should also be wary of the very serious implications of tearing this or that aspect of a given people's lived experience and worldview from its proper context and subjecting it to the deforming constraints and impositions of foreign ontological and epistemological commitments.[26] Thus, in attempting to learn about and from the worldviews and lifeways of Indigenous peoples, it is crucial that we avoid the mistake of constructing that which may seem nominally familiar in terms of what we might imagine to be correlates in our own lived experience. In short, we must endeavor to take seriously the voices, ideas, and perspectives we encounter on their own terms and in their appropriate cosmological contexts.[27]

We are confronted with this challenge immediately upon beginning to consider traditional Lakota cosmology, wherein existence is expressed as a circle rather than in the linear terms of Western cosmology. As one Oglala Lakota informant, Thomas Tyon, explained to J.R. Walker:

> The Oglala believe the circle to be sacred because the Great Spirit caused everything in nature to be round except stone. Stone is the implement of destruction. The sun and the sky, the earth and the moon are round like a shield, though the sky is deep like a bowl. Everything that breathes is round like the body of a man. Everything that grows from the ground is round like the stem of a tree. Since the Great Spirit has caused everything to be round mankind should look upon the circle as sacred for it is the symbol of all things in nature except stone. It is also the symbol of the circle that marks the edge of the world and therefore of the four winds that travel there. Consequently, it is also the symbol of a year. The day, the night, and the moon go in a circle above the sky. Therefore the circle is a symbol of these divisions of time and hence the symbol of all time.
>
> (Walker 1917: 160)

This account by Tyon bears unmistakable overtones of the Lakota sense of the intrinsic relatedness of all things. Moreover, as the celebrated Oglala *wicasa wakan* (usually translated as "holy man") Nicholas Black Elk made clear, the power that sustains life flows directly from one's connection to this circle of relatedness, a connection that is upheld, in part, via literal expressions of the circle in everyday life: "You will notice that everything the Indian does is in a circle. Everything they do is the power from the sacred hoop ... The power won't work in anything but circles" (DeMallie 1984: 290–1). Tyon concurred in this, citing it as the reason why the Lakota lived in round tipis which they arranged in a circle (Walker 1917: 160). And just as the power and unity inherent in the circle is important to the well-being of individuals, so too is it crucial to the health of the nation. The sacred hoop of the nation is a metaphor, derived from the camp circle, for the holistic unity of the Lakota people. Like the tipis that make up the camp circle, the nation is seen in terms of a hoop wherein no one constituent part is logically or implicitly prior to any other and such that all are equally necessary to complete the unity of the circle. The significance of the circle, then, is rooted in the assumption of an essential continuity from individual, through nation, to all elements of the cosmos, and back again. In fact, no one of these can be separated out from the others, since together they constitute a single totality encompassing all of Creation. Nature, therefore, is not something that must be overcome, with the result that the accent is on harmony over struggle; as Robert Bunge stresses, emphasis is placed on adjusting to nature, not subduing it (Bunge 1984: 94). In keeping with the endless unity of the circle, all things in the universe simply exist in a balance that was fixed long ago (DeMallie 1987: 31). Adjusting to this balance ensures its maintenance and, by extension, the security of all in Creation.[28] Contra the Judeo-Christian heritage, the Lakota were never cast out of their Eden; much to the contrary, they are inseparable from it.

The assumption of the fundamental interrelatedness of all things is expressed in the Lakota maxim, *mitakuye oyasin* – usually, if somewhat imperfectly, translated as "all are my relatives" or "we are all related." *Mitakuye oyasin* is in no way regarded as a normative proposition, but as a statement of simple fact whose falsity is so completely unthinkable that it may rightly be regarded as an aspect of traditional Lakota common sense. According to Fritz Detwiler, from this perspective, simply by virtue of their being part of the sacred hoop of the cosmos, "all beings are related in a way that reflects the ontological oneness of creation" (Detwiler 1992: 238). As Detwiler explains it:

> The Oglala understand that all beings and spirits are persons in the fullest sense of that term: they share inherent worth, integrity, sentience, conscience, power, will, voice, and especially the ability to enter into relationships. Humans, or "two-leggeds" are only one type of person. Humans share their world with Wakan and non-human persons, including human persons, stone persons, four-legged persons, winged-persons, crawling persons, standing persons (plants and trees), fish-persons, among others. These persons have both ontological and moral significance. The category person applies to anything that has being, and who is therefore capable of relating.
>
> (Detwiler 1992: 239)

From this perspective, given the emphasis on adjusting to – as opposed to subduing – nature, and inasmuch as other peoples are, like the Lakota themselves, related parts of a supremely holistic cosmos, bringing ruin upon them in warfare would be inconsistent with Lakota cosmological commitments. Moreover, it would be self-destructive since it would fragment the sacred hoop upon which all life depends. *Mitakuye oyasin*, then, expresses not only the interrelatedness, but also the interdependence of all elements of Creation.

Laurie Anne Whitt argues that "as an ethical and cognitive virtue" in many Indigenous societies, wherein it "mediates not only human, but human/nonhuman relationships," the notion of respect operates such that, "since everyone and everything has important functions, they deserve to be respected for what and how they are" (Whitt 1995: 243). And this outlook derives, in no insignificant way, from the assumption not only of epistemological diversity, but of cosmological diversity as well. Accordingly, as Harrod explains:

> Even though there were religious interchanges among groups, Native American peoples were not motivated to convert others, because they did not believe that one religion was true while the other was less true or even false. Evangelism and conversion were not the point of these religions. Indeed, to offer the power of one's central religious rituals to another was viewed as dangerous since such activity might cause a diminished relation of one's group to life-giving powers.
>
> (Harrod 1995: 103–4)

Similarly, according to Vine Deloria, Jr.:

> No demand existed … for the people to go into the world and inform or instruct other people in the rituals and beliefs of the tribe. The people were supposed to follow their own teachings and assume that other people would follow their teachings. These instructions were rigorously followed and consequently there was never an instance of a tribe making war on another tribe because of religious differences.
>
> (Deloria 1992: 36)

It should be noted also that if, as Deloria maintained, no wars were fought over "religious differences," this would almost certainly mean that divergent lifeways would not have been a source of derision either, given that, as with most Indigenous societies, spirituality for the Lakota was not ontologically separable from any other aspect of life or existence, however mundane. In this regard, the absence in most Indigenous languages of any pre-contact word by which to indicate religion or spirituality as discrete spheres is particularly telling (Kasee 1995: 84).

This broad outlook, which wrought no impetus to enforce conformity of others to one's own will or ways, was also reflected in the political structures of decision-making authority characteristic of Lakota bands. A band's council was called to convene whenever (and only as) needed to fulfill its collective decision-making function. Although membership was extended by formal invitation, all members of the band were free to speak in council.

Consistent in some ways with the principles of ancient Athenian democracy,[29] all decisions were required to be products of consensus rather than majority vote; so long as consensus could not be reached on a given question or issue, no decision could be rendered. This was fundamental to the Lakota conception of authority expressed as *Oyate ta woecun*, translated by Luther Standing Bear as "Done by the people" or "The decision of the Nation" (Standing Bear 1978: 129). Although a form of executive authority did come to prevail in matters of immediate urgency – such as when the band was under attack – it was completely specific to and coterminous with the special conditions that called it into being in the first place. The *akicita*, for example, performed a nominal and transitory policing function during buffalo hunts and were invested with considerable powers of censure in ensuring that the hunt remained a coordinated effort and that no individual did anything that might jeopardize its success. Still, even in this temporary form, authority was not automatically vested in any one designated individual or group, but was deferred to those most adept at dealing with the particular concern at hand.[30] All of this is not to say that the Lakota were without identifiable leaders. Individual bands were guided by *itancan* – patriarchs who could attain their positions only by way of positive attributes of character, earning them the respect and admiration of the band. Though they held a place of honor in council, the *itancan* were not possessed of any independent decision-making authority that could be made binding upon their bands or any individual members thereof (see Price 1994). To the extent, then, that they could ever presume to speak on behalf of their people, it would have to be on matters where collective decisions had already been reached in council. Moreover, the status of the *itancan*, contingent as it was on the reverence of their people, could evaporate quickly should they attempt to exceed their authority or otherwise fail to adhere to high standards of character (Powers 1975: 202–3).

None of this is to say that the pre-reservation Lakota were a people without conflict. Certainly, band councils had a need to resolve persistent deadlocks on important issues in respect of which consensus could not be reached. Dissenters in such cases would be subject to the discipline of peer and family pressure (Price 1994: 451). Such exhortation was grounded in an ethics of responsibility, expressed in the social expectation that individuals comport themselves in a manner consistent with "buffalo virtues," placing communal interests above individual ones after the manner of buffalo bulls, which would instinctively sacrifice themselves in defense of the herd (Rice 1991: 126). In the event that this too failed to break the impasse, resolution eventually came through the mechanism of secession – dissenters might join another existing band or, if their numbers were sufficient, found a new one (Price 1994: 451–2; Lonowski 1994: 154).[31] As all bands remained part of the Lakota nation and would still come together in the summer months to perform ceremonies and to take part in the communal buffalo hunts, secession was an accepted and legitimate mode of dispute resolution that implied no lasting enmity. Moreover, being a more drastic form of dispute resolution, it also served to deter intransigence by the majority and, simultaneously, prevented exercises of tyranny by preponderance of numbers. As in the view of the relation of humans to nature, the political sphere was thus constituted in deference to the cosmological emphasis on adjustment of human conduct so as to maintain balance.

Likewise, in the inter-national realm, conflict with other peoples involved efforts to restore balance perceived to have been temporarily lost. In this context, the existence of the revenge complex is particularly significant inasmuch as it both sustained low-intensity violence between groups and mitigated against disproportionate acts of retaliation – an exercise mandated by and subordinated to the imperative of maintaining/restoring balance.[32] Here too, then, the point is not to deny that conflict was part of the aboriginal condition but, rather, is to highlight the absence of a general anarchy. Far from an unrestrained "war of all against all," functional non-state mechanisms worked to furnish political order. What would have been unthinkable as a persistent feature of life on the pre-Columbian Northern Plains is large-scale exterminative warfare; such conduct would have been seen to jeopardize one's own well-being by threatening to break the sacred hoop. And all of this also remains consistent with the evidence of catastrophic conflict in the context of severe food shortages inasmuch as famine would almost certainly have bespoken a loss of cosmological balance.

Conclusion: the tyranny of orthodox social theory

Given the shared assumptions of the various academic orthodoxies briefly considered herein, it should be of considerable interest that the widely accepted accounts characterizing the aboriginal condition of Indigenous peoples as mired in interminable warfare are not, as may have been imagined, founded on unambiguous evidence unmediated by subjective interpretation. Equally noteworthy is the dearth of contact between scholars working in anthropology and history and those who make their disciplinary homes in international relations. And yet, we find the orthodoxies of these relative solitudes mutually invested in ontological commitments that both privilege the state as the sole locus of political order and render the aboriginal condition of Indigenous peoples as anarchic. This is revealing of the politics of academic disciplinarity insofar as it highlights how, in important ways, these fields have never truly been separated. More programmatically, it points up not only the profound ethnocentrism of scholarship situated in the orthodox traditions but also the importance of confronting their sites of origin, the travelogues of Europe's Age of Discovery, as foundational texts of the social sciences. To read contemporary realist-inspired international relations theory without also reading Hobbes is to miss much in the way of the dubious foundations upon which the former has been constructed. Likewise, when we read the philosophers of the Enlightenment without also reading the accounts of missionaries, conquistadors, and colonial administrators, we risk missing their centrality to the canons. Even so, their voices can be heard echoing through the legacy of social contractarian thought as well as in contemporary orthodox social theory, the colonial purposes they serve(d) all the while obscured but very much intact.

In January 2000, a group calling itself the Grass Roots *Oyate* (People) began what would become a lengthy peaceful occupation of the offices of the tribal government on the Oglalas' Pine Ridge Reservation in South Dakota. Among the group's objectives is the abolishment of the tribal government – a liberal-democratic representative form imposed under the US Indian Reorganization Act of 1934 (IRA) – and a return to traditional forms of political organization.[33] Their aspirations, then, are to (re)implement precisely that which orthodox social theory implicitly – and sometimes, as we have seen, explicitly – casts as implausible. The result is that Indigenous peoples are denied the possibility of a politics and are reduced instead to a political *issue*, itself confined to the domestic realm of the settler states in which they are situated. Such are the workings of advanced colonialism.

The immediate implications of this for people living on the reservation recall the instrumental use of Chagnon's writings by resource companies in Brazil. On Pine Ridge, as on many other reservations, IRA tribal govern-ments have often been implicated in serious mismanagement in areas such as the administration of social programs and stewardship over local mineral, grazing, and dumping rights.[34] The extent to which tribal councils are free from the leading or limiting influences of the settler state is also in question since, as Biolsi points out, the IRA constitutions had written into them "provisions for review or approval by the Secretary of the Interior" of actions undertaken by the councils (Biolsi 1985: 657). In the first half of the 1970s, American Indian Movement (AIM) activists joined traditionalist efforts to unseat the Oglalas' IRA council headed by Richard Wilson and replace it with a reconstituted traditional form of political organization. These devel-opments were met with the arrival of US Marshals on the reservation and extensive interference with the impeachment campaign; a sustained wave of political violence that left scores of traditionalists and AIM activists dead continued for several more years (Robbins 1992: 103–4). In combination with the material deprivations that so regularly attend reservation life, these are the very real consequences of the denial of traditional Indigenous polit-ical possibilities.

The idea of the savage in the state of nature also fulfills a vital rhetorical function in support of the contemporary settler state itself. Juxtaposed against the self-ascribed virtues of Euroamerican society, it justifies past conquests as well as subsequent and ongoing assimilative practices, even to the extent of making them seem morally imperative. Simultaneously,

Indigenous peoples – or at least their aboriginal lifeways – are conflated with the natural challenges once offered up by the "untamed" terrain on the American frontier. This phenomenon relegates all aspects of aboriginal lifeways – save, perhaps, for such markers and cultural accoutrements as have been appropriated into the semiotic performances of the settler state's own constructed identity – irretrievably to the distant past. This enables even those who might lament the (noble) savage's loss of natural freedom to accept it nevertheless as the inevitable result of "progress" and the steady march of "civilization"; in its contemporary manifestation, it renders the politics of the traditionalists as bewilderingly idealistic, even self-deluding. And all of these effects aid in the ideational production of Euroamerican society and the modern Western self. Even as it denies the possibility of a non-anarchical aboriginal condition, then, the Hobbesian impulse is essential as description of the bare life in opposition to which the virtues of the dominating society can be articulated. In this sense, the advanced colonial subjugation of Indigenous peoples is one with Euroamerican self-knowledge(s).[35]

The incommensurability between the ethnographies produced by the academic orthodoxies and the autoethnographic accounts by Lakota people themselves is also revealing of the extent to which the former are racialized. The conceptual indebtedness of orthodox anthropological and historiographical treatments of Indigenous peoples to the travelogues inexorably involves them not only in the material aspects of colonialism/advanced colonialism but with the rhetorical constructs of the colonial encounter as well. As the European empires expanded into the rest of the world, a dialectical relationship took hold between racial ideologies and the exigencies of material exploitation, each impelling the other (Loomba 1998: 113). This, in turn, was elemental in defining an emergent knowledge system that endorsed the discourse of savagery and the attendant idea of an anarchic state of nature. Constructed in terms consistent with the cultural logic of the Age of Discovery, these ideas fed back into it, reconfirming themselves. It is in their adherence to vital aspects of these same ontological commitments that the orthodox anthropological and historiographical literatures are most profoundly racialized. And, notwithstanding that it might make no explicit reference to race, orthodox international theory is exposed as being similarly and unavoidably racialized for having built upon this same ontological terrain – a terrain defined by commitments reciprocally constituted by and constitutive of racial ideologies.

To the extent that orthodox theoretical approaches to international relations exclude aboriginal knowledges and lifeways in deference to the familiar Hobbesian impulse, they are inseparable from the more comprehensive processes of invalidation by which the colonial subjugation of Indigenous people(s) is sustained. Though not directly culpable as purposeful agents, scholars working in this tradition, like their counterparts in the anthropological and historiographical orthodoxies, are nonetheless implicated in the ongoing project of advanced colonialism. It is in reproducing the hegemonic knowledges that invalidate many non-Western worldviews and lifeways that scholars working in these traditions exert a tyranny over Indigenous peoples. Articulated through research, writing, and (especially) teaching, the collective discursive power of orthodox scholars to define what is real, what is possible, and whose voices count can have considerable reach. The consequent denial of voice obscures the indeterminacy of dominant truth claims which, in turn, foreclose transformative possibilities and reconfirm the presumed naturalness of the hegemonic structures and ideas that enable the ongoing advanced colonial domination of Indigenous peoples. Here the inattention of the international relations orthodoxy is as significant as the attentions of those of anthropology and history. As Fabian reminds us, "writing need not have the Other as its subject matter in order to oppress the Other" (Fabian 1990: 767–8). Furthermore, if, as has been argued in this chapter, the commitments by which the denial of aboriginal knowledges might be justified do not stand up to critical scrutiny, we are left with the unsatisfactory circumstance that these selfsame commitments, by orienting the interpretation of ambiguous evidence, are themselves the sources of whatever putative proof can be invoked to support them. By extension, the invisibility of Indigenous peoples from the perspective of adherents to the orthodoxy of international relations is in some measure reproduced by the failure of these same scholars to see them. Though the particulars of their cosmological commitments may not be generalizeable to other Indigenous peoples, the case of the Lakota traditionalists alerts us to the imperative of engaging non-Western societies in their appropriate cosmological contexts and, not least, to the dangers of allowing Western philosophical commitments and inclinations to foreclose *a priori* the very possibility of such engagements. It also calls upon us to recognize that international relations theory is a powerful social force in its own right and is therefore susceptible to becoming an instrument of domination.

Acknowledgements

This chapter draws upon and repositions a line of argument that I first presented in Beier (1998). In its present form, it has benefited greatly from valuable comments by Samantha Arnold, Hugh Gusterson, Tami Amanda Jacoby, and Sandra Whitworth. I am also grateful to the editors and the other contributors to this volume for their thoughtful and supportive suggestions.

Notes

1   In the context of the argument that follows, I use the terms "Indigenous" and "aboriginal" in different and very specific ways. The former, I use in the manner of a proper noun in reference to the original human inhabitants of the Americas.

This treatment is in contradistinction to the more generalized "indigenous" which is more susceptible to appropriation by American-born persons of Euroamerican descent seeking to undermine claims to sovereignty by Indigenous people(s). In contrast, I use "aboriginal" as an adjective herein because, being more explicitly connected to the pre-Columbian past, it is less ambiguous in reference to aboriginal warfare or the aboriginal condition of Indigenous peoples.

2   There have been a few prefatory engagements with Indigenous North American empirical cases and epistemologies by scholars working in the field of international relations. To date, however, only one book (Wilmer 1993) has been published on the subject. Wilmer is also the author of "Indigenous peoples, marginal sites, and the changing context of world politics" (Wilmer 1996). Roger Epp (2000) identified and explored some of the problems, promises, and prospects for intersections between indigeneity and IR. For an attempt to engage the Great Law of Peace of the Haudenosaunee Confederacy as a security regime, see Crawford (1994). For a response to Crawford that disputes the reading of the Haudenosaunee Confederacy as a security regime, see Bedford and Workman (1997). But despite the important insights to be had from these and a handful of other contributions, all remain quite decidedly relegated to the margins of disciplinary international relations and few inroads have been made into IR curricula.

3   I make this point with considerable apprehension. While I think it is important to note that the Indigenous peoples of the Americas have achieved a degree of standing in the canonical international system, I do not wish to suggest that this ought to be the standard upon which the appropriateness of their inclusion in international relations be judged. Similarly, I am leery of any attempt to elevate Indigenous peoples in the popular imagination by way of reference to particular characteristics of social or political organization presumed as analogous or nascent forms of those of the dominating society. To do so is to fall into a form of evolutionist conjectural historicizing and to implicitly privilege Euroamerican forms of social and political organization by holding them up as evidence of an "advanced" society.

4   See also Stocking (1995: 940–1).

5   The Lakota, the Teton division of the Dakota people, may be better known by the name "Sioux," usually understood to comprise the aggregate of all Dakota peoples.

6   This bespeaks a more subtle and less instrumental working of colonial discourse than that suggested by Said's sense that imperialism and colonialism are "supported and perhaps even impelled by impressive ideological formations that include notions that certain territories and people *require* and beseech domination" (Said 1993: 9; emphasis in original). This might tend too much toward what Homi Bhabha has called "the transparent linear equivalence of event and idea" (Bhabha 1990: 292). That is, it seems to imply too unitary a connection between colonial discourses and actual colonial practices. See also Loomba (1998: 232).

7   For a discussion of how this factionalism generated conflict on the Pine Ridge Reservation in South Dakota culminating in the 1973 occupation at Wounded Knee, see Roos *et al.* (1980).

8   The first articulation of this idea is found in an essay titled "Subaltern studies: deconstructing historiography," in Spivak (1987).

9   Of course, there is a hint of this too in my own references to academic "orthodoxies," which in many ways defy the homogeneity I ascribe to them through the more particular points I want to make in this chapter.

10 See Mukherjee (1990) and King (1990).
11 According to Stuart Hall,

> "After" means in the moment which follows that moment (the colonial) in which the colonial relation was dominant. It does not mean ... that what we have called the "after-effects" of colonial rule have somehow been suspended. It certainly does *not* mean that we have passed from a regime of power–knowledge into some powerless and conflict-free time zone.
>
> (Hall 1996: 254)

12 In fact, as we shall see, orthodox accounts of the aboriginal conditions of Indigenous peoples are in many ways much more expressive of the dominating society. As Edward Said has argued, "Orientalism is – and does not simply represent – a considerable dimension of modern political-intellectual culture, and as such has less to do with the Orient than it does with 'our' world" (Said 1979: 12). In a similar vein and with specific reference to ethnography, Timothy Jenkins noted the related reductive and productive functions of conceptual dichotomies: "The use of the paired terms modern/backward says more about the world of the enquirer than that of the peasant. In the stereotype, peasants are survivals of the pre-modern, embodying its qualities which are defined against our own" (Jenkins 1994: 450).
13 As Mary Pratt noted, such renderings have been an important element in the legitimization of European conquest of Indigenous peoples (Pratt 1992: 186). And to this we might add that legitimization of this sort is as well conferred retrospectively as it was in the event.
14 See also Chagnon's seminal work, *Y,anomamö, the Fierce People* (1968).
15 A recently published popular book by investigative journalist Patrick Tierney (2000) implicates Chagnon, among others, in a scandal of apparently monumental proportions. A considerable tumult erupted in the autumn of 2000 when a widely circulated e-mail memorandum written by anthropologists Leslie Sponsol and Terence Turner – both of whom had seen galley copies of Tierney's manuscript – and addressed to the president and president-elect of the American Anthropological Association described Chagnon's work with the late anthropologist James Neel as well as Tierney's allegation that Neel might have deliberately incited a 1968 measles epidemic which, besides killing hundreds or perhaps thousands of Yanomami, also seemed to fit neatly with his research agenda. According to the memo, Tierney also alleged "that Chagnon has not stopped with cooking and re-cooking his data on conflict but has actually attempted to manufacture the phenomenon itself, actually fomenting conflicts between Yanomami communities, not once but repeatedly." The memo also noted Tierney's allegations of serious sexual misconduct by both Chagnon and French anthropologist Jacques Lizot – whose critique of Chagnon's work is cited herein – while in Yanomami communities. At the time of this writing, anthropology awaits the conclusions of a number of investigations into these various allegations. For their part, Chagnon and his supporters have vehemently denied the accusations.
16 Chagnon's choice of the word "fierce" to describe the Yanomami has thus become a contemporary functional equivalent of the label "cannibal," used to such great effect as a normative inscription upon those Others who have stood in the way of colonial aspirations since Columbus's first voyage to the Americas in 1492. See Motohashi (1999). Similarly, Loomba noted that "Spanish colonists increasingly applied the term 'cannibal' and attributed the practice of cannibalism to those natives within the Caribbean and Mexico who were *resistant* to

colonial rule, and among whom no cannibalism had in fact been witnessed" (Loomba 1998: 58–9, emphasis in original).

17 In Holm's view, militarization of Indigenous peoples was "a method of assimilation or subjugation, depending on the viewpoint, equal to, or perhaps more effective than, that of outright military conquest, conversion to Christianity or economic dependency" (Holm 1997: 462).

18 That Ewers does not seem to have felt compelled to propose an answer to the question of whence these animosities originally sprang is, once again, suggestive of a prior assumption of a Hobbesian state of nature.

19 For perhaps the most comprehensive inquiry into early Euroamerican accounts, see Berkhofer (1978).

20 See Sundstrom (1997). Winter counts are the basis of the traditional oral historiographical records of the Northern Plains peoples wherein each year is identified by way of association with some notable event.

21 Bamforth cited a count of at least 486, noting that perhaps 50 additional skeletons remain in place (Bamforth 1994: 106). P. Willey and Thomas Emerson offered a different explanation for the imprecision of the count: "Before the remains could be excavated by the USD Archaeology Laboratory, the remains of nearly 50 individuals were looted from the bank" (Willey and Emerson 1993: 265).

22 Noting that an incomplete second ditch had failed to enclose the expanded village before the massacre, Willey and Emerson speculated that the inner ditch fell into disuse because the village was not under constant threat of attack (Willey and Emerson 1993: 230–1). Such a view is consistent with speculation linking the massacre at Crow Creek to intermittent food shortages. It also reinforces the position that warfare was not endemic.

23 Though he is most accurately situated in the orthodoxy, Frank Secoy also noted that fortification increased in the post-contact period, observing that "the art of village fortification, long in existence, had been developed to high efficiency in defense against both the gun-equipped northeastern peoples and the horse-riding southwestern ones" (Secoy 1966: 72). Note that fortification is found to have increased in response to adversaries equipped with horses or guns, both of which were introduced by Europeans.

24 As noted above, Ferguson made no claim to the effect that warfare was absent from the aboriginal condition, holding only that the arrival of Europeans incited and intensified warfare among Indigenous peoples.

25 I follow Pratt in my use of the term "autoethnography," though with an important qualification. Pratt used the term to indicate a form of self-representation by colonized subjects which, because it engages with the ethnographical texts of the colonizer, is distinct from what is sometimes called the "authentic" voice (Pratt 1992: 7–8). Reflecting the fact that the autoethnographical voices of interest here are somewhat more complicated by virtue of their connection to oral literatures, my usage falls somewhere between the two. While each of the autoethnographies drawn upon herein must certainly have been influenced by the exigencies of life in what Pratt called the "contact zone" of the colonial encounter, the more communal nature of oral literatures suggests that textual revisionism is likely to move more glacially and less idiosyncratically than might be the case where single-author-ized written forms are concerned.

26 Indeed, it is precisely this mistake that Bedford and Workman (1997) found at the root of Crawford's attempt to render the Great Law of Peace as a security regime.

27 At this point, a note is in order regarding the choice of autoethnographies that follow. Difficulties in engaging the "Pristine Non," as described by Ferguson above, owe here to the practical disjunctures between oral literatures and the

Western conventions by which texts are author-ized. To highlight the contingency of orthodox anthropological accounts of Indigenous peoples, it is necessary to consult autoethnographical sources. In particular, I have drawn on Nicholas Black Elk, Luther Standing Bear, and Thomas Tyon. All three reached adulthood as members of pre-reservation Lakota bands and should thus be listened to at least as fully as twentieth-century anthropologists and historians. As a people with an oral literary tradition, the Lakota have no "hard" texts predating contact. Standing Bear, however, received a Western education and authored his own books. He is therefore not as readily dismissed as, lamentably, contemporary bearers of oral history might be. Additionally, testimony by Tyon (published by physician and ethnographer J.R. Walker) that draws on consultations he conducted with his own elders and other Lakotas around the turn of the century is quite well regarded. Accounts of their interviews with Black Elk published, each in their turn, by John G. Neihardt and Joseph Epes Brown bear heavy Christian overtones which have been the source of some considerable controversy. For this reason, I have drawn only on Raymond DeMallie's *The Sixth Grandfather* (1984) which combines the actual transcripts of the Black Elk interviews with a detailed study of the textual liberties apparently taken by Neihardt and Brown in their published versions. Walker and DeMallie are thus the surrogate bearers of the voices of Tyon and Black Elk respectively, their texts cultural transliterations of sorts from one literary medium to another. The conventions of Western academic writing are problematic here: there is no accepted means of referencing that would credit Tyon and Black Elk and, moreover, it might be regarded as a culturally insensitive mistake to try to individually ascribe oral literatures in this way. Theirs are, nevertheless, authoethnographical voices and as such are indispensable to us here. Of course, none of this should be taken to suggest that these or any other texts are ever free of the multifarious workings of domination and resistance that characterize the colonial encounter and its legacies.

28 Here, then, is the site of struggle at which people have sought, through both practical and spiritual means, to adjust to the transcendent balance of the natural order of which they are part.

29 Although certainly not underwritten by the same stratified social relations upon which the Athenian *polis* was constructed.

30 See Price (1994).

31 Stephen Cornell linked the reservation era loss of the ability to secede to the contemporary factionalism in many Indigenous North American communities (Cornell 1988: 38).

32 For a convincing hypothesis as to the sources of original conflict, see Biolsi (1984).

33 Eileen Janis, Grass Roots *Oyate*, personal communication, 20 February 2000.

34 See Churchill and LaDuke (1992).

35 The resultant identity-knowledge complex has proved remarkably resistant to critical re-evaluation. In 1991, for example, an exhibition at the US Smithsonian Institution's National Museum of American Art titled "The West as America: Reinterpreting Images of the Frontier, 1820–1920" was widely criticized by members of Congress, scholars, the press, and members of the public for the curators' interpretations of Frontier era art as racist, sexist, and imperialist (Price 1993: 230–1). One obviously incensed visitor to the museum complained: "Despite [the curators'] best efforts at 'political correctness,' they have produced a show whose visual impact confirms all that they detest – the expansion westward was good, desirable, and brought the 'New World' into the civilized mainstream" (Smithsonian Institution 1991: 8).

5

CULTURAL CHAUVINISM AND THE LIBERAL INTERNATIONAL ORDER

"West versus Rest" in Asia's financial crisis

L.H.M. Ling

Pushing reform after Asia's financial crisis (1997–8), the West's liberal international order has effected a strategic, triple move.[1] Not a cloak-and-dagger conspiracy, as some would dismiss it, this triple move rather reflects an openly calculated coordination of institutional interests to sustain Western capitalist hegemony in the global economy.[2] In this case, the liberal international order has sought to (1) (re)feminize Asia by discrediting the region's claim to a muscular, alternative capitalism; (2) (re)masculinize the role of Western capital in the region by buying out Asian capital at bankrupt prices; and (3) (re)hegemonize relations in the region, both domestically and internationally, by mimicking cold war power politics.

Neither conventional nor critical understandings of international relations (IR) adequately explain this triple move.[3] Conventional IR's Hobbesian scenario of "warre of all against all" might suffice if not for its liberal belief in the universal rationality of economic logic (Waltz 1979). That is, why would Western capitalists discipline Asian capitalists if they all *think* alike?[4] Moreover, why would such ideological disciplining take on gendered, neocolonial overtones? Critical theorists fare no better. Assuming the same of all capitalists, they are seen as either overlords of the state (Panitch 1994), exclusive members of a "neoliberal civilization" (Gill 1995a, 1995b), or suffering from capitalism's internal contradictions (McNally 1998). If so, then why would national identity or culture matter where corporate profit is concerned, especially in our current age of globalized finance, trade, technology, and production? Even if critical theorists recognize that rival camps of national capital may compete, they fail to answer a corollary question: Why do stereotypes of masculinity and femininity still drive this competition? These queries beget another: How does the liberal promise of "development" implicate the relationship between "developed" and "developing" economies, the West and the Rest?[5] Put differently, both conventional and critical IR overlook the meaning of global interactions, especially where they highlight relational struggles for ideology, organization, and power.[6] These necessarily involve historical–cultural understandings of who we are, what we do, and why we relate to "others" the way we do.[7]

This chapter offers an alternative interpretation of the Asian financial crisis based on what I call postcolonial IR (Ling 2001a). An analytical hybrid of social constructivism for method and postcolonial theory for an interpretation of politics, postcolonial IR reconciles these apparent paradoxes of power and rationality, capital and civilization, hegemony and development by positing five epistemological and normative principles:[8]

1   international relations reflects a collectivity or intersubjectivity of agent–structure relations (in constructivist terms) that sustain and reflect multiple identities and subjectivities (in postcolonial terms);[9]
2   first- and then second-order learning[10] ensues as problem-solving needs arise, reframing both the problem and its problem-solver in the process;
3   over time, systemic transformations result as learning cumulates and the rules of interaction are rewritten;
4   for this reason, agents and their institutions cannot escape a moral accountability for the world they create and re-create;
5   meaning in global relations thus redounds ultimately to the social values assigned to race, gender, class, and culture, particularly when problem-solving rules relate self to other.

From this skeletal framework, postcolonial IR fleshes out two specific concepts: mimicry and hypermasculinity. Homi Bhabha (1994) first articulated the notion of mimicry as a survival tactic for the colonized. It allows the colonized to try on, like a new accessory, the colonizer's reflected image in the body/site of the "native." A moment of political destabilization rather than fawning flattery, mimicry subverts the hegemonic convention that the colonizer is always separate from and superior to the colonized. Mimicry's artifice shocks the colonizer into accepting a possible parity with the colonized.

I update Bhabha's insight by differentiating mimicry into two types: formal and substantive. Bhabha's version of mimicry reflects first-order learning or what I call formal mimicry. It replicates an affect of the Self by the Other such as, for example, the current fashion of young Asians and Africans, whether living in the West or elsewhere, dyeing their hair blonde. In terms of economic development, formal mimicry can be found in a society without an indigenous, liberal tradition but which adopts an imposed or borrowed liberal ideology of limited state and unfettered market, plus all the developmental paraphernalia that come with it, such as commercially tied aid, foreign advisors, consultants, or experts, and First World rules, practices, and institutions (Escobar 1995). This mimic-economy would remain just that: dichotomized, superficial, contradictory, and forever emulative.

But other possibilities may arise. Over time, formal mimicry could evolve into a second-order version or what I call substantive mimicry.[11] What used to serve as surface copying (whether playful or imposed) now deepens into a cumulative strategy of integrated, more coherent problem solving, producing a hybrid sense of self and other. Arising from the interstices of contending worldviews, substantive mimicry fosters learning that draws on the cultural richness of *mélange* multiplicity without miring the problem solver in its divisive differences. Substantive mimicry, however, does not necessarily improve our lives; it merely resolves prevailing problems. For example, a highly gendered mode of economic development may emerge from the interstices of Western liberal masculinist capitalism ("economic man") and local patriarchal traditions ("father-state"). In East Asia, substantive mimicry sites women's bodies for utilitarian, economic production ("nimble fingers," "Singapore Girl"), self-sacrificing, generational reproduction ("good wife," "wise mother"), or lucrative, patriotic remittances (maids, nannies, nurses, and "entertainers" overseas). Substantive mimicry also draws on cultural resources outside liberalism's purview, such as father-state and son-corporations. Most distinctively, substantive mimicry articulates an innovative, internally developed ideology in contrast to formal mimicry's conventional, externally borrowed one.

Both types of mimicry destabilize self–other relations, but the hegemonic self's response to them differs markedly. Formal mimicry invites amusement, tolerance, even encouragement (after all, imitation *is* the highest form of flattery). But substantive mimicry provokes a punitive, disciplinary reaction. Now the other is competing against, not just imitating, the hegemonic self. As this chapter shows, liberals in the West could tolerate Asia's "miracle" growth so long as it remained formal mimicry: Asian elites paying ideological homage to the superiority of the Western, liberal model of capitalism. But Western liberals could not abide by substantive mimicry's formulation of a distinctive Asian capitalism, articulated most forcefully in the 1980s. Both the alternative itself and liberal responses to it reveal an underlying hypermasculinity at work.

Hypermasculinity demonstrates the transformative nature of intersubjectivity that lies at the core of postcolonial IR. Ashis Nandy (1983) initially identified hypermasculinity as a cultural pathology in colonialism. It justified barbaric acts of aggression, competition, power, and production as manly and masculine, while denigrating similar caricatures of welfare, nurturing, kindness, and consumption as womanly and feminine. With British rule in India as an example, Nandy showed how colonizer and colonized alike valorized hypermasculinity because it rationalized British colonialism while provoking local elites to prove their manhood, so to speak. In both, hypermasculinity induced an "underdeveloped heart" of sexism, racism, false cultural homogeneity, and banal violence.

I extend Nandy's hypermasculine pathology to the capitalist world economy. The players in and site of hypermasculine competition since colonialism may have changed, but its script of colonial power relations and underdeveloped hearts remains the same. Hypermasculine capitalism reconstructs social subjects, spaces, and activities into economic agents that valorize a masculinized, global competitiveness associated with men, entrepreneurs, the upwardly mobile, cities, and industrialization. It also assigns a hyperfeminized stagnancy to local women, peasants, the poor, and agrarian production. Hypermasculine capitalism, in short, is reactionary in nature.[12] For the formerly colonized, it recasts economic development into a retrieval of cultural–national manhood due to collective histories of castration by previous invaders, occupiers, or colonizers. For former colonizers, hypermasculine capitalism hoists a seemingly objective, universalistic rhetoric to cover a cultural chauvinism stoked by the rise of hypermasculinized others. For both, an underdeveloped heart results as hypermasculine capitalism demands ever more demonstrations of national or cultural manhood for fear of an imposed or revealed hyperfemininity.

Applied to the Asian financial crisis, postcolonial IR discovers the following:

1   *Intersubjectivity*. Contrary to its ideological commitment to a level playing field, liberal capitalism actually seeks a skewed intersubjectivity of "I lead, you follow."
2   *Learning*. Asian capitalism violates this intersubjectivity by evolving from formal to substantive mimicry, thereby shifting from hyperfeminized subordination to hypermasculinized competition.
3   *Transformation*. For this reason, the liberal international order aims to discipline Asian capitalism. Utilizing reform of crony capitalism as rhetoric, the liberal international order seeks to return power hierarchies in the Asia–Pacific region to their cold war configurations: (a) Western capital dominating Asian capital by buying out the latter at bankrupt prices; (b) the hypermasculine, developmental state regulating hyperfeminized society under the rubric of national recovery; and (c) depressed men exploiting women and other feminized subjects (children, minorities) for the health, wealth, and happiness of the patriarchal family–state–economy. Neither does the liberal international order itself escape these contestations. It, too, experiences internal jolts that underscore the reciprocal nature of hypermasculinity's underdeveloped heart.
4   *Accountability*. Elites in Asia and the West are jointly accountable for the Asian crisis and its aftermath. Both transfer the cost of the crisis to ordinary folk who had little to do with the massive lendings and borrowings of capital that transpired in the late 1990s in the region but now bear the brunt of its consequences.

5 *Meaning.* The meaning of crisis and reform, cronyism and liberalism, Asia and the West lies in their relationality. That is, each comes from and sustains the other. Hurting one damages the other, just as aiding the other helps oneself. From this realization comes our salvation from ever-expanding spirals of hypermasculine competition. We need to surrender the liberal myth that capital is objective, purely interest-driven, and culturally neutral. Economic calculation may obscure and sometimes overcome cultural prejudice, but not eliminate it, especially over the long run. The sooner we accept the existence of such local desires as cultural chauvinism in the global political economy – indeed, any relational basis to global interactions – the readier we are to devise a more democratic, humane, and culturally grounded future.

Before proceeding, a few caveats are in order. This chapter does not review the origins of the Asian financial crisis. Others have done so amply and with greater competence (Bullard *et al.* 1998). Neither does it debate the benefits of reforming "crony capitalism." Certainly, state and economic elites in Asia (especially when tied by family) have enjoyed an insular, mutually profitable relationship over the decades and deserve scrutiny. But so do crony capitalists in the West. (How else can we explain the longevity of crony capitalism in any economy, if not for the mutual reinforcement of *multiple* crony capitalists all over the world?) Rather, this chapter's focus remains IR theory building: that is, how does postcolonial IR help us achieve a better, more comprehensive understanding of global relations, with the Asian crisis as its latest manifestation, than conventional approaches? We begin with liberalism's implicit, intersubjective bargain of "I lead, you follow."[13]

Liberal intersubjectivity: "I lead, you follow"

Liberal capitalism claims to deliver a level playing field. It disallows any interference from exogenous factors on the field (the marketplace) or its players (the individual person or firm): family, society, nation-state, history, language, or culture. When exogenous factors (like the state) tamper with the market's self-regulating laws, liberals assert that "market failure" or "irrational *dirigisme*" results (Deepak 1985: 60). To liberals, the optimum condition for both individuals and markets is a context-free zone of buying and selling. That is, liberals treat individuals and markets as functionally identical or epistemologically interchangeable. Consumers and markets in Ecuador would act no differently from those in Zimbabwe or Belgium or Taiwan. All respond to universal laws of supply and demand, consumption and production, costs and benefits. With this radical individualism as premise, liberal capitalism declares itself the most democratic route to prosperity.

Liberal democratic theory thus asserts its necessity, superiority, and inevitability. Capitalist market practices, liberals claim, produce all the fundamentals of a democratic society: a revolutionary middle class, an active civil society, rational pursuit of individual interest that leads to self-censoring collective action, and so on. As Mancur Olson has observed, "the same court system, independent judiciary, and respect for law and individual rights that are needed for a lasting democracy are also required for security of property and contract rights" (1993: 572) . Further, liberals contend that globalization embeds democracy "in the depths of people's hearts and minds" (Sakamoto 1991: 122). To them, the fall of socialist governments in the former Soviet Union and Eastern Europe further affirms liberal capitalism as a transnationalized ideology of development. It represents "untrammelled international competition, celebration of the market, of wealth and self, anti-communism and anti-unionism" (Overbeek and van der Pijl 1993: 1). For East Asia's "neoautocracies," Minxin Pei concluded, it "is not *whether* [to democratize], but *when* and *how*" (1994: 102, emphasis added).

According to Francis Fukuyama (1989), history "ends" precisely for this reason. All peoples have realized, he proclaimed, that Western liberal capitalism offers the best venue to social, political, and economic fulfillment. Nonliberal governments and economies should emulate the developmental paths blazed by the industrialized West because modernization requires universal "stages of growth."[14] They become (re)defined as immature or underdeveloped. In contrast, industrialized economies represent advanced development, with attendant qualities of rationality, impersonal decision making, and specialization (Banuri 1990).

We begin to detect liberal capitalism's intersubjective bargain. In claiming what is (individuals respond to incentives), liberal capitalism slips easily into what should be (I have incentive X, so you should follow me). Partly, this bargain underpins all capitalist, market relations: "Buy my product not just because you need it but because you *desire* it." Indeed, liberals bank on this conflation of desire with choice and democracy. But liberal capitalism's implicit intersubjectivity bears specific configurations of race, gender, and class as well. These remain remarkably Western, white, male, and colonial despite liberal capitalism's global ambitions.

M.I. Franklin (forthcoming) finds that ads for global telecommunications companies,[15] for example, tend to replay themes of Western-style democracy ("pick and choose") based on a consumer cosmopolitanism ("a world of difference") guaranteed by big men, strong states. One ad from Deutsche Telekom shows three white male hands, stretching from business-suit sleeves, grasping one another by the wrist. The image suggests trust, friendship, and stability among the three. The ad's slogan assures the viewer that "Real international understanding starts here." One sleeve bears the stars and stripes of the American flag; the other two are less discernible. Another ad from Cable & Wireless suggests that yesteryear's "Great Game," when white men tromped through the world warring and profiteering to their privileged delight, has been replaced by another set of great powers: the world's telecom giants.

Similar images abound in *The Economist*, as noted by Charlotte Hooper (2000). They depict globalization and, by extension, global economic man, as a mix of "science, technology, [and] business" that exemplifies an "entrepreneurial frontier masculinity" (Hooper 2000: 67). It is ready to conquer new markets, new products, and new consumers. Even the very notion of cosmopolitanism is being colonized. Like Colonial Man before him, Cosmopolitan Man has the freedom, choice, and authority to straddle the world with "competence" and "mastery," not "surrender[ing]" to or "negotiat[ing]" with other cultures but imbued with a sense of "personal autonomy" that allows him to "exit" at will (Hannerz 1990: 239).

Cosmopolitan Man sets the stage for others as well. Elsewhere (Ling 1999, 1996) I have shown how commercial media in Hong Kong and Shanghai, from both domestic and international sources, subscribe to and propagate a notion of globalization and internationalization as societal mimicry of what is considered Western, modern, urban, industrial, upwardly mobile, and masculine. In turn, nonmimicry leaves behind the so-called traditional sectors and natives who are backward, rural, agricultural, socially stagnant, and feminine. The latter, for instance, scrounge for change in torn shorts and T-shirt, whereas modern capital's blazer-fitted profes-sionals swathe the globe with their shiny credit cards. It is hard *not* to surmise that "the developmental state" is supposed to mimic "reasoning [Western] man" (Manzo 1991: 6). Others, however, disagree.

Capitalist learning in Asia: from formal to substantive mimicry

Asian capitalism reflects substantive mimicry. Elsewhere (Ling 2001a), I have traced such hybrid, second-order learning to a history of institutional problem solving across two world-orders: Confucian governance and Westphalian capitalism. Confucian governance constructs the state as family relations writ large: that is, the state extends parental benevolence in exchange for society's filial piety. Westphalian capitalism is centered on individual self-interest expressed through marketplace commerce, in the name of the state, the firm, or an individual.

A Confucian mimicry of the liberal state results (Han and Ling 1998). Its public–private split is grafted onto the Confucian world-order's family-based governance to produce a public hypermasculinization of the state dictating policy to a privatized, hyperfeminized society. Together, they nurture a common progeny: son-corporations. These benefit from hyperfeminized society's nurturing and self-sacrifice (e.g., tax breaks, low wages, monitored unions) to enhance the hypermasculinized state's reputation and glory (e.g., greater profits, larger market shares, more authority domestically, higher visibility internationally). The hypermasculinized state also swiftly and severely punishes these son-corporations whenever they seem to transgress such parental-authority boundaries (Nam 1995).

Other examples of East Asia's Confucian-liberal hybrid include:

1   collective individualism, where the liberal individual – forever self-interested and rationally calculating – is placed within a Confucian collective like the patriarchal family–state–economy to enhance capitalist competition, particularly with other collectives;
2   utilitarian personalism, which licenses liberal utilitarian behavior within hierarchical structures like corporations or trade associations, to facilitate personal connections (*guanxi*) for economic gain;
3   an ideology of *patria economicus*, where the Confucian family-state redefines its mission to protect the welfare of the people in terms of gross national products and per capita income;
4   national calls for "learning for the state," which shifts the family-state's traditional monopoly on knowledge for political stability to business for economic development.

(Ling 2001a)

More subtly, substantive mimicry in Asia has led to a hypermasculine approach to capitalist competition. It frames developmentalism as a form of patriotic manhood: to catch up with the industrialized West, to gain independence from former and future imperialists, to fight communism (Japan, Taiwan, South Korea, Singapore, and Hong Kong), or to assert socialism with local characteristics (China). During the 1960s and 1970s, for example, Korea's government repeatedly exhorted its population to rapid economic development with the following slogans: "Let's fight to build!" (*ssaumuro konsolhaja!*), "Export is the only way to survive" (*such'ulmani salgilida*), "Total export war" (*such'ul ch'ongnyokjon*), and "Trade war!" (*muyokjonjaeng!*). Workers served as industrial or export "soldiers" (*sanop* or *such'uljonsa*).

At the same time, an international context of cold war power politics hyperfeminized these states. In receiving massive amounts of American military and commercial aid to deter communism in the region, they had to submit to American and European corporate dominance. Industrialization mixed with militarization invariably promoted prostitution and other "entertainment" industries in all the frontline economies, especially during the Vietnam War (Barry 1995). Asian capital thus served, pimped or otherwise catered to Western capital which, it claimed, sheltered the region with an economic and security umbrella.

Note this pep talk by a South Korean official to camptown prostitutes in the 1980s: motivating them to "service" the American military so it wouldn't withdraw from South Korea, he talked about their sister prostitutes in Japan who willingly sacrificed themselves to occupation forces after World War II so that the nation as a whole could reconstruct:

> The Japanese prostitute, when she finished with the GI, did not get up to go get the next GI (for more money) but knelt before him and pleaded with him to help rebuild Japan. The spirit of the Japanese prostitute was concerned with the survival of her fatherland. The patriotism of the Japanese prostitute spread to the rest of the society to develop Japan.
>
> (quoted in Moon 1997: 103)

This same process of substantive mimicry through hypermasculine competition applied to non-Confucian Asia as well. President Fidel Ramos of the Philippines, for example, referred to Filipina migrant workers – who have journeyed worldwide to work as maids, nannies, nurses, and "entertainers" – as "a vital export commodity [for] the Philippines' own economic strategy" (Rosca 1995: 524). He commended their ability to send back remittances but offered little to no governmental protections or recourse against the daily risks they faced with harassment, violence, and sometimes death. In the 1980s, Tien Suharto, the deposed dictator's wife, conveniently combined patriarchy with capitalism to solidify Indonesia's New Order Government:

> A harmonious and orderly household is a great contribution to the smooth running of development efforts ... It is the duty of the wife to see to it that her household is in order so that when her husband comes home from a busy day he will find peace and harmony at home. The children, too, will be happier and healthier.
>
> (quoted in Blackwood 1995: 136)

Hypermasculine capitalism drew on racial stereotypes as well. In Singapore, for example, women and minorities were often "neatly conjoined" in accusations of "runaway irresponsibility," requiring state-led supervision:

> [They are] believed to be most guilty of pursuing the noneconomy of pleasure (pleasure as, indeed, noneconomic): the female, and the "soft" Indian/Malay citizen, whose earthy sexuality, putative garrulousness, laziness, emotional indulgence, or other distressing irrationality conform to reprobate stereotypes of ethnicity and gender that have, in recent years, prominently found their way into public discourse.
>
> (Heng and Devan 1992: 347)

By the 1980s, Asian capitalism's domestic hypermasculinity started to turn outwards. Bolstered by a newfound prosperity based on the cheap labor and "nimble fingers" of its women workers, several Asian leaders[16] adopted what Mark Berger (1996) has called "yellow mythologies." They trumpeted an Asian way with Asian values, embedded in harmony, humanity, a long-term vision, and a Confucian version of folk democracy (*minben zhengzhi*). In contrast, they denigrated the West as lazy, inefficient, racist, and decadent. Glossing over any internal contradictions that might pertain, elites in Japan, Korea, China, and elsewhere in the region swaggered that they could finally say "no" to the West generally, and the United States specifically.[17]

Western liberals preferred to rationalize Asian capitalism as formal, not substantive, mimicry. Under pressure from the Japanese government, the World Bank belatedly issued a report in 1993 that lauded Asia's "miracle" economies with their state-led development as exemplars of liberal capitalism (Berger and Beeson 1998; Wade 1996; World Bank 1993). Elsewhere, Western liberals drew on older, colonial depictions to normalize relations between the two regions. *The Economist* suggested in the early 1990s, for instance, that a happy marriage should transpire between "mellow" (read: feminine) Japanese management practices and the cold, hard (read: masculine) edge of Western analytical skills (Hooper 2000: 67). But no one could continue to ignore what seemed like a paradigm shift in capitalist development (Gore 2000). Asia boomed with trade, finance, production, and technology. Many declared the dawning of an "Asian century" or "Asian renaissance" (Commission for a New Asia 1994) – that is, until the Asian financial crisis hit even before the century began.

Panicked withdrawals of foreign capital triggered the Asian crisis of 1997–8.[18] Indonesia, Malaysia, South Korea, Thailand, and the Philippines had enjoyed an almost twofold increase in net capital inflows from 1994 to 1996 (from $41 to $93 billion), which dropped suddenly (to $12 billion) in 1997 (Bello 1998a: 426). This run on money started with the Central Bank of Thailand defending the baht's value to the dollar, eventually losing $39 billion in reserves (Bello 1998a: 429).[19] By the end of December in 1997, the currencies of Malaysia, Indonesia, and the Philippines had hemorrhaged to 30–80 per cent of their previous value (Bello 1998a: 429). Indonesia's economy shrank by 13.7 per cent; Thailand's, 8 per cent; Malaysia's, 6.7 per cent (Symonds 1999: 1). Meanwhile, another crisis was brewing in South Korea. Its corporate conglomerates, the *chaebol*, had overborrowed to 10–40 per cent of their capital by 1998 (Bello 1998a: 432), amounting to approximately $160 billion (Johnson 1998: 17). And with stalled production and saturated exports, they had no way to pay it back. Korea faced a million new unemployed in 1998 (Bullard *et al.* 1998: 536). The "miracle" seemed shattered.

The International Monetary Fund (IMF) eventually loaned $17 billion to Thailand, almost $40 billion to Indonesia, and $57 billion to South Korea.[20]

Who's accountable for what? Liberal versus crony capitalism

Liberal elites in the West saw their chance and seized it. Smarting from almost two decades of hypermasculine taunts from Asia, they lambasted the region for its crony capitalism. Not only were the Asians wrong about the fundamentals for a healthy, modern economy, but they were also morally unfit to lead the global economy. "For it is the top-down nature of the Asian model itself that is the real cause of the crisis," declared a *Time Magazine* editorial. "This model bred complacency, cronyism and corruption ... The global economy is far too complex and fast paced for any bureaucrats to control" (quoted in Singh and Weisse 1999: 204). Japan, in particular, must end its "culture of deceit," declared another *Time* editorial, and pay for its irresponsibility of the past (Gibney 1998: 54) rather than pawning it off to others (Gibney 1997: 74). Some scholars who, just a decade before, had touted Asian institutions as a new model for late-modern capitalism now chastised the same institutions for being the problem (Haggard 1999).[21] Alan Greenspan, chairman of the US Federal Reserve, concluded that there is only one economic model for the world to follow and that is "the Western form of free-market capitalism" (quoted in Singh and Weisse 1999: 204).

Liberals in Asia also joined the model bashing. In their analysis of Japan's burst bubble economy, Michael Porter and Hirotaka Takeuchi conceded that the "model of corporate success has merit" but added that it "is dangerously incomplete" (Porter and Takeuchi 1999: 67). Governments are too narrow in their vision ("mistrustful of competition") and companies don't understand their own interest ("wrong approach," "undermine ... profitability"). "Fixing what really ails Japan," they prescribed, "will require fundamental changes in both government and corporate practices" (Porter and Takeuchi 1999: 67). As Bruce Cumings has noted, "the Americans have, paradoxically, had willing accomplices in Northeast Asian peoples who have sought to reform or nullify this same model [of state-led capitalism] themselves" (1998: 45).

This frontal attack took on viral metaphors.[22] The IMF and other international financial institutions (IFIs) warned that macromismanagement by unsavory crony capitalists may contaminate the rest of the world economy. Many in the United States, in particular, voiced concerns about catching the "Asian flu." Only liberally applied, stoically taken doses of structural adjustment administered by Western, rational experts could cure this economic virus.

More to the point, the Asian crisis allowed liberals in the West to flash their self-righteousness: that is, the West *should* lead and the Rest *should* follow. Thomas Friedman of the *New York Times* opined that Asian societies lacked the "software (regulatory agencies, banking controls, transparency, bureaucratic professionalism, civil society)" to match the "hardware (relatively free markets, free trade, open capital flows)" required by advanced, industrialized economies (quoted in Rao 1998: 1411). Another observer suggested that Asians need to develop certain (read: Western, masculine) values such as "directness" and "transparency" to counter their (read: Oriental, feminine) tendencies toward "circumspection" and "secrecy" (quoted in Rao 1998: 1411). *Time Magazine* likened the IMF to other "expeditionary forces" sent to Asia in the past (Lacayo 1997: 36). It labeled Treasury Secretary Robert Rubin's plan for US governmental action in the region, for instance, as "The Rubin Rescue" (Duffy 1998: 46).

This liberal rhetoric echoed an older era's lament. The "white man's burden" also sought to alleviate oriental despotism, purge exotic habits, and save the non-Western other from its various sicknesses. Not limited to unabashed poets of empire, this imperialist fiction had seduced critics of colonialism and capitalism as well. Marx, for example, complained that the "Hindoo ... like all Oriental peoples" subscribed to an "Oriental despotism" that "restrained the human mind within the smallest possible compass, making it the unresisting tool of superstition, enslaving it beneath traditional rules, depriving it of all grandeur and historical energies"; such "barbarian egotism" accounted for the Orient's "ruin of empires, the perpetration of unspeakable cruelties, and massacre of the population of large towns," rendering unto Orientals an "undignified, stagnatory, and vegetative life" (Marx 1972: 658). Anticipating Fukuyama's liberal triumphalism as an "end" to history, Marx predicted that England would serve as India's "unconscious tool of history," despite its "vil[e] interests" (Marx 1972: 582).

Table 5.1 summarizes the parallels between older, colonial invocations and contemporary metaphors applied to Asia.

It is not surprising that the IMF (supported by other IFIs and the US government) insisted on returning capital to the crisis economies as the only way to save them. This meant, of course, Western capital since there was none in Asia or elsewhere. Through its standard policy of liberalization, privatization, and deregulation, the IMF imposed cuts in government expenditures (usually in the social sector), credit tightening (through high interest rates), and emergency bank closures. Ordinary people, however, suffered the most under the IMF's lethal combination of increased prices, sudden unemployment, and stalled production.[23] In Thailand, IMF-imposed austerity measures reduced milk and school lunch subsidies by 40–50 per cent while both rice and bus fares doubled (Bullard *et al.* 1998). Because mostly small to medium enterprises in South Korea suffered immediate bankruptcy, a rash of "IMF suicides" spread throughout the country. Bank foreclosures exacerbated panicked withdrawals from non-foreclosed banks. An internal memo from the IMF admitted that its insistence on shutting down sixteen of Indonesia's insolvent banks dominoed into an economic free-fall in the country (Bello 1998b). Governments now owed more than ever. Thailand's foreign debt skyrocketed, increasing fourfold from 1988 to 1996 (Bello 1998b), yet it was still pressured by the IMF to incur more debt. Massive unemployment in the crisis economies mixed with a radical fall in wages with little or no social safety net inevitably erupted into labor

Table 5.1 Discourse of reform and neocolonial power relations in the Asian financial crisis (1997–8)

	Current metaphors for the crisis	Colonial invocations	Implicit power relations
General descriptions	Asian economic crisis full of "contagion"	"Sick man of Asia"	The Asian Other is the source of the problem: it is sick, emasculated, and needs cure/therapy from the healthy, masculine, doctor/scientist West
Immediate causes	"Crony capitalism", "macromismanage- ment", "poor governance"	"Oriental despotism"	Asia is backward, degenerate, and sensuous; West is progressive, virtuous, and stoic
Societal causes	"No [institutional] software … to match the [structural] hardware" needed for modernization, Asians too "circumspect" not "direct", too "secret" not "transparent"	"White man's burden"	Asia needs instruction from the West, Asia needs to submit to the West

strikes, food riots, and ethnic violence. A thirty-year dictatorship in Indonesia also crumbled. Though democratic forces in the country had long worked for such a day, it is hard to predict whether a democratic entity founded on at least partially externally induced instability can last.[24]

In so burdening the state, the IMF effectively transferred the cost of private overdraft to public payment, funded by local taxpayers.[25] Domestic capital at least paid the price of its irresponsible borrowing and investing in the form of debt, bankruptcy, and unemployment. But international capital ran happily to the bank to collect its repayment from the bankrupt government, courtesy of the IMF. It is this kind of "moral hazard," leaders of the IMF and World Bank and other IFIs now intone, that can be avoided through a new "international financial architecture" that ensures "account-ability" through "transparency."

The liberal international order seems to have won its ideological dog-fight. Capitalist mimicry in Asia, it hoots, was formal, not substantive, after all. A CNN report broadcast in late spring of 2000 inadvertently captured this triumphant mood. Announcing an end to the Asian crisis, the news

127

anchor turned to a regional "expert" for details on the subject. She seemed Asian American (based on her Chinese or Korean family name and American accent) and spoke with apparent authority. (It was unclear whether she was a CNN reporter on special assignment or an analyst from the region.) Her remarks were not unlike those made by most journalists: informative and quick. And, like most female personalities in the media, she was relatively young (late twenties to early thirties). What stood out was her hair. It was shoulder-length straight, parted in the middle, fashionably tousled, and completely *blonde*. This fact alone does not merit attention. But when placed within the context of the Asian crisis, this small detail in visual representation underscores the ideological chips at stake. In utilizing this young, Asian blonde woman to report on how the liberal international order has saved the day for Asia (and possibly the world), a mouthpiece of that very order (knowingly or not) was conveying a deeper, more subtle message. That is, Asian capitalism may have had its moment but, ultimately, it was no more than a tacky copy of the West like dyed blonde hair. Asia thus remains a pliant, feminized identity to the West's strong, white masculinity. Like *Madama Butterfly*'s Cio-Cio-san, Asia still *loves* Pinkerton–IMF despite the latter's cruelty.

Only Malaysia's Mahathir Mohamad openly spurned this interpretation of the crisis.[26] Closing the country's capital accounts, he vilified currency speculators as the world's "new imperialists":

> [They exhibit] cattle-like behaviour. If they cannot be done away with they should at least be regulated. Governments which harbour them and claim that they cannot control them should resign or be overthrown ... We are now seeing newer weapons of war, namely financial and economic weapons. And they are no less destructive, no less lethal than the rockets and the bombs.
>
> (Mahathir 1999)

Hyperbole aside, Mahathir has struck a chord.[27] Two years after the height of the crisis in 1998, the region presents an ambivalent picture of recovery.[28] If we focus on unemployment rates alone, we find that they have stabilized for South Korea and Thailand to less than their peak in 1998. Still, they register at a higher rate than before the crisis hit. In comparison, Malaysia has been able to control unemployment to a similar level despite refusing IMF intervention. Unemployment in Indonesia (the fourth most populous nation in the world), however, is rising, even after accepting the IMF's austerity package. Furthermore, labor unrest continues to rumble throughout South Korea as labor activists, employees, women, and migrants face continued hardships.[29]

Table 5.2 summarizes these unemployment rates for these four countries before and after the crisis:

Table 5.2 Unemployment statistics for Indonesia, South Korea, Thailand, and Malaysia

	1996–7	1998	2000
Indonesia	5%	10%	25%
South Korea	2%	7%	3.8%
Thailand	3%	6%	4.3%
Malaysia	2.6%	6.7%	2.8%

Sources: National Statistics Office, Thailand, 2000; National Statistical Bureau, Indonesia, September 2000; *IIJWorld Country Reports* (18 August 2000) (*see* www.iijworld.co.uk); *Seventh Malaysia Plan*, 1996–2000 (*see* www.epu.jpm.my/mservis/smp/title.htm); *South China Morning Post* (31 August 1998); Bullard *et al.* (1998).

Note: Indonesia has a current labor force of about 99 million, of whom 38.5 million are unemployed (National Statistical Bureau, Indonesia, September 2000).

Transforming the rules: cold war power hierarchies

It seems clear that the region is returning to cold war power hierarchies, both internationally and domestically. These include:

1 Western capital dominating Asian capital;
2 the hypermasculine state regulating hyperfeminized society;
3 men exploiting women and other feminized subjects.

Let us review each in turn.

Western capital dominating Asian capital

The liberal international order seems intent on returning Asia to its cold war dependency on the West, if not militarily then economically. The IMF's structural adjustment policies have achieved this goal to a certain extent already. As Walden Bello has testified before the US House of Representatives' Banking and Financial Services Committee, the IMF has

1 "worsen[ed] instead of alleviat[ed] the economic crisis in the region, raising the specter of a decade of stagnation, if not worse;"
2 brazenly promoted US administration interests in bilateral trade with and investment in Asia;
3 "prevent[ed] the Asian countries from developing innovative responses to the Asian financial crisis that would not be dependent on US taxpayers' money."

(Bello 1998b: 1)

United States trade representative Charlene Barshefsky has stated outright that "we expect these structural reforms to create new business opportunities for US firms" (quoted in Bello 1998b: 4). Even Robert Rubin, former secretary of the Treasury and now chairman of Citigroup, concedes that "the Asian financial crisis and the Mexican crisis were as much caused by the industrial nations' financial institutions as [the economies themselves]" (quoted in Sanger 2000: A1).

Indeed, Western capital is buying out Asian capital at bankrupt prices. Note, for example, the following:

- *Indonesia*. In March of 2000, the Indonesian Banking Restructuring Agency (IBRA), a post-crisis agency created specifically to sell bankrupt companies to foreign buyers, arranged for the Singapore-based Cycle & Carriage Group Limited (CCL) to buy a 39.5 per cent stake in Astra International, Indonesia's largest automotive company, for approximately $506 million. In August, IBRA and PT Holdiko Perkasa[30] raised about $47 million in cash from the sale of their 6 per cent stake in the Hong Kong-based First Pacific Co. Ltd., a conglomerate in telecommunications, property and banking, at a 4.8 per cent discount price.
- *Japan*. A recent report from the McKinsey Global Institute concludes that Japan needs to "open up" more to the international market to recover from its post-bubble bust. In particular, it suggests replacing Japan's small, family-based retail shops with an American K-Mart, corporate model (Lopez 2000b). In July of 2000, the Mori government announced its decision to abandon a bailout plan for the retailer Sogo Co. Ltd at $17.3 billion, prompting the *Australian Financial Review* to crow:

  > The influences of globalisation and market forces are becoming irresistible in Japan and it is fitting that another Western vulture fund, Cerebus – the dog at the gates of Hell – is the first to have stuck its hand up as interested in the remnants of Sogo.
  >
  > (Lopez 2000a: 2)

- *South Korea*. For the first time, the Korean government is allowing foreign companies to buy shares in state-run monopolies (Cumings 1998: 65). Toward this end, Korea Electric Power (Kepco) will permit foreigners to buy up to 30 per cent of its stock in shares (Burton 2000: 1). Foreign direct investment (FDI) in Korea reached $15 billion in 1999, a historic high (Hong 2000). Korean capital markets, now almost entirely open to foreign investors, are rebounding spectacularly. The Financial Supervisory Committee (FSC) reported on 4 February 1999 that "31 national security companies in Korea made a profit of 1 billion dollars during the fourth quarter of last year"; at the same time, the Korean branches of twenty-four foreign security companies "enjoyed a profit of 120 million ... which was three times greater than the same period of 1997" (*JoongAng Ilbo* 1999). Conversely, Ford Motor Company's decision to not purchase the debt-burdened Daewoo Motor, an affiliate of Korea's second largest *chaebol*, caused the Korean stock market to plummet by 8 per cent in one day.[31] The government is turning to General Motors–Fiat as an alternative buyer, hoping to entice it by reducing Daewoo to a "firesale" price (Lopez 2000c: 3).[32] Such corporate buy-outs follow a trend since the crisis: Renault now owns 70 per cent of Hyundai's car operations, Samsung Motors;[33] foreign investors have acquired 50 per cent of Hyundai's flagship corporation, Samsung Electronics; and DaimlerChrysler bought 34 per cent of Mitsubishi Motors in March and 10 per cent of Hyundai Motors for $400 million in June (Sunday Business Group 2000). The list goes on.[34]

- *Thailand*. DBS Thai Danu Bank, now partly owned by Singapore's DBS, will soon sell 30.6 billion baht in bad loans to National Finance and a unit of America's Lehman Brothers at 29 per cent of the loan's face-value price (*Economist* 2000).

Even liberals in the West admit that the IMF may have gone too far. "Encouraging inflows when exchange rates and local asset values are so depressed creates the image and the reality of arranging bargain-basement deals for foreigners" (Tobin and Ranis 1998). Such discriminatory action, cautioned Walden Bello (1998b), will lead to virulent anti-Americanism in the region.

The hypermasculine state regulates hyperfeminized society

Meanwhile, Asia's post-crisis states are rearing, once again, a self-righteous, hypermasculine front to domestic constituents.[35] Two prime examples are *chaebol* reform in South Korea and Anwar Ibrahim's "sodomy" trial in Malaysia.

Shortly after the IMF bailout in 1998, Kim Dae Jung's government enacted a series of *chaebol* reforms. It developed a new cooperation system (*nosajeong*) between labor, business, and government to break down the *chaebol*'s monopoly power (Chang 1998). In so doing, the reform has strengthened, not diminished, the role of the Korean state in relation to national capital (Mo and Moon 1999). Indeed, this relationship recalls Korea's cold war developmental years (1960s–1970s) when the state firmly controlled the *chaebol* even while nurturing it. Some scholars speculate that this was Kim Dae Jung's secret agenda for resorting so quickly to IMF intervention.[36] It allowed the government to stem rising political independence from newly emergent financial elites and the *chaebol* that serves as their power base (Ghosh *et al.* 1998).

The Malaysian government's prosecution of Anwar Ibrahim, former finance minister and deputy prime minister, on charges of sodomy indicates state hypermasculinity of another kind. One interpretation of this seemingly inexplicable case is that contending hypermasculinities were at work. The Malaysian state needed to flex its muscle, so to speak, to the liberal international order given its constant castigation of Mahathir as a madman or fool for rejecting IMF intervention. Although several domestic factors contributed to Mahathir's response to the political crisis that accompanied the financial fallout, it is also clear that Mahathir asserted his power in hypermasculine ways by simultaneously targeting an internal link to the liberal international order, his closest political rival Anwar Ibrahim. Leader of a new generation of religiously conservative but economically liberal Malaysians, Anwar had risen quickly and impressively in Mahathir's party, the United Malays National Organization (UMNO), since his entry into the party in the early 1980s (Chin 1997; Mohamed Jawhar 1996; Ho 1994). Though named Mahathir's heir apparent, Anwar deviated too much from the old master, especially in economic matters. The financial crisis crystallized their ideological tug-of-war when Anwar favored IMF intervention and Mahathir rejected it outright. On 20 September 1998, one day after being dismissed from his government posts, Anwar was arrested on three counts of "sodomy".[37] Mahathir subsequently announced a series of sweeping reforms to tighten Malaysia's money markets, currency exchange, and share trading. A year later, the government basks in its hypermasculine defiance of the IMF with a stabilized currency and checked unemployment. Meanwhile, Anwar faces fifteen years in prison (six years for corruption and nine years for "sodomy") even though at least two of his alleged victims admitted that their confessions had been coerced and faked.

Depressed men exploit women and other feminized subjects

Hypermasculinizing the self requires hyperfeminizing all others, including internal ones like women and minorities. The Malaysian government, for example, has urged women to sell their jewelry and invest the money in bonds as a patriotic gesture. They need to control their impulsive consumption of foreign luxury items, the government reasoned, in order to concentrate on buying local products. Malaysian official rhetoric has recast the crisis, also, as an opportunity for families to reunify and enhance communication between spouses, parents, and children. That is, in the heyday of miracle growth, men tended to spend too much time at work and entertainment. Today, the crisis returns father and husband back to the family, but he should be pampered and cared for during this time of (national and individual) "depression." The South Korean government has deployed similar tactics in negotiations with labor unions. It appealed to housewives, for example, to dissuade their worker-husbands from going on strike against their corporations and, by extension, the patriarchal family-state.

For women, hypermasculine competition entails more than the usual catastrophe of "first fired, last hired." They suffer from its effects at all ages and in all circumstances. The rising cost of school fees and books in the crisis economies, for instance, have forced parents to withdraw girls from school in favor of more valued brothers. Many young girls are forced into or agree to early marriages to relieve financial burdens on their parents. In Korea, unwanted pregnancies have increased by 77.7 per cent since the crisis. In the Philippines, many desperate parents are encouraging or selling young daughters into prostitution (Symonds 1999). Conversely, the cost of contraception has increased the likelihood of unwanted pregnancies while a greater supply of young girls sold to brothels has lowered the price of prostitutes (Kristof 1998).

Hypermasculine competition rapes as well, as evidenced by mob violence against ethnic Chinese women in Indonesia.[38] During the May riots of 1998, approximately 1,200 people died, of whom ethnic Chinese were the most targeted. At 3 per cent of the population but owning 70 per cent of the economy, the Chinese have long attracted local outrage. But the recent rapes of ethnic Chinese women during the riots are unprecedented in scope and motivation. Volunteer Team for Humanity, a Jakarta-based Catholic organization, has documented 168 cases of violence against ethnic Chinese women, of which 130 were rapes (Human Rights Watch 1998a: 5). Witnesses reported that perpetrators shouted the following as they looted, burned, assaulted, and raped: "Scoundrel Chinese! Damaging our country!" "Because you are Chinese, you are raped!" (Volunteer for Humanity 1998). Many perpetrators mutilated their victims' sexual organs during or after raping them. Where Mahathir emasculated an internal other (a political rival) with ironic charges of "sodomizing" another man, Indonesia's mob rapists physically raped the internal other's woman with equally ironic charges of economic, if not moral, culpability. Such fantasies of revenge always exact a price. Whether it comes in the form of societal sanctions or individual guilt or both, the rapist self and his heirs for generations to come will not – cannot – escape the reciprocal legacy of violence induced by hypermasculinity's underdeveloped heart.

The meaning of it all: underdeveloped heart for self and other

So, too, does the Western, liberal self pay for such violence. Many today, for instance, talk openly of a crack in the fabled "Washington Consensus" (Gore 2000). Composed of key institutions in the US government along with multilateral institutions like the IMF, the World Bank, and other organizations of the United Nations (UN), the Washington Consensus has anchored the liberal international order since the end of World War II. A further layer of elite think tanks, universities, and individual scholars, mainly headquartered in Washington, DC, but also located elsewhere in the world, surrounds the Washington Consensus, providing it with an intellectual "protective belt" (Lakatos 1970) to ensure its ideological legitimacy and reproduction.

One source cracking the Washington Consensus has been an ultimate insider: Joseph Stiglitz. A former high-level cadre at the IMF, Stiglitz has exposed the organization's cultural and economic chauvinism.[39] Far from a level playing field, it underscores all too clearly liberalism's implicit subjectivity of "I lead, you follow":

> Most importantly, did America – and the IMF – push policies because we, or they, believed the policies would help East Asia or because we believed they would benefit financial interests in the United States and the advanced industrial world? And, if we believed our policies were helping East Asia, where is the evidence? As a participant in these debates, I got to see the evidence. There was none.
>
> (Stiglitz 2000: 60)

Indeed, all the Bretton Woods institutions are now under critical scrutiny. A study conducted by the UN University's World Institute for Development Economics Research (WIDER), with support from its Division for Social Policy and Development and the Ministry for Foreign Affairs, Finland, decry the "badly outdated political and economic foundations" of the UN, the World Bank, the IMF, and other international institutions. They need to be overhauled, the study warns, "before a crisis induced by globalization forces the changes required" (WIDER 2001). Aside from some general recommendations,[40] the study emphasized the need to transform the ethos of UN institutions:

- The UN needs to reduce its economic dependency on rich states, which tend to compromise its policies.
- An Economic Security Council should be created to "ensure that the United Nations provides an institutional mechanism for consultations on global economic policies and also, wherever necessary, [an] international regulatory authority."
- The IMF needs to be weaned from its "one size fits all" approach to currency crises and to practice what it preaches: greater transparency, democracy, and accountability.
- The World Bank should shift from its current role of moneylender of last resort to a pro-active, development institution.
- A new financial architecture must manage global macroeconomics.

- A system of governance must oversee the activities and operations of transnational corporations (TNCs).
- International "public goods" and "public bads" should receive greater facilitation/regulation.

(WIDER 2001)

The Wen Ho Lee case offers further insight into liberalism's institutional wobbliness. The US government's arrest and prosecution of Dr Wen Ho Lee, a Taiwanese-American scientist at the Los Alamos National Laboratory in New Mexico, paralleled in timing, if not motivation, the liberal West's "expeditionary forces" to eradicate crony capitalism from a financially wrought Asia.[41] The Clinton administration singled out and jailed this 60-year-old computer scientist on *suspicion* of selling the "crown jewels" of America's nuclear program to China – the same government to which it had granted "most favored nation" trading status – though he was never charged with espionage. After a year-long trial in 1999, the government's case devolved into one count of mishandling classified data in exchange for dismissal of the other fifty-eight charges that had been levied against Lee. His punishment was nine months of jail time, which he had already served.

The Lee case has pointed out the racialized character of the pillars of liberal democracy identified by Mancur Olson: "the ... court system, [the] judiciary, and respect for law and individual rights" (Olson 1993: 572).[42] Not only has the judge in the Lee case apologized for the unfair, demeaning, and punitive treatment of the defendant (Scheer 2000: 12), but members of Congress and the *New York Times*, two institutions that epitomize the workings of a liberal democracy, now hurl mutual accusations of leaks, distortions, half-truths, and other manipulations that account for the Wen Ho Lee fiasco. In an unprecedented move, the *New York Times* has confessed to a journalistic *mea culpa* for its coverage of this story (*New York Times* 2000: A2). Though still defending its reporters as "fair-minded" and "persistent," the *Times* admitted that it could have pursued the story more critically and evenly. One reflection in the editorial raised, for me, the specter of an enduring stereotype: the "inscrutable" Asian. Upon hindsight, the *Times* admitted, it could have inquired more into Lee's personal history so that he could have been "humanized" for readers. Why was this an afterthought only?

Some may hail this case as a triumphant moment of liberal self-rectification, but I am less optimistic. If not for its high visibility, this case would not have been called upon to confront its internal contradictions: the "private vices" of racial profiling and anti-Asian hysteria that are all too often excused in the name of liberalism's "public virtues" of commerce, trade, and national security. Contrary to Adam Smith's famous adage, private vice does not necessarily lead to public virtue. Instead, one tends to sanitize the other

– unless and until we reassess liberalism in light of postcolonial analyses of race, gender, class, and culture.

Conclusion: need for postcolonial IR

The liberal response to Asia's financial crisis ultimately provokes an uncomfortable realization: liberalism tricks. Liberals in the West would allow the other to develop if and only if the latter remains at the formal mimicry level, thereby retaining a certain degree of economic control and ideological superiority. But once substantive mimicry ensues, competition involves more than capital or firms, profit and loss. It turns into a battle between self and other, native and foreigner, colonizer and colonized. The "politics of resentment" (Higgott 1998), it appears, do not affect only Asian elites. They motivate elites in the West as well.

Economic competition *per se* cannot account for such animus. After all, global capitalist elites share interdependent, if not common, interests and stakes. Rather, liberalism's fundamental flaw is its cultural insularity. Protected by hegemony's privilege, Western liberals have not had to confront their own underdeveloped heart in proclaiming a universal capitalism for all when it is, as the Asian crisis makes clear, only for us and not them.

This reassertion of cold war power politics in economic development may trigger its own round of mimicry. Whether it will stay at the formal level or evolve into substantive mimicry remains to be seen. Cold war mimicry, however, differs from capitalist mimicry in one significant respect: the former is inherently dangerous. Its structure compels each agent or player to exhibit more and excessive bouts of hypermasculinity simply to stay in the game.

In Asia, this process seems underway already. Some may bow to US hegemony for now,[43] but others are seeking to develop Asia's own capacity for an economic counter-strike. One suggestion has been the formation of a $100 billion-endowed Asian Monetary Fund (AMF). Sakakibara Eisuke, Japan's former Vice-minister of Finance for International Affairs, first raised this proposal in August of 1997 but the US immediately and definitively vetoed it. Recently, ministers in Asia are reviving the AMF concept (Goad 2000) along with several others to enhance the region's capacity to deal with future financial crises: strengthening regional capital markets by mobilizing savings (Adlan 1998), developing large efficient securities markets (Tsui 1998), promoting broad-based, pro-active domestic investors, enhancing free trade and investment, and possibly creating a Far Eastern Economic Community (*JoongAng Ilbo* 1999).

Still others are learning from Mahathir's successful defiance of the liberal international order. Even Japan, though deep in a post-bubble recession, has had enough. In a speech to the Foreign Correspondents' Club in Washington,

DC, on 16 March 1999, Japanese ambassador Kunihiko Saito warned of a rising nationalism in Japan due to unfettered American criticisms and encroachments since the collapse of its bubble economy: "I'm not worried about the problem yet, but I don't think we should forget that only 50 or 60 years ago we made some big mistakes, and one of the reasons, in my view, was excessive nationalism" (Saito 1999).

How can we escape these ever-expanding spirals of hypermasculine competition? Herein lies postcolonial IR's true contribution. Given its epistemological and normative commitments to intersubjectivity, learning, transformation, accountability, and meaning, postcolonial IR demonstrates our ability to "make our world(s)" (Onuf 1989). With mimicry as evidence, we know that such world-making occurs on a daily basis, ranging from individuals to institutions to societies to global systems. With hypermasculinity rising, we know also that hyperfeminized groups, whether biologically male or female, have a common stake in building coalitions across races, genders, classes, and cultures to subvert this global calamity. Postcolonial IR offers a unique insight not found in conventional or critical IR. That is, international relations is not only about inter-state power politics, as emphasized by conventional theorists. Nor do capitalism's internal contradictions, on the one hand, or neoliberal civilization, on the other, as identified by critical theorists, explain all. Rather, these derive from more fundamental, *relational* processes. These reveal the mutual embeddedness of constructs like self and other, mimicry and defiance, hyperfeminization and hypermasculinization.[44] From their interstices, hybrid strategies will (must) evolve that build upon, rather than deny, the postcolonial *mélange* that accounts for who we are, what we do, and why we relate to others the way we do.

Acknowledgements

Comments from the editors of this volume, Geeta Chowdhry and Sheila Nair, have greatly enriched this chapter. I thank, also, the following for their insightful comments: Anna Agathangelou, Tim Emmert, Marianne Franklin, Rogan Kersh, and Herman Schwartz. A debt of gratitude goes to the following for their research assistance: Tim Emmert, Chris Innocent (*Jakarta Post*), Nipatsorn (Kitty) Kampa (Ministry of Foreign Affairs, Thailand), and Nussara Saratsawang (formerly of the *Bangkok Post*). I am grateful, also, to the Miami School of International Relations, located at the University of Miami and Florida International University, for inviting me to present this paper at its seminar series in December of 2000. Of course, I alone bear responsibility for the contents of this chapter.

Notes

1 By liberal international order, I·mean an inter-state system of capitalist world politics based on an ideology of individualism, competition, private property,

and limits on state power. Its main proponents are governments that uphold such an ideology and their affiliated private and public agencies like "the Wall Street–Treasury–IMF Complex" (Wade and Veneroso 1998; Bhagwati 1997), the European Union (EU), World Bank, Citigroup, and so on. My usage of the liberal international order also draws from Cox (1987).

2 If we can accept that institutions "think" (Douglas 1987), can "learn" (Argyris 1992; Argyris and Schon 1978), and have "interests" (March and Olsen 1984), then it is only logical to conclude that they can learn to coordinate their thinking and interests to formulate an overall strategy to ensure not just survival but hegemony as well.

3 By conventional IR, I refer primarily to (neo)realism and its economic branch of (neo)liberalism. By critical IR, I refer to Marxian or Marxian-based analyses with specific attention to its latest intellectual offshoot, Gramscian globalism. I recognize that critical IR encompasses other schools of thought, most notably postmodern or dissident IR. The latter, though, tends to overlook issues of political economy or materiality in its theorizing (Krishna 1993). For this reason, I concentrate on (neo)realism, (neo)liberalism, and Gramscian globalism as the relevant markers of IR theorizing for the Asian financial crisis.

4 By discipline, I do not mean the usual tides of competitive profit and loss that lift or sink firms in a capitalist economy. Instead, I use the word discipline here to underscore a specific kind of institutional policing that is ideological, not economic, in nature.

5 These terms have a contingent, socially constructed nature. Clearly, distinctions between developed or developing economies and the West or the Rest cannot be sustained consistently. For example, Northern Ireland is located geographically and culturally in the West but economically in the Rest. I thank Rogan Kersh for this example.

6 This classification of international interactions into ideological rule (hegemony), organizing structures (hierarchy), and power relations (heteronomy) comes from Onuf (1989).

7 By self and other, I refer to the full spectrum of constructed identities and subjectivities that range from, and interlink, societies, institutions, and individuals.

8 For an explanation of this constructivist–postcolonial hybrid, see Ling (2001a). For constructivism's articulation of its five epistemological principles, see Ruggie (1998).

9 I define identity as societal assignments of who we are, and subjectivity as who we believe we are. For instance, society may identify an individual as a black woman or simply a minority, when she may embrace a personal subjectivity of, say, an artist of black, Cherokee, Filipino ethnic background.

10 First-order learning involves immediate problem solving, such as discovering that applications of aloe oil can heal burns or other damage to human skin. Second-order learning revamps one's understanding of the problem itself. The aloe oil incident, for example, may inspire an entirely new interpretation of holistic, organic healing rather than passive doctor–patient relations based on pharmaceutical drugs as prescribed by conventional, clinical medicine.

11 Clearly, individuals journey from formal to substantive mimicry all the time, depending on their personality and psychology. More to the point here is the ability of institutions to evolve from formal to substantive mimicry. To this end, more comparative and empirical research is needed to determine the specific conditions that spur this turn. A cursory review of Asian and African developmental histories suggests that elite problem solvers seem more able to institutionalize substantive mimicry in economic development when the state is

grounded in local traditions, rather than created *de nuovo* under the yoke of colonial modernity. The situation in Latin America is more complicated since elite
problem solvers in local sites were, for centuries, the colonizers themselves
(Todorov 1999).

12 Hypermasculinity differs from R.W. Connell's (1987, 1995) notion of hegemonic masculinity. Whereas the latter refers to a tradition of masculinity that
society has perpetuated historically and culturally, the former takes form in reaction to challenges to hegemonic masculinity. Thus hypermasculinity is always
reactionary in nature. For more on this difference, see Ling (2001b).

13 I recognize that power mongers will distort any school of thought or tradition
to suit their interests. Hence, liberalism *per se* does not necessarily advocate an
implicit intersubjectivity of "I lead, you follow." However, I contend that liberalism's precepts allow such rhetorical sleights of hand given their resistance to
self-reflection. For more on liberalism's non-reflexivity, see Arblaster (1984).

14 The language may seem anachronistic, stemming as it does from postwar
modernization theory. But its underlying presumptions still hold, as evidenced
by contemporary treatments of globalization (Scholte 2000).

15 For example, Cable & Wireless, Deutsche Telekom, France Telecom, AT&T, and
British Telecom.

16 These included Singapore's Lee Kuan Yew, Malaysia's Mahathir Mohamad,
Japan's Ishihara Shintaro, and, to a lesser extent, South Korea's Kim Dae Jung.

17 For example, how can elite rule, so precious to the Asian values discourse, ensure
democratic choice when it offers no protections for popular dissent (Ling and
Shih 1998)? Also, what does it mean for hypermasculine capitalism in Asia to
say no to its counterpart in the West when all engage in crony capitalism, illicit
or otherwise?

18 Of course, currency speculators differ in interest and substance from portfolio
investors and foreign direct investors (I thank Rogan Kersh and Herman
Schwartz for emphasizing this distinction). Nonetheless, the actions of one affect
those of the other. When currencies devalue drastically they invariably undermine any locality's attractiveness to outside investors. At this point, the only
difference among them is how quickly they could pull out their capital.

19 In 2000, the baht had risen to only half its value before 1997 (*The Economist*
2000a: 6).

20 Just by way of comparison, it is worthy to note that Korea's second largest
chaebol, Daewoo, owed $78 billion in debts in 1998.

21 Of course, there were exceptions as well; see Johnson (1998).

22 In contrast, the Chinese-language press characterized the financial crisis as a
terrible storm or typhoon.

23 See, for example, *Business Week* (1998), International Labour Organization
(1998), and Oxfam International (1998).

24 See the World Socialist Web Site (1999), published by the International
Committee of the Fourth International (ICFI), which contends that the elections
of 7 June 1999 more accurately reflected a counter-coup by Indonesia's bourgeois elite to salvage what they could from Suharto's fall.

25 For example, a foreign investor would provide credit to a local commercial bank
which would lend cash at commercial interest rates to a local borrower. The
crisis hit when the local borrower could not generate any profits to pay back the
bank loan. The bank, in turn, could not pay back its credit (and associated
interest payments) to the foreign investor. All the lenders and borrowers, so far,
are private sector actors. The IMF's bailout plan, however, insisted that the state,
through its central bank, pay back its loans to the foreign investor by drawing
on its foreign reserves and extracting local savings accumulated largely from

taxes. The foreign investor, whose irresponsible lending flooded the region with capital in the first place, has not lost any income in the process. Indeed, he or she may have profited given drastic changes in exchange rates (usually in favor of the hard currency) and continued interest payments guaranteed by the IMF bailout.

26 This stance, however, has not kept Malaysia from currying foreign investments for its economy.

27 Even some in the West concede that Mahathir may have had a method to his madness (Barro 1998).

28 See, for example, the Asian Development Bank's *Asia Recovery Report*. In its regional overview, the report notes positive growth rates in all the crisis-affected economies but also states that the region continues to suffer from three enduring legacies of the crisis: "heavy debt, skittish investors and greater household insecurity" (Asian Development Bank 2001).

29 Labor in South Korea remains unconvinced that it will benefit from the economy. The *Korea Herald* reported that "150,000 workers went on strike in the Jan.–July period, surpassing the total number that participated in walkouts last year and marking the highest seven-month figure in nine years" (Kim 2000). Another 5,000 bank employees are expected to lose their jobs this year (*Korea Herald* 2000). Amnesty International reported that fifteen trade unionists and political activists were arrested in July 1998, another twenty in February 1999 (Amnesty International 1999). As of this writing (1 April 2001), hundreds of workers and students are protesting against the government's restructuring plans, which have laid off thousands of workers at Daewoo Motor Co. and Korea Telecom.

30 PT Holdiko Perkasa was established as part of the debt settlement agreement between IBRA and the Salim Group.

31 Ford bought Kia Motors in 1998.

32 The sale would involve four operations within the Daewoo *chaebol*: Daewoo Motor Sales, Ssangyonng Motor, Daewoo Capital, and Daewoo Telecom. GM also owns 10 per cent of the Japanese automaker Suzuki and 20 per cent of Ishikawa and Fuji Heavy Industries (Shameen 2000). It remains the largest automobile manufacturer in the world.

33 Renault also owns Japan's number two car manufacturer, Nissan.

34 The *Far Eastern Economic Review* reported a 27 per cent increase in foreign capital in South Korea since 1998, involving the following takeovers or joint ventures: "Germany's BASF and Daesang Lysine, British Telecom and LG Telecom, Germany's Commerzbank and Korea Exchange Bank, Belgium's Interbrew and OB Brewery, and the US-based supermarket giant Wal-Mart and Korea Makro" (Lee 1999: 58).

35 One exception is the Thai government's response to the financial crisis. For example, it has emphasized re-employment policies rather than foreign capital investment. However, this pattern of negotiation with more powerful international forces while maintaining an independent, third-way path is reminiscent of the Thai state's strategies during the cold war.

36 Could it be coincidence that two years later, Kim received the Nobel Peace Prize for his efforts in democratizing and unifying South Korea?

37 He was accused of committing "sodomy" with three men: his adopted brother, a lecturer in Islamic philosophy, and his chauffeur.

38 Documentation of these cases remains difficult. See Human Rights Watch (1998a).

39 Stiglitz was forced into early retirement from the IMF due to these unwelcome remarks.

40 For example, greater civic, not just governmental, representation in the UN through a Global Peoples' Assembly, modeled after the European Parliament, to run parallel to the General Assembly; a Volunteer Peace Force to depoliticize intervention by the United Nations and enable it to provide a prompt collective security response wherever humanitarian emergencies arise; greater attention to and coordination of cross-border movements of people.

41 Many would protest that working-class whites like Richard Jewell (who was falsely accused of the 1996 Olympic Park bombing in Atlanta) suffer from a miscarriage of justice as much as wealthy minorities like O.J. Simpson, who are able to escape justice altogether. However, the fact that liberal institutions seem to discriminate equally on the basis of class or income as much as race does not lend greater credibility to their fairness, a crucial criterion of any democracy.

42 One could argue that the George W. Bush administration, placed in office in 2001, represents a conservative backlash to patch over and reinforce these internal contradictions of the liberal state and, by extension, the liberal international order.

43 As Korea's former prime minister, later ambassador to the United States, put it recently: "The model is now clear. It's not Japan, it's the West. The current crisis has convinced almost all people that the old style doesn't work" (Cumings 1998: 71).

44 For a more conventional, economic-based argument towards this end, see Radelet and Sachs (1997).

6

"SEXING" GLOBALIZATION IN INTERNATIONAL RELATIONS:

Migrant sex and domestic workers in Cyprus, Greece, and Turkey

Anna M. Agathangelou

> The national bourgeoisie organizes centers of rest and relax-
> ation and pleasure resorts to meet the wishes of the Western
> bourgeoisie. Such activity is given the name of tourism, and
> for the occasion will be built up as a national industry ... the
> little Brazilian and Mexican girls ... the ports of Acapulco and
> Copacabana – all these are the stigma of this deprivation of
> the national middle class ... [This class] will have nothing
> better to do than to take on the role of the manager of
> Western enterprise, and it will in practice set up its country as
> the brothel of Europe.
>
> (Fanon 1965: 153–4)

> It's a processing center for prostitutes ... Girls are brought
> here. They have no money and their passports are taken away.
> They become the property of the rings. Within a few years
> they are full-time prostitutes. They say they are "processed."
> And then they are sold to other rings in Europe or the Middle
> East.
>
> (Lazos quoted in Murphy 1998: 2)

Sex work, prostitution, sex trade, sex trafficking, and domestic work are
concepts that evoke both a sense of morality and criminalization in the
global context. The global trade in women, a lucrative "shadow market,"
generates from 7 to 12 billion dollars annually (Hughes 2000). While these
sexual relations suffuse international relations (IR) and constitute a lived
experience, the field as an intellectual discipline continues to retain the
(neo)realist fiction that IR is really only about competing states making
rational choices independent of gender and sexual relations. Theoretical
analysis of the sex trade remains underdeveloped in contemporary IR and
international political economy (IPE), despite feminist critiques that have
brought it to the forefront of policy and scholarly attention (Enloe 1990;

142

Moon 1997). What would the disciplines of IR and IPE look like if we took seriously concepts such as desire economies and sex trade?

To date, no single study in IR has systematically examined the social organization and movement of sexual labor within the peripheries. Such studies of globalization typically focus on the upper circuits of capital relations, such as the increased level of international trade, the internationalization of production and financial markets, and the promotion of commodity culture, thereby missing the significance of lower circuits such as tourism. The significance of the reproduction of labor, food preparation, janitorial or custodial jobs, and the sex industry to tourism are thus also neglected in the conventional study of globalization. A prominent feature of globalizing social relations is the sexualization and commodification of female migrant labor within peripheral sites and the accelerating exchange of money for bodies (Ling 2001a). New global arrangements no longer depend solely on movements from the industrialized North to the developing South or from poor Third World countries to the First World. For the first time, these movements are occurring within and between developing nations and depend extensively on the migration of women. While it has been assumed that globalization is about the movement of the cosmopolitan class (Kempadoo and Doezema 1998),[1] the constitution of the transnationalized cosmopolitan class is intimately intertwined with notions of women (and men) as the providers of service and sexual pleasure. Such services and pleasures are integrated into "desire" economies.

Differences across race, ethnicity, and nationality are crucial elements in sex and domestic work. These axes of power act as organizing principles that determine who will do what, when, and for whom in the desire economies. According to Fanon (1965), the national bourgeoisie in Third World contexts organizes sites of relaxation and pleasure to service the desires of an emerging transnational cosmopolitan class that includes both Western and Third World consumers. This desire economy is sexualized, racialized, and commodified. For example, those who offer the services are mostly foreign by culture, language, and race to the customer within the peripheries. Both the "otherness" and the affordability of sex and domestic work are sources of desire for clients. Moreover, the sexual labor and use of women's bodies for consumption in Third World sites cannot be viewed in isolation from the global political economy's generation of profits. Desire economies generate profits for some agents of the peripheries and much more for Western elites of the global economy. According to Kempadoo, "local and national economies, [and national industries, with help from their states' legislative and regulatory bodies] ... sustain global corporate capital, First World identities, and masculine hegemony" (1999: 18). Even when female labor migration is acknowledged as crucial in the restructuring of the world economy, the discourses surrounding the migration of sex and domestic workers within peripheral sites do little more than sensationalize the phenomenon. US activists, Congressional leaders, and some scholars are speaking up, calling for a ban on sex trafficking, but most of these discourses end up arguing that the economic and political conditions of postcolonial countries push women into brothels and sex trafficking rather than explaining this phenomenon transnationally. Thus, these discourses once more constitute Third World peripheries as spectacle, a product of the First World's gratuitous othering and its consumption of the "exotic," "primitive," and "degenerate."

This chapter explores the silences accompanying female sex and domestic labor migration in discourses of IR and mainstream perspectives on globalization. It further examines the implications of these silences for the theory and practice of IR, drawing on the desire economies in peripheries such as Cyprus, Greece, and Turkey to substantiate the above claims. I use "peripheral" instead of "Third World" here to permit the inclusion of Greece, whose tourist economy[2] is one of its major income-generating industries. I also show how the discourses of IR frame how we read, understand, and intervene in transnational capitalist relations.

Sexing, racializing, and recolonizing the worker of globalization

New global arrangements and movements, including the transfer of female workers from one location to another, characterize the current phase of the world economy. Transnational tourism, intimately related to the sex economy, is likely to become the largest industry in the world within a decade (Leheny 1995: 367). In addition to its financial power, this industry shapes the practices and identities of its producers and consumers, including the identities of nation-states within which it resides. Despite the growing significance of the tourist trade, the two major schools of thought in IPE, liberal internationalism and Gramscian political economy, by focusing on the upper circuits of the global economy, have ignored the movements of female workers and their relationship to international tourism.

The liberal internationalist discourse, a master discourse in IPE,[3] argues that globalization comprises market responses to integrate "finance, production, telecommunications, and the media on a world-wide scale" (Chang and Ling 2000: 29). For these scholars globalization is different from internationalization or the "geographic spread of economic activities across national boundaries" (Dicken 1992: 1). Moreover, they argue that the state's role is reduced and should be focused on "educat[ing] the consuming public with better information" (Chang and Ling 2000: 29). The master liberal discourse sees labor movements in terms of transnational wage differentials, which encourage migration-for-employment. It suggests that migrants follow market forces for a better allocation of resources around a given economic space:

> In the neoclassical economic framework ... labor moves from places where capital is scarce and where labor is plentiful (hence remuneration to the worker is low) to areas where capital is abundant and where labor is scarce (hence remuneration is high).
>
> (Wood 1982: 300)

The conditions that incite people's movement in specific directions represent market forces translated into the social realm (Straubhaar 1992). As *homo economicus*, migrants calculate the costs and benefits of each option, including emigrating, and decide accordingly. Liberal scholars debate whether economic factors affect the individual's decision to migrate or if noneconomic factors such as emotions, politics, or ideologies are involved. Lim argues that in the end, the analysis remains the same insofar as these noneconomic factors are given a utility value and are thus counted as economic ones (Lim 1992: 133–49). But the *homo economicus* that neoclassical economists write about is the highly educated professional. This theory favors the highly educated professional's activities to the exclusion of the women who typically service them (Mohanty 1997). It also renders invisible a major reason for this transnational migration-for-employment: that (re)productive or sex labor (domestic and sexual) is central to the process of globalization and capital accumulation and is used toward the development of desire services of the global economy to meet the demands of the emerging capitalist class. It follows that states' demands for foreign female workers stem from "enhanced personal purchasing powers during a period of declining supply" of local female workers (Chin 1998: 4). This focus on wage differentials and costs and benefits eclipses the process by which states have become extensively involved in facilitating labor migration of both domestic and sex workers (Rosca 1995). For example, in southern Cyprus, each family who decides to buy the domestic labor of a woman applies to the state by depositing 600 Greek Cypriot pounds (approximately $1000). Both the Greek Cypriot state and other states like the Philippines work with each other to make possible the transfer of female labor to Cyprus into homes and businesses that can afford it. The Filipino state under President Ramos sent women abroad despite international protests over the treatment of Filipina domestic workers overseas. For him, they are "a vital export commodity [for] the Philippines' own economic strategy" (Rosca 1995: 524).

A focus on the choices of the individual state and those of the *homo economicus* misses the politics behind such movements of sex and domestic workers. Their reproductive labor, for example nursing, child care, cooking, and cleaning, and the provision of sexual pleasure, are utilized by masculinized states and their agents to (re)colonize women. In other words, what is obscured is that reproductive labor is an extension of sexual relations between men and women, reestablishing domination and control over women's lives and bodies (Chin 1998). In the service of neoliberal utilitarianism, this state

145

power is not neutral, but sexualized and racialized: women are constructed as commodities or assets and the property of men within nation-states and within the geopolitical context of global capitalism. Many feminist critics have begun to challenge theories of IPE, claiming that they frequently privilege masculine notions of power. Feminists critique the choice to focus on the upper circuits of globalization and its agents, while devaluing the lower circuits such as tourism and (re)production as feminine, weak, and irrelevant in the study of transnational movements (Peterson 1996; Pettman 1996; Ling 2001a). Other feminists (Eviota 1992) argue that the social, political, and economic arrangements organizing reproduction are naturalized.

In contrast, Gramscians and Gramscian Marxists conceptualize globalization as the political project of a transnational historic bloc (Cox 1987; Gill 1995a; Rupert 1995). For Cox (1987), liberal capitalism constitutes a world hegemony that ensures the dominance of certain capitalist production processes and relations. This bloc embodies a set of ideologies that validate the supremacy of leading states, their power, and the dominant social classes. It is formed by cross-national, cross-cultural global classes, who "uphold mutual interests and ideological perspectives" that institutionalize "common criteria of interpretation ... and common goals anchored in the idea of an open world economy" (Cox 1993: 254). The major focus of the historic bloc is the profits and privileges of capitalism, including its relations of production, rendering invisible the widening gaps between rich and poor. For this reason, Gramscians advocate the building of counter-hegemonic movements to address the contradictions engendered by a capitalist world economy. However, traditional social movements like labor will need to mobilize beyond their conventional base and build coalitions with feminists, environmentalists, and peace activists if such counter-hegemonies are to occur (Chang and Ling 1996). While Cox recognizes that a focus on "manual industrial workers" as the major agents of class struggle and social change is insufficient, he neglects how identities other than the manual industrial workers become included or affirmed as potential agents of class struggle. How should such affirmed identities strategize, and on what grounds should they intervene in transforming liberal capitalism?

Cox and other Gramscian Marxists raise a critical question about the coalitions and solidarities that must emerge if a social transformation is to take place. Their questions remain unanswered for several reasons. First, Gramscians fail to see that liberal capitalism's restructuring of the global economy depends on a (re)colonization of peripheral sites and bodies that is made possible through a series of silences and invisibilities. Inflecting and drawing upon indigenous asymmetries, ideologies, and forms of exploitation, liberal capitalism racializes certain kinds of work and constructs workers within such industries as nonworkers. If, for example, the market constitutes reproduction as natural through particular ideologies, then workers doing that kind of work are not compensated because they are *supposed* to do that kind of work. Also, there is a lack of theorization regarding those labeled as nonworkers (lower circuits, informal sectors, household) and the links among capitalism, colonialism, and the gendered and racialized nature of surplus extraction and exchange of cash for bodies. This renders invisible the very close "connection between how these jobs are defined and who is sought after for the jobs" (Mohanty 1997: 11). Finally, (re)productive labor – a central process of globalization and capital accumulation through the constitution of desire economies – is not brought into the same analytical field as production. On the contrary, at times it is collapsed under production, and thus its relevance in the reorganization of global relations is missed. Cox is adamant about the common material basis that must be rendered visible if these affirmed identities are to be mobilized toward democracy[4] and "people's power" but he ignores the sexualized and racialized dimensions of such struggles. This chapter utilizes a postcolonial re-reading of globalization and IPE to expose the (re)colonizing strategies of liberal internationalism and the exclusions of critical international political economists regarding female sex and domestic migrant labor.

Postcolonial readings of globalization

The analysis in this chapter draws from various theoretical strands, including the Marxist or socialist perspectives of Mies (1986; Mies *et al.* 1988) and O'Brien (1987) and the postcolonial critiques of Alexander and Mohanty (1997), Grewal and Kaplan (1994), and Chang and Ling (2000), among others. These authors theorize individually or collectively about how international inequalities (colonizer/colonized, production/reproduction, feminine/masculine, worker/nonworker, global/local, center/periphery) are historically constructed by colonial and neocolonial practices.

Marxist feminists provide insights about how class and gender identities are produced and acknowledge that the struggles over the construction of hegemony are informed by class and gender politics. They critique traditional Marxism's focus on production and the universal proletariat and argue that hegemony's formation depends on ideological assumptions that naturalize men as universal productive beings and women as nature. Further, Marxist feminists reformulate Gramsci's notion that the working-class consciousness was based on economic reality, and that this reality, mediated through civil society, was nonhomogeneous and contradictory (O'Brien 1987: 255).[5] The concept of hegemony, O'Brien argues, is not a byproduct of culture depicting the flexibility of class hegemony, but rather it depicts patriarchal hegemony, a relation in which the reproduction of labor power is subsumed under the mode of production. Within that relation, women's productive labor is collapsed into general labor, and women's work is constituted without value (Mies 1986: 48). The two infrastructures of history that O'Brien addresses are the daily reproduction of individuals (economic activity) and the daily reproduction of the species (the birth and sustenance of the new generation). Civil society is thus the site where specific forms of contradiction are mediated that emerge from three sources: the economic substructure where contradiction emerges as class struggle, the reproductive substructure where contradiction emerges concretely as gender struggle, and the tension between an individual worker's survival and the survival of her household. However, O'Brien's critique still misses the effect of recolonization practices in the construction of power relations, both in production and (re)production processes. Direct colonization and subordination of postcolonial societies in the international system precipitate substantially different expressions of sexual, racial, and class relations, both transnationally and nationally.

O'Brien's retheorization of the relations of production and reproduction is further complicated through the work of Mies (1986) and Mies *et al.* (1988). These feminists contest the "narrow, capitalist concept of 'productive labor'" or the wage labor production of surplus for capital, arguing instead for a more general concept of the productivity of labor.

> In contrast to Marx, I consider the capitalist production process as one which comprises both: the superexploitation of non-wage laborers (women, colonies, peasants) upon which wage labour exploitation then is possible ...? It is not compensated for by a wage ... but is mainly determined by force or coercive institutions. This is the main reason for the growing poverty and starvation of Third World producers.
>
> (Mies 1986: 48)

Mies *et al.* (1988) provide a framework to analyze the oppression and exploitation of women, workers, and colonized people across various modes of production and historical social formations. Through their work, we are able to explain the construction of social differences in relation to colonization and the development of asymmetrical divisions and appropriation of both (re)productive and surplus labor as part of an integrated world system. Sexual and racial differences are not seen as epiphenomenal or purely ideological. On the contrary, these different forms of productivity (wage, subsistence, colonization, reproductive labor) are all mutually imbricated and the subject occupies multiple and contradictory places within them. However, like critical IR theorists such as Cox, their work remains within the political economy of the world systems and structural approach. They do not typically disassemble putative categories such as West, Third World, race, sexuality, and class. Further, Marxist feminists have not systematically engaged postcolonial intellectual skepticism and understanding of the transnational economic, cultural, and social forces that have shaped these received categories.

The work of Marxist feminists does several things for postcolonial feminism. First, it challenges the idea that the major agents of production are masculine proletariat workers. Second, it claims that (re)production is a process that liberal capitalism uses as a colonizing strategy to exploit women's labor. Thus, (re)productive labor (broadly defined) is central to the process of capital accumulation. Third, they suggest that social differences such as sexual and racial ones are not separated from the economic sphere as ideological differences. On the contrary, these differences are informed by the asymmetrical relations of power among different people, and different countries within the broader context of global capitalism. Their insights are useful for centering a materialist analysis within postcolonial feminism, one that accounts for the integration of sex, race, and class differences as relational, interlocking, and socially constructed systems of the same process of labor exploitation. In making explicit the gendered and class nature of production and (re)production processes, their agents and the material structures that inform these relations, Marxist feminism intersects with the postcolonial project.

Postcolonial theorists argue that the imperialist project shapes the postcolonial world, its relations with the West, the production of postcolonial and western identities, and the struggles over identity in national communities. In addition, these theorists pay special attention to representational issues and the production of meanings around culture, gender, race, and sexuality. They venture beyond the dichotomies of self/other and masculine/feminine, and deconstruct categories such as Europe, West, Third World, and race. An example of this move is given in *Tensions of Empire* (Cooper and Stoler 1997) where an attempt to bring colonies and metropoles into the same analytical field is made, thus highlighting that strategies for generating and managing notions of racial, national, gender, and sexual differences in the colonies run parallel to processes occurring simultaneously in the metropoles. Their work calls for methods that consider how nations, gender, race, work, and movements emerge within a transnational context of hegemony building.

These feminist and postcolonial critiques highlight several issues that are critical to the analysis of globalization and desire economies. I argue that a political economy of desire is a significant aspect of globalization and transnational relations, but that it has been made invisible by the strategies of conventional and critical IPE analyses. I therefore explore the recolonizing strategies of global capital, rethink the category "worker" in her productive and (re)productive roles, and suggest the possibilities for social change.

First, I suggest that the way the worker is identified in the transnational context and the literature on globalization is informed by a colonialist logic that focuses on irreconcilable oppositions such as "history-making capitalist economies vs. history-lagging non-capitalist ones; wealthy centers vs. exploited peripheries; transnational firms vs. territorially bound states; globe-straddling cosmopolitans vs. locally bound parochials" (Chang and Ling 2000: 32). This dichotomous categorization of the relations between local and global, West and the rest, tends to privilege an emphasis on macro-corporate processes such as finance, production, trade, telecommunications, and the subjects and agents who populate this global economy – the abstracted consumers and producers such as professional workers, citizens, and cosmopolitans (Chang and Ling 2000). However, I suggest that the concept of the worker is historically, socially, and politically constructed. The construction and naturalization of this concept in IPE makes invisible the different colonial practices through which this worker becomes racialized and sexualized. These workers are not "disembodied persons who traverse across time and space, but corporeal women and men whose choices and movements reflect their gendered, racialized, and class-based identities in the worlds they inhabit" (Chang and Ling 2000: 33).

Second, the globalization literature in IR and IPE also focuses narrowly on the structural production and implementation of ideology rather than its social embeddedness. However, attention needs to be paid to the "circulation of meaning" and the discursive economy that informs globalization. Thus, power must be understood as ideologically produced in institutions and consciously articulated into cultural or social practices. For example, discourses about the bodies of Eastern European female workers in Cyprus, Greece, and Turkey revolve around how the "blondes of Russia and Rumania" come to these countries because their own nation-states are poor. They are the women who "lead astray" indigenous men. A Turkish Cypriot woman said the following about Rumanian croupiers in northern Cyprus:

> Imagine you are a man, single. Of course you look at women, and try and talk to them. If you are a *terbiyeli* [decent] woman you look away, you don't talk back, or you just return their *merhaba* [hello]. But if you say: [in English] 'Hello, you are very nice,' and invite them to your house, of course the young man will go.
>
> (Scott 1995: 399)

Naturalizing male and female sexuality, this story affirms a liberal capitalist order that is sustained by racialized and gendered hierarchies. This narrative privileges the "good" Cypriot men and their women over the "bad" women of other ethnic backgrounds who tempt Cypriot men. Men are susceptible to "other" women's charms because it is their nature to be sexual, and thus it is natural for them to desire them and accept their invitations. In contrast, there is a corresponding vigilance about the presence of Rumanian women in Cyprus because these women threaten to "modernize," and therefore destroy traditional values. These understandings about women's and men's sexuality are rooted in transnationalized, racialized, and sexualized discourses, affirming that men can involve themselves sexually any time they want without any social consequences, whereas women cannot. Emphasizing the commodification of women's and men's sexuality, these discourses are not fully explained by the politics of nationalism and state policies. They are structurally produced, share similarities to parallel narratives produced in other social contexts, and take a very local and nationalized form. What informs the circulation of this discourse?

Both the social context and these discourses impact the asymmetrical (re)production of power for men and women. For example, circulating discourses about the Rumanian woman's morality in relation to the Cypriot woman's seem to suggest that Rumanian women should not be protected by the state or the authorities in Cyprus if they are sexually harassed or assaulted. Their indecency is what leads them to this condition. Similar discourses are available transnationally in other local contexts. Questions about the politics of an invitation by a Rumanian woman to a Cypriot man become reduced to questions of culture. For example, sex workers are conceptualized as "international whores" (Jumilla 1993) for the consumption of men who enact and choose "whiteness." Racial and sexual discourses circulating transnationally about sex workers are used locally in decisions to hire and purchase the services of sex and domestic workers. In Cyprus, many imply that Rumanian women are here to be consumed because they are beautiful and sexy, unlike women from Sri Lanka and the Philippines who are hired to do domestic work. However, these stereotypes are used to marginalize sex workers' claims about sexual violations committed upon their bodies and their narratives which rightfully demand a secure place within the national community in which they work. These stereotypes further minimize the complexity of life choices for sex workers and marginalize their agency. Obscured is the fact that these women come to Cyprus to find work in response to the demands of consumers of the desire economy. While these discourses constitute a shared notion of ideal "whiteness," and its prescriptions for white normality, they also affirm the power of the people who abide by such discourses, like the Cypriot women, albeit asymmetrically.

When deconstructed these discourses seem to support particular industrial and other policies that reinforce the subordination of women, whereby surplus created by the former is siphoned into men's and some women's hands through various direct and indirect mechanisms. Both the sending and receiving states actively structure, facilitate, and sustain a globalized, gendered economy. For example, the Cypriot state, via the Department of Labor and Foreign Affairs, supervises the import of these female workers by deciding who can and cannot afford them. Sending states like the Philippines marketed "overseas contract work as part of a national development policy" (Rosca in Chang and Ling 2000: 524). These gendered processes, practices, and meaning structures assign and reflect historically constructed notions of masculinity and femininity that are also class-based, racially specific, and culturally defined (Chang and Ling 2000). For example, many of the professional women in Cyprus do not challenge the patriarchal rules that demand that women do household work and the relegation of women to feminine servicing work, such as nursing, teaching, domestic services, and prostitution. On the contrary, they hire domestics to do their (re)productive work, such as cooking, taking care of the children, and cleaning house, claiming that they pay them "enough money to buy the world back home." For men of all classes, paying Rumanian women for sexual pleasure is a favorable choice because it is, in a sense, cheaper than sexual relations with Cypriot women. Typically, this gendering process reflects a patriarchal power structure that glorifies men, masculinity, and manhood and denigrates women, femininity, and womanhood and assigns women to certain occupations in the global political economy. However, these processes are also racialized.

> [T]he social structure of accumulation is actually configured around race. The relations of production, in other words, cannot be separated from the racial relations of subordination. Further, the reproduction of the objective conditions necessary for the expansion and consolidation of capitalist modes of social relations, ipso facto demanded a deepening of the "mundanity" of racism. Colonial racism, therefore, should not be seen as (superstructural) consequence of economic imperialism, but as the organizing principle through which specific forms of surplus-value extraction took place.
>
> (Persaud 1997: 174)

Citing Fanon, Persaud claims that "class domination was over-determined by structural racism, 'sexism' and a relatively permanent state of violence" (1997: 174). In light of this critique, it is possible to envision the racialized nature of the desire economy where black bodies are hired to do domestic work and white bodies are exoticized in the sex industries of Cyprus, Turkey, and Greece. The following section utilizes the insights of postcolonial materialist feminism to analyze the racialized and gendered transnational movement of female workers in these countries. What are the processes of domination and exploitation upon which the formation of desire economies depends, and what are the politics informing such processes?

Sexing and racializing desire economies: Cyprus, Greece, and Turkey

Three processes constitute the desire economies of Cyprus, Greece, and Turkey: (1) the construction of women's (re)productive labor as a natural resource, (2) the commodification and (re)colonization of reproductive labor, and (3) the criminalization of the working class. Viewing these processes

152

through a postcolonial, materialist lens problematizes the ways in which workers, (re)production, and agency are constituted, and makes visible that (re)colonization is integral to the creation of desire economies.

> [S]exualized, gendered, cross-cultural bodies ... have histories of production in the United States [and Western Europe] at the nexus of academic and nonacademic discourses. These histories are histories of tourism and exploitation. They are histories that simultaneously seek and produce commodities as queered fetishes, feminized fetishes and nativized fetishes.
>
> (Patel in Alexander 1998: 281)

In trying to analyze how desire economies constitute themselves, Patel foregrounds the imperial, which allows us to see both the interdependence and competition between what are currently referred to as "peripheral" and "metropole" capital. A discourse pervasively employed by the media and IR theorists is the peripheral as spectacle, and this discourse represents women in the sex trade as victims of backward, peripheral economic patriarchies that are struggling to survive against all odds. Simultaneously, these narratives universalize the peripheries as regions where violence and abuse of women is commonplace. This kind of aberration

> occurs in relation to a First World that is seldom included as violating its women. The First World, imperialist, militaristic, violent, and exploitative, is rarely present in this visual evidence of [spectating]. Its absence constructs the authoritative and objective viewer and rescuer, always outside of history.
>
> (Grewal 1998: 502)

The constitution of desire economies is closely linked to the histories of colonialism, production, and (re)production in the United States and Western Europe, the leaders of the current global order. However, IR and IPE discourses construct the social relations in peripheries as if they are outside this historical production. The formation of desire economies,[6] a fundamental process of (re)production, depends on naturalizing women's labor and sexualizing their bodies, and these processes are constituted through the commodification of black and white women's bodies, the policing and criminalizing of the working class, and the myths of opportunity, femininity, masculinity, and racism (e.g., white slavery).[7]

Since the late 1980s, Cyprus, Greece, and Turkey have pursued neoliberal economic strategies such as the promotion of tourism, an industry that continues to grow in strength. This strategy is a result of domestic financial institutions such as the World Bank and technocrats working in alliance to reconfigure the position of these countries in relation to transnational flows of labor and capital in the transnational economy. These regions, which are marketed as providers of services, draw upon sex and domestic labor commodities from Sri Lanka, the Philippines, Eastern Europe, Ethiopia, and Brazil.

Cyprus draws most of these workers from Eastern Europe, such as Russia, Rumania, and Albania, and the Philippines, Sri Lanka, and mainland Turkey. These women workers constitute one among several groups entering northern Cyprus but they have a "particular status, reflected in the special regulations governing their entry into the country, which arises from their association with prostitution" (Scott 1995: 387). Some of these women travel to Turkey to engage in prostitution, and from there, travel to northern Cyprus. The women who come to northern Cyprus depend on their employer to deal with entry visa requirements and health and blood tests. Since the work permits and permissions are agreed upon by the employer rather than the employee, changing jobs requires permission from the state through the new employer. If women are brought to the country as a group, some formalities are waived, for instance health exams. However, if a woman is traveling alone to find a job, she must produce a visa and health certificates before embarking on a plane from Istanbul (these workers can enter northern Cyprus only through Istanbul because the Turkish republic of northern Cyprus is acknowledged by only two states internationally). Arbitrariness in the implementation of rules leaves women vulnerable.

As noted earlier, in southern Cyprus each family who decides to buy the domestic labor of a woman applies for her by depositing 600 Greek Cypriot pounds. The Greek Cypriot state and states like the Philippines work with each other to make possible the transfer of female labor to Cyprus and into homes and businesses that can afford it. For the Greek Cypriot state, domestic laborers are "a temporary solution so that they can meet some needs of Greek Cypriots. Our goal is to 'export' them if tendencies toward unemployment appear" (Hatzikosta 1998: 3). Additionally, in southern Cyprus Eastern European pimps have recruited young women for prostitution. Most of these women entered either illegally after authorities were bribed or on temporary three-month work permits. In most cases, the employers forced sex workers to surrender their passports and stay beyond the terms of their work permits (Bureau of Democracy, Human Rights and Labor 1999a).

Turkey draws most of its workers from Albania, Bulgaria, Moldova, Rumania, and Ukraine. African and Asian women use the country as a transit point to other countries in Western Europe. Even though the state claims that there is no trafficking in Turkey, in 1998 there were arrests, and in most cases, deportations, of 6,700 women from Rumania, Moldova, and Ukraine. In 1997, 7,000 Rumanian women were deported. This number rose to 11,000 in 1999 (Bureau of Democracy, Human Rights and Labor 1999b). Greece imports women for domestic and sex work from the former

Soviet satellites, Albania, Bulgaria, and Rumania. It is estimated that there are 20,000 domestic and sex workers in Greece. According to media sources, some police officers force illegal immigrants to have sex and then channel them into prostitution rings (Bureau of Democracy, Human Rights and Labor 1999c).

Why do these workers migrate? Feminists such as Shrage (1994) and Kempadoo (1995) argue that a large percentage of sex customers seek workers with a racial, national, or class identity that differs from their own. "Sex industries depend upon the eroticization of the ethnic and cultural Other [which] suggests that we are witnessing a contemporary form of exoticism which sustains postcolonial and post-cold war relations of power and domination" (Kempadoo 1995: 75–6). Shrage explains that Western men demand women "different from their own" (1994: 142) because of "culturally produced fantasies regarding the sexuality of these women," fantasies connected to "socially formed perceptions regarding the sexual and moral purity of white women" (48–50). This logic guides not only white Western men but also the practices of men and women in the peripheries when deciding to hire domestic and sex workers. Asymmetrical relations are produced in these countries through the (re)production of raced and classed masculinity and femininity.

All three countries import women to respond to the desires of an emerging middle class and the desires of men and women buying services through the tourist industry. Most of the women who come to these countries are seeking better living conditions for themselves and their families. The restructuring process in the economy of their countries has changed to the extent that it has left much of its population (especially women) without jobs (ICFTU 1997). Despite suggestions from liberal internationalism that supply factors (such as poverty, inadequate educational employment, the growth of transnational crime) and demand factors (demand by employers) are what push women from Eastern European and other countries to move to Cyprus, Greece, and Turkey to seek jobs, these factors do not tell us the whole story. What kinds of (re)productive processes, relations, and discourses does the formation of desire economies depend on in peripheral contexts? For what purpose and for whose benefit?

Domestic and sex workers as natural resources

The formation of desire economies relies heavily on professionals from the upper circuits who consume the services (and bodies) of women from the peripheries. Within this relationship, these women are constituted as natural resources or objects for the use of the new emerging professional class of men and women in these three countries as well as professionals in multinational corporations. My interviews in Cyprus, Greece, and Turkey suggest that hiring domestic and sex workers to do (re)productive labor is a means of

accessing gendered and racialized power. Nirmala[8] discusses her employment in southern Cyprus:

> Loulla brought me here to help with the children. Life in Sri Lanka
> was very difficult. My husband and I divorced a while back. Loulla
> brought me here for a year. She paid me $300.00 before taxes and I
> was left with $270.00 after taxes. She will wake me up everyday at
> 6.00 a.m. and ask me to clean the house, wash the clothes, help her
> with cooking, and then take me to the family restaurant. I will have
> to work there till 1.00 a.m.
>
> (Author interview 1995)

Nirmala's arrival in Cyprus is a result of several forces. Loulla, a Greek
Cypriot woman, is buying these services from another Third World country
through Nirmala. She argues that Nirmala is in Cyprus to make much more
money than she would at home, and thus she intends to extract as much
work as possible for the 180 Cypriot pounds a month that she is paying her.
The abject conditions to which Nirmala is subjected would be unacceptable
under any other circumstances, and Loulla would have a difficult time hiring
a Cypriot woman to do this work for $300.00 per month. However, these
facts are marginalized and obscured through the colonial myths that
supplant the racial subjectivity and labor of her employee with the sexualized "native" who can endure all in trying to ensure the (re)production of the
next generation. Within this "sexual narrative of consumption those
providing services are never positioned as agents" or wage workers but are
rather naturalized as the poor and despondent who are to be provided a job,
room, and board by the emerging upper- and middle-class women of Cyprus
(Alexander 1997: 295).[9]

The pay and working conditions of Bulgarians, Rumanians, Russians, and
Ukrainians compare unfavorably with those of the British croupiers who
previously dominated the profession, and who were earning 100 pounds
sterling five years earlier for similar jobs. The British women were less
subject to the controls and restrictions on their social life than these women
are now. Scott cited a British former croupier who said that "there would
have been a strike if they'd tried to do that to us" (1995: 398). Additionally,
British women could terminate their contracts any time and still become
hired anywhere in the world without much difficulty. It is different for new
immigrants. Restructuring in the former Soviet bloc and restructuring
within Cyprus, Greece, and Turkey have led to conditions that make
possible female migrations for sex and domestic work. For example, in
Albania the rate of unemployment has hovered at 30 per cent. This leads
Albanians to sell girls "usually to the mob in Italy or Greece for up to
$10,000 according to a study done by an Albanian women's organization"
(Montgomery 2001). In an interview with several women working on a

cruise ship, two women told me that they did not like their job but it helped them to earn enough to send money home to their families. They both had children staying with their parents and had to make enough money to bring them to Greece. Another woman was sending money to her sister so that she could go to school.

Greek and Turkish Cypriot women of upper and middle class seem to equate true femininity with unbridled control over women from other peripheral countries. When women like Loulla argue that domestic workers should be doing so much work for so little compensation, this reaffirms their power over the migrant worker. In this sense, domestic work provides women (and men) with opportunities to manage and control both themselves and others. Thus, taking into account domestic labor, a form of sex work, in Cyprus, Greece, and Turkey allows us to view this work "beyond the boundaries of reproductive domestic work, the emasculation of men, and the feminization of the Third World" (Kempadoo and Doezema 1998: 27). It allows us to see this (re)productive work as integral to the (re)structuring of the global economy. Eleni, a working-class Greek Cypriot woman, 30 years old, who befriended Nirmala, talked to me about the abject conditions imposed by Loulla:

> I used to visit her when Loulla was not home. In the beginning she would cry and show me her dry and bloody hands. She would tell me about her headaches and her hurting teeth. Finally, it seems that she became accustomed to her pain. I do not think you can get used to it but what can you do? If you have family back home to feed and no job, what can you do? I asked Loulla a couple of times about her mistreating Nirmala. She responded that the money they make here can buy them the world back home. She "killed" [not meant literally] the poor woman.
>
> (Author interview 1995)

When Eleni found out that Nirmala was being mistreated, she questioned Loulla about her relationship with her domestic worker. Loulla's response revealed her class politics as it is gendered and racialized. To her, Nirmala makes enough money to buy the world back in Sri Lanka. Domestic work as a relation of sexual power and as productive and reproductive labor is integral to the local and global economy and it is a site upon which the First World and the new emerging transnational class reconstitutes its power. In hiring a migrant domestic worker, not only does she get services at harshly exploitative rates, she also reconstitutes herself as more powerful in relation to both Eleni and Nirmala. Furthermore, the relationship among Loulla, Nirmala, and Eleni is anchored in ideologies that draw upon masculine and feminine notions of protectionism, property, and individual opportunity and success. These ideologies are also heterosexual and are premised on normative definitions of women as mothers and nurturers. The explanation given to Eleni by Loulla about her domestic laborer was one of protectionism as well as support: "the money they make here can buy them the world back home." However, these interactions mystify the structural conditions within which this relationship becomes possible. The idea of women as servants is based on the assumption that women's labor is a natural resource and thus does not cost the same as men's labor. For example, Greek Cypriot women of middle and upper-middle class who move upward in class via professionalization hire women from the Philippines, Sri Lanka, and Eastern Europe to continue doing the household chores and care for their children and the elderly. In this relation, patriarchal and capitalist understandings of production (in this case, professionalization) and reproduction are sustained in an asymmetrical relation to each other, with production at the top of the hierarchy and reproduction at the bottom. Moreover, professional upper- and middle-class women do not question their role in the (re)production of a world system.

The subordination of the woman of color and the working-class woman is critical in the process of reconstituting new forms of power. We see in the interview a reflection of the patriarchal/capitalist double standard that dominates the local context around male and female work: the new emerging professional woman uses women of color and of the working class to do all (re)productive work for little compensation because as women they are expected to nurture and sustain the members of the household. Thus, professional women in Cyprus, Greece, and Turkey are guided by the racialized patriarchal and capitalist logic of colonization which sees women of a certain race and class as "nature". Professional women do not question why women from Sri Lanka, the Philippines, or Cyprus should be doing this reproductive labor for very little compensation because it frees professional women from domestic work and also enables their power over domestic workers. In these peripheral sites, a new emerging middle class is co-implicated in the very processes of violence and recolonization that originated in heterosexual "Western" capital.[10] This class colludes with the hegemonic nation-state in seeking to consume the labor of women of particular races and is also complicit in recirculating earlier colonial myths about (re)productive labor as being "natural." As Mies (1986) informs us, this allows for the superexploitation of women's work. In sum, the transnational hegemonic code constructs women's labor as a natural resource, and we see the existence of class- and race-based parallels in the regulation of women in diverse social locations.

These transactions are premised on racializing labor and the economy, which in turn allows for the (re)production of global power in sexual, racial, and class terms. Liberal capitalism as a structure does not shy away from creating markets where none existed before, or from boosting existing ones, from finding new areas to colonize. There was indeed a time when racial and sexual capital wanted nothing to do with the "backward" Cypriot, Greek, and Turk[11] consumers. "Now it seems that the same crises that have come about as a result of aggressive transnationalization and expansion, have forced ... [metropole] capital to consume on the same site" with peripheral capital (Alexander 1997: 293),[12] with the masculine and white capitalist class at the top, black females of working class at the bottom, and women of other peripheral contexts as the co-implicators in the production of Western modernities or more specifically capitalist–patriarchal relations.

Commodification of (re)productive labor

Women who work as both sex and domestic workers are objectified and commodified. Within Cyprus, Greece, and Turkey, women work as *artists* or *Natashas* in dance and nightclubs. In Cyprus particularly, women dance and offer their sexual services to not only Cypriot men but tourists, businessmen, United Nations soldiers, and men still working at the British bases in Cyprus. These women are subject to strict surveillance at their jobs, and some of them, depending on the conditions under which they enter the country, are not allowed to shop unsupervised. These restrictions are implemented because their bodies are seen as sexual commodities and thus any kind of opportunity to develop non-monetary relations undermines the possibility of the employer receiving their commercial value. Irena explains:

> No matter how upset we were, the customers persisted in wanting us to sit on their laps. I couldn't speak to them because they were mostly Greeks and Arabs. We had to act sexy knowing quite well that if we didn't we were not going to make enough money to pay back what we owed. We drank with them because we had to sleep with them.
>
> (Author interview in Larnaca 1995)

In this interview, both Greek and Arab men buy access to sex workers' bodies. These men expect "unbridled sexual access to willingly objectified women" (O'Connell and Taylor 1998: 41). In addition to their location as migrant workers, commodification of sex plays a major role in positioning these women in the global political economy and also how they will be treated. Altink (1995) interviewed women from the Dominican Republic, Ethiopia, and Brazil who suggested that they came to Greece after they needed to earn a living because their husbands were not earning enough money back home. They were recruited by an intermediary who promised them enormous salaries in comparison with Dominican standards and brought them to Greece. After they arrived in Athens they were taken to the "tourist office" in a seaside resort and began working right away at eight o'clock that night. One of the women said the following:

That first night I was like a piece of furniture. Punters could only look at me, not touch me. I didn't want to do that kind of work. Why would I do my best to attract customers? Surely not to line the pockets of the bosses. Later on I only had intercourse with them if I couldn't avoid it. And those customers smelled. I continually argued about money with this self-styled impresario, the proprietor of the club. Since I couldn't refuse customers, I wanted to be paid for entertaining them.

(Hermana quoted in Altink 1995: 91)

These women are targeted racially on different levels: from racisms embedded in structures, and cultural imperialism refracted through transnational discourses on prostitution and domestic labor. Labor-importing states decide who will enter as a prostitute or as a female domestic worker on the basis of economic, racial, and ethnic calculations. For example, images of the exotic are intertwined with ideologies of racial and ethnic difference: the *Natashas* and *artists* are defined as "others" and always in comparison to the racial and ethnic background of the client and his attached property, women of his own ethnic, racial, and class background. In both northern and southern Cyprus, women who are considered legitimate workers for the sex trade are the exotic green- and blue-eyed, white-skinned women from Rumania, Russia, and the Ukraine. It should be noted that other issues of virginity and age complicate this story. A working-class Turkish woman shared the following story with me:

He teaches at our university. We have two kids together, a son and a daughter. He and I were together for twenty years till he found this Rumanian, green-eyed, blond woman. He came home one day and he gushed to a friend of ours about his new green-eyed, blond woman. "She is beautiful and she worships me unlike Turkish women who want your money but will not give you all you want in bed." I was so angry at him for leaving me for this younger blond woman and also concerned that he might catch AIDS. What does she have more than me?

(Author interview 1995)

This woman's husband was enamored by the other woman's ability to provide him with everything that he wanted in bed. Although his wife speaks angrily, she does not inform us why she is angry. In the interview, she repeats three times that the new woman her husband left her for is green-eyed, blond, and younger. From what this Turkish woman imparted, I gathered that Turkish men equate true masculinity with having younger, lighter women next to them. There is a sense in which Turkish men attempt to restore their masculinity by finding sex workers who will presumably satisfy all their needs, unlike Turkish women with whom their relationship is circumscribed by traditional norms.

The logic guiding these politics stems from colonialism, which still informs the construction of the hierarchical stages of a female worker: a woman who is white-skinned with green or blue eyes becomes the object of ultimate masculine desire and sexual exploitation. This heightened exoticization of the sexuality of white-skinned women is a way of doing two things: valorizing peoples and cultures and "concurrently also constituting them as projections of western [and eastern] fantasies" (Rousseau and Porter 1990: 7); they can be exploited because of their commodified beauty and sexuality. Furthermore, these women's sexualized and racialized labor becomes a marker of danger and pollution to the members of the world economy: these women are here to sell their white bodies but at the same time pose danger for the tourists who buy them, and can pollute public morality, health, and the family if they are left unsupervised. Altink argues that some of the women from Colombia when going through Cyprus were not even provided with condoms despite the public rhetoric of regular health exams by the state (1995: 96). Such investment reduces surplus value and increases costs, which in turn increases production costs, something the state tries to avoid in favor of efficient production. Further, Altink (1995) claims that in southern Cyprus, when groups of young, virginal women arrive from the Philippines, they are allowed to participate in sex work. However, these are exceptions. A Greek Cypriot, working-class, 35-year-old domestic laborer had this to say about these racial distinctions:

MARIA: Most of the domestic female workers are from Sri Lanka, the Philippines, and sometimes from Bulgaria. These women could not find a job back home and they all have kids that need food and clothes. They come here because somebody tells them in their country that there are jobs and they can earn money for their children. These women are not considered to be sexy and dangerous enough to steal the husbands of women who hire them because most of them have children and families. These women are expected to be good servants for the rich women in cities. I know this woman, called Lito, and she has a black maid.

INTERVIEWER: What do you mean by "black"?

MARIA: She is from Sri Lanka. Not only does she clean their house starting at the crack of dawn but she is also teaching their kids how to speak her language. The kids know her language better than Greek.

INTERVIEWER: How is Lito treating her domestic laborer?

MARIA Ah ... she is treating Houanita quite well, better than Eleni who used to beat up her domestic worker. Hers is from the Philippines.

(Author interview 1998)

There are distinctions made between black female workers and the other female sex workers who are considered sexy and dangerous. Such racial distinctions between the "good" and the "sexy and dangerous" female servants reinforce limits on national and ethnic membership. However, material (re)structuring is leading to other kinds of relations not necessarily envisioned by the agents and managers of the state: the transformation of the Greek, Turkish, and Cypriot citizen through interaction with domestic and sex workers, and ultimately, the (re)organization of the state itself into a regime that serves the interests of the emerging global capital class, and that (re)organizes production and (re)production globally.

These men (as well as women) who can afford in a transnational context to buy the services of these sex workers do so by commodifying their services in bars, hotels, and cruise ships. For them, the labor of these workers is a commodity to be sold and bought, especially the labor from white bodies. Women's participation in this commodified (re)production process is expressed consistently through comments like the following by Kostantina:

> She is Rumanian. They come here and they steal our husbands. Ever since my husband went out with her, he lost his brains. He lies in bed fantasizing about her and I ask him all the time if he is thinking of her and he nods "yes" as if we are acquaintances and not husband and wife with two children.
>
> (Author interview 1999)

These comments reveal the heterosexual/patriarchal myths and expectations by which women in Cyprus abide. Cypriot women point to a few Rumanian sex workers as evidence that Rumanian women are all "loose" husband thieves. However, these comments make invisible the violent processes of (re)colonization and control over women's bodies, whether Rumanian or Cypriot. The same liberal capitalist–patriarchal relation that allows men to ignore their wives' needs enables them to consume sex from Rumanian women: men using women as commodities.

Policed and controlled through particular rules and laws, these relations render sex and domestic workers vulnerable to their employers and clients' practices once they are out of public spaces and in private homes, hotel rooms, bars, and cruise ships. A Bulgarian woman, who worked on Louis cruise ships, said she started working at five o'clock in the morning, making beds, doing laundry, and fending off her employers' advances, and then she danced in two night shows, and of course, depending on the night, provided "companionship" to some of the tourists (Greek, German, British, French, and Arabs) on the ship. When I asked her what she thought about all this work, she replied, "It is okay because I will be able to save enough soon to be stable financially." A construction worker and a man who owns a grocery store who frequently booked cruises on this line said that two things made the trip worthwhile: gambling and the blondes from Rumania. The middle-class manager stated the following:

> This woman I met on one of the cruises from Cyprus to Egypt. She was Rumanian. She talked to me at the casino, we went to her room and I gave her 30 pounds.
>
> (Author interview)

This quotation reveals a set of social relations defined by commodification in which the woman is a means to the constitution of masculinity and femininity through pleasure. Sex and domestic workers often discount the risks of violence and AIDS when faced with the potential payoff of financial stability. Working as sex and domestic workers is a more certain path to financial gain than other kinds of work back home.

Why do women place themselves in a context of violence and uncertainty? Women from these different countries decide to move to Cyprus, Greece, and Turkey as a result of the globalized changes in several sites. The decisions of these women are determined not only by local factors (e.g., the change of socialist economies into market economies, and ethnic conflict) but by the location of Cyprus, Greece, and Turkey in the transnational economy of tourism. These nation-states are daily becoming desire sites through (re)colonizing practices: importing women from other peripheries, selling their (re)productive labor for very little, and constituting sex and domestic workers as objects and spectacles of consumption. These decisions by states are also guided by the need for foreign investment in tourism in these countries. Just as international investors see Cyprus and Turkey as a site of cheap labor, and offshore activity that brings white clients, international tourists know it as a place to buy cheap sex. Other factors that influence their decision are "ideoscapes" or the images of the world that the international media produce and disseminate (Appadurai 1991: 25).

Violences: criminalization of the local and transnational working class

Another major process leading to the formation of desire economies is the criminalization of the local and foreign working classes. This opportunity or success myth is (re)produced within the boundaries of these countries. The state rhetoric is that "we need to learn to live with people of different ethnicities, religions, and who speak different languages especially in relation to our integration to the European Commission, which possibly will bring to Cyprus workers from European countries." However, middle-and upper-class women within Cyprus treat black women from countries such as

Sri Lanka and the Philippines differentially, and frequently with violence because of their race, gender, and class:

> Unfortunately, it seems that there is a larger difficulty, when it comes to people from countries of the "third world." More welcome, are, for example, Europeans who work in large corporations ... finally, the treatment of foreign workers in Cyprus is inhumane ... Either we accept them or we will have a problem. We have the previous problem of the Western countries. They brought foreign workers when they needed them and then started developing a whole racist movement against them with all the incidents and tensions that we have observed. The same can happen in Cyprus. Even when you have laws to control their entrance, it is inevitable when the door opens for issues to go out of control. An example today is that nobody knows how many are legals and how many are illegals.
>
> (Prodromou in Hatzikosta 1998: 3)

Liberal internationalists claim that the professional worker is the one who counts in transnationalization processes. Similarly, the Cypriot media discourse argues that the European businessman is more welcome, and therefore more valued. The entry of sex and domestic workers is presented as a potential problem with chaotic implications in the Cypriot context. Thus, the Greek Cypriot state, despite attempts to control the illegals, ends up supporting this process of globalization by opening its doors to the service economy as a crucial strategy of (re)producing its power and the upper- and middle-class purchasing power, and the legitimate members of the world economy's global power. According to the dominant discourses of globalization circulated by most leaders of the political parties, these states not only have to compete in the international tourism market but they also have to come up to par with the European countries' economies in order to better integrate themselves into those economies. However, to manage and control the contradictions that emerge out of these transnationalized processes, all three states criminalize and police legal and illegal workers.

Policing the foreign "criminals" (domestic and sex workers, along with others) and also the local working classes is about more than simply sex and ethnicity. It is about the kind of sexuality, race, and ethnicity that endangers the nation and "promotes citizenship." Not everybody can be a citizen, especially the bodies and subjects who are nonproductive and do not offer economic gains for the survival of the new emerging transnational state. As the state moves to reconfigure the nation, it simultaneously "resuscitates the nation as heterosexual and 'white'" (Alexander 1997: 6) and makes invisible the criminalization of citizens (national and international) who are consumed and managed locally.

Conclusion: possibilities for transforming the hegemonic neoliberalist project

> There will be no feminist revolution without an end to racism and white supremacy. When all women and men engaged in feminist struggle understand the interlocking nature of systems of domination, of white supremacist capitalist patriarchy, the feminist movement will regain its revolutionary progressive momentum.
>
> (hooks 1995: 107)

I have theorized the contradictions inherent in the globalization project by examining the participation of Cyprus, Greece, and Turkey in the import of labor for the lucrative desire economies. A postcolonial feminist materialist analysis challenges the intersecting histories of colonialism, capitalism (commodification and naturalization of women's work and bodies) and nationalism. A postcolonial materialist feminist orientation allows us to critique the practices of peripheral nation-states, their hegemonic and transnational discourses and inequalities that cut across peripheral sites. But how are transnational sex and domestic workers in conjunction with the local working class to resist the neoliberal project and to create more egalitarian and democratic spaces? How are these workers who recognize and experience both familiar and new histories of disenfranchisement to work together for change?

Greek, Turkish, and Cypriot working-class women are forging alliances with migrant sex and domestic workers to transform the current exploitative structures. They use their agency to achieve an inclusive vision of social transformation by (1) exposing how the postcolonial nationalist and transnational discourses of naturalization, commodification, and the myths of opportunity and white slavery are strategies of colonization at different places simultaneously; (2) understanding how these individuals and groups of people are exploited and oppressed by various methods that "keep them in place;" (3) recognizing that they as agents can envision their futures because they carry not only the scars of oppression and exploitation, but also the memories of survival and self/collective empowerment; and (4) (re)interpreting the strategies utilized by capitalist and patriarchal discourses and practices (nation-state, citizen, freedom, and democracy) toward (re)envisioning social justice and constituting a feminist democracy. All of these different transformative processes are ridden with contradictions and tensions:

> A non-essentialist position does not imply a nonbelonging to a group, nor does it imply loss of agency or of coalitions and solidarities. For some feminists of color, identity politics remains central ...

which can enable a politics through positions that are coalitions, intransigent, in process, and contradictory.

(Grewal 1994: 234)

Sex and domestic workers are a force to be reckoned with in these three nation-states and within the European Union. According to the Greek Cypriot Ministry of Labour's statistics for 1995, foreign nationals working in Cyprus reached an all-time high of 24,000 persons or 8.5 per cent of the working population. Of this group, domestic workers comprised the majority, numbering about 4,000 persons (Agathangelou and Ling 1997). While other official statistics are not yet available, government officials of Greece and Turkey do assert that the phenomenon of migrant sex and domestic workers continues to grow. This feminized proletariat could ally with counterpart groups in a newly transnational European Union. In 1990, women accounted for approximately 50 per cent of the foreign population in Europe's industrialized economies.

Transborder alliances are equally problematic. Even when the peripheral nation-state mediates with transnational capital to constitute the desire industries as a strategy to create jobs for some people, it is still actively participating in the commodification of women's labor and bodies. It is informed by local and transnationalized practices and ideologies of servility and service-ability that depend on a set of commercial productions: the black maid, and the exotic and erotic white beauties to be consumed for sexual pleasure. However, sex and domestic workers along with members of the local working class are challenging these contradictions, which in turn challenges conceptualizations of race, peripheral nation-state, civil and human rights, freedom, and democracy. Women who stand at the intersections of gender, race, class, sexuality, and nationality are speaking up and telling a story different from the one told by agents of the state and the women and men who hire sex and domestic workers. In the interviews with these workers, the contradictions of the nation-states' practices and ideologies become apparent. I close with two interview excerpts, the first from an individual interview with Sophia, a 55-year-old working-class woman who used to be a domestic laborer, who discloses that her son had just hired a Filipina domestic worker:

Did my son forget when I used to work as a domestic worker? I hope not. Otherwise, he could participate in the same torture I experienced when I was working to feed him and help him grow and go study abroad ... Why do the rich need their houses cleaned? Why don't they do it? And I wonder why I lost my job. I lost my job because they had to pay a little more to me than they pay the Sri Lankans and the Bulgarians who are my friends and are exploited. They work for nothing!

(Author interview 1995)

Sophia's words bring to the fore the memories of some of the local working class. She reminds us how restructuring is another strategy to disenfranchise some Cypriots and people from Sri Lanka and Bulgaria. The crucial point here is that the new emerging middle and upper class, some of whom are children of working-class mothers, collude with transnational power structures by exploiting these women and treating them as servants. Her friendships with Sri Lankans and Bulgarians emerge out of these same structures of exploitation. One of her friends who worked as a domestic worker for five years in Cyprus is now married and lives next to her house in her community. These two women talked about their own exploitation and oppression and their need to work as domestic workers:

SOPHIA: I used to get up very early and catch the bus to go to work. I will leave my 5-year-old son behind with my sister and I will worry the whole day about his well-being. I will take care of Maria, Antonis, and many others and my sister will take care of my son. These were scary times for me.

(Author interview 1995)

GALENA: Scary times for me when I was in Bulgaria. My husband left me with two kids and I did not have any savings to take care of their basic needs: food and clothing. I left Bulgaria for a better life and I left them behind with my parents. I came here for a better life. But my boss was torturing me till I decided to leave this family. I came here to find a job and a better life. It was all for a short time. Now, I got married here and found a new country.

(Author interview 1995)

These stories are the seeds of creating alliances and new relations. The mobility of sex and domestic workers engenders the potential for the development of new social relations. When Galena says that domestic workers migrate with dreams of success but they remain unrealized, she makes the first step toward the creation of a critical consciousness regarding the capitalist myth of opportunity. However, their lived practices present them with ways of challenging the effects of normalizing and regulating women's lives through racialization and nationalization. These stories undermine the stability of categories such as Cypriot and Bulgarian woman, Cypriot and Bulgarian worker, nation, race, and class.

Female migrant laborers are now organizing. A Filipina domestic laborer, Rosalyn, told me that all domestic laborers meet every Sunday and discuss possible connections with other Filipinas in both the Middle East and Europe:

We come together and share stories and strategies to help women who are new in Cyprus and do not know how to rid themselves of their contracts when they work under very bad conditions. The state does not support them. On the contrary, the state always ends up supporting the employer. Domestic workers in the Middle East and Europe are working with us to mobilize resources and legal knowledge that can be utilized against the local employers.

(Author interview 1995)

The study of sex and domestic workers broadens our understanding of agency and feminist struggles. It demonstrates that globalization's subjects are agents who simultaneously collude and resist the practices of the heterogeneous structures in the new millennium. Caught in geopolitical shifts, and carrying overlapping geohistories, sex and domestic workers along with the local working class require a "differential consciousness," which unites them. This new and differential consciousness permits men and women in peripheries to "self-consciously break and reform ties to ideology ... [to] permit the achievement of coalition across differences" (Sandoval 1991: 15). In the case of Cyprus, Greece, and Turkey, we see emerging agents of change and alliance building in the subjects who work collectively with others and engage in a mutual critique of their location in the oppressive capitalist structures. When these workers recognize and contest their positions in the global political economy, they are able to negotiate transnational solidarity.

Acknowledgements

The author wishes to thank Kyle D. Killian, Geeta Chowdhry, and Sheila Nair for their invaluable comments and suggestions for revising the several versions of this article. Many thanks to the other participants of the ISA 2000 workshop: L.H.M. Ling, Marshall Beier, Shampa Biswas, and Randolph B. Persaud.

Notes

1   Mohanty (1997: 13) following Mies (1986) stated that traditionally we understood the worker as male. However, this silences women's labor and its costs, and that women are agents who are capable of making their own choices. The constitution of this class depends on the services and labor of what is relatively constituted as the working class.
2   Greece's "per capita income places [it] above only Mexico and Turkey among the member nations of the organization for Economic Co-operation and Development" (Thomadakis 1995: 147).
3   Master here refers to the discourses that inform the ordering of international political economy inquiries and the ways that such inquiries legitimize and delegitimize pursuits of knowledge.

4 Cox does not refer to liberal democracy here but rather to a participatory kind of democracy that allows the possibility of redistributing resources and the constitution of a just society.

5 Gramsci's understanding of consciousness and ideology as nonhomogeneous and contradictory allows us to explore racist ideologies within the working class and within trade unions (Hall 1986: 26).

6 Alexander argues that both

> the generative scripts of heterosexual tourism and those of gay tourism ... traverse a similar imperial geography and draw upon similar epistemic frames to service an imagined "Western" tourist. The similarity requires our political attention for it suggests that material and ideological gestures of recolonization may not be the province of heterosexual capital alone.
>
> (1998: 281)

I agree, and thus, when discussing sexual relations in different contexts, I suggest that we sustain a deconstructive postcolonial mode and we can do that by focusing on the relationship of imperial capitalist relations especially in the context of production and (re)production which do not only assume heterosexuality but also a "queer fetishized native" (Alexander 1998: 287).

7 See Doezema's (1998) work, which engages systematically the discourses about the "trafficking in women," and argues that there is a re-emergence of the myth of "white slavery."

8 All of my interviews were conducted between 1995 and 1999 in Nicosia and Larnaca, Cyprus. The names of the interviewees are confidential; therefore I have used pseudonyms within the text of this chapter.

9 See also http://www.unifemeseasia.org/Resources/Traffick2.html.

10 Desire economies exist in both the peripheries and metropoles. The difference between these two kinds of desire economies is (1) peripheries' cash inflows depend to a large extent on this kind of economy because of their location in the global economy, but this is changing; and (2) capitalist development in its globalized form does not distinguish sites so much as long as new consumer markets are created that can be colonized. See Alexander (1998: 287) for a similar argument.

11 We still see this refusal in the debates surrounding the issue of Cyprus and Turkey joining the EU. In the case of Cyprus, the debate is linked to the militarization of the North by Turkey, and thus debates around Cyprus joining the EU constantly bring to the fore that its entry will be contingent upon resolving the ethnic conflict between Greek and Turkish Cypriots. Muftuler-Bac has argued that "Turkey's failure to uphold democracy justifies the EU's rejection but at the same time conceals an aspect of the EU's reservations about Turkey: its perception of Turkey as the other of Europe" (1993: 240).

12 Alexander (1998) uses this logic to explain the interdependence and competition between heterosexual and homosexual capital. This logic applies to the relation between metropole and marginalized capital.

7

IN ONE INNINGS

National identity in postcolonial times

Sankaran Krishna

This chapter examines the issue of national identity in postcolonial societies by focusing on a West Indian cricketer named Shivnaraine Chanderpaul from Guyana.[1] Still in his twenties, Chanderpaul has established himself as one of the most reliable batsmen in the West Indies cricket team and one of the premier batsmen in the world.[2] As a cricketer of Indian origin (his ancestors moved from India to British Guyana in the nineteenth century as indentured laborers on sugar plantations) Chanderpaul's location is complicated in interesting ways. Contemporary Guyana's population is about 50 per cent East Indian and about 38 per cent African in its origins. When Chanderpaul made his test debut for the West Indies against the visiting English (the erstwhile colonial power that left Guyana as recently as 1966), Guyana was wracked with ethnic tension between the Guyanese-Indians and Afro-Guyanese. A recent election had brought to power the political party closely affiliated with the East Indian population, unseating the party affiliated with the island's black population. There was some rioting in the streets and a perception that the elections were not entirely free and fair. It was in this tense political climate that Chanderpaul played his inaugural test innings.

The crowd at the Bourda Oval in the capital city of Georgetown was vectored by a complex and fascinating set of identity positions. Guyanese-Indians obviously identified with "their boy" and were keen to see him succeed. Most Afro-Guyanese wanted to see a fellow-national come good, especially because the Guyanese have always felt that they are discriminated against in gaining selection to the multinational Caribbean test team, which was dominated by white players in the colonial era, and in later decades by players from Barbados, Jamaica, and Trinidad. Moreover, the West Indies were playing against the visiting English, a country whose imperial history and colonial mindset possibly lingered more strongly in cricket than in many other realms of encounter. Yet surely the Afro-Guyanese, even as they rooted for Chanderpaul, were unable to forget the fact that he was not one of "us" but of "them" – that he represented a national fragment that symbolized the ethnic tension of the moment.

Through the figure of Shivnaraine Chanderpaul, this chapter attempts to map out the multiple and dynamic trajectories of national identity in a post-colonial setting. One of the most intriguing aspects of the Guyanese context is that it muddies hierarchies of race, ethnicity, class, and gender in exceedingly complex ways. This is not a historical context in which one can easily isolate the imperial/colonizing classes from those whom one might classify as subaltern or colonized. Indeed, in some ways, the entire population of Guyana (with the exception of the "original" inhabitants – the Arawak Indians who today constitute less than 4 per cent of the population) owes its presence in that country to imperialism, and can claim a subaltern status in regard to global political economy in recent centuries. How does one adjudicate between ethnic fragments that emerge as a legacy of the period of imperialism and battle over entitlements in a postcolonial national order? This paper marks an effort to think about the contentious issues involved in such an adjudication. While it makes no pretense toward finding answers or solutions, I submit that such contestations between ethnic fragments, nearly all of whom can legitimately lay claim to a position of subalternity arising from the colonial/imperial era, are likely to become a prominent feature of many postcolonial settings in the years to come. The challenge to any claim of a unified postcolonial perspective emanating from these struggles is a profound one – the political and social issues herein are complex and resistant to easy solutions.

A second impetus of this paper is the suggestion that the territorially bounded practices of national citizenship and static international relations are perhaps too leaden-footed to match the dexterous footwork of a Guyanese–West Indian cricketer of "East Indian" origin. "Identity" is not here regarded as a static set of attributes that characterize a person – identity changed, flowed, reversed, and reinvented itself, and metamorphosed in the course of just two hours that day at the Bourda Oval when Chanderpaul walked in to bat. Rather, identity is seen as a constantly dynamic and performative practice, as something based in part on a historical inventory that memorializes past encounters but also something that changes with dazzling speed within a single moment. Nuances and inflections in that inventory surface on different occasions and under different provocations. In other words, this paper regards identity as a performative practice that connects an individual to a continuously changing social setting. It is moreover incompletely under the control of the so-called protagonist.

In thinking about such questions, I eclectically combine the work of a postcolonial theorist such as Edward Said with that of a continental thinker such as Martin Heidegger. I suggest that postcolonial scholarship may have to give up the pretense of a deferred overcoming, a politics of transcendence, in trying to deal with historical contexts in which issues of nationality, race, class, and gender cannot be arrayed in terms of victimizer and victim. This chapter ends with a meditation on the sort of democratic and pluralist comportment, one that denies the dominant, morally transcendent mode of national becoming, that might serve us well in such situations.

On worlding

I suggest that a useful place to start reframing the question of identity in less territorially bounded and more mobile and mediated ways might be a discussion of the idea of "worlding" as found in the work of Martin Heidegger. For Heidegger, the pursuit of knowledge is not so much a matter of uncovering a reality that awaits our efforts in this regard, nor ought we to assume the complicity of knowledge in our efforts to grasp it. Drawing from a Hellenic and tragic sensibility rather than a Cartesian and subjective will to knowledge, Heidegger constantly foregrounds the fact that every effort at knowledge is ineffably accompanied by a simultaneous and unavoidable concealment of the plenitude of being from which that which is sought is "disclosed." As he explains in his discussion in *Being and Time*, phenomenology means "to let that which shows itself be seen from itself in the very way in which it shows itself from itself" (Heidegger 1988: 58). Another way of putting this is to say that we never ever encounter reality *de novo*, through an act of discovery, or as the subject encountering an object, but that we encounter it through categories and experiences that form our very sense of existence. In an exceptionally lucid and accessible interpretation of Heidegger in this regard, Rudiger Safranski noted the following:

> He [Heidegger] asks: How do we experience reality before we arrange it for ourselves in a scientific, or value-judging, or world-view approach? ... We [then] think in line with this pattern: there is a perceiving ego, and this ego encounters something, an object, and in that object the ego gradually notices a number of properties. Heidegger now wants to draw our attention to the fact that things do not encounter us like that in reality ... One should try not to talk "about" the acts of perception, one should not dredge up convenient theories, but instead one should perform the act and simultaneously, follow it with attention. Attention should therefore be focused on attention ... we first perceive a diffuse, albeit significant, world-context, arriving at a "neutral" object only by way of abstracting from the natural act of perception. If we view the process from a customary theoretical viewpoint, we reverse it – we let it begin at the seemingly "neutral" thing to which we then assign properties and which we then place in the appropriate segment of a context with the world ... *"worlding" means it assembles a whole world, in terms of time and space.*
> (Safranski 1998: 93–6, emphasis added)

To clarify Safranski's clarification of Heidegger, we encounter reality as a moment of disclosure, as an act of knowing but from within and against a larger background of concealment. Reality appears itself – to use the word "appear" in a verb-form consistent with Heidegger's own usage. Yet it is this simultaneous disclosure/concealment that is forgotten in the Cartesian elevation of the knowing subject – and it is this knowing/not knowing that Heidegger constantly battles to rescue. Its rescue is of critical import for him: parallel to Weber's notion of the disenchantment of modernity in an age of instrumental rationality, for Heidegger it is the historical emergence of a knowing subject who inexorably proceeds to compartmentalize knowledge, to elevate technique, to forget the plenitude of being from which perception selectively selects, that forms the source of his critique of modernity as a quintessentially "de-experiencing" experience.

Among other things, this Hellenic emphasis on the pursuit of knowledge as a simultaneous and tragic act marked by concealment means that it is, as Michael Dillon (1996) demonstrated so effectively in his work on security, less enamored of a desire to control, subdue, and bend reality to our wishes – it rather emphasizes the incompleteness of knowledge, of every act of knowing as simultaneously an act of concealment. It is not accidental that so many of the Greek tragedies of the classical age therefore center on the concealment of parentage, on the double entendres inherent in a play of language, on the protagonist not knowing his true lineage, and so on. Time and time again, the protagonist is marked not by his knowledge of his genealogy or his foretold destiny, but precisely by his not knowing what everyone else, including the audience, already does. Indeed, it is often the protagonist's relentless quest to unearth the "truth" of his parentage or his foretold destiny that marks the beginning of his end, the reason for his undoing. Among other things, the tragic sensibility deflects hubris, sensitizes us to the dangers inherent in a pursuit of a singular truth, and draws our gaze to the ultimate impossibility of a will to knowledge in a world where the sign is neither complete nor legible.

What is of crucial import for this chapter is the idea of worlding that is Heidegger's neologism and his means to resist de-experiencing. He suggested that it is through worlding – that is, the idea that every encounter with reality, every act of perception, is an act of "assembling a whole world, in terms of time and space" (Safranski 1998: 96) – that one resists the modern technical subjectivity that for all its practical advantages and comforts is ultimately alienating and impoverishing of life. To put it differently, every act of perception congeals within itself genealogies of time and space – of histories, of movements, of past encounters, of that whole plenitude of being that go into the background conditions of every contemporary encounter.

Heidegger's political problems are all too well known to merit repetition here. I allude of course to his association with Nazism in Germany. Unsurprisingly, his notion of worlding is confined exclusively to a European philosophical, or more accurately, a phenomenological context. It is in this regard that I find the work of Edward Said in his magisterial *Culture and Imperialism* (1993) an extraordinary supplement to Heidegger's notion of worlding. Said contrapuntally rereads certain emblematic and canonical texts of Western literature, music, and theater to demonstrate the implicit spatialization that allowed for their emergence and for their consolidation as canonical. He takes the idea of worlding as an act of assembling a whole world behind each text, a global set of possibilities that underlie them, and shows how differently these canonical texts can be read and appreciated when one places them in a genealogy that is attendant to questions of imperialism, displacement, conquest, exploitation, and the differential accumulation of wealth, status, and privilege "elsewhere" – an elsewhere that never seems to merit explicit elaboration in a self-referential metropolitan world. As Said convincingly demonstrated, to reread these works in a context of worlding is to enrich our understandings of them, to better appreciate the global contexts that underlay their appearance and form, and the background conditions that silently inform the wealth and status of so many protagonists in the Victorian novel, a nineteenth-century opera, an impressionist painting, and so on. His injunction to read these acts of artistic production contrapuntally can be interpreted as an injunction to "world" them – and thereby to place them in genealogies of time and space. It is fashionable to critique such a process of worlding as an instance of reductionism, or of economic determinism, especially through a vacuous overvalorization of aesthetics as a realm that ought to be devoid of material concerns and interests. As any fair reading of Said would undoubtedly show, to the contrary his work reminds us that aesthetic practices have ever been imbricated with material ones and that is precisely why one ought to take them seriously. As Said himself responds in this context:

> It would be silly to expect Jane Austen to treat slavery with anything like the passion of an abolitionist or a newly liberated slave. Yet what I have called the rhetoric of blame, so often now employed by subaltern, minority, or disadvantaged voices, attacks her and others like her, retrospectively, for being white, privileged, insensitive, complicit. Yes, Austen belonged to a slave-owning society, but do we therefore jettison her novels as so many trivial exercises in aesthetic frumpery? Not at all, I would argue, if we take seriously our intellectual and interpretative vocation to make connections, to deal with as much of the evidence as possible, fully and actually, to read what is there or not there, above all, to see complementarity and interdependence instead of isolated, venerated, or formalized experience that excludes and forbids the hybridizing intrusions of human history.
>
> (Said 1993: 96)

What Said brings to Heidegger's notion of worlding is essentially world politics – it gives that concept the edge that allows me to take worlding from the realm of phenomenology to a sunny afternoon at the Bourda Oval in Georgetown, Guyana, where a nervous 19-year-old man awaits his turn at bat. The crowd – moving, restless, calypso-singing, and carnivalesque – awaits as well. They will all have to wait a little longer for I now turn to the historical narratives that "world" that moment at the Bourda – the reasons that make this encounter an extraordinary one even as test matches go.

The underbelly of El Dorado

Guyana is an Amerindian term meaning the "land of waters" and it was once home to the Arawak Indians. By the sixteenth century, European settlers and prospectors had already landed in the country and in 1595, Sir Walter Raleigh in his book *Discoverie of the Large, Rich and Beautiful Empire of Guiana*, noted that it is

> a country that hath yet her maidenhead, never sackt, burnt nor wrought. The face of the earth hath not been torn, nor the virtue and salt of the soil spent by manurance, the graves hath not been opened for gold, the mines not broken with sledges.
>
> (quoted in Glasgow 1970: 6)

In the fervid mythology of the new world, Guyana was constructed as the city of gold, the original El Dorado, through an act of imagination. Raleigh never set foot on Guyana and when the first settlers did, they found a swampy land whose interior was forbidding and uninhabitable by the sedentary and agrarian societies of the old world. The first Africans were transported to Guyana in 1621 to work as slaves on the sugar plantations – nearly all along the thin strip of a coastline. At this time, Guyana was a Dutch colony and would remain so until 1803 when it was wrested from them by the British. The history of slavery in Guyana is replete with blood and violence, but also with resistance, as the famous slave uprisings at Berbice in 1763 and the revolt of 1823 attest.

The occasion for importing indentured laborers from "India" was the abolition of the slave trade in the late 1830s. From the very beginning, this import of labor was to constitute the Indians as scabs and black-legs. They were imported to produce a surplus or reserve army of labor for the plantations, not because of any demonstrable shortage of labor in Guyana. Upon emancipation the Afro-Guyanese fled the plantations to the towns and would much rather starve or become vagabonds than re-enter the hated plantations at the wage levels of the period of slavery. In the new dispensation, they hoped the market would force up the wages paid to plantation labor. The entry of Indian (and smaller numbers of Chinese) indentured labor ensured that the plantations could continue as before, paying little more than subsistence wages. As Glasgow notes, "immigration was used as a technique for getting the [black] laborers back to work on the plantations. The raison d'etre was to provide a stimulus to induce the newly emancipated slaves to become a free labor force" (1970: 69–70). The historian K.O. Laurence observes in his encyclopedic comparative history of plantation labor in Guyana and Trinidad that the intended role of Indian labor was quickly fructified:

> In 1848, when the Creole laborers in British Guiana went on strike in search of higher wages, they had been conscious of the Indian indentured laborers as people whose presence was a serious hindrance to their prospects of success, perhaps indeed a fatal obstacle. In 1856, Guianese Creoles were complaining that the Indians undercut their wages and that they were taxed to pay for importing them.
>
> (Laurence 1994: 279)

The recruitment zones for the indentured laborers in India were some of the most impoverished regions (eastern United Provinces, and some parts of Orissa, Bihar, and Bengal) – areas that had been repeatedly ravaged by famines in the nineteenth century. Given that frame of reference, the new immigrants settled for wages and conditions that seemed to the Afro-Guyanese definitive proof that Indians were docile and untrustworthy stool pigeons of the plantation bosses. The Indians, having been suddenly torn asunder from the webs of tradition and caste, clung to the remembered village with a tenacity that evoked contempt in the European plantation owners and managers, and the Afro-Guyanese.

It is important to note that these immigrant laborers did not see themselves as having left India for Guyana – that nationalist consciousness would emerge only much later as they rewrote the story of their passage. In the mid-nineteenth century a category called "India" had a rather limited social ambit, if any at all. It was only in the late nineteenth century that even elites in domestic society began to think of themselves along such lines. It would be many decades, if ever, before the subaltern classes from which indentured labor was recruited began to frame their identity in terms of a nation-state called India. And when they did, ironically, in various diasporic spaces such as England, South Africa, Fiji, Guyana, and Mauritius, they would rewrite their emigration within an international geopolitical imaginary – thereby further energizing the nationalist movement back home.[3] As Lord Acton noted long ago, "exile is the nursery of nationality" (in Anderson 1998: 59).

All through the nineteenth century and until 1917, when the practice was ended due to pressure on the colonial administration by a newly emergent and self-conscious Indian "national movement," indentured labor entered Guyana with the hope that it would be a temporary affair, and that after saving a certain amount of money, they would return home. And a sizable minority did return. Yet the belief in the imminence of a return to the homeland, along with the tenacious hold on religious and social practices from back home, imparted to the Indian community in Guyana (and in the Caribbean more generally) a cultural resilience that contrasted sharply with the Afro-Guyanese. It is unsurprising that this produced a feeling of intellectual and social superiority among the Guyanese-Indians *vis-à-vis* the Afro-Guyanese. To the Indians, the Afro-Guyanese seemed unmoored from any cultural tradition or civilizational heritage – accentuating the stereotype of the Afro-Guyanese as a superficial mimic of plantation managers and one given to pursuit of fleeting pleasures rather than stoic investment for the future.

Over the nineteenth century the Indians concentrated in the rural areas, hardly intermarried with the Afro-Guyanese, resolutely clung to their ways from back home, and continually regarded their connections with the land as transient and destined to expire when they caught the slow boat home. The Afro-Guyanese, on the other hand, saw their ancestors as having shed blood to rescue the land from the swamps – they had moved "100 million tons of water-logged clay" as the historian Walter Rodney put it (quoted in Williams 1991: 163). They were the ones who had made the plantations possible at all and who had nobly resisted slavery, as shown by the revolts. They had helped the Indians in their initial years in the new land and had received little or nothing in return. Afro-Guyanese perceptions of the Indians meshed rather well with that of the plantation managers too. The situation in the second half of the nineteenth century is best exemplified in this quote from the British Guyanan newspaper *The Working Man*, which noted that

> They [the Indians] proved dogged, sullen, obstinate, alike pernicious to themselves, planters and the community at large. To mention a few defects: idleness and theft ... vindictiveness which is hydra-headed and exhibits itself in ... wife and other murders and often suicide on the most frivolous pretenses.
>
> (quoted in Laurence 1994: 281)

These historical residues of a plantation economy inform the habitus of everyday life in contemporary Guyana. As Brackette Williams finds in her ethnography, the Guyanese distinguish "making a living" from "making life" (Williams 1991: 56–7). The former refers to a person's industry, his skill and ambition, and his ability to achieve material rewards and results. The latter refers more to the quality of one's life, and it includes sociability, enjoyment of life through participation in organized and casual community occasions, and an other-regarding calculus in most things. Afro-Guyanese and Guyanese-Indians hold contrasting images of each other in this regard. Both feel that whatever the other group's ability to make a living, they are woefully bereft of any ability to "make life" – the more substantial and social of the two categories. In a deft arraying of the various ethnic groups, a common stereotype runs as follows: "East Indians live to work, Amerindians work to live, Africans work when all else fails, and Portuguese and Chinese work only long and hard enough to accumulate sufficient capital to let it work for them" (Williams 1991: 56–7).

These stereotypical images are characteristic of many a plantation economy. What they collectively accomplish, as Adamson (1972) points out in a work written at a time when the transcendent idea of class solidarity still held out some hope, is a society marked by division. He notes:

> the real tragedy of post-emancipation Guyanese history is that the common experience was not (could not be?) felt or perceived. Instead it was the divisive aspects of life – ethnic, cultural and economic – that captured the consciousness of all important groups in the colony.
>
> (Adamson 1972: 266)

Or, they exemplify the "plural" society in J.S. Furnivall's sense of the term: a society characterized by stubborn and enduring fractures of various ethnic groups rather than their commingling into community.

The postcolonial dispensation in Guyana, predictably, has carried this fractured inheritance into an enumerated world of democratic politics based on universal franchise and ethnically based ideas of entitlements. There have been instances of ethnic riots and of political breakdowns as the institutions of governmentality give new meaning and content to the divisions of a plantation society. It is literally this world that Shivnaraine Chanderpaul brought with him into the middle when it was finally his turn at bat in the Bourda Oval on 19 March 1994.

Within the boundary of the Bourda

When Chanderpaul walked to the middle that day, the West Indies were already in an impregnable position. Their star batsman, Brian Lara, was just out for a blazing 167 runs studded with twenty-five fours and two sixes, and his team had the English on the run. As one report of the match proceeds to tell it:

> There was an even LOUDER ROAR from the Guyanese crowd as its native son, 19 year old Shivnaraine Chanderpaul strode to the middle. There were signs in the crowd saying "The Little Terror,"

"WI's youngest gun" and "Simply the Best." He looked a little tense and it must have been for this kid ... Critics saying you were a surprise selection. Playing to keep your place knowing that a failure may be your end. His first scoring stroke (a single) was greeted by another roar. But he had the Bourda really ROCKING with his second scoring stroke as he crashed Fraser through backward point for 4.

(Cricinfo Match Report 1994, emphases original)

And it went on and up from there. Chanderpaul compiled a flawless sixty-two runs on his debut. As he reached his half-century, the crowd erupted and play was held up as a section invaded the pitch to convey their congratulations to him personally. Chanderpaul himself was sorely disappointed at not getting to a hundred.

While the entire crowd at the Bourda seemed to embrace him as one of their own at the end of his innings, the situation must have been quite different at the beginning. A quick dismissal, a failure in his inaugural innings, would have immediately energized many a traditional stereotype – that the Indians often flatter to deceive, that they cannot rise to the occasion, that they are susceptible to pressure, that his place really ought to have gone to someone else, and so on. In a sense, it was only as Chanderpaul consolidated his batting during the course of his innings, it was only as he moved through the thirties and forties and toward his half-century, that the crowd at the Bourda began to coalesce behind him as Guyanese. It was only as it became gradually evident that his first innings was something that might be called a success, an occasion worth celebrating, that the "national" identity of Guyanese-ness triumphed over the fragmentary identity of Guyanese-Indian. It was not that his identity was ever a secure and static entity – rather I wish to emphasize the extraordinary mobility and fluidity of his identity position in the course of a single appearance at bat, which lasted a little over two hours.

At the instant of his success, on a superficial gloss it would seem that the Bourda had momentarily escaped the narratives that worlded that encounter. For example, stepping outside a history that has kept the Guyanese from marrying across racial lines, one female voice carried right across the ground as it was heard to say: "If this Chanderpaul think he marry a foreigner he think again!" Her comment could not alter a reality in which women have been the sites on and through which ethnic identity and insularity has often been produced, policed, and reproduced through the taboo against interethnic marriage. Indeed, it is precisely that insular reality produced through gender that makes the female fan's comment a compliment at all. In the suggestion that there ought to be a forgetting of that reality, this woman was bestowing Chanderpaul's inaugural innings with sociopolitical distinction – her comment made the moment extraordinary. Another lady, selling biscuits and sweets by the side of a potholed road, noted that "I like dis boy, he so young and he play all de shots." What was especially signif-icant, according to the reporter, was the fact that both these comments came from the Afro-Guyanese, who also predominated among those who invaded the pitch when he reached his fifty (Roebuck 1994).

It would be tempting to see the incident at the Bourda as a step in the eventual consolidation of Guyana into a tolerant, pacified, and pluralist (in the un-Furnivall sense of the word) nation-state. Such a redemptive hope in the triumph of pluralist nationalism, however, overlooks a simple fact: the very reason Chanderpaul's debut innings at the Bourda Oval acquired signif-icance is the controlled tension that underlay it. It is precisely that it was overdetermined by historical narratives of suspicion, ethnic fragmentation, hostility, stereotypes, mutual recriminations, and uneasy fellowship that gave the moment its charge, its energy, and its explosive potential. The match was poised on a political hair-trigger, an ethnic stand-off was still unfolding in the neighborhood of the cricket ground which rendered the occasion incredibly alive and fraught with both life and danger. And, of course, Chanderpaul's virtuoso performance became all the more appreciable and praiseworthy precisely because of that background. Were Guyana a blank space marked by ethnic commingling, pacified histories, the amica-bility and intermixing of its various fragmented populations, his inaugural test match would not have been the event that it was. What makes it remarkable is precisely what the telos of nationalism, or for that matter any of the other narratives of socialism, neoliberal global modernization, and so on, would seek to deny: that differences are constitutive of our social life, they embed our narratives with meaning and endow our actions with signif-icance. To seek the transcendence or erasure of such antagonistic difference would at some level seek to remove the very stuff that makes our social life both social and living.

In somewhat different ways, Edward Said and Martin Heidegger prize the antagonistic differences that underlie and produce significance in social life. Throughout his *Culture and Imperialism*, Said points out that imperialism was a joint social formation, one that inevitably partook (albeit differen-tially) of the intersecting cultures and to the mutual constitution of both. It was an adversarial and a violent encounter, marked by the dispossession of peoples, their frequent conversion into the homeless and the migrant and the refugee, by racism, and by exploitation. It was inevitably also a process that threw into violent, irreversible, and inescapable contact ways of thinking, writing, making music, painting, governing, and other aspects of aesthetic and material comportment. That encounter was "globalization" – but not in the sanitized and apolitical sense that is now popularly attached to the term. Imperialism and colonialism produced the off-stage of Jane Austen's novels just as much as they underwrote the more febrile brilliance of a Rizal or the supranational imaginings in some of Tagore's prose. Despite the mutual constitutiveness of imperialist and colonized identities, the imperialist imaginary was constructed around notions of racialized, gendered, and cultural difference. But imperialism's greatest victory may yet be denied to it if we refuse the temptation, as a consequence of conquest and reaction, to retreat behind essentialized, static, and singular identities. Or as Said avers,

> No one today is purely *one* thing. Labels like Indian, or woman, or Muslim, or American, are not more than starting-points, which if followed into actual experience for only a moment are quickly left behind. Imperialism consolidated the mixture of cultures and identities on a global scale. But its worst and most paradoxical gift was to allow people to believe that they were only, mainly, exclusively, white, or black, or Western, or Oriental. Yet just as human beings make their own history, they also make their cultures and ethnic identities. No one can deny the persisting continuities of long traditions, sustained habitations, national languages, and cultural geographies, but there seems no reason except fear and prejudice to keep insisting on their separation and distinctiveness, as if that were all human life was about. Survival in fact is about the connections between things ... reality cannot be deprived of the "other echoes that inhabit the garden." It is more rewarding – and more difficult – to think concretely and sympathetically, contrapuntally, about others than only about "us."
>
> (Said 1993: 336, emphasis original)

It is the agonistics of everyday life in postcolonial Guyana that render Chanderpaul's cricketing debut a meaningful occasion for a world of politics. To revel in that moment is not so much a forgetting of politics, or a diminution of the strained histories that connect Guyanese-Indians and Guyanese blacks, but precisely to appreciate the extraordinary politics that underwrites the occasion. It is an unwarranted underestimation of the Guyanese crowd to think that one could predict finally and correctly how they would comport themselves during Chanderpaul's test debut – in large part that would depend on what happened during the course of the game itself. There was a palpable excess of possibilities that day at the Bourda Oval. And if that is not the essence of a sporting encounter, or the essence of politics, I don't know what is.

Conclusion

Heidegger regards this plenitude of histories and possibilities that intersect every moment of existence as the very stuff of being. He is impatient with a moralistic politics that seeks, through a technical and instrumental

181

rationality, to transcend the agonistics of encounter. For what seems at first gloss a "solution" to the human predicament turns out, upon closer examination, precisely the negation of freedom and the possibility of political life. In contrast to the benign and pacifying narrative of the eventually assimilationist nation in a context such as Guyana, Heidegger forces us to not only face up to the worlded narratives that ethnically fragment that space, but to moreover live that reality in the here and the now. Or, as he notes:

> it is not rift as a mere cleft is ripped open; rather, *it is the intimacy with which opponents belong to each other* ... This rift does not let opponents break apart; it brings the opposition of measure and boundary into their common outline.
>
> (Heidegger in Dillon 1996: 56–7, emphasis added)

The narratives that constitute Guyanese-Indians and Guyanese blacks are intertwined, written into each other, and jointly worlded in specific ways. The agonistics of their encounter have produced an intimacy so that each belongs to the other. Resisting the temptation to banalize the differences that constitute them into the assimilative story of the nation, or to drop anchor in a content-less "syncretism," I prefer to regard the intimate enmity of their encounters as the possibility condition for the enactment of politics – a politics that by giving up its quest for a pacific transcendence in the hereafter may perhaps enable us to live in the here and now.

Notes

1 This paper is a preliminary inquiry into a question that I suspect will obsess me for some years to come: in multi-ethnic, postcolonial societies, how does one adjudicate between the competing claims for social justice and fairness between national fragments that are each, in their own way, marked as victims of a history of imperialism, capitalism, and colonialism? I do not offer much by way of an answer here, but I suspect that this could be the central political, social, and economic question faced by postcolonial spaces in the new century. It is time to start thinking seriously about the sort of political comportment that might be appropriate to face this challenge. My thanks, first and foremost, to Randolph Persaud for our many conversations about Guyana, cricket, and race, that impelled me to begin here rather than elsewhere. Thanks are due, as well, to many colleagues for their insights and encouragement, especially Itty Abraham, Michael Shapiro, Konrad Ng, Simon Dalby, Geoffrey Whitehall, and Jon Goldberg-Hiller.
2 Guyana is a former British colony on the northeast shoulder of the South American continent. It is flanked by Venezuela on the west, Surinam on the east, and Brazil to the south. The "West Indies" collectively refers to a group of countries in the Caribbean basin that together constitute an international cricket team. In other words, a cricketer invariably has to first come to national prominence (in Barbados or Guyana or Trinidad or Antigua, etc.) before being selected to play for the multinational West Indian cricket team.

3 One instance of the geographical imaginary that informed the indentured laborers from the subcontinent is especially poignant. A group of them, thoroughly disoriented by the passage and the strange surroundings they found themselves in, deserted the plantations and went off into the uninhabited inland of Guyana – someone had told them that they could find their way back to their villages in India if they did so. This is one indicator of the mental maps that informed these indentured laborers, which certainly bore no resemblance to a modern atlas.

8

THE "NEW COLD WAR"

Secularism, orientalism, and postcoloniality

Shampa Biswas

It is clear that the multiple phenomena now increasingly categorized under the rubric of globalization have both universalizing and fragmenting tendencies. Emphasizing the simultaneity of the homogenizing and heterogenizing thrusts of globalization in the late twentieth-century world, Roland Robertson points to the twin processes embodied in "the particularization of universalism (the rendering of the world as a single place) and the universalization of particularism (the globalized expectation that societies ... should have distinct identities)" (Beyer 1994: 28).[1] It becomes possible through Robertson's analysis to see the universalization of the nation-state as an ideal cultural–political form of collective identity, one aspect of the homogenizing thrusts embodied in "the particularization of universalism," and in that sense very much a product of globalization. The now globalized expectation that nations exist and deserve their states provides the normative foundations for most contemporary international organizations as well as embodying the aspirations and political demands of many disenfranchised people around the world, despite the recent badgering the nation-state has taken from many quarters. It is then perhaps less curious that a vast literature in international relations has accepted so unproblematically this nation-state framework and has been so notoriously oblivious to the constant and ongoing production and reproduction of the nation-state as a unique historical entity. Yet one of the most striking outcomes of this lack of attention to processes of nation and state production has been the neglect of the other side of globalization – the heterogenizing thrusts that Robertson has described as the "universalization of particularism." We live in a world, Robertson claims, in which not only has the "expectation of uniqueness" become institutionalized and globally widespread, but the local and the particular itself is produced on the basis of global norms (Robertson 1995: 28). In other words, the globalization of international norms has produced not just the legitimacy of the idea of the nation-state, but also the expectation that such nation-states should embody unique and distinct identities. But it is only recently with critical constructivist, postmodern, and feminist writing in international relations that identity – and in particular the cultural constitution of particular nation-state forms – has begun to be theorized.

However, despite this neglect of processes of identity-construction, the theoretical commitments of mainstream international relations (IR) to a foundationalist ontology of nation-states have presupposed a particular imaginary of the nation-state *form*. The undertheorized and ahistorical nation-states that inhabit the anarchical "state of nature" within realist IR have drawn on and sustained particular normative conceptualizations or visions of the good life – imaginaries that derive from the developmentalist trajectories and modernization narratives that have undergirded much of the thinking and writing on the history and future of the nation-state.[2] In other words, my contention here is that the expectation that all societies (should) aspire to the nation-state form is then also simultaneously an expectation about the form that such nation-states (should) take – rational, industrial, democratic, and most important for the purpose of this paper, "secular." This is not entirely surprising. Robertson points out that along with the need to assert an identity, the participation of nation-states in the world system and the legitimation of their statehood also encourages states to subscribe to the global norms of secularism. The pressures to conform to a particular nation-state form – that is, a secular form – can of course only be more urgent in the context of the liberalizing and democratizing imperatives of contemporary globalizing forces. If the secularity of the nation-state form has indeed been unspoken and taken for granted in accounts of international relations, it is then clear why the global resurgence of religious nationalisms has elicited a certain amount of incredulity from scholars and commentators on world politics. If the onward march of secularism, so unremarkably accepted by disciplines like international relations and sociology which were beholden to different variants of modernization theory, seems to be suddenly and surprisingly interrupted by this new global upsurge of religion, this surprise is evidence of the epistemological inability to theorize the contradictory pressures emerging from the need to conform to a particular, i.e. secular, nation-state form and to formulate a distinct national identity, the cultural resources of which no doubt often come from religion.

There are two central purposes to this chapter. The first part attempts to examine how deep-seated ontological commitments to a modernization paradigm explain why attempts at explaining the "return" of religion find themselves mired in untenable tradition/modernity binaries and why the sense of alarm and foreboding on the impending "new cold war" generates certain kinds of orientalist anxieties. In addition to a tendency of much of this response to the resurgence of religion to congeal around the "global threat of Islam," many such accounts remain framed by what I call a "reactive epistemology" – explaining religious nationalisms as some form of reactions to modernity – an epistemology that both presupposes and reproduces a troublesome and problematic Western secularism/Eastern fundamentalism ontology. In taking a postcolonial approach to the study of global politics, my purpose is to indicate how certain kinds of representational practices are complicit in the reproduction of international hierarchies.

Problematizing the orientalist biases that emerge from attempts at explaining religion in global politics, the second part of this chapter interrogates the category of "secularism" as it has come to designate a particular and problematic conceptualization of global modernity. It seems clear that contemporary religious nationalisms are in many ways as thoroughly implicated in the modernist project as are contemporary secularist agendas, even when the former speak in the name of an unmodern "tradition." Yet the celebrations of secularism as a marker of a progressive modernity are thereby hardly muted. I claim that such celebrations of secularism derive less from what one might call the "successes" of secular tolerance, and much more so from their association with a particular characterization of modernity – the ideal of a Western liberal-democratic vision that undergirds the ontological commitments of international relations. Yet, as I demonstrate below, it is precisely the imbrication of secularism with the liberal-democratic/national project that reveals its limitations – where religion becomes the arbiter of different and potentially antagonistic political communities, the "problem" of accommodating religious difference within a liberal–secular polity becomes utterly complicated by the workings of structural power, and brings to the fore unsettled conceptions of (religio-)national identity. In other words, the rationalized and de-religionized public domain remains a liberal fantasy in any context where power renders democracy incomplete and the national imagination hegemonic. In Britain, the politicization of a marginal and racialized postcolonial Muslim community has radicalized religio-political differences in a manner that has simultaneously revealed the limitations of British liberalism and secularism. That the chauvinistic and exclusivist Hindu nationalist party currently in power in India calls itself secular reveals both the symbolic resonances of a concept that was critical in the imagination of a liberal, democratic, modern postcolonial India and its perverse operations in the contemporary period. Indeed, that one might draw comparisons between the British and the Hindu Right versions of secularism reveals certain kinds of originary limitations of the liberal-democratic national project in the postcolonial world, despite the hasty prognosis of the "end of history."

If the history and theory of secularism has been so marred by its imbrication with power, can we, and should we, attempt to reclaim its democratic possibilities in the context of the various intolerances and violences that have also been unleashed by the religio-political visions offered by some asecular movements around the world? This is a question taken up in the conclusion to this chapter, which speculates about how one might conceptualize a postcolonial politics of resistance beyond the deconstruction of the essentialized categories that undergird the ontology of international relations.

Responses to the global resurgence of religious nationalisms

At a certain level, it seems clear that religion is back in the reckoning in international politics. New editions of world politics textbooks have found it necessary to add chapters and sections on religion and nationalism. It seems as though the empirical reality of the worldwide resurgence of religion in politics can hardly be overlooked any more. The rising influence of the Christian Right in the United States, the growth of Evangelical and Pentecostal movements in Latin America with various ties to US political interests, the different varieties of Islamist movements in the Middle East, North Africa, sub-Saharan Africa, and parts of South-East Asia, the religionization of the conflict in Bosnia–Herzegovina, the increasing influence of the Orthodox Church in postcommunist Russia, the foray of Hindu nationalism into mainstream politics in India, and the politicization of Buddhism in the anti-Tamil Sinhalese politics of Sri Lanka as well as in Myanmar are just a few prominent examples in a much longer list. This empirical reality led the MacArthur Foundation to fund a six-year American Academy of Arts and Sciences project, called *The Fundamentalism Project*, out of which five volumes of encyclopedic lengths on a number of empirical studies of religious movements in different parts of the world have been produced.[3] How have scholars and journalists thinking and writing on this subject responded to this phenomenon? What kinds of questions are being raised about the role of religion in contemporary international politics?

Secularism and modernization

At one level, there is a certain amount of incredulity associated with the observation that religion is back. Much of social theory based on the modern narrative of progress and reason, whether liberal or Marxist, premised itself on the inevitability of the regression of religion from public/political life. If the Enlightenment principle of secularism that banishes religion away from the public realm of politics had never been as firmly entrenched as expected even in the Western liberal democracies where it took root, many expected this to be a sign of an incomplete modernity that had not fully blossomed worldwide.

> Sociological theory based on the notion of the one-way trajectory is modified only to the extent of admitting that special conditions may *delay* the death of religion. Death may be postponed but not averted. Or, alternatively, sociological theory locates the key element in the one-way trajectory not as outright extinction, but as a marginalization whereby religion is "no more" than a leisure time pursuit.
>
> (Martin 1991: 467)

The presence of religion in public/political life has been dismissed in the social science literature as constituting residual vestiges or isolated reactionary responses. For instance, most early works on political development found religion to be an obstacle to modernization and expected secularization of the modern state to be a prerequisite, and hence inevitable, in the process of modernization and development.[4] But the recent intensification of religious passions, in both the East and the West, has led scholars to question increasingly the inevitability of secularization. This questioning is particularly marked within the discipline of sociology, where scholars have been critiquing the Secularization Thesis, which posited that, in the progressive unfolding of modern history, secularization was to be an accompaniment of modernization.[5] In general, to the extent that these different varieties of modernization theories were premised on the expectation of progressive secularization, the resurgence of religious passions and the increasing intensity of religio-political demands been met with some degree of surprise.

The new cold war

At another level, and particularly marked within accounts of international politics, are those who ask whether the rise of religious nationalisms constitutes a new source of conflict in the post-cold war world. The most prominent here, of course, is Samuel Huntington's work on the rise of civilizational conflicts, in which notwithstanding the confusing array of markers used to designate civilizational boundaries, religious conflict (and in particular the division between the Islamic world and the Christian West) receives clear prominence of place (Huntington 1993).[6] But this question is also raised by several other journalists and scholars, writing at different levels of theoretical sophistication and from different political positions. But what is most interesting about much of these analyses is that even though the conflict is often presented as that between secular versus religious nationalism, the analyses often congeal around the "threat" of Islam. For instance, whether the rise of religious nationalisms portends a new source of global, binary conflict is also raised in Mark Juergensmeyer's book *The New Cold War? Religious Nationalism Confronts the Secular State*, albeit with considerably more nuance than Huntington (Juergensmeyer 1996). Juergensmeyer envisions the possibility of a new cold war in the future which like the old cold war would be "global in its scope, binary in its opposition, occasionally violent, and essentially a difference of ideologies" (Juergensmeyer 1996: 2). This opposition would be between what he at different places describes as "new forms of culture-based politics and the secular state" and "religion in its various forms, and the European and American model of secular nationalism," but in a telling phrase he gives away that it is "the West (now aligned with the secular leaders of the Soviet Union) [that] confronts [this] opposition" (Juergensmeyer 1996: 2–7). By the end of the book, this opposition is much clearer:

[O]ne can foresee the emergence of a united religious bloc stretching from Central and South Asia through the Middle East to Africa. With an arsenal of nuclear weapons at its disposal and fueled by American fear of Islam, it might well replace the old Soviet Union as a united global enemy of the secular West.

(Juergensmeyer 1996: 201)[7]

Like Huntington, Juergensmeyer also approaches this topic from what might be called a Eurocentric perspective, but unlike Huntington's much more defined prognosis for the future and the call for security preparedness in the face of such perceived threats to the West, Juergensmeyer leaves the question a little more open and calls for increased empathy and under-standing to prevent the possibility of a new cold war along religious lines. But to reiterate, despite such differences, there is an interesting (and disturbing) tendency of analyses that find in the rise of religious nation-alisms a new source of global, binary conflict to congeal around the "threat of Islam."[8]

I turn now to the questions that the global resurgence of religious nation-alisms have raised with respect to the issue of "modernity." Much as this resurgence has unsettled the acceptance of the inevitability of secularization, commentators have struggled with the implications of the "anti-modernist" thrusts of religious movements for the progress of modernity. I therefore explore some of the complicated issues that the rise of religious nationalisms has raised with respect to modernity by examining how the rise of religious nationalisms has been explained in the literature. In particular, I would like to highlight the orientalism[9] that undergirds such explanatory attempts.

Explaining religious nationalisms: the orientalism of "reactive explanations"

A large bulk of the literature on religious nationalisms is premised to a large degree on a pejorative and unproblematic construction of such nationalisms as anti-modern or reactionary (reacting to modernity). This is true even in accounts that recognize the connections of contemporary religious move-ments to various modernist projects. Even though it is generally recognized that many such movements are quite adept at the instrumental use of modernity, especially the use of modern technology, religious nationalists are generally seen as anti or pre-modern, with the generally benign and progres-sive character of modernity being assumed even when its problems are identified.

In the five mega-volumes of *The Fundamentalism Project*, Marty and Appleby quite consistently found the central substantive similarity among the various movements covered in the project to be reactive, described at different places as "*reaction* to secular modernity" (Marty and Appleby 1994: 5; emphasis added), *reacting* against "the erosion of traditional society and fighting back against the encroachments of secular modernity" (Marty and Appleby 1995: 6, emphasis added), and being a "religiously inspired *reaction* to aspects of the global processes of modernization and secularization in the twentieth century" (Marty and Appleby 1993a: 2; emphasis added). But more specifically, what are the particular aspects of modernity and modernization that these movements are reacting to or against? The editors of *The Fundamentalism Project* found that fundamentalisms have to be understood as responses to certain aspects of the late nineteenth and twentieth centuries – an "unstable era of rapid urbanization, modernization and uneven rates of development with the withdrawal of Western colonial forces from the third world," the "vulnerability to totalitarian dictators and military regimes," the "social and economic dislocation and deprivation upon migration to the cities," the "conditions of misery and exploitation experienced by millions of subject peoples," the "anonymity of city life," the "weakening of traditional social controls," and the "absence of familiar community values." In their words,

> these conditions of upheaval and disorientation have provided an opening, an undeniable aggregate need, for alternative philosophies, structures, and institutions that would retain certain traditional values even as they reflected adjustments to the potentially overwhelming pace and shape of change.
>
> (Marty and Appleby 1991: 823)

Or as they point out in another place,

> religious fundamentalisms thrive in the twentieth century when and where masses of people living in formerly traditional societies experience profound personal and social dislocations as a result of rapid modernization and in the absence of mediating institutions capable of meeting the human needs created by these dislocations.
>
> (Marty and Appleby 1993b: 620)[10]

Similarly, Emile Sahliyeh, in concluding her introductory chapter on global religious resurgences, says that the "social upheaval and economic dislocation that were associated with modernization led to this renewal of traditional religions" (Sahliyeh 1990: 16).[11] In general, in such accounts, religious nationalisms are presented as (traditionalist) reactions to the dislocations and alienations of modernity. It is this mode of explanation that I term "reactive explanations" here.[12]

If the epistemologies underlying such reactive explanation presuppose a narrative of progressive secularization as part of their commitments to, and

visions of, modernity, it is not surprising to find that explanations of the
return to religion take recourse at least at some level to the tradition/moder-
nity binary. But to understand religious nationalisms as simply "reactive" is
problematic for a number of reasons. At a certain level, these kinds of explanations derive too literally from the rhetoric of such movements, and can be
too easily dismissive of the particular and complicated challenges posed by
them. Clearly, contemporary religious nationalisms contain within them
certain visions of the "modern" that do not have any simple relationship to
unmodern antiquities, and raise certain kinds of moral questions that derive
from and speak to modernity in a host of different ways. Nor is the question
of the distance of such visions from what one might call Euro-modernity so
easily settled. For instance, in addition to the use of modern technology in
the imagination (and dissemination) of contemporary religious communities
are the compromised relations of many such movements with the nation-
state project or to different aspects of global capitalism – whether it is the
Christian Right in the United States or the Hindu Right in India.

But even more significant for my purpose here is the issue of representation, such epistemologies carrying within them particular and problematic
self/other constructions. It seems to me that reactive explanations often tend
to slide into orientalist dichotomies that end up connecting two binaries –
First World/Third World (or West/East) with secularism/fundamentalism –
which leads to the problematic and untenable opposition between "Western
secularism" and "Eastern fundamentalism." It is interesting for instance that
even though the *Fundamentalist Project* attempts to cover a variety of
different empirical case studies spanning several different geographical areas,
the theoretical overviews that attempt to analyze fundamentalisms as reactions to modernity seemed to focus almost exclusively on the Third World.
It seems almost as though, notwithstanding Marty and Appleby's attempts
to think of fundamentalisms as a global issue, their theoretical presuppositions as to the connected binaries of the traditional/modern and Third
World/First World creep into their analysis. For if indeed religious nationalisms are a reaction to modernity, and modernity is a characteristic
primarily of (and from) the West (as those editors do seem to think), then
such movements should perhaps emerge more "naturally" and more widely
in the West.[13] Yet the bulk of the empirical studies in the project are from
the Third World, most notably the Middle East.[14] Hence, religious nationalisms insofar as they exist in the West become peripheral to Western
modernity, but essential to the East.[15]

Further, it seems curious in that light that despite this focus on the third
world, the editors of *The Fundamentalism Project* pay much less explicit theoretical attention to postcoloniality. For if religious nationalisms are to be
understood as anti-modern, the articulation of modernity with postcoloniality is critical in understanding both the emergence and the appeal of
such nationalisms in the Third World. Religion is often the site that

provides the symbolic and mythic resources for the construction of tradition, and if modernity-as-colonialism is to be opposed, religion often proves invaluable in that opposition. Like Marty and Appleby, Ashis Nandy also finds the force of religious nationalisms in South Asian politics in the displacement and alienation that have followed the industrialization and urbanization of "mega-development" in India. In this scenario, Nandy points out, religions provide the "metaphor of continuity" that become "potent myths" in politics (Nandy 1996). This metaphor of continuity, in other words, is a postcolonial means of recuperating a (continuous) tradition in the face of a (disjunctive) modernity. For instance, it can be claimed that the anxieties and dislocations generated by globalization and economic liberalization have created the "conditions of possibility" for the appeal of the culturalist discourse of the Hindu nationalist Bharatiya Janata Party (BJP), which provides this kind of "metaphor of continuity." Yet these conditions of possibility don't provide an adequate explanation of the success of the BJP without understanding the discursive mechanisms through which the party balances the ambivalences that emerge from the contradictory desires for "mimicry" and "authenticity," which are a fundamental aspect of the postcolonial condition. Inevitably, such reactions remain connected to the modernist project in numerous ways, even as they react to modernity. It can be argued, for instance, that the BJP in one sense enables Indians to become modern, but in what it interprets as the Indian way. In other words, the use of religion-as-tradition cannot be understood without analyzing the complex negotiations of such reactions on and with the turf of modernity.

One of the central questions raised in the preface of a special issue of *Daedalus* on "Religion and politics" is

> whether the remarkable capacity of the world religions to survive in very different social settings, and with quite new dimensions and forms, does not attest to the fact that modernity, while influencing all established institutions, cannot destroy those that continue to respond to man's [*sic*] deepest needs, to understand suffering, age, and death, to respond to new societal cravings, but to do so in quite distinctive and different ways?
>
> (*Daedalus* 1991)

Accounts of the world that draw on the tradition–modernity dichotomy always put religion in the former category. Yet if modernity has influenced all established institutions, how can we understand the persistence of religion without understanding how it speaks to, with, and from modernity? Notwithstanding the different levels of theoretical sophistication from which they might be posed, "why religion survives" or "why modernization fails to destroy religion" are questions that ultimately emerge from within a modernization paradigm that is founded on the tradition/modernity dichotomy. One of the most problematic discursive effects of such ontological commitments to developmentalist, modernization narratives is the production of orientalist binaries that reclaim secularism as a marker of a progressive Western modernity, simultaneously condemning both religion and the Third World to a "temporal paucity" or an "essential barbarity." Yet what might we learn from the history of secularism as a liberal-democratic modern project? The next section interrogates the category of secularism as it has come to designate a particular characterization (and celebration) of progressive modernity.

Rethinking secularism

Secularism raises the issue of the proper relationship of religion and politics in modern societies, and its birth as a principle of good government is often traced to the Enlightenment period of European history and its displacement of the authority of the Church in matters of political governance. In the narrative of progressive modernity, the separation of religion from politics (and science) forms one of the constituting principles of the modern condition. The sense of alarm that religious claims to identity cause is partly because such claims are seen to transgress the "legitimate" sphere of religion in modern polities (in the private realm), which the idea of secularism defines and hence constitutes. Jose Casanova points out that in a sense the principle of secularism is constitutive of modernity (1992). According to Casanova, as "inaccurate as it may be as an empirical statement, to say that 'religion is a private affair' is nonetheless constitutive of Western modernity in a dual sense." First, since religious freedom, in the sense of freedom of conscience, is chronologically the first freedom, and freedom of conscience is intrinsically related to the right to privacy (in the institutionalization of a private sphere free from government and ecclesiastical intrusions), it serves as the precondition of all modern freedoms, and hence constitutes the very foundations of modern liberalism and modern individualism. Second, the privatization of religion also refers to the process of institutional differentiation (the separation of the economy and the sphere of politics from ecclesiastical control) that is constitutive of modernity (Casanova 1992: 17–18). Secularism here refers to the "privatization" of religion – not that traditional religions lose all social salience (in directing individual lives, behaviors, beliefs), but that they lose public salience as they are relocated to the private sphere.[16]

It is not uncommon to accept unproblematically the success of this privatization of religion in Western liberal democracies. For instance, Marty and Appleby conclude their third volume in *The Fundamentalism Project* on the note that the institutionalization of the public/private distinction, and more importantly the privatization of religion in Western democracies, makes "fundamentalism ... less likely to dictate the course of national self-definition" (1993b: 640).[17] The taken-for-granted articulation of Western democracy with secularism underlies many accounts and commentaries on religion and politics. However, even if this articulation of secularism with modern democracy can be taken as self-evident, the extent to which the formal separation of religion from politics can restrain the actual influence of religion on politics is questionable.[18]

Now, even if Western secularism is in general accepted as a given, the United States is one case that has always intrigued scholars and problematized that assumption. The question of the religious identity of the "American nation" has clearly marked public debates about immigration, alcohol consumption, sabbath observance, and especially public education, so that Kenneth Wald wrote that religion functions as a "silent cleavage" in American politics (Wald 1991). Based on the consistently high-church religiosity and the resilience of religious organizations in the United States, sociologists such as Andrew Greely have been some of the first to argue strongly against what he called the "secularization myth" (Greely 1972). Greely argued that religion has always fulfilled certain essential needs of the human condition, and even with the institutional separation of different spheres in modern society, religion continued to have significant social and individual relevance. Coming from the functionalist school within sociology, the conceptualization of Robert Bellah's "civil religion" in formally secular states was an attempt to show that religion in the modern world does not disappear, so much as it is transformed (Bellah 1992).[19] Rather than banishing religion from the public, public religions take new cultural forms. In such an analysis, religion is an institution that performs a socially integrative function by creating the normative consensus that holds a society together. As Bellah has pointed out, the religious accent of secularism in the United States, as evidenced in the inaugural speeches of presidents and the rhetoric of other public speakers and the religious nature of public ceremonies, provides religious legitimacy for the state and gives nationalism a religious aura.[20] It seems to me that it may be useful to understand the recent resurgence of the Christian Right in US politics as deriving from this religiously inflected (even if politically marginalized) space. The articulation of Christianity with the American way of life in the Christian Right discourse can only resonate if one understands the invisible religious undertone of secular US politics.

Some scholars believe that the secularization thesis holds only for Europe. Critiquing the "tendency to identify the truly modern moment as what occurs in Western Europe" so that other places exhibiting vigorous religiosity are somehow behind, David Martin points out that secularization was a product of the specific historical circumstances obtaining in the battle between the Church and Enlightenment in Europe, and the sociological model of secularization best applies to Europe (Martin 1991: 466). Hence, even though non-European contexts (and he includes examples from North America, Latin America, and the Middle East) are influenced by the European experience, they are not determined by it, and should not be expected to follow some universal social logic encapsulated in the European experience.[21] Similarly, Peter Berger points out that even though the world today is massively religious, with vigorous upsurges of conservative religions worldwide, Western Europe, with its "massively secular Euro-culture," is an apparent exception where the secularization thesis does hold (Berger 1996–7).[22]

However, the very exceptions that these authors are forced to note (see notes 21 and 22) suggest the inadequacy of holding rigidly to the secularization thesis, rather than looking at the specific and different ways that religion and politics are articulated in different socio-historic situations. Roland Robertson points out that rather than taking literally the term "separation" (of the Church and state) one needs to examine the "structure of conjuncture," which means "paying attention to the ways in which church and state are coordinated" (Robertson 1987a: 9).[23] The theme of civil religion has been one way of conceptualizing this conjuncture, and even though it has usually been applied to Western societies, most notably the United States in which Christianity has been the dominant religious tradition, this is also true of other formally secular contexts such as India, where a dominant religion coexists with a variety of other religions. Similarly, Talal Asad has pointed out that the

> separation [of religion from the state] has always involved links between 'religion' on the one hand and public knowledge, moral identity, and political processes on the other (varying, of course, from one Western country to another). It is not just that the separation ('secularization') has been incomplete, but that even in Western liberal societies 'modernized religion' and 'secular culture' have supported each other in crucial, if often indirect, ways.
>
> (Asad 1992: 3)

Hence, it is important to look at how secularism has been articulated in particular socio-historic circumstances, and how the principle of religious tolerance that underlies secularism has fared in practice in the presence of visible religious minorities.

Let us first look at the West European context. Of the many religious groups in different parts of Western Europe, Islamic minorities have clearly problematized the taken-for-granted tolerance of European secularisms. Starting in particular with the large-scale migrations of postcolonial populations to meet the labor needs for the reconstruction of post-World War II Europe, the Muslim presence in contemporary Western Europe has become both more permanent and visible. There are now sizable settler Muslim communities from the Middle East, Africa, and Asia in many West European countries, with some cities like Bradford in Britain and Marseilles in France seeing the increased participation of Muslim groups in local politics.[24] The salience of the "Islamic issue" in Europe arises not merely from the growing physical presence of Muslims, but from the concrete demands that Muslims, organized largely in mosque institutions, have increasingly come to place on the state – demands for provisions for burial procedures, worship times and places, ritualistic animal slaughter, education of children, and so on. Institutionalized measures for ensuring the building of mosques,[25] slaughtering in the ritually prescribed way,[26] and having schoolgirls exempted from coeducation classes have been demanded and to some extent met. Such demands have also encountered great resistance, but much more significantly this resistance is expressed in terms of a challenge to "core" (read Christian) national values, and is taken as indicative of the marginal relation of ethnic and religious minorities to mainstream national values.

The "Rushdie affair"[27] in Britain was one particularly contentious and internationalized instance of the numerous episodes within Western European nation-states involving Muslims that have brought into prominence cultural issues of national identity. If the politicization of Islam within Britain could at all be ignored until then, the Rushdie affair made the religious identity of ethnic minorities an irreversibly political question, revealing the fissures and gaps in a taken-for-granted British secularism, by bringing the issue of religious difference into the center of political debate. At a most basic level, the Rushdie affair revealed some of the ambiguities of British secular law, as for instance with respect to the blasphemy laws that protect Anglican Christianity, but not other religious communities. At the time of the Rushdie affair a demand for the extension of these laws to Muslims met with at least one clearly articulated Conservative position that argued against the extension on the grounds that Britain was essentially Christian.[28] During the height of the Rushdie controversy, newspapers and television almost unanimously condemned the "fundamentalism" of Britain's Muslims[29] – the general brandishing of Muslims as intolerant and fanatical spanned the political spectrum in the popular press, and the entire debate became centered around the "fit" of Muslims into a (Christian) liberal society, sometimes with Christian tolerance clearly juxtaposed against Muslim intolerance (Parekh 1990; Asad 1993). Rather than raise legitimate questions about the role of religion in public life, this response to the Rushdie affair raised two kinds of questions, both of which reflect the limits of British secularism. First, questions raised about the incompatibility of Islam with Western liberalism makes one ask whether compatibility is always rendered problematic in the face of radical difference. On the face of it, there is no reason why Muslim demands (for the ban on publication, for the extension of blasphemy laws) could not be accommodated by the British state, or more importantly, why such demands, even when they could not be accommodated, should be seen as external to a liberal-democratic political system. Second, and related to raising questions on the place of Muslims and Islam in a Christian and post-Christian society, the response to the Rushdie affair clearly revealed the cultural core that lies at the heart of a secular–liberal national imagination, so that the "otherness" of Muslims became constituted as the radical difference that raised the first question of compatibility. In bringing up the question of the place of non-European religious and cultural minorities in the context of a secular hegemony, the significance of the Rushdie affair lies in pointing to the limits of a taken-for-granted British secularism. Not only did this episode reveal the gaps in the existing secular legal structure, but, much more telling, it brought into prominence the Christian face of British secular hegemony within which Muslims and Islam remained cultural others.

However, the Western secularism/Eastern fundamentalism framework not only fails to problematize the questionable articulation of the West and secularism, but also leaves no epistemological space for understanding the forms of secularism (and their own perversions) that exist in the non-West.[30] It might be easy, for instance, to dismiss the contemporary prominence of Hindu nationalism in India to a failed secularism, revealing some basic, backward, traditional Indian-Hindu religiosity lurking beneath an imposed secularist veneer. The uncertain terrain marked out by the secular Congress party which held state power for most of India's postcolonial history before the BJP came to power – sometimes clearly revealing its Hindu face and at other times manipulating religious issues for narrow partisan interests – already makes any accomplishments of Indian secularism somewhat suspect. Yet it is also unquestionable that the postcolonial imagination of India as a "liberal-democratic/secular" nation-state has lodged Indian secularism quite securely both within the existing political discourse and in at least one dominant version of the Indian common sense (Madan 1993).[31] In other words, secularism is very much a part of the existing political vocabulary in India with a certain resonance in the Indian political idiom, especially among the Indian middle classes, and frames much of the imagination of "modern India" among these groups. Part of this resonance comes from the articulation of secularism to a liberal-democratic discourse that is seen as just, progressive, and modern. At the same time, secularism also functions as an ideological anchor in the Indian imagination that enables the distinction of "tolerant" India from its authoritarian, military, and religiously "intolerant" Islamic neighbors in Pakistan and Bangladesh, and thus helps demarcate and constitute the "Indian self" from its own "barbaric others."

Hence it is the case that in more than half a century of postcolonial Indian nationalism, secularism has been successfully articulated to the Indian "nation" within a liberal-democratic discursive framework, from which its unsuturing becomes difficult at best and politically futile at worst. Even the BJP – the Hindu nationalist party currently wielding governmental power – cannot forsake the claim to secularism without impairing its political image. It is not unsurprising, then, that the BJP – whose antipathy to minority religious communities in India is hardly in doubt – claims to be a secular party, rejecting what it names as the alien and anti-Hindu "pseudo-secularism" of prior governments, and claiming the essential tolerance of Hinduism as a cultural resource for its own version of "positive secularism." However, that the category of secularism is not rejected is not simply a cunning manipulation of a political symbol. Without dislodging the critical articulation of secularism with the imagination of the Indian nation-state, the BJP rearticulation of secularism is simultaneously the reproduction of a modern identity and a renewed process of othering – a rearticulation made possible only by tapping into a larger common sense among middle- and upper-class Hindus in India about the cultural core (read Hindu) of India and a prejudice about the democratic, pluralistic, and tolerant thrusts of Hinduism *vis-à-vis* Islam and Muslims. That the "self" of Indian secularism has always existed by virtue of the "other" of Islamic fundamentalism has made possible what is the more clearly chauvinistic and intolerant version of BJP secularism.

The category of secularism, carrying with it the authorizing signature of the West, has been used to mark out, condemn, and constitute the Third World as the space of an unmodern religiosity – whether it be the British liberals responding to the Muslim "fanatics" in the wake of the Rushdie affair, or the BJP secularists celebrating their modernity *vis-à-vis* Pakistanis or Indian Muslims. Indeed, it has been done in the name of, and in defense, of tolerance and justice – the normative commitments of a progressive modernity and history. But clearly therein lie the dogmas and exclusions that have been carried by secularism itself – not only marginalizing all those diverse peoples, modes of being and living, and visions of utopia that remain inflected with religious orientations, but also denying the possibilities of being secular in ways not transcribed through a discourse of Enlightenment rationality. The imbrication of secularism with an impoverished liberal-democratic/national project that remains impervious to the operations of power clearly renders it suspect. Any simple demarcation of public secularity from a private religiosity can hardly be expected to settle the exclusions of vulnerable religious minorities (the real problem of democracy) or make the nation representative (the question of religion in national identity). Yet secularism as the signifier of a liberal-democratic/national project of modernity continues to bear the badge of honor, a pride of place that also then allows it to exclude and hierarchize. This is what calls us to rethink secularism.

Religious othering through race, class and gender

As inadequate as it may be epistemologically, the reproduction of the Western secularism/Eastern fundamentalism binary yet serves interests and carries material consequences at many different levels. It is clear that the discursive processes of othering explored in this chapter are marked by the multiple intersections of race, class, and gender. It may be argued for instance that the prejudices of Western secularism make religion a new kind of racio-cultural marker – whether it be in marking out the bodies of an immigrant underclass of color in the New Europe or in marking out the contemporary face of underdevelopment, i.e. those not yet assimilated to, or those marginalized by, the current trends of globalization. As demonstrated with respect to the Rushdie affair, and as evidenced in the increasing severity of European immigration regulations for people of color, the question of Islam's ability to co-exist with secular/liberal-democratic principles has become yet another state device to enforce racial exclusions. It is no accident that the signifier "immigrant" still signifies "black" in a Britain where most immigrants are in reality white, and where most blacks called immigrants are in reality British-born (see Gilroy 1993). In the United States, the image of the Islamic terrorist that has become well entrenched in everyday common sense through the media and popular culture has made the Arab-American population particularly vulnerable to nationalist frenzy during moments of crisis (see Said 1997). Hence, the immediate aftermath of the Oklahoma bombing saw on the one hand the extremely irresponsible speculation by political leaders and journalists on the Middle-Eastern characteristics of the event and explanations for Islamic Jihad in the United States, and on the other hand, and partly as a result, cases of abuse and violence directed at ordinary Arabs and Arab-Americans, not unlike the ones unleashed during the Gulf War.

While gender has not been an explicit part of the analysis of this chapter, it is also clear that the secularism/fundamentalism divide has often signified the celebrations of Western modernity via a measure of the position of women. For instance, it is the sign of the "woman in veil" that still marks the face of backward patriarchy, masking the myriad of gendered and racialized practices and effects of contemporary (secular) globalization – the feminized labor force of color of export-promotion transnationalism, the feminization of Third World poverty as a result of structural adjustment programs, the new modes of commodification of Third World women's bodies and sexualities as in the sex-tourism industry, and so on. The veil as a signifier of Muslim women's oppression has had a very long history in the imagination of the West, symbolizing in Western eyes "the most visible marker of the differentness and inferiority of Islamic societies" and has functioned as a powerful symbol for a variety of colonialist, nationalist, and feminist interventionist projects (Ahmed 1992: 152). Uma Narayan has suggested that while practices affecting women have always served the process of defining "the Self *in contrast* to the Other" in colonial encounters,

> [p]ractices affecting women that involve a significant measure of
> the "spectacular" (such as *sati*) or a significant amount of "hidden-

ness" (such as the seclusion of women in the *zenana*, *purdah* and veiling) seem to provoke a special interest and fascination in the projects of contrasting cultural self-definition.

(Narayan 1997: 66)

Contemporary representations of Muslim women in the veil, not uncommon in the Western media and commentary, only bolster the image of the "liberated First World" woman *vis-à-vis* the "oppressed Third World woman" – a combined product of gendered and racialized difference as has been pointed out so well by Chandra Mohanty. These representations not only efface the multiple meanings of the veil as understood by veiled Muslim women, but also conceal the less spectacular and hence many mundane varieties of modern–secular gender oppressions that continue to exist (Mohanty 1991b). Just as the feminization of factory labor in off-shore multinational production can be individually empowering while structurally exploitative for Third World women, the veil has been adopted by Muslim women for a variety of reasons that are not reducible to the state-enforced coerced veiling (or de-veiling) in many other situations. Yet in the secularism/fundamentalism binary the Third World woman, determined and oppressed by religious fundamentalism, can only be rescued through secular modernity, rather than seeing such interventions as what Leila Ahmed in a different context called "the substitution of the garb of Islamic-style male dominance for that of Western-style male dominance" (Ahmed 1992: 161).

Orientalist constructions that continue to treat religion as an atemporal, essential, static realm of backward patriarchy, implicitly if not explicitly, rely on a Western-style secular modernity, usually imagined along liberal-democratic lines, as the harbinger of racial and gender equality. Yet, it is these very constructions that mark out new exclusions, and are deployed in new exclusionary ways – exclusions with clear racial and gendered implications. Neither religion nor secularism, as they take political shape within particular socio-historic conditions, are devoid of the traces of race, class, and gender. But the Western secularism/Eastern fundamentalism binary, and the progressivist teleology that undergirds it, masks and indeed reproduces a racialized and gendered construction of the Third World that has real material effects for people of color in the First and the Third World.

Conclusion

There is no dearth of scholarship and commentary on world politics now announcing that "religion is back." Not only is the empirical reality of the worldwide upsurge of religion in politics increasingly recognized, but there are some who have called this upsurge "the new cold war." However, an analysis of the scholarship and commentary on the new cold war reveals the orientalist biases that frame such analyses – the celebrations of (Western) secularism as a marker of a progressive modernity are made possible through the simultaneous constructions and denunciations of (Third World) fundamentalisms. Such analytical predispositions are reflective of deep-seated ontological and epistemological commitments to modernization and developmentalist frameworks of analyses – commitments that undergird much of what is taken for granted in international relations orthodoxy.

Much of this chapter has focused on the issue of representation as it pertains to accounts of religion in global politics. The production of knowledge through which the Third World once again is condemned to an unmodern barbarity is clearly reflective of the operations of power in a postcolonial world. Darby and Paolini point to the impoverished conceptualization of power in international relations orthodoxy, despite the prominent status assigned to the analysis of power in the relations among states (Darby and Paolini 1994). However, even critical-postmodern approaches to IR with their focus on representational and discursive power have been curiously inattentive to the Third World.[32] This paper has looked at the production of international hierarchies through the representational practices of communities of scholars and commentators writing on religion in global politics, pointing to the ontological and epistemological commitments shared and reproduced through this process. However, to focus on representational devices in the reproduction of hierarchies is not to ignore or underestimate the material and structural bases of international power. Indeed, it is the very existence of such material inequities in the global distribution of economic and political resources – inequities being notoriously widened in the current context of economic globalization (the final triumph of the modernization paradigm?) – that makes it imperative to focus on the cultural and discursive processes through which such inequities are sustained and reproduced. Discursive processes of "othering" have very real effects, and these must be revealed and resisted.

The Western secularism/Eastern fundamentalism binary that frames much of the writing and thinking analyzed here is problematic because both fundamentalisms and secularisms exist in Western industrial democracies as they do in the postcolonial world – each taking different hues and shapes in different contexts. To take the postcolonial notion of "hybridity" seriously would be to pay more attention to the complexities of the modern condition as found in an increasingly interconnected (but unequal) world. But the celebrations of (Western) secularisms are also problematic because it has been the very imbrication of secularism with the liberal-democratic/national project, along with their mutual articulation with a certain vision of progressive modernity, that has also rendered its workings suspect – an issue demonstrated with the British and Indian cases mentioned above. A postpositivist approach to IR might then possibly see the project of secularism as one more grand, totalizing, Enlightenment narrative that simultaneously enables and renders invisible a whole host of exclusions and marginalizations

– of the Third World, of religious minorities within secular hegemonies, and religiously inspired or asecular visions of the good life. I see this deconstructionist stance implicit in any postpositivist approach – questioning and problematizing the discursive presuppositions and teleological narratives underpinning a discipline – as critical to a postcolonial approach to IR, carrying within it a radical and subversive position that is inherently political.

Yet one is confronted at once with the politically urgent task of recognizing the exclusions and marginalizations (against religious minorities, women) that also lie at the heart of many different religiously inspired political visions – whether they be Christian, Islamic, Hindu, or Buddhist. My purpose in highlighting the epistemic violence conducted via the celebrations of secularism is not then to privilege that over the physical violence and other exclusions effected in the name of religious nationalisms around the world. To point out that religion has become the way to mark the Third World (or any non-rationalist, asecular version of modernity) as the site of otherness is not to condone the forms of intolerances committed in the name of religion, whether in the First or the Third World. Wherever such intolerances exist, they must surely be resisted, a resistance only more urgent in the context of the violences that have also accompanied the resurgence of religion around the world.

Can the category of secularism be used as a tool of such resistance? How might the democratic potentialities of the category be excavated against the violences of religiously based movements and orders? Here I find the concept of "strategic essentialism" as theorized by many scholars – postcolonial, post-Marxists, feminists, and others – very useful (see Krishna 1993). To the extent that secularism can be deployed as a political-oppositional category, contingently and strategically, to resist the effects of power, there are surely grounds for its deployment. For instance, it makes political sense for Muslims in Britain to seek certain kinds of legal protections from the state in the name of secularism, as it does for activists in India resisting the rising influence of the BJP to lay claim to a certain vision of the secular. Here, the association of secularism with the ideals of justice and democracy can be a resource of resistance. But to fix this category in the name of, or for the purpose of, resistance must be done provisionally and contingently, recognizing the dogmatisms, exclusions, and violences that have also occurred in and through secularism. Trying to carve out a new political space between or beyond what he calls the "the conceits of secularism" and forms of religious or theocratic dogmatisms, William Connolly has recently suggested "not to eliminate secularism, but to convert it into one perspective among several in a pluralistic culture" (Connolly 1999: 11).[33] Indeed it seems to me that political circumstances in many parts of the world make it necessary to both retain some notion of secularism, and simultaneously guard against its hegemonizing effects in the context of power.

Notes

1 See also Chapter 6 ("The universalism–particularism issue") in Robertson (1992). In his more recent work, Robertson has offered the concept of "glocalization" to emphasize this simultaneity. See also Robertson (1995).

2 Darby and Paolini seem to point to this co-construction of international relations theory and modernization theory in suggesting that "the discipline (of IR) was shaped by the interests and ideals of the Enlightenment, and ... has been deeply involved in the global elaboration of Western reason and modernity," modernity, as they point out, being "deeply implicated in the nation-state and development projects" (Darby and Paolini 1994: 390).

3 See Martin E. Marty and R. Scott Appleby (eds), volumes 1–5 (1991–5). Even though the project claims to be global in scope, the emphasis on the Middle East across the volumes is unmistakable.

4 See Donald Eugene Smith (1970) for one of the most systematic comparative accounts of the process of secularization that accompanies the process of political development in the course of modernization. Smith draws on the work of scholars like Lucian Pye and Gabriel Almond who posited that differentiation and specialization of social and political spheres was a prerequisite for modernization and development, which leads to the assumption that "religion is in general an obstacle to modernization" (Smith 1970: xi). In the face of the contemporary surge of religious movements, Smith continues to emphasize the limits of religious resurgences, claiming that the contemporary reality is less of a generalized religious resurgence and more a part of a cyclical movement that will eventually witness a downswing (see Smith 1990). For a brief and general survey of the literature on political development, and in particular for an account of the diminishing role of religion in modernization theory, see Wuthnow (1991).

5 For a well-known early statement of secularization theory within sociology see Peter Berger (1967). Related to his work (with Thomas Luckmann) on the social construction of reality, Berger argued that religion as a type of overarching symbolic universe (a meaning-system) can provide integration, legitimation, and most important, meaning, to the chaos, complexity, tragedy, injustice, and uncertainty of "everyday reality." Yet he argued that as modern (industrial capitalist) society became structurally differentiated and rationalized, it set in motion an irreversible process of secularization (both at the level of consciousness or "subjective secularization" and at the social-structural level or "objective secularization"). Further secularization also sets in motion "pluralism" (or "demonopolization") and the competitiveness of the market leads to the "bureaucratic rationalization" and commodification of religions, which in its turn contributes to the "crisis of credibility" of religions in modern societies as the authority of established religions to provide integration, legitimation, and meaning declines. For a good overview and critique of Berger's views on religion and secularization, see Wuthnow (1986). But more recently, Berger has himself come to question his earlier work, arguing now that the secularization theory to which he himself contributed, was "essentially mistaken." See for instance Berger (1996–7). See Hadden and Shupe (1989) for a very good collection of essays that question secularization theory from several different perspectives. For a review of theories on secularization, see Casanova (1984). For an early critique of the secularization thesis based on the persistence of American religiosity, see Greely (1972). For an attempt to rework secularization theory in the light of religious resurgences, see Chaves (1994).

6 Huntington's article was clearly an attempt to substitute the old cold war paradigm with a new post-cold war one. In his words, "Civilizations are the natural successor to the three worlds of the Cold War" (Huntington 1993: 187).

7 In the very next paragraph, Juergensmeyer went on to add that

> [s]uch a conflict might be compounded by the rise of new religious radicals in Europe and the United States, including not only politically active Christians but also members of newly immigrant communities of Muslims, Hindus, and Sikhs who might support their comrades at home. A nascent cult of cultural nationalists in Japan and elsewhere in the Far East might also be in league with what could become the West's new foe.
>
> (Juergensmeyer 1996: 201)

It is still interesting that all of these religious radicals, regardless of where they are located, would be the *West*'s new foe.

8 Why this rise of religious nationalisms might take a cold war form is less thoroughly analyzed by most scholars who point to the emergence of a new cold war along religious nationalist lines. This "global threat of Islam" scenario recurs with some regularity in the popular media, and sometimes shows up in the public pronouncements of state leaders and policymakers in the West. It is important to point out here that there have always been critical voices in the Western academy and the media that have also resisted this demonization of Islam. John Esposito (1992) has been one of the most consistent and vocal voices in this group. In general, the critiques take several different expressions. There are those who argue that Islam is expansionary only within the *umma* (the community of believers) and seeks neither confrontation, nor domination of the non-Muslim world. See for instance, Karabell (1996). There are others who argue that Islamic fundamentalism lacks the military or economic strength to pose a threat to the Western world. See for instance Rubinstein (1994). *The Economist* has taken a fairly conventional complex-interdependence approach in downplaying the significance of an Islamic threat and arguing for the need to build better trade relations and economic ties with Middle Eastern and other Muslim countries, as well as urging Muslim countries to liberalize and democratize. See "Living with Islam" (Economist 1995b) and "Islam and the West" (Economist 1994b); both cover stories explicitly attack the Islamic threat argument. John Esposito, through his numerous writings and public lectures, has perhaps done the most in empirically discrediting the notion of a monolithic Islam in the Western media, and has pointed to the many differentiations among Islamic organizations, movements, countries, and cultures. See also Piscatori (1986) for a similar critique of the threat of Islam. The book by *New York Times* foreign correspondent Judith Miller (1996) makes a similar point about the heterogeneity of Islamic movements in the Middle East, but remains framed by, and serves to reproduce, many orientalist stereotypes.

9 My use of the concept of orientalism is drawn from Edward Said's (1979) groundbreaking work on the construction of the East through the representational devices of Western canonical literature.

10 I would like to point out, though, that as far as these different volumes of *The Fundamentalism Project* are concerned, this is less a critique of individual chapters, some of which are quite theoretically sophisticated, but more of the overall theoretical framework within which the project is situated, as laid out in the editorial commentaries in each of the volumes.

11 It is interesting that an account such as Emile Sahliyeh's which attempts to correct such reactive explanations does not seem to move significantly beyond that framework. Sahliyeh proposed "to advance a more sophisticated explanation to the phenomenon of religious resurgence," by moving "beyond viewing religious renewal as being primarily a response to grievances and deprivations" (1990: 300). The combination of four factors that she listed as part of this explanatory framework include: (1) the failure of secular ideologies to provide solutions to socioeconomic and political problems; (2) the uneven impact of economic modernization within and among Third World countries in exacerbating poverty and unemployment; (3) outside threats to group identity and political integrity; and (4) the availability of organizational resources for effective mobilization (see her "Religious resurgence and political modernization" and "Concluding remarks"). The first three in the list clearly seem part of a reactive explanation and the fourth does not significantly move us beyond that level by focusing almost entirely on an instrumental use of modernity.

12 The reactive nature of such explanations is also evidenced to a degree in the definitions of modernity in such analyses. The question of "what is modernity" is rarely, if ever, addressed in most studies of religious nationalisms. For Marty and Appleby, modernity by default is whatever fundamentalists claim to oppose. Hence to whoever "listens to the rhetoric of the ayatollahs, rabbis, priests, and pastors who call attention to religion and who often exploit it, 'modernity' is a kind of code word for any of the erosive forces that threaten self-identity" (Marty and Appleby 1997: 9) or modern "is a code word for the set of forces which fundamentalists perceive as the threat which inspires their reaction" (Marty and Appleby 1991: vii). It is interesting that in introducing the first volume the editors clarified that "[m]odern cultures include at least three dimensions uncongenial to fundamentalists: a preference for secular rationality; the adoption of religious tolerance with accompanying tendencies toward relativism; and individualism" (Marty and Appleby 1991: vii). Yet these three aspects do not receive much theoretical explication in the rest of the volumes.

13 Regardless of the genealogies and historical origins of particular modernist projects, I find the conflation of modernity with the West problematic. Here I find Eric Wolf's (1997) monumental work on the study of modern (capitalist) history through understanding the mutual encounters of the European and non-European worlds (without erasing questions of power) quite illuminating. In exploring the contemporary resurgence of Islam worldwide in the context of globalization, Pasha and Samatar (1997) also emphasized the need to move away from Eurocentrism by locating the place of Islam in the "coconstruction of globality." In other words, my own analysis is sympathetic to understanding modernity as global, shaped by a variety of different interactions in different parts of the world, but influenced by multiple and overlapping levels (from local to global) of power hierarchies.

14 This is not an empiricist argument about indicating bias through counting the number of cases devoted to a particular topic, but rather is a larger claim about epistemology that enables writers to see the world in particular ways (where does religion exist?) and pick cases accordingly. While many works on global religious nationalisms have tended to focus overwhelmingly on the Middle East, David Westerlund (1996) attempted to redress the balance by bringing together articles that look at the rise of religious nationalisms in North and Central America, Europe, Africa, and Asia. Yet it is interesting to see that the authors of the different articles in the book often got caught up in the attempt to differentiate Christian fundamentalism from anti-secularist movements in other religions.

15 Even a book such as Mark Juergensmeyer's, which pays close attention to the self-descriptions of religious nationalists in the Third World and is conscious of the many modernist aspects of such movements, ultimately remains wedded to this secularist/fundamentalist–East/West dichotomy. It is common for journalistic commentary on Third World religious nationalisms to reflect this East/West dichotomy – whether it be the "centuries-old hatreds of Hindus and Muslims" in the coverage of Hindu fundamentalism in India or the "fanatical Islamic terrorists" in the coverage of elections in Algeria. Islam in particular continues to receive this kind of journalistic treatment.

16 See Casanova (1992) for an excellent discussion on the variety of ways in which the public/private distinction is drawn with respect to religion. Casanova pointed out that since the liberal conception of politics tends to confuse state, public, and political, the disestablishment of religion is understood and prescribed as privatization as well as depoliticization. He has also drawn on the feminist critique of the public male/private female split to show how the historical process of the privatization of religion is a process of feminization in which religion (and morality), exempt from public rationality, is consigned to the sentimentalized sphere of the private (see especially pp. 20–37).

17 This is immediately contrasted with the lack of such distinctions in Islamic thought.

18 When thinking of the relation between religion and politics, most analyses remain tied to the dichotomy between secularism and theocracy. Sometimes, a third category is added to accommodate the "gray areas." For instance, Hallencreutz and Westerlund (1996) made distinctions between a "confessional policy of religion" (where a particular religious tradition or community is politically privileged, and religion and politics are in close interaction, this including theocracies such as Iran), the "secular policy of religion" (which presupposes at least a formal separation of the religion and the state, with individual and corporate religious freedoms granted to more or less extent), and the "generally religious policy on religion" (where the state is guided by religion, but not institutionally attached to any particular religion, such as in Indonesia).

19 The title of Bellah's book *The Broken Covenant* reveals his belief in the continuing erosion of religious and moral values in American society in the face of the rational, technical, utilitarian ideology of self-interest.

20 The institutionalization of this norm is evidenced in the decision in the 1950s to amend the Pledge of Allegiance to refer to the United States as "one nation under God." But this concept of "civil religions" has been looked at differently by other authors. In Robertson's analysis for instance, civil religions have to do with identity issues experienced by formally secularized societies. In his words, the "globally legitimated secular state," even though lacking the "aura of the genuinely sacred," and with religion being constitutionally denied, has often, even if unintentionally, drawn religious interests into it to give expression to its particularistic identity (Robertson 1987a: 43–7).

21 But, as he pointed out in the course of the article, there are three factors that qualify the applicability of the secularization thesis even to Europe. On the one hand, the particular historical conditions that gave birth to the principle of secularization in Europe no longer obtain in contemporary Europe, and with the discrediting of liberal and Marxist views of history, perhaps a new kind of space for religiosity is opening up. Second, even within Europe, major national communities or subnational communities that had experienced alien and external rule had often found their major resource and source of identity in historic faiths. This is true for instance in the cases of Poland and Ireland, and in the Basque country, Croatia, and Brittany. Third, similar to the second group

are the new migrant Muslim communities in contemporary Europe (Martin 1991: 465–74). One could add to this list the protracted conflict in Northern Ireland.

22 But even he recognized the survival of religion in Western Europe, mostly Christian, despite widespread alienation from organized churches, which to him indicates "a shift in the institutional location of religion, rather than secularization" (Berger 1996–7: 8). He also pointed to an international subculture composed of "secularized" people with Western-type higher education, especially in the humanities and social sciences, that even though a minority, are very influential, and provide the official definitions of reality (through the education system, the media of mass communication, and the legal system). Hence, he pointed out, religious upsurges "have a strongly populist character," being also "movements of protest and resistance *against* a secular elite," sharing a "globalized *elite* culture" (Berger 1996–7: 8).

23 In his words, "for if church and state were truly – as opposed to constitutionally – separated, there would be no society at all" (Robertson 1987a: 9).

24 In Britain, for instance, the demographic concentration of Asian Muslims in particular areas gives them significant political leverage at the level of the ward in local council elections, and in particular constituencies in parliamentary elections (although due to the absence of a proportional representation system, the latter may not translate into significant influence at the national level). Both the Conservative and the Labour parties have departments to deal specifically with Asian (and black) voting issues, and have had to increasingly address Muslim issues.

25 See Eade (1993) for an excellent analysis of case studies in two areas of London in which the public debate on the issue of the construction of mosques led to a discourse on community belonging that took a religio-cultural form, pitting the white residents of the areas or the "real locals" (uniting "well heeled gentrifiers and working class 'Cockneys' in a defence of tradition"; p. 40) against the "alien" encroachments of Muslim outsiders or the "foreigners." Eade's analysis is excellent in demonstrating how the physical presence of Muslims and Islam politicizes space and community around a discourse of race. Mosques in particular have been politicized because they have served not just as places of worship, but also for building of community, organizations, and networks providing services and organizing issues and demands for Muslims in Britain and elsewhere. See Nielson (1989, especially pp. 230–3) for a discussion of different mosque-based and other organizations and political movements of British Muslims. See also Joly (1995) for a detailed discussion of such organizations in Birmingham, and Lewis (1994) for a comprehensive account of such resources in Bradford. (Birmingham and Bradford contain some of the heaviest concentrations of British Muslim populations, and the majority of this population is concentrated within a few inner-city electoral wards.) Gilles Kepel (1997) has argued that the mosques that sprang up in the early years of post-world war immigration were encouraged by the British state to stabilize these communities and make them into a more efficient and compliant workforce, and worked as well as a form of communalism that marked off the proletarian Muslim populations from the native working class, thus preventing class solidarity (see especially Part II, "The Britannic Verses"). It is only later that mosques became problematic as they started becoming centers for political activity.

26 See Husbands (1994) for a brief anecdotal account of the introduction of *halal* meats into two local education authorities' schools, which raised outcries across the spectrum from animal rights activists to those who expressed cultural revulsion at barbaric practices. Interestingly, as Husbands pointed out, much of the

anti-*halal* rhetoric made possible an easy slippage from the argument that ritual slaughter was barbaric to the implicit corollary that Muslims were barbaric.

27 The Rushdie affair refers to the huge response to the publication of Salman Rushdie's *The Satanic Verses*. The publication of the book despite objections made to Penguin by Muslim groups, the resulting demonstrations in many parts of the world including the celebrated Bradford book-burning episode, and the issuing of the *fatwa* (religious edict) by Ayatollah Khomeini against Rushdie, brought up much public debate and commentary in the Western world. The Rushdie affair had important policy implications, as diplomatic ties with Iran were severed by many European countries, soon after diplomatic and trade relations between Iran and Europe had been strengthened after the cease-fire in the Iran–Iraq war in August of 1988.

28 There had been an attempt in 1978 to abolish the blasphemy law, but the House of Lords rejected it on the grounds that Britain, its institutions, and the monarchy were still essentially Christian and deserve protection by the law, and that abolition could lead to an abundance of blasphemous publications (from Dyson 1990: 68).

29 For a collection of press articles on this issue, see "The international response" and "Reflections," in Appignanesi and Maitland (1990). For an analysis of the press coverage of the Rushdie affair, see Cottle (1991) and Parekh (1990).

30 It might be argued that one of the political implications of analyses that end up constructing a Western secularism/Eastern fundamentalism opposition is that they create the basis for the easy rejection of secularism in the postcolonial world as alien and imperialist. For many religious nationalists in the postcolonial world, secularism can be rejected less for its substantive content and more for its association with Euro-Christianity.

31 Madan argued that regardless of its genealogy and despite its contestations, it is still possible to talk of something unique and particular called "Indian secularism." However, this is not to argue that the Indian meaning of the term is innocent of its Western genealogies, or that modernizing elites in India no longer find its reference in a Western discourse on modernity. It is true, as Chatterjee pointed out, that the continuing "use of the term secularism is ... an expression of the desire of the modernizing elite to see the 'original' meaning of the concept actualized in India" (1995: 13–15). In many ways, as Sankaran Krishna pointed out, the use of neologisms like "Indian secularism" reflects the ambivalences of an imitative nationalist discourse that simultaneously attempts to stake out its unique historical significance (1994: 195). See Chatterjee (1986) for a fuller discussion of some of the contradictions of a "derivative nationalism" for postcolonial societies.

32 See Krishna (1993) for an eloquent demonstration of this point.

33 Connolly's suggestion to engage the thought-imbued visceral register of subjectivity and intersubjectivity within a (disenchanted) public/secular domain that has been both impoverished and rendered dogmatic by its insistence on a de-religionized public rationality/ethics is to take seriously and critically engage with the multiple visions and passions of the good life offered by religiously inspired groups and movements, while also recognizing why the commitment to secularism (albeit not as a singular, authoritative arbiter of public reason) remains critical.

9

A STORY TO BE TOLD

IR, postcolonialism, and the discourse of Tibetan (trans)national identity

Dibyesh Anand

The question of Tibet has been neglected in the study of international relations (IR). Although Western infatuation with Tibet can be witnessed in the outpouring of support from prominent Hollywood stars and recent films like *Seven Years in Tibet*, the Tibet question has remained marginal in IR. I therefore seek to theorize the construction and expression of Tibetan (trans)nationalism, one crucial element of the Tibet question, within a wider argument for a postcolonial approach to IR. While arguing that the study of IR needs to have a dialogue with postcolonial theory to understand the complexity of the Tibet question in general, and the discourse of Tibetan diasporic (trans)nationalism in particular, this chapter also highlights the limits of current postcolonial theorizing. A redefinition of IR, which moves it beyond its conventional concerns, allows us to take on board the question of Tibet since "Tibetanness" is a typical postcolonial narrative of identity politics that combines processes of migration with the human desire for fixity.

Reconceptualizing IR away from its moorings in realist and liberal paradigms involves questioning its ontological, epistemological, and methodological concerns. To combat conspicuous elements of geographical parochialism within IR is important. While various strands of the so-called third debate have critiqued the conventional theories and widened the self-definition of IR, it still remains mainly Western in orientation. Postcolonial international theories that draw upon the literature of critical international theories and postcolonialism are useful for addressing this Eurocentrism in IR. The task is not only to look at issues affecting people in the non-Western world, but also to examine old themes of state, power, war, and peace from new and different perspectives. For example, conventional IR pays attention to Tibet mostly in terms of its role in Sino-Western relations or Sino-Indian border disputes, denying subjectivity to the Tibetans. This resonates with the early twentieth-century British preoccupation with Tibet's role in the "Great Game" – the imperialist rivalry between the

British and the Russians in Asia. In contrast, a postcolonial analysis of the Tibet question entails considering new issues such as imperialism, history, diaspora, and identity as well as scrutinizing conventional IR.

The interrogation of the Tibet question as a problem of world politics, with its constitutive element of diasporic (trans)national identity, tests the limits not only of conventional IR but also of current postcolonial theorizing. The first part of the chapter situates my stance on postcolonialism and argues for a shift in the concern of postcolonial theory away from its focus on dialogue between the Third World and the West. Though the West,[1] as an ideational construct as well as a recognizable political entity, is a crucial element in arguments about Tibet, the controlling power here is the postcolonial state of China. Further, the bulk of the Tibetan diaspora lives in the postcolonial states of India and Nepal, highlighting the need to shift the analytical focus from the West/non-West axis to a transnational one. In the second part of the chapter, various facets of the Tibet question are introduced, underlining the argument that such a complex problem in the contemporary world requires a postcolonial IR. The focus then shifts to Tibetan (trans)nationalism within the diasporic population, highlighting the power of representational regimes in constituting and containing the discourses through which collective identity is expressed. In these discourses Tibetanness can be seen as a typical postcolonial narrative of identity politics, as it is constituted and contested by dominant and resistant discourses of nationalism, culture, gender, class, race, and religion. To better understand the Tibet question in international studies, we need to explore the possibilities of postcolonial analysis.

Interrogating the postcolonial

As discussed in the introduction, the term "postcolonial" is often seen as a temporal marker that demarcates the colonial era from the period of formal political independence. However, this conception of postcolonial is problematic and lacks a critical edge. The term with its prefix "post" carries with it the implication that colonialism is a matter of the past, trivializing colonialism's economic, political and cultural traces in the present international political and economic life. Where would Tibet fit in? It was never a European colony, though it was for some time under British influence. Ironically, it was colonized by postcolonial China at a time when the rest of the world was witnessing movements for decolonization. However, if we use "postcolonial" to mean a different approach, one that signifies the continuing impact and relevance of colonial practices, the contours of our analysis shift dramatically. Thus, rather than debating whether Tibet is a postcolonial entity or not, our attention shifts to analyzing colonial practices and knowledge formation around the Tibet question from a postcolonial theoretical perspective.

Postcolonial theory emerged to challenge knowledge production in the West about non-Western peoples. Highlighting the links between knowledge formation and its impact on the politics of everyday life, the epistemic violence committed by these knowledges often has wider implications as it shapes (and influences) policy-making processes. The postcolonial focus on micropolitical concerns is significant as it is here that the real effects of knowledge regimes are felt. It is herein that the strength of postcolonial theory lies – in its refusal to fix and discipline itself. Universal ideas and their unproblematic global implementation are eschewed.

However, such a retheorization of politics does not necessarily imply jettisoning macropolitical questions.[2] Though the specificity of "big" political questions is negotiated and resisted at an individual and local level, the big questions often have a containing and constraining influence on postcolonial theorizing. One such macropolitical question is related to the issue of self-determination. Postcolonial theory has had a variety of analyses regarding the state, ranging from an early cognition of struggle for national identity to later skepticism about nationalist projects (for a range of views see Memmi 1968; Said 1978; Chatterjee 1993). While a skepticism of nation- and state-building projects is understandable given the exclusions that nationalism has enabled, it cannot be denied that there are many groups who seek to define their collective identity in terms of nation and collective aspirations in terms of state. For the Indian diaspora it might be comfortable to talk about failings of their nation-state, but for the Tibetan diaspora it is a luxury they can hardly afford.

The postcolonial focus on the interrogation of ways in which the West continues to spin a web of knowledge–power regimes in the non-Western world is also critical for understanding the Tibet question. Postcolonial theory contributes substantially to our understanding of imperialism, representation, identity, diaspora, and resistance. However, there is little analysis when it comes to nationalism,[3] sovereignty, self-determination, and domination by postcolonial states (largely because of its skepticism of macropolitical ideas). While it may be true that the application of Western ideas has allowed powerful states to assert their dominance regionally, it is not enough to leave the analysis at this point. Interrogations of Western ideas have to be accompanied by questioning the particular dynamics of power exercised by regional hegemons like China in Tibet, India in Kashmir, and Indonesia in East Timor. While postcolonialists have contributed substantially by studying resistance to state-building projects from the perspectives of gender and indigeneity, there is also a need to take into account resistance coming from those identifying themselves as distinct nations, or as distinct ethnic groups. The discrediting of nationalism as a liberating ideology by second and third wave postcolonial scholars does not mean that all those who mobilize themselves in the name of nationalism are now operating under some sort of "false consciousness." For instance, Tibetans adopt a different language keeping in mind the audience, ranging from the rhetoric of human rights to the right of self-determination, from autonomy to secession. Postcolonial theory needs to recognize the writings of first-wave postcolonialists and take such issues into account to be more meaningful to many people living within the Third World. As Scott has argued, the thrust of the argument now should be to move away from postcoloniality's politics of theory to a new theory of politics where "the accent is on *political* rather than cultural criticism" (Scott 1999: 19).

As the discussion of the Tibet question in the next section will show, the West has played a crucial constitutive role in the construction of a Tibetan identity. Therefore, postcolonialism signifies a position against imperialism and Eurocentrism – an argument to lay bare the complicity of knowledge production concerning cultural others and representational regimes within the dominant power structures. However, since knowledge about Tibet is produced not only in the West but in China, India, and Nepal too, Tibetans thus have to negotiate their identity discourses at different levels, depending upon the kind of representational regime in which they are operating. This entails a shift in focus from dialogue with the metropolitan to transnational dialogue with other Third World discourses (Williams and Chrisman 1993: 16–17).

Western ways of knowledge production and dissemination in the past and present are objects of study within postcolonial studies for those seeking an alternative means of expression. As argued in this volume, the enterprise of IR theory is one such Western knowledge formation that can be interrogated from a postcolonial perspective (also see Darby 1997a; Jabri and O'Gorman 1999; Krishna 1999; Paolini 1999). However, a prescriptive blueprint for postcolonial IR is neither feasible nor desirable; a postcolonial analysis would differ according to the historical, cultural, and geopolitical contexts involved. One such issue that illustrates the usefulness of a postcolonial approach to IR is the question of Tibet within world politics.

The Tibet question

Even though the issues raised by the Tibet question are international in scope and there is an increasing recognition that it remains one of the unsolved problems in world politics, Tibet hardly figures in the IR literature. Even when it comes up, it is either as a footnote to the cold war[4] or as a pawn in Sino-Western or Sino-Indian relations. This neglect reflects a web of strategic interests of major Western powers, IR's focus on relations between states, and finally IR's ethnocentrism. All this was evident after 1959 when China acquired complete control over Tibet, giving up the uneasy accommodation with the Dalai Lama-led Tibetan government that lasted for ten years. Despite international condemnation of Chinese action through either strongly worded statements such as those of the International

Commission of Jurists or feeble statements in the United Nations General Assembly,[5] the states of the world accepted the Tibet question as an "internal" matter of China. Realist and liberal strands of IR theory with their preoccupation with sovereignty seem incapable of engaging with the complexity of the Tibet question, though the emergence of critical schools within the field suggests the potential for a better understanding. There are many constituent dynamics of the Tibet question in the contemporary world and though critical IR can contribute to an interrogation of some of these, others are better captured through postcolonial analysis.

The Tibetan issue can be studied in terms of themes including sovereignty/suzerainty, imperialism, human rights, representation, identity, nationalism, diaspora, and transnationalism. An approach that not only highlights the interlinkages between these themes but also emphasizes the need for some sort of dialogue between critical IR and postcolonialism better addresses the complexity surrounding it. Critical international theories provide sophisticated investigation of some of the themes like sovereignty, representation, and nationalism; but themes of imperialism, diaspora, Western representational practices, and transnational identity are better understood through the lens of postcolonial theory.

The question of historical status

Regarding the status of Tibet *vis-à-vis* China, various concepts are deployed including sovereignty, suzerainty, independence, autonomy, vassalage, protectorate, overlordship, and colony. However, for the most part, it is sovereignty that is asserted and contested. On the one hand, the Chinese state makes historical arguments to buttress its claim of sovereignty over Tibet; on the other, Tibetan exiles and their supporters make counter-claims and assert that Tibet was for all practical purposes independent from China. Though both sides mobilize history to make their claims, the concept of sovereignty is often left unproblematized. Crucially, the revolutionary communist regime that took over China in 1949 has no qualms in staking claims over Tibet based on a debatable imperial legacy, which it denounces in other spheres. The Chinese, who during the nineteenth century rejected the Western model of international relations as alien, exert with a vengeance their control over Tibet using the modern European concept of sovereignty. It is important that in the process they also ignore the different worldview within which the Mongol and Manchu emperors interacted with Tibet. Unlike the British, who used suzerainty and autonomy to designate Sino-Tibetan relations, since 1905 the Chinese have consistently argued that their position is that of a sovereign and not suzerain. At the beginning of the twenty-first century, even though there is no space for suzerainty within international law and politics and all the states recognize the Chinese claim of sovereignty over Tibet, the pro-Tibet lobby contests the assertion of sovereignty by highlighting the difference between suzerainty and sovereignty within international law. As Oppenheim argued: "Suzerainty is by no means sovereignty. It is a kind of international guardianship, since the vassal State is either absolutely or mainly represented internationally by the suzerain State" (Van Praag 1987: 107).

The genealogy of the modern idea of sovereignty also reveals its close nexus with European imperialism. Until the first half of the twentieth century, the international community of states was based on a double standard. While the "civilized" world (read as Europe, and later the United States and Japan) had a right to sovereign statehood, the rest was open to various forms of imperial control as a "degree of civilization necessary to maintain international relations was considered as one of the conditions for statehood" (Hannum 1990: 16). The Tibetan example is typical of how imperial efforts throughout the non-European world were empowered by Western understandings of non-Western states. Not only did imperial powers actively delegitimize non-Western modes of sovereignty, they also refused to recognize the intricacies of non-Western inter-state relations (Strang 1996). It is within this context that during the turn of the nineteenth–twentieth century the traditional Sino-Tibetan relationship was considered by the British as irrational and lacking legitimacy for not conforming to modern ideas of diplomacy. For a large part of the nineteenth century, to the British in India, Tibet was a "forbidden land" ruled by "strange lamas" under some form of Chinese control. While some, including Bogle, named the control as "sovereignty" (Markham 1876: 195), most used the term "overlordship" or "suzerainty." This was based on the presence of Chinese *amban* (resident) in Lhasa, claims of the Manchu emperor, and refusal of the Tibetans to clarify the situation. Due to their own familiarity with feudalism and with the Chinese international system of tributary relations, it is not surprising that the British interpreted Sino-Tibetan relations in terms of suzerainty and protectorate. British policy in the case of Tibet was shaped by conflicting dynamics, including nonfeasibility of direct colonization, strategic location as a buffer state in Central Asia, commercial interests in the Chinese Empire, and so on. These conflicting interests dictated the ambiguous policy where Tibet's relation with the Chinese Empire was seen in terms of Chinese suzerainty and Tibetan autonomy. Through a memorandum on 17 August 1912 the British government clarified its stance that "while recognizing the Chinese suzerainty, they were not prepared to admit the right of China to interfere in the internal administration of Tibet" (Foreign Office 1920: 41). Thus, "outer Tibet would become an autonomous state under Chinese suzerainty and British protectorate" (Foreign Office 1920: 43). The failure of the British to understand the complex relation had as much to do with their heady faith in the superiority of European norms as with their conflicting interests in the region.

Traditionally, political actors interpreted and understood their inter-state relations in vocabulary familiar to them; Sino-Tibetan relations were no exception. The same relationship could have been understood by the Chinese imperial officials in terms of Confucian tributary relations, and by the Tibetans as Buddhist *mchod-yon*.[6] This does not validate the primacy of either worldview, but reveals the complexity of the issue involved. Grounding the relation in some universally accepted terms was unnecessary within the Chinese as well as Tibetan worldview, and personal, moral, and spiritual overtones were a significant part of their relations; however, brutal takeover was not. The influence of the *amban* varied according to many factors including the strength of the Dalai Lama. Even when China had "the upper hand" (Bataille 1992: 33), Tibet "enjoyed local autonomy over domestic matters" (Grunfeld 1987: 57), and more significantly, on the basis of simple experienced reality, Tibetans did not consider themselves Chinese (Barnett and Lehman 1998). However, this traditional relationship became problematic when the socio-cultural and political environment was altered first by the arrival of Western colonial powers in Asia, and second by the transformation of the traditional Chinese Confucian-dominated polity toward a more occidental type of political system that produced a republican China and the growth of Chinese nationalism (Shakya 1999: xxiii). As the Chinese have adopted modern diplomatic language, since the early twentieth century, they have begun to assert their relationship in terms of sovereignty. Tibetans on the other hand were late in adjusting to the modern world and continued to refuse to comply with any treaties between British India and China concerning Tibet. Thus, it was a "forceful interpretation of Sino-Tibetan relations in terms of European international law and *praxis* of (British) imperialism" (Norbu 1990: 67) that lies at the genesis of the Tibet question; it was not some intractable nationalist and historical conflict between Chinese and Tibetans. Westernization of international relations made it inevitable that when China gained control over Tibet in 1951, it was no more the traditional symbolic relationship, but an absolute rule. For the first time in its history, through the Seventeen Point Agreement, Tibet acknowledged Chinese sovereignty (there was no space left for ambiguous terms like suzerainty) in writing.

Thus, extrapolation of Western ideas to a situation where people operated on the basis of a totally different worldview has had serious ramifications and has facilitated the victimization of many communities like the Tibetans. Further, lack of serious consideration of imperialism within IR has contributed to IR's conservatism and lack of understanding of several international problems such as Tibet. While critical theories in IR have contributed to the deconstruction and problematization of sovereignty, its linkages with imperialism tend to be overlooked and may be better understood by applying a postcolonial analysis.

Productive power of representations

The power of representation and discourse is also critical for understanding the Tibet question and Tibetanness.[7] As postcolonial works drawing upon Foucauldian ideas have argued, this power not only constrains and contains, but is also productive of certain identities (Said 1978). The very idea of Tibet and what it means to be Tibetan is constructed and contested within the matrix of identity and representation discourses, thus making it an integral part of the Tibet question. Representations have productive influence over the discourses of Tibetanness (Tibetan identity) since the Tibetans, especially those living in the diaspora,[8] self-reflexively appropriate these images as a part of their own identity.

When studying the issue of representation and identity in the specific context of Tibetans, I make a fine but important distinction here between the poetics and politics of representations of Tibet. These distinctions relate closely to two streams within social constructionism–semiotic and discursive approaches to representation (Hall 1997). On the one hand, the semiotic approach is concerned with how language produces meaning, the *poetics* of representation. On the other hand, a discursive approach is concerned with the effects and consequences of representation, its *politics*. A semiotic approach would entail examining how Tibet is imagined within the Western world or in China by looking at popular as well as statist discourses. In this chapter, both the poetics and politics of representation are discussed.

The importance of Chinese representational regimes for the Tibet question warns against reducing postcolonial critique to a turning of "all people from non-Western cultures into a generalized 'subaltern' that is then used to flog an equally generalized 'West'" (Chow 1993: 13). Knowledge production about Tibet, especially since the mid-twentieth century when the Chinese communists consolidated their political control, is no longer the preserve of Europeans. Very much in the tradition of orientalist scholarship and British imperialist writings, manufacturing of the scholarly truths about Tibet within the Chinese academies is implicated in the service of the political regime. Chinese representation of Tibetans as essentially backward, primitive, and barbaric is witnessed not only at the popular level, but more dangerously within state discourse too (see Jingsheng 1998; Kolas 1998). Analysis of Chinese representations of Tibet (related to Western Sinology, and its constituent "red China" image that prevailed during the cold war) shows how Tibetans, like most of the non-Han peoples, are an exotic but backward people necessitating Chinese leadership to help them progress.[9] Apart from the claim of historical sovereignty, Chinese communist nationalism has also justified its control over Tibet in terms of its modernizing role, its overthrow of the feudalism existing in pre-1959 Tibet, and its liberation of serfs and women (see Makley 1997, 1999). The debate about the validity of these class[10] and gender analyses of "Old Tibet" is not our concern here. But it is sufficient to underline that these representational practices have serious implications for Chinese policy about Tibet. For instance, in the name of liberating Tibetan women from the clutches of tradition, not only has the Chinese state attacked religious practices and structures, but it has also forced women to undergo "family planning" (see Kikhang 1997: 110–16).

The thematic as well as structural content of Chinese representations resonates with Western representations of Tibet. The *exotica Tibet* (henceforth used as a shorthand for the exoticized – both positive and negative – representations of Tibet), which represented a Shangri-La, a place with spirituality and peace, requires a detailed treatment that is not possible here. (For a detailed treatment see Bishop 1989 and 1993; Lopez 1998; Schell 2000.) One can only sketch a very brief outline. Geographically and culturally, Tibet's peripheral place enabled many Europeans and Americans to use it as an imaginative escape, as a sort of time out, a relaxation from the rigid rational censorship of their own society (Bishop 1989: 7). This explains the unease of many Westerners with the modernization of Tibet under the aegis of the Chinese state. Hence writings about Tibet are sometimes "conservative protests against modernism, the masses, and the changing world order" (Bishop 1989: 15), and at other times "counter to the globalising tendencies" of modernization (Neilson 2000). The presence of contradictions within Western imaginings of Tibet is not new. Since the beginning of the twentieth century, there has been "a play of opposites: the pristine and the polluted, the authentic and the derivative, the holy and the demonic, the good and the bad" (Lopez 1998: 10). While some held disparaging views about Tibet, others extolled it. Strategies of essentialism, reductionism, and stereotyping are common to positive as well as negative representations. Thus, debasement and exoticization are part of the same representational regimes.[11] Both sides flatten Tibet's complexities and competing histories into a stereotype that operates through adjectives.

This *exotica Tibet* was not confined to a cultural sphere. It influenced and was in turn influenced by the political processes at work. Accounts of British Indian officials like Bell and Richardson show that their "more prosaic view did not destroy this exotic representation but tacitly encouraged it" (McKay 1997: 207). The importance of *exotica Tibet* in our understanding of the Tibet question lies in the impact it has had on the very construction and contestation of categories of Tibet and Tibetans – the politics of representation. The language of stereotype about Tibet "not only creates knowledge about Tibet, in many ways it creates Tibet, a Tibet that Tibetans in exile have come to appropriate and deploy in an effort to gain both standing in exile and independence for their country" (Lopez 1998: 10). Interaction with Western audiences is a very important dynamic shaping Tibetan identity and Tibetanness in the diaspora. This area has received substantial attention from scholars only since the last decade of the twentieth century (Klieger 1994; Korom 1997a, 1997b; Harris 1999). The examination of a politics of representation informed by the discursive approach locates expositions on Tibet in the context of imperialism, neocolonialism, nationalism, orientalism, and development. It also focuses on the implication of such exercises in image making on those who are subjected to it – the Tibetans. There is no doubt that initially at least Tibetans had little control over the way they were represented in the outside world and thus had to negotiate within the representational regimes already in place. For instance, since for Western "Tibetophiles" the practice of Tibetan Buddhism is the only cultural expression though which exiles can perpetuate the dream of their lost paradise, Tibetans often have to make their case in terms of threatened extinction of a unique culture (Harris 1999: 38). Rather than painting Tibetans as mere victims, it is now recognized that they have been active in appropriating and internalizing Western representations, and in creating and presenting their own cultural, political, and religious identity. Soliciting international support has been one of the main strategies of the Tibetan diaspora elite. Support in the form of "Free Tibet" movements is often based on the image of "Tibet as [a] defenseless underdog, a spiritual society that was minding its own business only to get crushed under the jackboot of an aggressive, materialist overlord" (Schell 2000: 206). Even the cultivation of this victimization paradigm reflects the agency of Tibetans. Though the Tibetan global publicity campaign consciously portrays Tibetans as victims of Chinese oppression, this does not deny them their subjectivity. They have made conscious and extensive use of Western discourses, such as psychology, philosophy, physics, personal growth, and holistic health, in their attempts both to communicate with Westerners and to reconstitute themselves in conditions of exile. Tibetans have also colluded with, as well as contested, various Western images of Tibet (Bishop 1997: 67).

Thus, representations have played a constitutive and performative role in identity discourses among Tibetans. This is true not only in the arena of cultural identity but also regarding political identity, especially in the diaspora. While recognizing the asymmetrical power relations involved, we may look at Tibetanness as a product of creative negotiations of diasporic Tibetans with dominant representational regimes, as a process of resistant appropriation of dominant identity concepts including transnationalism, sovereignty, indigeneity, universal human rights, and diaspora.

Tibetan (trans)national identity: a postcolonial conundrum

An important aspect of the Tibet question involves unpacking various narratives of Tibetan (trans)national identity as promoted by the "Tibet movement," which consists of Tibetans in the diaspora as well as their non-

Tibetan supporters. Tibetanness, with a unique mix of nationalism, trans-nationalism, and internationalism, lies at the heart of the Tibet question. The fact that the most sophisticated articulations of Tibetanness come from Tibetans living in diaspora contributes significantly to this. This is compounded by the lack of political liberties within Tibet. As Kolas argued, the Tibetan diaspora elite recognize that religious and cultural identities have inferior currency as opposed to national identities as a source of polit-ical legitimacy in the contemporary world (Kolas 1996). Operating within this international political environment, it therefore comes as no surprise that Tibetans have appropriated the hegemonic language of sovereignty, autonomy, and nationalism to make their case. In fact, imagining Tibet as a nation is to a large extent, a post-exilic phenomenon.

The dynamics that play a constitutive role in the articulation of a distinc-tive Tibetan national identity are significantly transnational too; thus it is impossible to speak of Tibetan nationalism without a "trans" – bracketed or not – national side to it. Modern Tibetan identity has strong constructive elements of transnationalism including those that emphasize the environ-ment, peace, spiritualism, international human rights, universal compassion, and eclectic religious beliefs. The constituency of Tibetan supporters often overlaps with that of many other transnational social movements.

The crucial and constitutive role played by a globally networked political cultural system of Tibetophiles is peculiar. This system can be studied by looking at the conspicuous phenomenon of Tibet-support groups (TSG is used here as an umbrella term for disparate organizations such as the Tibet Support Group, Friends of Tibet, Free Tibet, Students for Free Tibet, and so forth) which are more often than not run by non-Tibetans. Though the effec-tiveness of campaigns organized by the transnational network of Tibetan supporters may be debated, it cannot be denied that their protests often get extensive media coverage. Visits of senior Chinese officials anywhere in the world seldom occur without a protest by some TSG. Given that Tibetans occupy a minuscule position in terms of numbers as compared to other dias-poric groups, and that Tibet is not high on the priority list of many states' national interest, theirs is a surprisingly high-profile case evoking support from people cutting across national boundaries. Common to Western supporters and Tibetan refugees is a shared belief in the iconic image of the Dalai Lama, and strong advocacy of non-nationalistic (transnational) causes, including world peace, environmental responsibility, indigenous sovereignty, human rights, and non-violent activism. It is this adoption of an inclusivist cosmopolitan agenda and the approaches adopted to achieve it that gives the Tibet movement its geopolitical significance.

The transnational reach of the Tibet movement is also highlighted by the alliances it strikes with other supranational (and even national) movements and organizations ranging from Amnesty International to the Transnational

Radical Party, Chinese dissidents in exile to Jewish religious groups, Unrepresented Nations and People Organization to environmental organizations.

Though the odds are stacked against the Tibetans in the real world, at least in the virtual world it is a radically different situation. An overwhelming number of websites on Tibet are pro-Tibetan.[12] To a certain extent, Tibet Online, which claims to serve as a virtual community space for the Tibet movement, succeeds in its aim of leveling the playing field by leveraging the Internet's ability to harness grassroots support for Tibet's survival (Tibet Online 2001). Though there is a substantial gap between success in the virtual world and success in the real world, with the virtual world increasingly governing the real there may be a glimmer of hope for the Tibetan cause.

At the same time, one cannot deny that such a transnational support base also constrains the nationalist aspirations of Tibetans themselves as it is more often than not based on an image of Tibetans as inherently peaceful. The towering personality of the Dalai Lama and his principled stance on nonviolence contributes significantly to this. The support is often conditional upon Tibetans remaining as "passive" victims. As Tsering Shakya remarks, unlike other international political problems such as the Palestinian one, the Tibetan issue is seen more in terms of sentimentality. He argues that "if the Tibetan issue is to be taken seriously, Tibet must be liberated from both the Western imagination and the myth of Shangri-la" (Shakya 1991: 23). The inability of the Tibetans to muster any support among the existing states is also disturbing. Here one may point to one of the paradoxes of the Tibetan situation *vis-à-vis* the Palestinians. While the support for Palestinians comes overwhelmingly from Third World countries, a similar support is conspicuous by its absence when it comes to the Tibetans. In fact, one often comes across references to Jewish organizations offering support to the Dalai Lama and the latter in turn expressing his desire to learn from the Jewish experience of diaspora. But we do not hear of serious efforts on the part of the Tibetan government-in-exile to form linkages with the diasporic communities like the Palestinians, who also experienced forced occupation in the recent past.

The growing Tibet movement can be looked at as an "emergent form of transnational, intercultural political activism, one that is dependent upon the complex production and circulation of representations" of Tibetanness in arenas cutting across various boundaries (McLagan 1997: 69). At the same time such a complex relationship between Tibetans and non-Tibetan supporters of Tibet can also be comprehended by using a vocabulary indigenous to Tibetans, that of *mchod-yon* – a term that refers to a patron–client relationship. Tibetans have historically operated with dominant external powers on the basis of this principle, and in contemporary times it is the Western supporters who occupy the position of patron. As Klieger has put it, the "patron/client dyad is a warp and weft upon which ideas of Tibetan identity are woven" (1994: 22)

The transnationalized aspect of Tibetanness deriving from globalized discourses, however, is not an end in itself, as in many other postcolonial movements, but is more a means to an end – preserving a distinctive culture while at the same time garnering support for reclamation of a homeland. As Venturino points out, for much of the Tibetan diaspora the Tibetan national imagination is a *means* to a particular political end – national independence for some, and genuine cultural autonomy for others (1997: 98–112). While such claims to essential culture and an original homeland are looked at skeptically within some postist discourses, in the case of Tibetans it is not difficult to appreciate the need for such essentialist claims. This is not to deny the constructed character of these identity claims, but to show that these claims may be seen in terms of strategy or tactics. Tibet's constitution as a globally dispersed culture and its contradictions, together with geopolitical claims, productively complicate notions of genuine national desire and demonstrable ethnic integrity – phenomena quite common in the postcolonial world.

Apart from directing sympathy toward nationalism and transnationalism, the Tibetan question also draws attention to the constitutive role of internationalizing principles. As Malkki argues, the dominant imagination of the international community is not a cosmopolitan or supranational world, but "an *inter*national one, a world where *globality is understood to be constituted by interrelations among discreet 'nations'*" (Malkki 1994: 41). The idea of appealing to some benevolent international community out there is quite strong among the Tibetans. There is a presumption that without the support of this community, nothing substantial can be achieved. At the same time, there is also an awareness that too much investment should not be put into this idea, as China's geopolitical and economic importance could overshadow or undermine the international community's support for the Tibetan cause. Often the appeals are made not to this community that is understood as a community of distinct nation-states, but to transnational groups. For instance, women activist organizations such as the Tibetan Women's Association direct their activities toward international governmental and non-governmental organizations (2001).

Tibetanness is a discursive product of nationalism, transnationalism, and internationalism. Some constitutive tensions that play important roles in Tibetanness[13] include assertions of essentialist national claims that draw support from transnational ideas and movements; stylized tropes of representation and resistant politics of identity; the imperative of deploying a limited (masked as universal) vocabulary of identity while modifying it for strategic purposes; a desire to return to homeland while negotiating the realities of refugee life; the need to preserve culture while trying to adopt and adapt to radically different circumstances; and hybridity and ambiguity *vis-*

à-vis essentialism and resistance. Despite significant differences within the Tibetan community, the stress is on presenting a united front. This also affects the question of women's liberation within the Tibetan society, as a united struggle for Tibet is the priority. Often a feminist critique might be seen as a "stab in the back" (Devine 1993: 6). In highlighting the difference in approach between Western nuns (initiates in Tibetan Buddhism) and the Tibetan nuns living in exile, Havnevik pointed out that though the former have instigated some positive changes in the socio-cultural position of nuns, their "aggressiveness" and "insensitivity" stands in contrast to the humility among the Tibetan nuns who proceed in "accordance with the sentiments in the Tibetan community rather than against them" (Havnevik 1989: 205). Even though Tibetan women are very active in organizing resistance to the Chinese state (evident in the high degree of participation by nuns in protest marches in Lhasa) and support for the nationalist movement in exile, many observers have noted that gender equality is far from an achieved goal (Willis 1987). Tibetanness represents unity in hierarchy; "it is most generally a shared orientation to male-dominated Buddhism as a marker of positive difference from the Chinese" (Kapferer quoted in Makley 1997: 8–10).

However, conceptualization of Tibetanness as a postcolonial identity narrative highlights the fact that recognition of the contingent nature of identity does not preclude collective identity claims. It simply draws attention to the strategic nature of such claims. This position is afforded by a discursive approach to the identity question, something that draws together in postcolonial theory, but also increasingly in critical IR.

Conclusion

A postcolonial IR approach to the Tibet question involves unpacking various constituent themes, including those dealing with the power of representation and (trans)nationalism. Critical international theories help investigate macro-political themes such as sovereignty, nationalism, self-determination, and representation. However, for others, like the historical legacy of imperialism, epistemic violence, transnational identity discourse, experience of migration, and transculturation, we need to look at postcolonial theory. The fact that the Tibetan case is not only about the West versus the non-West also raises uncomfortable questions for the postcolonial enterprise, questions that underline the argument for at best a resistant appropriation of ideas. Putting Tibetanness under a postcolonial scrutiny implies not an abandonment of the subject but a reconceptualization that refuses to privilege certainty over doubt, identity over difference. Tibetanness helps many Tibetans make sense of their migrant experience, while at the same time being a product/process of identity politics oriented toward the goal of reclaiming the homeland.

Acknowledgements

I thank Jutta Weldes, Barry Hindess, P. Christiaan Klieger, Nitasha Kaul, Philip Darby, and Arie M. Kacowicz for their useful comments on different versions of this essay. I am also grateful to the editors for their encouragement and suggestions.

Notes

1 Throughout the modern period, the idea of the West did not reflect an already existing society; rather it was essential to the very formation of this society. Hall put forward strong arguments for considering modernity as the story of "the West and the Rest" (Hall 1992: 275–332).

2 For an interesting analysis of macro issues and postcolonial theory from a feminist perspective in political economy, see Kaul (2000).

3 Here, we find earlier postcolonial thinkers like Gandhi, Fanon, Memmi, and others, more helpful. Often, they sought to separate nation from state and deploy it in service of other, more inclusive, forms of political community (Gandhi 1998: 121).

4 For an analysis of CIA operations in Tibet during the early years of the cold war, see Knaus (1999).

5 The International Commission of Jurists in Geneva brought out two reports on Tibet around the time, and has continued to do so since then. *The Question of Tibet and the Rule of Law* (1959) and *Tibet and the Chinese People's Republic* (1960) were the first two. The United Nations General Assembly has passed three resolutions on Tibet: 1353 (XIV) 1959; 1723 (XVI) 1961; and 2079 (XX) 1965. For details on these as well as other international resolutions on Tibet, see Department of Information and International Relations (Tibet) (1997).

6 While some have argued that *mchod-yon*, patron–priest relations, was the main characteristic of the Sino-Tibetan world (see Klieger 1994), others have clarified that this was more about personal relationship between rulers and not about statehood (Barnett and Lehman 1998). According to Shakya, the concept indicates that the Tibetans viewed the Chinese emperor only as a secular institution, which is far from the case; Manchu emperors for instance were often referred to as *Jampeyang Gongma*, the incarnation of Manjushri (1999: xxiii).

7 Even though critical IR has started taking the issue of representation seriously (Shapiro 1988; Doty 1996b; Campbell 1992, 1998; Weldes 1999), the focus is more on the generative and legitimizing role played by representational regimes in certain foreign policies of dominant states and less on the impact of these practices on the represented. This necessitates bringing postcolonial theory, with its emphasis on productive dimensions of representations, into discussion.

8 The emphasis on Tibetans living in exile does not deny the fact that Tibetans living within Tibet also have to negotiate with Western and Chinese representations (see Goldstein and Kapstein 1998; Barnett and Akiner 1996; Schwartz 1996; Adams 1996, 1998).

9 The notion of the lack of development in Tibet being due to "cultural backwardness" has been very strong in Chinese state policies ever since the 1949 Seventeen Point Agreement. Development as a rationale for Chinese control is also found in the writings of those sympathetic to the Communist regime (Suyin 1977) as well as many Chinese dissidents (Xu 2000). Unfortunately this has resonance with the self-justificatory tone of the civilizing mission within Western imperialism.

10 Tashi Tsering's autobiography provides a nuanced reading that critiques the rigid class structure of traditional society as well as his disillusionment with the Chinese rhetoric of a "free" Tibet. Instead of seeking to provide simplistic answers, through his experience of growing up as a "serf" in "Old Tibet" and a revolutionary in "New Tibet," Tsering argues that the question is far more complex. See Goldstein *et al.* (1997).

11 For a discussion on rhetorical tropes common to Western representations of the non-West see Spurr (1993).

12 In a search in Netscape with Google using the word 'Tibet', of the first hundred links only three were not connected to the Tibet movement (dated 15 February 2001).

13 For a detailed discussion of dynamics constituting Tibetanness in the diaspora, see Anand (2000).

10

POSTCOLONIAL INTERROGATIONS OF CHILD LABOR

Human rights, carpet trade, and Rugmark in India

Geeta Chowdhry

Twelve-year-old Iqbal Masih, a former bonded child laborer in the carpet industry and a child rights activist in Pakistan, was killed in April 1995 near Lahore, Pakistan. Pakistan police claimed that his death had nothing to do with his activism for children's rights and against bonded child labor.[1] The life of Iqbal Masih provides an important example of the brutal exploitation of children in many industries across the world. While his heroic struggle against child labor echoes the desires of the global child rights movement to ban child labor, his death near Lahore, violent and tragic, is symbolic of the costs of struggle to those outside the circuits of power. It can also be read as a commentary on the global faultlines surrounding child labor.

Iqbal Masih's story is not an aberration in the global political economy. Two hundred and fifty million children work in the world today; 120 million are employed in full-time work and 130 million combine work with other noneconomic activities, including going to school (International Labor Organization 2000–2).[2] Asia is estimated to have 153 million, Africa 32 million, and Latin America 17.5 million economically active children between the ages of 10 and 14 (Kebebew 1998). UNICEF has estimated that 10–40 million children work in India alone (UNICEF 1997).[3] The government of India maintains that the number of child laborers in India is 2–20 million, and that the number has been reduced by a third in the past two years (Cox 1999). In contrast, the Commission on Labor Standards and International Trade has reported that the incidence of child labor in India grows at an annual rate of 4 per cent, as economic liberalization increases the cost of living and unemployment (Tucker and Ganesan 1997). Despite disagreements on the degree of child labor in national and global economies, child labor is at the center of current national and international concern and policy.

The importance of child labor for the study of international relations (IR) and international political economy (IPE) cannot be underscored enough. Since discussions about child labor are often situated at the intersections of human rights, social movements, and international political economy, understanding the issue of child labor requires, at the very least, an interrogation of the production and circulation of commodities created using child labor. Further, global discourses on child labor are generally invoked in the context of North–South relations, and depend on the "production and circulation of meanings" for their appeal.[4] Thus problematizing the production and circulation of meanings around child labor is essential for understanding the ways in which this phenomenon works to (re)produce North–South identities and relations of power. Such a problematization requires that we situate child labor "in the current conjuncture of global capital" (Cheah 1999) in which commodities and meanings, including meanings surrounding identities and rights, are produced. Consequently, debates surrounding child labor are instructive not only in uncovering the human rights struggles of a "globalized civil society," but also in underscoring the geopolitical dimension of human rights discourses that includes the "internationalism and the nationalisms that are sustained by it" (Grewal 1999: 337). Although heartrending stories of child labor have spurred international attention and international social movements, they have also obfuscated the workings of global capital and geopolitics that are engendered through the telling of the child labor story. Thus, situated at the intersections of human rights, social movements, and international political economy, discourses on child labor provide us with a unique opportunity to examine the workings of power in a postcolonial world. In this chapter I suggest that human rights and labor discourses on children have become important symbols of transnational geopolitics that provide us with critical insights into the exercise of power. By focusing on child labor in the carpet industry, this chapter explores these discourses by examining the production and circulation of commodities and meanings at the international and national level. I argue that both international discourses on child labor, which are heavily influenced by the language of universal human rights, and national discourses generally premised on a culturally relativist human rights position are situated within the "force field of global capitalism" (Cheah 1999: 13) and provide economically and culturally similar and moribund arguments about human rights and child labor.[5] In addition, an alternative postcolonial reading of child labor, human rights, and international political economy, which unveils the racialized, gendered, and class underpinnings of the human rights regime and makes visible the hierarchies of power within international relations, better unfolds the complexity and the geopolitics that surround child labor discourses.

This chapter is organized into four sections. The first addresses the limitations of current IPE and IR theorizing, including a critique of the human rights literature, and suggests a postcolonial alternative for the study of child labor. The second section discusses the history of child labor in the carpet industry in India and its integration into the global economy. It also analyzes US mainstream media and policy discourses on child labor, their claims to a universal human rights stance, and their relation to international capital. The third section analyzes Indian discourses on child labor in the carpet industry and examines the ways in which these discourses are structured by their relationship to capital. In the final section I discuss transformative possibilities by focusing on the voices of children and the various strategies of resistance used by activists seeking to eradicate child labor in India.

International relations, human rights discourses, and postcolonial mediations

Since the issue of child labor, as discussed above, is located at the intersections of IPE, IR, and human rights, this section begins by exploring the ways in which debates surrounding child labor are situated in these fields. I believe that conventional theories of international political economy and international relations provide only limited tools for understanding the complexity of child labor. Further, I suggest that even the human rights literature, with its seemingly oppositional universalist and culturally relativist positions, produces a moribund analysis of child labor. Finally, I explore the ways in which a postcolonial reading of human rights, and thus child labor, is significantly different and provides an alternative and more complex reading of the struggle over labor and human rights.

Child labor and international political economy

Craig Murphy and Cristina Rojas de Ferro (1995) suggest that although orthodox IPE provides multiple frameworks for understanding the production and circulation of commodities, it is curiously silent about the production and circulation of meanings. Further, they argue that the relationships between universalizing tendencies in global capital and "regimes of representation," which are critical in the maintenance of global power, have also been overlooked by orthodox IPE. Although there is little scholarship in IPE that directly explores child labor in the global economy (for exceptions see Kent 1995; Schoenberger 2000), I examine the methods and concepts utilized by the dominant schools of IPE to assess their validity for understanding child labor.

Since I contend that understanding child labor in the global economy requires an examination of the production and circulation of commodities as well as meanings, orthodox political economy with its focus mainly on commodity production provides little assistance for understanding the latter. Whereas Marxist IPE with its focus on the fetishization of commodities provides valuable insights into the exploitation of labor in commodity production, it too does not relate the importance of representational issues, i.e. the circulation of meanings, to material analysis. Although orthodox liberal and Marxist political economy can tell us different stories about the production of commodities in the Third World and the consumption of these commodities in the West – carpets are produced in India and consumed in Germany and the United States of America – both these perspectives fail to articulate the ways in which these stories about production and consumption constitute and sustain different subject identities, say for example North–South identities. In other words this literature does not discuss the ways in which the discourses of child labor, i.e. the circulation of meanings around child labor, sustain the production of global hierarchies in a postcolonial world.

Critical IPE, particularly postmodern and poststructural approaches, deconstruct and "make strange" the received nature of knowledge and its links to the production of identity. However, they generally ignore the racialized, gendered, and class basis of this identity, and claim that a foundationalist essentialism pervades scholarship which seeks to locate power in structured inequalities and hierarchies (Ashley and Walker 1990a, 1990b). In contrast, the work of some critical feminist scholars who link the production of commodities to the production and circulation of gendered knowledge provides some insights for the analysis of child labor (see Mies 1986; Waring 1988; Kuiper and Sap 1995; Kabeer 1996). According to Waring (1988) for example, the gendered construction of the discipline of economics and the systems of national accounting make invisible women's labor; since much of women's labor remains a part of the private realm and the unorganized sector of the global economy, it is rarely factored into the gross national product of a nation. Feminist economists have long argued for including the "household as an economic site," as they examine the value of unpaid work and the "gendered processes in the paid labor market" (MacDonald 1995: 175–97). Applying the insights of critical and feminist scholarship to understand child labor can be useful, for it enables an examination of the gendered international labor processes in which children's labor is often made invisible and where children, like women, suffer from wage differentials. Further, these insights also facilitate an exploration into the discursive economy of child labor.

The postcolonial political economy perspective, utilized in this chapter, deploys the insights of both critical feminist and Marxist scholarship by situating child labor not only in the internationalization of global capital, but also in the gendered constructions of a globalized economy. More significantly, this perspective also foregrounds race, gender, and class and their imbrication with the capital, knowledge, and representation that surrounds child labor.

Child labor and international relations

Whereas discourses of child labor in IPE are either negligible or frequently centered around discussions of commodity production and capital accumulation, child labor in international relations is generally situated within the literature on human rights and international law. The "norms" school focuses on the dissemination of human rights norms through the agency of transnational social movements (Risse-Kappen 1995; Keck and Sikkink 1998; Donnelly 1999; Risse *et al.* 1999).[6] One of the shortcomings of the norms school, as discussed by Sheila Nair in this volume, is that it does not "interrogate its own liberal presumptions" about human rights and disturbingly assigns the liberal version of human rights with a universal moral force. Further, this school does not investigate the links between global capital and human rights violations. By their own admission, Risse *et al.* focus on "norm-violating states" and "norm-violating governments" (1999: 5). They do not concern themselves with the human rights violations of transnational or multinational corporations and international financial institutions. Thus these violations of the global economy do not feature in their work; they are most concerned with the violations of political rights by states and governments (Chowdhry and Beeman 2001). Since child labor and children's rights are heavily imbricated with global and national capital, the norms school on human rights thus fails to provide the tools necessary for analyzing child labor in the global economy.

Discourses on human rights in IR usually tend to cluster around a universalism/relativism binary (Washburn 1987; Rentlen 1988, 1990; Pannikar 1992; Perry 1997; Wilson 1997; Woodiwiss 1998; Booth 1999; Donnelly 1999). In international debates, child labor is often examined under the simple dualisms of universal human rights versus cultural relativism (for a discussion see Smolin 1999: 11–16). On the one hand, child labor evokes a "universal moral" discourse, against which only a few dare to speak out. In this genre an impassioned rhetoric, activism, and scholarship seeks a total ban on child labor. On the other hand, a "practical" and cultural relativist discourse suggests that the poor economic conditions of Third World countries dictate the need for child labor. Accordingly, these scholars suggest that economic development will end child labor in these countries.

Universal and relativist human rights

Although universalist and relativist analyses of human rights are seen as discrete and oppositional, there is much in common between them. I claim that both the universalists and relativists use "culturalist" arguments to promote their cause. Whereas the universalist discourse advocates global human rights on the basis of a universal human culture, or what it means to be human, their epistemological and ontological roots are ensconced in the imperial juncture and colonial readings of "native" culture. The contradictions

229

between their universal claims and parochial roots, and their claims to justice while their practices are rooted in colonial injustice, have contributed to their skeptical reception in much of the postcolonial world. In addition, the links of universal human rights claims to the current project of modernization, including modernization theory (Grewal 1999: 338) have also made it suspect to some in the Third World. The relativists suggest, however, that different histories have enabled different cultural understandings of rights which should be respected globally. It is interesting that both refer to culture as an entity and not a process, and both homogenize and reify culture. In addition, the imbrication of these culturalist arguments with global capital limits their analytical usefulness for understanding child labor.

Universalists, or proponents of universal human rights, argue that since human rights are embedded in a universal notion of humanity and are not tied to the practices of any one nation, they should be applicable universally. They assume that the discourse of human rights, or what it means to be human, is universal in its application, is beneficial to all people, and thus is – and should be – exportable (Elshtain 1999). Some cultural anthropologists and other human rights scholars have ventured beyond this international "secularism" to suggest that standards of human rights are not only a part of an individual's status as a person, but are a part of "a more complex story of the modern secular concept of what it means to be truly human" (Asad 1997: 111).

According to Asad (1997) the exporting of European versions of universal human rights to the Third World began with European colonization and is imbued with references to modernity and progress. Although itself premised on the violation of human rights, European rule often legitimized its presence in the colonies through its claims to eliminate certain forms of "inhumane" native cultural practices. Colonizers often outlawed what they claimed were culturally peculiar and inhumane practices of indigenous societies in the name of progress and *mission civilisatrice*.[7] Recent feminist scholarship on colonial cultural projects has placed gender and women at the heart of colonial constructions of indigenous cultures (see for example Spivak 1985, 1987; Abu-Lughod 1986; Mani 1989; Ahmed 1992; Narayan 1997). Descriptions of oppressive cultural practices that target indigenous women and the barbarity of the indigenous men who invented, sanctioned, and promoted such practices haunted the colonial imagination and often became the basis for marking the boundaries of civilized/human and barbaric/inhuman societies. For example, "oppressive" practices like veiling were often centerpieces in Western narratives about their "humanizing mission" (Ahmed 1992: 149–50).

These gendered and racialized images of identity and difference about Western and Third World people that were used to bolster the colonial project were not simply descriptive projects; rather they were "inevitably implicated in the discursive and political struggles that marked the colonial encounter" (Narayan 1997: 15). In addition, the obvious complicity of the racialized and gendered colonial project with international capital was significant. Consequently, current claims to universal human rights are mired in the political antagonisms of the colonial encounter and tend to be viewed with suspicion by many in the postcolonial world. For example, the 1948 Universal Declaration of Human Rights (United Nations 1948) is seen by critics as rooted in the experience of the Enlightenment, the particularities of a post-Second World War Europe, and the dominance of the United States in the international political economy. Thus, it "is universal only in pretension, not in practice, since it is a charter of an idealist European philosophy" (Wilson 1997: 4). Indeed, it has been argued that international human rights are a ruse for the exercise of realpolitik in which the United States (and the West) emerges as the leader of human rights (Lazreg 1979).

The close association of universal human rights with the colonialist project has an important historical and economic legacy. The racialized and gendered colonialist projects that attempted to redefine culture through "Western eyes" forever embroiled human rights and culture in the discourses of geopolitics. As a consequence culture and human rights have become symbolic and expedient tools of identity marking, as well as tools of inclusion and exclusion in discourses of resistance.[8] Further, universal human rights discourses continue to be used in the service of global capital. As Pheng Cheah (1999), among others, points out, human rights are used to protect US (Western) business and state interests. According to Cheah, the deployment of international financial and trade regimes in "neo-mercantilist" ways secures Western economic hegemony and destroys potential economic competition. These efforts

> should therefore be seen in a continuum with the curious homology between the ... (Western) use of human rights universalism to justify encroachments upon the national sovereignty of the developing south and the attempt of industrialized countries to increase the freedom of TNCs.
>
> (Cheah 1999: 25)

Ironically, but not surprisingly, these transnational corporations (TNCs) lobby against unionization and environmental standards, violate labor rights, and use child labor.

Although "relativists" are quick to point out the political, economic, and cultural shortcomings of the universalists' claims, their arguments are ironically similar to the latters'. First, relativists' claims are also premised on culturalist arguments; they suggest that different cultures have specific understandings of human rights and thus should not be subject to monolithic and so-called universal (read Western) human rights laws. Unlike the universalists' desire to level differences in the promotion of a universal humanism, the relativists valorize differences, suggesting that rights be culturally and historically contextualized (Rorty 1993; Dworkin 1977; Gellner 1982). According to cultural relativists, a Western, individualistic, liberal, legalistic assumption of human nature is prevalent in the universalists' assumptions of human rights. Hence focusing on universal human rights in which individual and community rights are seen as diametrically opposed is ethnocentric and Eurocentric (Obiora 1997). Further, according to relativists, international human rights law as presently constituted by the United Nations is also fundamentally grounded in Western understandings of individual rights and thus operates with a "normative blindness towards indigenous peoples," who may claim communal rights to land ownership or political self-determination (Falk 1992: 48).

Second, although relativists underscore the proximity of the universalists' human rights project to Western colonialism and capitalism, their position is also situated within the conjuncture of global capital. Nations deploying a relativist position often suggest that the location of their countries at early stages of development and their consequent preoccupation with issues of economic development, leads to the displacement of "first generation" human rights in their agendas. In these articulations economic development and political–civil liberties are oppositionally positioned and culturally based economic arguments become a decoy for ignoring civil and political rights. Further, authoritarian rulers have also often objected to the universal applicability of human rights to mask and rationalize their own violations of these rights (Tharoor 1999–2000) and their complicity with national and global capital as they pursue "crony capitalism" and policies that enhance the accumulation of capital and promote foreign direct and portfolio investments.

Notwithstanding the merits of both the universalist and relativist arguments, the limitations of these arguments are enormous. Both suffer from similar constraints in their understanding of culture and are equally compromised by their association with capital. Hence their analysis is of little value in understanding human rights and child labor. Cultural relativist claims to an authentic, fixed, and immutable culture are problematic, as is their tendency to valorize, homogenize, and reify culture (Sen 1997; Wilson 1997; Tharoor 1999–2000). The "contested, fragmented, contextualized and emergent" nature of culture is rejected by the relativists (Wilson 1997) who argue that an authentic indigenous culture exists and is domestically inclusive and dominant. The oversimplification of this argument not to mention the dangers are evident. As Amartya Sen suggests, "the rhetoric of cultures, with each 'culture' seen in largely homogenized terms, can confound us politically as well as intellectually" (1997: B11). It can also serve to oppress minority cultures in the body of the nation. Similarly and ironically, the universalist stance rejects the definition of culture as fluid, contested, and historically specific. In seeing Western civilization as the birthplace and natural reserve of desirable human values, universalists also naturalize culture as given, fixed, and immutable. In addition, the imbrication of both discourses with global capital leads them, sometimes in concert, to sanction oppression against indigenous and other forms of human rights struggles,[9] bolster existing power arrangements, and delegitimize those providing challenges to hegemonically defined boundaries of culture and power.

Postcolonial mapping of human rights

Uncomfortable with the cultural or moral nihilism of the universalists and relativists I, like postcolonial feminist scholars Grewal and Kaplan, refuse "either of these two moves" and explore instead the possibility of human rights activism (and analysis) across "cultural divides" (Grewal and Kaplan 1994: 2). While advancing a postcolonial perspective on human rights that is historically grounded and context specific, I suggest that scholars should locate their analysis of human rights in the imperial juncture. The importance of the imperial juncture for understanding human rights and child labor stems not only from its links to universal human rights claims and from its own history of human rights violations in its colonies, but also from the role that colonialism has played in the racialized and gendered constructions of the North and South. The discursive economy of representation and hierarchy embodied in these constructions has significant implications for the unequal distribution of power between the North and South (Said 1978; Spivak 1987; Mudimbe 1988; Mohanty 1991b) and thus for child labor and human rights.

As discussed previously, the intersection of knowledge and power was central for sustaining colonialism; colonial projects constructed indigenous cultures as morally inferior and mandated reform along "universal" (Western) lines. A significant finding of postcolonial feminist scholarship on human rights and indigenous cultural practices was that many of these practices were not necessarily remnants of a precolonial era; rather they were the result of the practices of codification, representation, and control by the colonial state (Mani 1989; Ahmed 1992). Thus, postcolonial scholarship on culture and human rights does not argue in favor of the universal or culturally relativist position; rather it seeks to uncover "the operations of power in relation to knowledge formation" and codification that existed historically and "that are emerging in the contexts of globalization at the turn of the century (Grewal 1999: 338). For example, how does the idea of human rights circulate? What are the identities and relations of power that are constituted through the circulation of this idea? How does this idea facilitate the dissimulation of power and workings of global capital? Here identity and meaning as well as material and political power can be understood as cultural contests (Alvarez *et al.* 1998) where culture and identity are constructed through the circulation of regimes of knowledge. Although postcolonial approaches have been mistakenly critiqued for focusing solely on cultural politics and neglecting the material impact of global capitalism (see Introduction), this chapter attends to such criticism by exploring the embeddedness of the universalist and nationalist discourses in the global capitalist economy.

The influence of subaltern studies on postcolonial scholarship and the consequent subaltern challenges to the elitist nature of Indian historiography also have significant implications for a postcolonial understanding of human rights. The subaltern project shifts "the crucial divide from that between colonial and anticolonial to that between 'elite' and 'subaltern'" (Loomba 1998: 200), focusing on the exclusions that nationalism has enabled (Chatterjee 1993; Lazarus 1994; Parry 1994; Illiah 1996; Prakash 1994, 1997). Situated between the global and national discursive economy, child labor claims can be better understood by utilizing subaltern insights to explore both its colonial–global and national–elite dimensions.

Constructing identity: child labor, global capital, and representation

To appreciate the extent to which race, gender, and class are insinuated in global and national discourses on child labor, we must explore how these discourses are implicated in the imperial moment, and the "conjuncture of global capital," and the ways in which they construct North–South identity and reinforce global hierarchies. This section begins by outlining the history of the carpet industry in India and linking its integration into the global economy with the British colonial project. Next, I explore US media and policy discourses to suggest that they reflect a universalist position on child labor, one that obfuscates the role of global capital in child labor. These discourses revitalize an orientalist discursive economy and consequently reinforce the hierarchy between the North and South (Said 1978).[10]

The global economy and child labor in the carpet industry

The origins of the carpet industry in India can be traced to the end of the sixteenth century, around 1580 AD, when the Mughal emperor Akbar invited Persian carpet weavers to set up a royal workshop in the emperor's palace in India.[11] Although Akbar is credited with the introduction of carpets into India, his son and grandson, Mughal emperors Jehangir and Shah Jehan, are said to be responsible for bringing Indian carpets to their current international prominence (Waziri 1986; Saraf 1986; Juyal 1993).[12] Carpets woven during their reign are displayed in museums across Europe, including the Victoria and Albert Museum in London. A few are also housed in the Jaipur Museum in India (Saraf 1986).

About 80 per cent of the carpets currently produced in India are from the carpet-belt of Mirzapur and Bhadohi in the state of Uttar Pradesh. A popular account states that in 1857, during the first war of independence, soldiers from the Mughal army were waylaid on the Grand Trunk Road near the villages of Madhosinh and Ghosia located between Mirzapur and Bhadohi (Juyal 1993). Another account claims that in response to the 1857 war of independence, carpet weavers fled from the city of Akbarabad, now known as Agra, and sought refuge in the villages of Madhosinh and Ghosia. In both these accounts these refugees took up carpet weaving to make a living and soon the area of Mirzapur–Bhadohi came to be associated with carpet production.

However, it was not until the industry came to the attention of British international capital that large-scale carpet production and consequently a restructuring of the industry occurred. In the late nineteenth century when India was under British colonial rule, the carpet industry drew the attention of Mr Brownford, a Britisher, who established E. Hill and Company in the village of Khamaria, followed by the creation of H. Tellary in Badohi and Obeetee in Mirzapur (Waziri 1986).[13] Although prominent colonial firms like the East India Company, Mitchel and Company, and Hadow and Company were also involved in carpet production and trade in the states of Punjab, Kashmir, and other carpet-producing areas in Uttar Pradesh,[14] it was Mirzapur–Badohi that acquired a prominent national and international position in the handmade carpet industry.[15] According to Juyal (1993: 13), Mirzapur–Bhadohi accounts for 85–90 per cent of the total value of carpet exports with an annual turnover of two billion US dollars; the "Indian carpet industry has become almost synonymous with what is commonly known as the Mirzapur–Badohi carpet belt" (Juyal 1993: 13).

Since the carpet industry was traditionally located in households, it employed family labor, using children as apprentices in the production of carpets. However, the integration of the carpet industry into the global economy forever changed the nature and structure of the industry in India. The successful exhibition of Indian carpets at the 1851 Great Exhibition in London drew the attention of international buyers and producers and further embedded the industry in the international political economy. Subsequently, as noted above, many British companies invested in the carpet industry in India. Whereas the integration of the carpet industry into the international economy reinvigorated carpet production, it also led to a transfer of control from local weavers situated in household-based economies to British merchant traders located in international capital. Since the industry was now geared largely toward exports, Western tastes and Western markets became increasingly influential in carpet production, leading to the decline in quality of Indian carpets (Juyal 1993).[16] In addition, this integration increased the exploitation of carpet weavers, including children. Since then, the carpet industry has been one of the major sources of export from India and control of carpet production continues to remain in the hands of merchant traders, who are now mostly Indians (Juyal 1993).

One of the significant impacts of the internationalization of carpet trade was that child wage labor and bonded labor were introduced into an industry dominated by child apprentices. Because of social and state vigilance the incidence of bonded labor has been on the decline. The Child Labour Act of 1986 prohibits the use of child labor in twenty-five hazardous industries, including the carpet industry.[17] However, the Indian carpet industry still employs about 300,000 children in all stages of carpet production including pre-processing, weaving, and carpet finishing activities such as dyeing and washing (Tucker 1997).[18] Official statistics citing an independent survey taken by the National Council of Applied and Economic Research claim that child labor is on the decline; from 8 per cent (of total weavers employed) in 1992 to 5.1 per cent in 1997 (Misra 1999). Unofficial statistics suggest that the percentage of bonded labor far exceeds those of wage earners (McDonald 1992; Juyal 1993; Mehta 1994; Dutt 1995). The argument of "nimble fingers" has often been used to explain the demand for child labor in carpet weaving. Proclaiming the mythical nature of this argument, activists have argued that the wage differential between children and adult weavers better accounts for the degree of child labor in that industry.

Carpet manufacturers and traders claim that the "decentralized" and "cottage" nature of the carpet industry prevents any kind of monitoring by them; loom owners in the villages and in their own houses can use child labor without the knowledge of manufacturers and traders. However, according to Juyal, this picture is seriously misleading on several accounts. Despite claims by the carpet manufacturers about the decentralized nature of the carpet industry, it is a highly controlled industry with contractors, subcontractors and manufacturers coordinating all the production and distribution activities to maximize exports. Thus the carpet industry has always had an "organized" sector, in which various carpet production related activities, with the exception of weaving, have occurred. More recently carpet weaving itself is being done in factories, further increasing the organized component of carpet production. In addition, it was the carpet manufacturers who introduced and fostered the "unorganized" sector in order to undercut the power of organized labor in carpet production. Thus, the integration of the carpet industry into the global economy, the increase in global demand for carpets, the consumer demand for finer and cheaper hand-woven carpets internationally, and the desire for increasing profit margins in the carpet industry have contributed greatly to the increase in child labor.

How is child labor, which increased through the carpet industries' integration into the global economy, represented in global and national discourses? According to David Campbell, the

> discursive economy of identity/difference allows us to think of discourse (the representation and constitution of the "real") as a managed space in which some statements and depictions come to have greater value than others ... and participation in the discursive economy is through social relations that embody an unequal distribution of power.
>
> (1994: 161)

The location of Western mainstream media in the North and their global reach engenders the weight given to their analysis. As explored below, because Western media discourses on child labor are widely disseminated they are able to naturalize certain understandings of child labor, and also revitalize North–South identities and unequal relations of power.

Representing child labor: universalism in mainstream US media discourse

Ronald Inden (1990) discusses the relationship between "imperial formation" and imperial knowledge in *Imagining India*. He suggests that "universalizing discourses, the world-constituting cosmologies, ontologies, and epistemologies" of "those who presume to speak with authority" for others, are central to the imperialist project (Inden 1990: 36). The knowledge of these "hegemonic agents" is privileged by the economic power they command, and is legitimized by its reference to objectivity and rationality, thereby appropriating the power to represent the "other" (Inden 1990). With attention to child labor in general (although information specific to India is included as well) this section explores the "imperial formation" around child labor, suggesting that the role of the mainstream media in the production and circulation of meanings is critical to the emergence of a "common sense" around these issues, which leads to an obfuscation of the interconnections between human rights and capital. The role of the media in forging a common sense around identity and global economic and foreign policy has been explored by scholars such as Herman and Chomsky (1988) and Said (1997), among others. For example, Said (1997: 47) suggests that daily newspapers, "mass-circulation news magazines," and television and radio networks "constitute a communal core of interpretations providing a certain picture of Islam" to the United States. Further, he adds, US media coverage of foreign countries not only constructs their identities but also forges US identity and "intensifies interests 'we' already have there" (Said 1997: 52). Using these insights, I suggest that US media representations of child labor play a significant role in constructing global hierarchies and relations of power, and reflect both the concerns and limitations of the universalist position on human rights.[19]

Space, location, and power

I begin with a discussion of spatial metaphors and the implications of such metaphors for knowledge and power. I agree with Agnew that "representations of space are not isolated, idiosyncratic or marginal," rather they are "deeply embedded in ... intellectual fields" (Agnew 1994: 87). These intellectual fields, as Said (1978, 1994, 1997) and Inden (1990) have pointed out, are shaped by imperial histories and current conjunctures of power. Hence "by always foregrounding the spatial distribution of hierarchical power relations, we can better understand the process whereby a space achieves a distinctive identity as a place" (Gupta and Ferguson 1992: 8). Critical to spatial metaphors is the drawing of boundaries, or "distancing," a technique that race theorists suggest is key to the construction of "other" and "self." I argue here that the spatial representations by Western media and Western policymakers around child labor reinscribe colonial identity, hierarchy, and power. The location of home, where child labor flourishes, is not simply informative; rather it constructs self and other, North and South in orientalist ways to establish difference and hierarchy. Since the discourse of morality is so central to child labor investigations, the location of child labor becomes at once an immoral and irresponsible terrain in contrast to a moral and responsible location in which such practices do not occur. These discourses on child labor establish home and location along the binaries of Western/non-Western, developed/developing, First World/Third World, rich/poor, and importing/exporting nations, with only the latter being directly implicated in child labor practices.

Central to these discourses of child labor is the underlying assumption that the spatial divisions between nations are not merely territorial, they are also identity (culturally) driven. The presence of child labor practices in non-Western countries, like India, becomes a trope used to demarcate cultural and national boundaries. India is constructed as the spatial and cultural other where child labor is heavily used, while Western countries are the self set apart from any direct culpability for child labor. By interrogating these representations, I am not suggesting here that they are fictitious; child labor is indeed prevalent in India and the exploitation of children needs to be addressed. Rather I am suggesting that multiple "communities of interpretations" (Said 1997) exist around child labor that are often at odds with each other. While the mainstream US media is a dominant player in these communities, its discourses are often reductive and provide simplistic, identity and geopolitics driven analysis of the "other." In addition, I suggest that the spatial distancing visible in mainstream US media discourses often elides the imbrication of the West in child labor practices and the centrality of spatial metaphors in the construction of culture, nation, and global hierarchy.

However, "since a labor activist revealed that daytime TV talk-show co-host Kathy Lee Gifford's line of sportswear was produced by youngsters working long hours in a Honduran sweatshop" (Berlau 1997: 20), some media sources and policymakers have begun to acknowledge that Western countries are implicated in the practice of child labor. Nevertheless, they portray them generally as recipients of goods made from child labor rather than being directly implicated in its practice. Note for instance this statement by Senator Tom Harkin when he is describing what his bill, the Child Labor Deterrence Act, seeks. According to him, the bill

> prohibits the importation of any product made in whole or in part by youngsters under 15. In addition, the bill directs the US Secretary of Labor to compile and maintain a list of *foreign industries* and their respective countries of origin that use child labor in the production of exports to the US. Once such a foreign industry has been identified, the Secretary of the Treasury is instructed to prohibit the entry of any of its goods.
>
> (Harkin 1996: 74, emphasis added)

Senator Harkin is clearly holding foreign industries responsible for child labor. Even in these instances where US businesses and US consumers are implicated in the consumption of goods made from child labor, it is often alleged that "few US investors and even fewer US consumers would knowingly buy products made from the sweat and toil of children" (Moran 1997). Senator Tom Harkin also supports this assumption about US consumers and businesses:

> I do not believe that American consumers knowingly would buy products made with child labor, but, most often they don't know. Moreover, no respectable importer, company, or department store willingly would promote the exploitation of children.
>
> (Harkin 1996: 74)

Typically, even though many may highlight Western engagement – as consumers and importers – in child labor practices, the onus for child labor practices is placed squarely in the hands of non-Western countries. The West is implicated only in an indirect way, as consumers of goods made from child labor or as corporations that contract out to "irresponsible" subcontractors.[20]

An important failure of this discourse is that it rarely mentions the use and practice of child labor in the Western world, say, for example, in migrant labor practices in agriculture or sweatshops in the United States. Similarly, although Nike or other Western corporations may get mentioned for the violation of child labor, a closer look reveals that it is not the parent company Nike but its subcontracting unit in a Third World country that becomes the focus of these discussions. Even in these cases, child labor is seen as an aberration; it is generally implied that only non-Western forms of capital use child labor and it is not integral to the structure of capitalism. In addition, how Western capitalism gets implicated in child labor practices is also rarely addressed. In fact the following comment is typical of mainstream media's position on the role of capitalism *vis-à-vis* child labor: "some critics blame capitalism, others the children's parents" (Economist 1994a: 46).

In these representations of child labor practices the non-Western and Western world once again gets recreated in the colonial mold; repugnant cultural practices of the non-Western world encourage child labor, signaling inhumane traditions and lack of modernity in the "dark continent(s)." This discourse constructs the cultural identity of the non-Western world as traditional, as backward, and as a violator of human rights. In a replay of colonial imagery, the West gets represented in contrast to the non-Western world as enlightened, as modern, and as respectful of human rights.

The "modern self" and the "traditional other"

The moment of contact more than 500 years ago, when Columbus set out to "find" India and "discovered" the Americas, was sustained not only by brutal colonial practices but by a discourse machinery that legitimized the colonial presence (see Said 1978). Central to this process of legitimation was the construction of racialized and gendered identities of the other that were inferior to the European self. Post-World War II modernization theory, dominant in the field and practice of development studies, further cemented these classifications along a racialized and gendered modern/traditional binary. Whereas the characteristics associated with being modern – rationality, strength, belief in science and technology, achievement orientation, association with mental work – are also the characteristics associated with masculinity, characteristics associated with being traditional like irrationality, superstition, weakness and passivity, fatalism, association with manual work, ascription, and emotion are also associated with femininity. In addition, modern characteristics were ascribed to white Europeans while traditional characteristics were associated with Africans, Asians, and Latin Americans.

This modern self/traditional other dichotomy is also evident within the Western discourse of child labor as demonstrated, for example, by the statement "no *reasonable* person can support child labor" (Economist 1995a: 13; emphasis added). Myron Weiner, a prominent political science expert on India, and more recently an "expert" on child labor in India, has argued that the incidence of child labor in India is less a function of its poverty and more a function of its belief systems:

> (T)here is historical and comparative evidence to suggest that the major obstacles to the achievement of primary education and the abolition of child labor are not the level of industrialization, per capita income and the socio-economic conditions of families, the level of overall government expenditures in education, nor the demographic consequences of a rapid expansion in the number of school age children, four widely suggested explanations. India has made less of an effort ... than many other countries not for economic or demographic reasons but because of its attitude of government officials, politicians, trade union leaders, workers in voluntary agencies, religious figures, intellectuals, and the influential middle class toward child labor and compulsory primary education.
>
> (Weiner 1996: 287–9)

Weiner argues that there is an essential Indian attitude that cuts across state and nonstate workers, religious leaders, different ideologies, and intellectuals as well as the entire middle class! According to him this attitude results from India's religious and caste system, which advocates "that some people are born to rule and to work with their minds while others are born to work with their bodies" (Weiner 1996: 31). Weiner, in an orientalist move, suggests that the essence of India and being Indian is premised on religious and cultural inequality. Weiner's analysis suggests that no one can escape the "Indian way of thinking" because Indian culture is homogenous, rigid, immanent, and unchanging. This depiction of child labor as a function of characteristics uniquely Indian – the Indian attitude – constructs child labor in primordial ways. For Weiner, it is the excrescence of Indianness, not a function of global or national poverty, nor a pathology of modernity that leads to the prevalence of child labor in India.

The homogenized and undifferentiated view of Indians and Indian attitudes articulated by Weiner is also partially reflected in the writings of Pharis Harvey, a prominent child labor activist who currently heads Rugmark in the United States.[21] Although Harvey has generally provided a more sophisticated analysis of child labor, even linking it to the "integration of the world's poor areas into production for the global markets" (Harvey 1995: 3), implicit in his article is the argument that Indian religions tolerate and support a social hierarchy. He contrasts this to Christianity, writing that the "gospel does not allow us to assign higher value to some of God's people than others" (Harvey 1995: 2). However,

> Christians do not stand alone in their opposition to child labor; in India the lead is taken by reform groups of Hindu and Muslim

faith. But the impact of Christian faith on this problem is profound. Kerala, where Christianity is strongest, has had the most success in coping with child servitude.

(Harvey 1995: 6)

He acknowledges that this may be in part due to the values of equality espoused by the communist governments in Kerala, but he holds that "Christian concepts that value women, oppose caste discrimination and emphasize education" are responsible for the reduced incidence of child labor in Kerala (Harvey 1995: 6). Although Harvey, unlike Weiner, has admitted that Hindu and Muslim faith groups are organizing against child labor, he calls them "reform groups," implying that mainstream Hindu and Muslim groups in contrast are deeply embedded in the hierarchies that create child labor. While this may be true, it is equally true that Christianity has been acutely located in global injustice at an unprecedented scale. The pivotal role played by Christianity in colonization is not a secret. Neither is it a secret that institutional Christianity has supported capitalism. The uncritical glance that Harvey bestows on Christianity is therefore surprising. More significantly Harvey also ignores the impact of Kerala's matrilineal system on the education and empowerment of women and children.

The links to "imperial formations" about India, rather than to an essential corporeal reality are evident in this discourse. India and Indians have been classically represented as deeply embedded in Hinduism and caste, and an Indian way of thinking has been cited as the main cause of child labor in India. According to Inden (1990), the orientalist literature on India has argued that the key to understanding India is Hinduism, which they consider integral both to its otherworldliness and to its caste system. Further, Hinduism is often presented "as a sponge," "as a 'mysterious amorphous entity,' one that is palpable yet lacks something" (Inden 1990: 86).

What is the essence that Hinduism – and, therefore India – lacks? It is what I refer to as "world-ordering rationality" ... Implicit here is also the idea that Hinduism is a female presence who is able, through her very amorphousness, and absorptive powers, to baffle and perhaps even threaten Western rationality, clearly a male in this encounter. European reason penetrates the womb of Indian unreason but always at the risk of being engulfed by her.

(Inden 1990: 86)

Western child labor imaginaries are built on the edifice of these earlier gendered and racialized mythologies, which reinforce the hierarchies that enable the West, its institutions, and its activists and scholars to be constructed as the masculine, moral rationalists in contrast to a feminized, immoral, and irrational India.

Imbrication with capital

In the representations of child labor explored above, the West is often constructed as the savior of children in India, and Western (read universal) understandings of human rights are given a critical role in the elimination of child labor in India. These discourses, however, do not generally locate this problem in world capitalism; rather, in a replay of colonial and modernization analysis, they seek the reform of Indian (Third World) cultural attitudes and of feudal working arrangements. For example, George Reisman, a professor of economics at Pepperdine University, claims that the only way to eliminate child labor is to advocate "saving, investment, economic freedom and respect for property rights" (quoted in Berlau 1997: 4). The ideological dogmatism behind these claims is apparent. For Reisman, economic freedom and respect for property rights, i.e. unfettered capitalism, will bring an end to child labor. A number of scholars like Reisman have conflated capitalism with human rights. However, critics have exposed the myths of such a conflation by pointing to the human rights violations brought about by the internationalization of capital. For example, critics have demonstrated that the "processes set in motion by international capital (through the IMF)" in India have led to increases in poverty and consequently child labor, as well as cutbacks in the state budget (Forum of Indian Leftists 1996: 6). These cutbacks have not only limited the capacity of the Indian state to offer welfare policies but have also led to a steep drop in the education budget (Forum of Indian Leftists 1996: 6). The universalists who seek to ban child labor but do not locate their critique in the global economy fail to grapple with the complexity of child labor, and their solutions often service Western nationalist and business causes.

Further, these critics have also pointed out that the discourse of universal human rights is insinuated in global capital. One such example has been the move by the global campaign against child labor to link labor standards and trade. The United States and European nations (with the exception of Britain and Germany), many Western non-governmental organizations (NGOs) working on child labor and human rights, and several US policy-makers – notable among them Senator Tom Harkin – have argued for linking labor standards to trade, suggesting that child labor is "illicit" protectionism by the Third World, providing an "unfair" comparative advantage to it (Smolin 1999: 4–8). Although critics are convinced of Harkin's moral conviction on issues of child labor, they question the timing of these proposals. The Forum of Indian Leftists (FOIL), a group of progressive Indians active in the United States and elsewhere, asks: "why did Senator Tom Harkin ... propose a bill ... to fight child labor in industrially backward nations in September 1994?" (1996: 2). According to them, the 1991 Multilateral Trade Negotiations, an outcome of the 1986 General Agreement on Tariffs and Trade (GATT), includes the Agreement on Textiles and Clothing which will be integrated into GATT in 2003. India's quota for textiles was raised in this agreement. The Forum of Indian Leftists has suggested that the Child Labor Deterrence Act was a way to help the US textile industry "equal input costs" so that they did not lose their share of the US market. Implicit in this argument is the claim that the universal human rights discourse is situated within global capital and knowingly or unknowingly services it. The next section examines how the cultural relativist discourse is also situated at the intersections of capital.

National discourses on child labor in India

There are multiple national discourses on child labor in India and it is indeed undesirable to present them collectively in any kind of a homogenous way. In this section, I focus on the discourses of the state and carpet manufacturers, to explore how they are shaped by cultural relativism and situated in relation to capital. I begin by noting the prevalence of child labor in the Indian carpet industry and the importance of the carpet industry to the Indian economy.

Despite the provision of child labor legislation in the Indian Constitution, including the Bonded System Abolition Act (1976) and the Child Labour Act of 1986, the incidence of child labor continues to prevail in the carpet industry in India (Chowdhry and Beeman 2001). As previously mentioned, unofficial statistics suggest that about 300,000 children continue to be employed in the carpet industry in India (Tucker 1997). The carpet industry is one of the most lucrative export industries in India. Export earnings from the sale of Indian carpets have been increasing, from US $316.13 million in 1993–4 to $478.68 million in 1998–9, an increase of about 51 per cent (Juyal 1993), with the biggest share of exports going to Germany and the United States.[22] Thus the carpet industry is critical to the Indian economy, particularly in the age of neo-liberalization.

The All India Carpet Manufacturers' Association (AICMA)[23] and the Indian government, represented by the "parastatal" Carpet Export Promotion Council (CEPEC)[24] claim that the human rights demands of Western NGOs and policymakers to ban and regulate child labor in the carpet industry are neo-mercantilist and advantage the interests of Western nations in a competitive global economy. They suggest that the human rights organizations in Germany and the United States, which have been central to the struggle for eliminating child labor, like Bread for the World, Misereor, Terre des Hommes, and the Robert F. Kennedy Center for Human Rights, may have argued for the abolition of child labor on moral grounds, but their work serves the interest of Western nations and a larger agenda of Western labor and business protection.

Trade sanctions, and the effort to link labor standards to trade, are also seen as promoting the interests of Western capital and Western states. AICMA and CEPEC have argued that since child labor in India as in other

Third World countries is the result of poverty, trade sanctions and labor standards will only result in more poverty and thus more child labor:

> Any such action as restrictions on imports of hand-knotted carpets by traditional buyers on the basis of adverse publicity about the alleged exploitation of child labor will be a retrograde step as it would certainly kill the carpet industry resulting only in increased levels of rural poverty.
>
> (CEPEC quoted in Juyal 1993: 28)

They point out the tragedy of Bangladesh where the mere threat of sanctions had contradictory effects and "forced" children from the textile industries into other more dangerous work. In contrast, Senator Tom Harkin of the United States, who introduced the Child Labor Deterrence Act in 1992 to ban the import of goods made with child labor, does not believe the authenticity of UNICEF reports that suggest that sanctions may have contradictory effects. According to a UNICEF report, the threat of sanctions induced panic among Bangladesh garment makers who then laid off child workers. According to UNICEF, some of the children ended up in more hazardous industries like prostitution or welding (Fairclough 1996):

> Asked by Insight to comment on the UNICEF report, Harkin's spokesman denied the authenticity of the UNICEF conclusion without explanation, faxing the response: "There is no evidence that ... the children dismissed from their jobs in Bangladesh entered more dangerous working situations."
>
> (Harkin in Berlau 1997: 3)

The differences between the positions of Harkin (read universalist) and AICMA and CEPEC officials (read relativist) are telling. Harkin does not believe that an economic and cultural relativism needs to be deployed to understand the complexity of child labor. For him it is an evil that needs to be completely and immediately expunged (Layla 1998). In contrast, both CEPEC and AICMA, staking an economic and culturally relativist position, claim that while they too find child labor morally undesirable, the needs of poor families as well as those of developing economies necessitate a more contingent stance on child labor.

It is interesting that child labor activists in Asia, like Kailash Satyarthi, who routinely challenge AICMA and CEPEC on child labor issues, partially agree. In an interview with the author Satyarthi suggested that while he supported Senator Harkin's Child Labor Deterrence Act, he also opposed the protectionist clauses in the bill (Satyarthi 1992, 1994).[25] Assefa Bequele, a Bangkok-based child labor expert at the International Labor Organization (ILO), stated that "trade penalties may actually be counter-productive"

(Fairclough 1996). The comments on trade sanctions of Butterflies, a non-governmental organization in India, also reflect a similar position:

> The campaign for the use of trade sanctions against child labor in developing countries is another variant of the same abolitionism (foreclosing the option of labor as a tool of survival) ... Such a campaign would contribute to extending the power of developed countries over the supply chain to the Western market, thereby dominating the terms of international trade.
>
> (Butterflies 1998: 51)

Despite the agreement on trade sanctions and labor standards, there is little else that activists, carpet manufacturers, and government officials agree on. While the latter point to poverty and the culture of poverty in their analysis, many of the more progressive Indian activists see child labor as rooted in the exclusions of national history. They argue that the economic relativist position of India, like the universalist position of the West on child labor, is equally located in the forcefield of global and national capital.

Nation, capital, and its exclusions

As stated earlier, child labor in the carpet industry is an outcome of poverty. However, I believe that poverty is "an outcome of unequal access to productive assets, structurally in-built inequities and a pattern of development which further accentuates these factors" (Butterflies 1998: 50). The peripheral position of the state in the global economy also accentuates these exclusions. Chatterjee (1993) has discussed the subaltern exclusions of India; according to him, *dalitbahujans*, *adivasis*, poor women, and others who do not own the means of production and have been rendered socially and culturally marginal were not included in and continue to be excluded from the nationalist project. In contrast, the Indian nationalist project, particularly in its neo-liberal avatar, has always included business, state, and elite interests. Further, since the nature of the Indian state frames the relationship of state and society, it is not surprising that poor children, 80 per cent of whom come from the families of *dalitbahujans* and *adivasis*, are in a structurally disadvantageous position *vis-à-vis* the state because of their class, caste–ethnic, and gender backgrounds. Household-level surveys conducted by B.N. Juyal bear this fact out for the carpet industry where more than 90 per cent of child labor comes from the "scheduled castes/tribes, the lower backward castes and low status groups within the Muslim community" (Juyal 1993: 61). These children and their families are "caught in the aporetic embrace between a predatory [international] capitalism and an indigenous capitalism" seeking to compete (Cheah 1999: 26) even though the power of indigenous capital to compete is often caught in the cracks of global hegemony. Those supporting universal human rights ask for total abolition of child labor. However, they are often unwilling or unable to change the structure of global capitalism or national power relations. Hence, the certainty for poor children to either remain in abysmal poverty or become even more precariously located in it is real. Similarly, those supporting a culturally relativist position also do not provide a way out of this poverty for children. The explanation that development will bring an end to child labor barely hides the class bias of the state. Waiting for development does not lessen the anxiety of waiting and the cruelty of poverty; development may prove to be ephemeral, if it has not proven so already. Child labor thus remains caught in the global and national faultlines of capital.

Agency, resistance, and reform

The significance of resistance for challenging dominant discourses and practices surrounding child labor cannot be overstated. Resistance ranges from activism and the recovery of children's voices to unveiling the discursive economy that surrounds child labor. While previous sections have been an effort at the latter, the following pages discuss the activism surrounding child labor and the recovery of children's voices.

Child rights activists have worked hard to bring child labor to the attention of national policymakers. Kailash Satyarthi and Swami Agnivesh have been at the forefront of the campaign to free bonded children employed in the Indian carpet industry. Through the raids conducted by Bandhua Mukti Morcha (the Bonded Labor Liberation Front) many bonded children have gained their freedom. Although, according to Satyarthi, the work of freeing bonded children was initially rewarding, it was also disheartening to see either the same children returned to bondage or their replacement by other children. In 1986, Satyarthi and other activists formed the South Asian Coalition on Child Servitude (SACCS). Given the export-oriented nature of the carpet industry, and the fact that in 1998–9 Germany and the United States accounted for 68 per cent of these exports, Satyarthi worked with German and US activists to initiate a consumer boycott. Further recognizing the limitations of boycotts alone, Satyarthi and other activists established Rugmark, a label that declares that no child labor was used to make the carpet.[26] Rugmark has used its revenues to establish schooling programs for children. In addition, they have also created Balashraya, where freed bonded laborers are housed, educated, trained, and "rehabilitated" into society. They have also assisted their graduates in finding work. Ironically, some of their graduates have taken up work in the carpet industry. However, charges of anti-nationalism and being Western agents have been leveled against Satyarthi and Rugmark. For example, focusing on the adverse publicity about the carpet industry (and India) that was generated by the exposure of its use of child labor, CEPEC commented that "the adverse publicity as such can be termed as an act which is anti-Indian and the government should take immediate action against such acts before it is too late" (CEPEC in Juyal 1993: 28).

However, the repeated efforts and pressure by activists in India and abroad led to the development and implementation of the Child Labour Act of 1986. In response AICMA leveled counter-charges against the government and the child rights activists. In a 1991 *Carpet-e-World*, the carpet industry journal, the manufacturers suggest that it is the conspiracy of the government and the activists to keep these children poor. While the government has been accused of formulating an impractical law that has created labor-related bottlenecks for the carpet industry and impaired their ability to increase carpet exports and acquire hard currency, Swami Agnivesh has been singled out as wanting "poverty to continue so he can continue to serve them [the poor and their children]" (Juyal 1993: 27).

How does resistance and agency get represented in child labor discourses? Despite the efforts of Satyarthi, Agnivesh, and numerous other activists as well as organizations like Butterflies, it is interesting but not surprising that US media have associated the efforts to eradicate child labor mostly with the Western world. For sure, the efforts and money of German activists and organizations like Terre Des Haufe, Bread for the World, and Misereor have been critical in establishing Rugmark in India. However, these organizations have worked in concert with their Indian partners, and the leadership of Indian activists has been central to the success of Rugmark. It is discouraging to note that despite this partnership mainstream US media generally ignores the role of Indian activists and places greater emphasis on Western actors. This is indeed in direct contrast to the efforts of child labor activists around the world, such as Kailash Satyarthi, who have been instrumental in bringing the plight of child labor in the carpet industry to the forefront and in establishing Rugmark. Satyarthi has recently been the chief architect of the Global March Against Child Labor. He has also testified on issues of child labor to the UN Commission of Human Rights. Another Indian activist, Swami Agnivesh, the crusader against bonded child labor, has worked tirelessly for the eradication of child labor. Butterflies, Bandhua Mukti Morcha, Mukti Ashram, and the Committee for the Eradication of Child Labour (a composite of twelve organizations) are a few of those working on issues related to child labor in India. That the 12-year-old child labor activist from Pakistan, Iqbal Masih, was gunned down in 1995 for his activism on child labor issues should certainly guarantee him a place in the annals of child labor activist history. The Bonded Liberation Front of Pakistan and the organizations listed for India were responsible for bringing the plight of child labor in the carpet industry to the attention of the world. However, in a Tarzan type version of human rights, popular media articles give very little agency to "natives." They are mostly portrayed as the perpetrators of injustice, rarely those who seek to undo injustice despite ample evidence to the contrary.

Further, the voices of children are missing from both the nationalist and universalist discourses. It is assumed that since they are children, their voices do not matter. Once again there is no monolithic position that is articulated by all children. On the one hand, working children's organizations like Programa Muchacho Trabajador (PMT) in Peru and Ninos y Adoloscentes Trabajadores (NATS) with branches in Latin America, West Africa, India, and Thailand in Asia are contesting the United Nations policy to abolish child labor. They are "instead trying to build a worldwide structure to give them a voice in matters that concern them" (Boukhari 1999: 1). Their positions are pragmatic. They suggest that the United Nations should make a distinction between exploitation and work. Concerned for Working Children in India, like their counterparts NATS and PMT, argue that "inhuman and dangerous categories of labour, like slavery, prostitution, drug trafficking, and work harmful to health" should be "regarded as punishable crimes" and not work (Boukhari 1999: 2). However, arguing against a legal minimum age and consumer boycotts, they suggest that child labor activists and the United Nations should work to establish safe working conditions and decent wages for them (Boukhari 1999; Cisneros 1999). In essence they are asking for the formation of a children's union. In December of 1994, the Campaign Against Child Labour organized a conference in Chennai in which about 1,000 child laborers participated.

> The youth demanded access to education "near our houses," free books and uniforms ... and jobs for their parents (who struggle with debt), and daycare for their siblings. In the meantime they hoped for some rights in the workplace – some form of unionization as an interim measure.
>
> (Prashad 1999: 4)

On the other hand, many children seek to end child labor and participate in education and training toward a better future. For example, working children across the world participated in the Global March Against Child Labor and asked for an end to child labor and for the privileges of a safe world that middle-class children have. Child laborers in India have actively participated in the "Bachpan Bachao Andolan" (Save Childhood movement) which is a South Asian anti-child-slavery organization whose chairperson is Kailash Satyarthi. The activities of the children range from demonstrations to sit-ins (*dharnas*), protesting against a range of child labor abuses. Children working in the carpet industry support the ban on child labor and ask for rights to a universal education. "Thirteen-year-old Mohan," a child laborer in the carpet industry "has a dream: he wants to be a superintendent of police" and he wants to make sure that no child should be made to work for a living

(SACCS 2000). However, some children whom I interviewed at Balashraya also supported better working conditions and wages for themselves. Different than the universalists and cultural relativists, these children appear to have recognized their vantage point as workers in the global economy.

Conclusion: postcolonial considerations on child rights

In summary, this chapter suggests that the binary classification of human rights discourse into universal and relativist dichotomies does little to increase our understanding of child labor, provides only moribund arguments about human rights more broadly, and serves only to obfuscate the role of capital in child labor. It further claims that a postcolonial examination of child labor provides us with an analysis that is more revealing about the project of global hierarchy, within which power is in part sustained by racial, gender, and class inequities. The intersection of knowledge and power in child labor representations and the ways in which the script of nation and nationalism works in the service of children's rights in supporting and challenging the universal and relativist constructions of child labor is better uncovered through a postcolonial analysis.

What is one to make of all this? By exploring the ways in which the universalist discourses, unknowingly or knowingly, service Western nationalisms and capital interests, I am not suggesting that child labor abuses do not occur in the Third World. Indeed, statistics on child labor in Africa, Asia, and Latin America are staggering when compared to child labor in the West. Rather, I suggest that the failure of universalists to place child labor in the "aporetic embrace" of capitalism and global and national power hierarchies compromises its moral stance. Similarly, the moral limitations of the relativist arguments have been highlighted as is their location in competing capitalist claims. In contrast, a postcolonial analysis calls for a comprehensive approach to child labor in which the role of child labor in the production and circulation of commodities, as well as meanings, is interrogated. In this chapter I have explored the interconnections between global and national discourses and their imbrication with capital. Further, I have argued that despite the work of Satyarthi and Butterflies, among others, little attention is given to them compared to Western activists and organizations, which again points to the role of race and nation in (re)producing global hierarchies. I have also highlighted modes of activism that hinge on the recovery of children's voices and the interrogation of the discursive economy surrounding child labor. Finally, a postcolonial analysis has implications for global activism as well. It suggests that activists be cognizant of the power hierarchies and dangers that underlie the easy rhetoric of both the universalists and the relativists.

Acknowledgements

I thank the children of Balashraya who welcomed me into their midst and were willing to share their stories and their hopes. I also thank AICMA and CEPEC members, Mr Kailash Satyarthi, and Rugmark officials in Mirzapur –Bhadohi, New Delhi, and Germany who discussed their work with children and who helped me develop a better understanding of the issue. In addition, I thank Mark Beeman, Sheila Nair, and Jessica Urban for their comments on the manuscript.

Notes

1 Iqbal Masih had worked in Pakistan's carpet industry since he was six. After being rescued from bondage by the Bonded Labor Liberation Front of Pakistan (BLLF-P) in 1992, Masih joined it and became its president. He was honored for his work by the Reebok Human Rights Foundation in December of 1994 in Boston. He testified to the International Labor Organization on behalf of bonded children. He was killed in April of 1995 by 120 pellet wounds to his back. His death, it was assumed, was caused by the "carpet mafia" in Pakistan. The initial police report did not contradict this story. However, a later report stated that he was shot by "a local farm worker named Mohammed Ashraf" who was surprised by Masih "in a compromising act with a donkey" (Harvey 1995). The BLLF-P and other human rights organizations in Pakistan and around the world demanded that the Benazir Bhutto government conduct an impartial investigation.

2 Some social activists disagree with global and national statistics on child labor, arguing that the incidence of child labor is much higher. For example, some activists and agencies have placed the number of children working globally as 400 million rather than 250 million.

3 The estimates of child workers vary in agency reports. Although UNICEF reports an estimate of 10–40 million child workers in India, Human Rights Watch gives a figure of 60–115 million, and the World Bank reports 44 million. The ILO reports that 14.4 per cent of all children between the ages of 10 and 14 work (UNICEF 1997; ILO 1996).

4 According to Craig N. Murphy and Cristina Rojas de Ferro, international political economy is "not only about the production and circulation of 'things' ... political economy is also about the circulation of meanings" (1995: 63).

5 Although Pheng Cheah (1999) did not address child labor, he has provided an acerbic critique of human rights.

6 Risse *et al.* (1999: 7) discussed the process through which "principled ideas ... become norms". They suggested a five-phase spiral model in which the flow of human rights is often from the West to the non-Western world.

7 The following report of British colonial authorities on the practice of hook swinging provides us an example of the interconnections between colonial discourses on modernity, progress, and human rights.

> It is, in my opinion, unnecessary at the end of the nineteenth century and, having regard to the level to which civilization in India has attained, to consider the motives by which the performers themselves are actuated when taking part in hook swinging, walking through fire, and other barbarities. From their own moral standpoint, their motives may be good or they may be bad; they may indulge in self-torture in satisfaction of pious vows

fervently made in all sincerity and for the most disinterested reasons; or they may indulge in it from the lowest motives of personal aggrandizement, ... but the question is whether public opinion in this country is not opposed to the external acts of the performers, as being in fact repugnant to the dictates of humanity and demoralizing to themselves and to all those who may witness their performances. I am of the opinion that the voice of India most entitled to be listened to with respect, that is to say, not only the voice of the advanced school that has received some of the advantages of western education and has been permeated with non-Oriental ideas, but also the voice of those whose views of life and propriety of conduct have been mainly derived from Asiatic philosophy, would gladly proclaim that the time had arrived for the Government in the interests of its people to effectively put down all degrading exhibitions of torture

(Dirks in Asad 1997: 119)

According to Asad the offensiveness of "hooking" and a particular notion of human and humanity was invoked to justify the ban on such practices. Voices of Westernized Indians and of those who while immersed and trained in "Asiatic philosophy" wanted to reform indigenous culture, in essence all those voices who were seen as closer to the project of modernity and progress, were utilized in the restructuring mission of Western morality.

8 It is important to note that the charges of "foreignness and alternity" are not reserved only for those outside national boundaries wanting to impose universal human rights, but are also made against those whose struggles challenge received notions of culture, nationalism, and development within national boundaries.

9 The indigenous struggles I refer to here are distinct from the claims of the relativists about an authentic indigenous culture. By indigenous I mean groups, like the *adivasis* who are protesting the building of the Narmada dam, who are at the margins of society and who have been denied a voice in the development project. In addition, groups who seek self-determination outside the national context can also be included in this category.

10 For an elaboration of orientalism see the Introduction.

11 This section on the history of the carpet industry is based on Chowdhry and Beeman (2001).

12 Even though "Sir George Birdwood in the Industrial Arts of India (1880) believed that carpet manufacturing existed here before the Moughals there is hardly any evidence to show that it was an organized industry" (Saraf 1986: 49).

13 H. Tellary was created by Mr A. Tellary whose grandson Otto Tellary became the founding member and first president of the All India Carpet Manufacturers' Association (AICMA). Obeetee was founded by Okay, Bowden, and Taylor; the name stands for their initials.

14 According to Juyal, many British traders were involved in the carpet trade, particularly as revenues from the indigo trade were not forthcoming. The success of Indian-made oriental carpets at the Great Exhibition in London in 1851 cemented the involvement of British merchant traders in the carpet industry (Juyal 1993).

15 Whereas Kashmir has been another significant center of carpet production in India, particularly silk carpets, India has cornered only a relatively small portion of the international market. More recently, the "civil war" in Kashmir has led to a further decline in its share of the world carpet trade.

16 The change in tastes initiated by British control of carpet production is evident in the carpet commissioned for the London-based Gridler's Company by Robert Bell, master of the company and director of the East India Company. The carpet, which is on display in the company's hall in London, has the company's coat-of arms, the figure of its patron saint holding the Bible. At the bottom is the legend "Give Thanks to God" (AICMA 1986: 1).

17 Tucker (1997) listed the twenty-five industries in which child labor is prohibited as: *beedi* making (an indigenous type of cigarette); carpet weaving; cement manufacture; cloth printing; dyeing and weaving; manufacture of matches, explosives and fireworks; mica cutting and splitting; shellac manufacture; the building and construction industry; manufacture of slate pencils; manufacture of agate products; manufacturing processes using toxic metals and substances, hazardous processes as defined by section 87, and printing as defined by section 2(k)(iv) of the Factories Act of 1948; cashew and cashew nut processing; soldering processes in electronic industries; railway transportation; cinder picking, ash pit clearing or building operations and vending operations in railway premises; work on ports; sale of fireworks; and work in slaughterhouses.

18 Pre-processing activities involve opening yarn to make balls (*kablis*), and sorting of yarn (*berai*). Weaving involves sitting at the loom and knotting the carpets.

19 I examined articles on child labor from mainstream media sources including the *New York Times, USA Today, US News and World Report, Time Magazine, The Economist*, and *Newsweek* during 1994–2000. Although *The Economist* is a British magazine, I included it in this sample to get a sense of child labor representations in the English-speaking Western world. I have tabulated findings for those who are interested. I am grateful to Jessica Urban for her assistance.

20 Very few articles that I read discuss the use of child labor in Western businesses, whereas more articles mention that Western businesses import goods made with child labor.

21 Rugmark was created by the efforts of Indian and German child labor activists. The label claims that no child labor was used to make the carpet. For further information see Chowdhry and Beeman (2001). In the summer of 2000, I conducted interviews with representatives of Rugmark in India and Germany.

22 Other importers are Britain, Japan, Canada, Sweden, Italy, Australia, France, and Switzerland.

23 I interviewed AICMA officials in Badohi in June of 2000.

24 In the summer of 2000, I interviewed the chairman and other members of CEPEC in New Delhi, India. The data on export earnings from the carpet trade were provided during this interview.

25 I interviewed Satyarthi in New Delhi in the summers of 1999 and 2000.

26 See note 21.

HUMAN RIGHTS AND POSTCOLONIALITY

Representing Burma

Sheila Nair

In 1991 Aung San Suu Kyi, the Burmese dissident, won the Nobel Peace Prize for her struggle against Burma's military authoritarian government, and her persistent advocacy and defense of human rights and democracy in her homeland. At the time she was in the third year of house arrest under the ruling State Law and Order Restoration Council (SLORC) in Burma, and had become the key figure leading a movement for democracy and human rights in that country.[1] The figure of Suu Kyi, female nationalist icon and symbol of resistance to the Burmese military, emerges forcefully in accounts of human rights and democratization in Burma. The Nobel Prize further underscored her visibility and presence in the movement. Michael Aris, Suu Kyi's late husband, wrote after learning of her award,

> Many will now for the first time learn of her courageous leadership of the non-violent struggle for restoration of human rights in her country. I believe her role will come to serve as an inspiration to a great number of people in the world today.
>
> (Suu Kyi 1991: xxix–xxx)

Even as she emerges as the main "voice" of Burmese resistance and chief human rights advocate, the struggle for democracy in Burma remains a complex and complicated story involving a range of participants and multiple contestations. The Burma human rights and democracy campaign is simultaneously national and global, and a testament to the contested and unsettled terms of governance in a postcolonial state.

Like other human rights cases, Burma's location in the contemporary transnational and liberal discourse may be attributed to the investigation, documentation, and analyses of the government's human rights record by Western governments, non-governmental organizations, and international organizations. In the United Nations, for example, human rights violations in Burma have been the subject of some debate and censure. A recent UN report notes that, "At the very worst, we are faced with a country which is at war with its own people. At the very best, it is a country which is holding its people ... hostage" (Burton 1999: 32).[2] The Burmese regime, however, consistently denies the claims of its accusers and maintains that it "fully subscribes to the human rights norms enshrined in the Universal Declaration of Human Rights" (UDHR; U Win Aung 1998: 5).[3] In reality, the Burmese state has not only ignored the provisions of the International Bill of Rights made up of the UDHR and its related covenants, but claims that what it does within its own borders is in accordance with key principles of international law concerning state sovereignty and noninterference. The sovereignty principle enshrined in international law enables the military government in Burma to secure its place in international relations, reasonably assured that Burma's internal politics are affairs of state and do not invite international intervention.

The emergence of a dominant liberal human rights discourse on a global scale has been central to how the West imagines Burma as a space where human rights violations recur. The production of this discourse implicates not only the United States and other major Western powers, but also non-governmental organizations (NGOs) and institutions shaped in important ways by Western knowledge and power such as the United Nations. The liberal discourse has engendered efforts to translate human rights principles and norms into practices, particularly in the postcolonial world, where states violating these norms and principles are frequently the target of criticism from human rights groups and Western governments. Attention to human rights violations in the postcolonial world and campaigns to end such abuses grew in number and density in the last few decades of the twentieth century. Approaches to human rights in the IR literature tend to address these questions from a predominantly liberal perspective, one that explores the impact of human rights norms, transnational social movements, and advocacy networks on state violators of human rights, and their implications for sovereignty claims (e.g. Donnelly 1998; Keck and Sikkink 1998). However, the liberal approach, which also privileges civil and political rights violations in its critique, is less able to account for the failure of long-standing international campaigns on human rights to impact state practices in countries like Burma, despite the "success" of such campaigns in other areas (Nair 2000).

Mired in Western social and political thought and histories, the hegemony of the liberal discourse on human rights poses other pertinent questions, such as what are the key dispensations, limitations and contradictions of this discourse? It is evident that despite claims of an emergent global civil society and the creation of a transnational human rights regime, which presumably forces norm-violating states to be more accountable for rights abuses, powerful states may also insinuate themselves in the liberal discourse and appropriate it. Hegemonic economic and political interests and objectives complicate and compromise transnational, particularly northern-based, movements' efforts to call attention to human rights abuses by postcolonial states, demonstrating the persistent tensions that abound in the liberal approach to human rights in IR.

The gap between international human rights norms and the principles espoused by transnational movements and actual human rights conditions suggests the need for an alternative reading of the human rights discourse. This chapter addresses how and why a postcolonial approach enables us to better grapple with the silences and erasures that accompany the dominant liberal discourse on human rights, offers a different vantage point for exploring the human rights discourse on Burma and the location and power of key contributors to this discourse, and furthers our understanding of the political possibilities and limits of a human rights critique.

Liberal meditations, postcolonial interventions, and human rights

Although activists, academics, intellectuals, and governments may disagree on the universality of human rights norms, the notion of human rights as a liberal discourse having its origins in European social and political thought is seldom disputed. On one hand, those who celebrate the emergence of a transnational human rights regime, for example, typically raise it within the context of the evolution of universal human rights norms and laws in the post-World War II era, but are equally cognizant of the historical development of these ideas in the West which were preceded by the expansion of universal systems of suffrage, self-determination, and representative government (Lauren 1998). On the other hand, those who resist the human rights discourse and its universal claims also refute its presumptions concerning liberal ideals and Western morality as the basis of governance and rule, and question the ontological givens of human rights. In fact, we can find more extreme views in both positions that ignore all truth claims made by the other side, thus resulting in something of a philosophical impasse. The practical implications of this debate not only constitute an important stumbling block to the development of an effective transnational "rights regime," but also beg the question of why repression by state forces and powerful groups on a mass scale, as in Burma, continues to be perpetrated in clear defiance of existing international covenants and human rights principles. Despite the presence of an important relativist strain in human rights thought, the liberal discourse remains hegemonic and sustains the dissemination of core international human rights principles and values. However, the liberal discourse suffers its own erasures although it renders human rights as universal, timeless, and inclusionary.

International relations scholarship, long preoccupied with anarchy and order, and sovereignty and security, has belatedly addressed the phenomenon of an emergent transnational human rights community made up of networks and movements, seen as actors or agents challenging the state-centeredness of IR. However, recent efforts at theorizing and developing a rigorous framework for the analysis of human rights issues in IR mostly privilege a liberal understanding of the growth and dissemination of human rights norms and principles, and its effects in world politics. There are at least three related problems associated with the dominant liberal position on human rights in the literature. First, this human rights literature fails to interrogate its own liberal presumptions and invests the discourse with a normative, moral force that inflects analysis and critique. Much of the literature focuses on the role of transnational networks and celebrates the development and dissemination of universal human rights principles within and by such networks. Since it also approaches human rights as an "issue area" and privileges the role of international human rights NGOs and transnational networks in securing states' acquiescence to human rights norms and principles, it gives less attention to states' authoritative and creative reinvention of the human rights agenda and local initiatives to engage it. One example of the latter is the establishment of official and government-appointed human rights commissions, which despite addressing human rights violations can provide some legitimacy to a government being accused of the same. The IR literature on human rights usefully suggests that the formation of transnational human rights networks may lead to an erosion of sovereignty claims in so-called domestic matters, and in the context of human rights violations such an erosion is critical to addressing the problem.[4] However, the unevenness and unpredictability of states' adherence to the liberal human rights model and the continuing power of sovereignty claims are evident in the prevalence of human rights abuses around the world, and the inability of international bodies to properly intervene in these situations, even in situations where genocide is being perpetrated (Pieterse 1997; Falk 1999).

The second problem is the IR literature's neglect of the impact of economic globalization on the creation and maintenance of an effective human rights framework. Clearly not all of IR is guilty of this lapse as the homogenizing and fragmentary effects of globalization are addressed at some length in critical international relations, particularly by Gramscians. However, even in critical IR, significantly less attention is given to human rights issues than to other types of contradictions generated by globalization, such as the development of global capital regimes. In a recent essay that draws attention to how global capital compromises the claims of human rights discourse, Pheng Cheah argued that the three voices in "existing human rights practical discourse," namely those of Western governments, Asian governments, and human rights NGOs in the South, are caught within the "force field of global capital" (Cheah 1999: 13). According to Cheah, human rights NGOs have to negotiate with shifting interstate relations within an unequal global economic order. As such, their claims are irreducibly susceptible to cooptation by competing states on both sides of the North–South divide at the very moment they are articulated.

(Cheah 1999: 28)[5]

The liberal discourse on human rights has been challenged by both progressive left critics such as Noam Chomsky, and rightist authoritarian leaders in Asia such as Mahathir Mohamad. To many critics the liberal discourse is compromised by its complicity with capital, which significantly reworks its political implications.[6] Further, by privileging a particular liberal definition of rights, the discourse underscores its relationship to a specific global class formation, one that cannot fully account for economic, social, and cultural injustices and inequalities whose protection forms an integral element of international covenants.

A third problem is that the dominant liberal perspective in IR is situated within an Enlightenment discourse in which the notion of human rights is presumably embedded, but one that also sanctioned slavery, white racism, colonialism, and imperialism (see also Chowdhry in this volume). International relations scholarship has been on the whole remarkably silent on these tensions, and on the ways in which knowledge is constructed in the realm of human rights and culture. Meanwhile, Western-based human rights organizations such as Amnesty International and Human Rights Watch also sustain an international politics and discourse that is intrinsically liberal, even if their work as activists has consistently foregrounded and made visible human rights violations. Neo-Marxist critics have drawn attention to class conflict and dialectical materialism which, they argue, underpin colonialism and imperialism, and presently neocolonialism, but there is very little mention of the racialized and gendered dimensions of colonial and neocolonial discourse and policy. The work of First World or Western feminists on the gendered foundations of international relations and international political economy has been central to making problematic and reevaluating arguments concerning so-called core IR principles such as sovereignty, order, and security (e.g. Peterson 1992a; Tickner 1992; Sylvester 1994). However, feminists writing in IR, with some important exceptions referred to in the introduction to this volume, do not properly address the implications of overlapping hierarchies constituted by race, class, gender, and cultural difference in their critiques.[7] For more insight into these aspects of international discourse and the cultural bases of Western dominance, one must turn to mainly "non-IR" works in interdisciplinary areas such as cultural studies and postcolonial theory, whose belated inclusion in IR debates is itself noteworthy.[8]

Postcolonial studies, inaugurated by Edward Said's *Orientalism* (1978), attends to these concerns, which have been long-standing in a body of writing not discernible as "postcolonial" in its inception. For example, analyses of race and cultural representation in colonial discourse can be found in the writings of nationalists for whom the intersections of race, culture, and class were central to the maintenance of colonial rule. These critiques took one step further the "Marxist understanding of class struggle as the motor of history [which] had to be revised because in the colonial context the division between the haves and have-nots was inflected by race" (Loomba 1998: 22). Works by such anticolonial thinkers as Frantz Fanon (1967) and Albert Memmi (1965) reflect an acute awareness of the power of cultural and racist constructions – the "othering" of colonized peoples – and the simultaneous appropriation of subjectivity by the colonizer. These writers did not view the inflection of race and cultural representation in colonial discourse simplistically, but rather explored its origins, meanings, and locations. Summarizing the key contributions of colonial discourse analysis, Loomba argued that it interrogates the assumptions of Western science and philosophy and in doing so reveals the "spectacular" as opposed to the insidious nature of colonial power. Instead of disabusing the connection between race and culture, for example, the development of Western scientific knowledge in the nineteenth century solidified it (see Loomba 1998: 57–69). Western scientific knowledge is also manifested in the present in discourses of modernization and human rights where representation of the "other" is re-worked in a more liberal vein.

Postcolonial analysis necessarily excavates and retrieves the intersections of race, culture and class in human rights discourse, not to excuse human rights abuses in the postcolonial world, but instead to ground them in their historical complexity. It is therefore perfectly appropriate, and in fact necessary, in the view of many Third World human rights activists like the Malaysian social critic and political activist, Chandra Muzaffar, to decry the "horrendous human wrongs" inflicted by Europeans "upon the colored inhabitants of the planet," while at the same time condemning human rights abuses in the Third World. In fact, for such activists "Western colonialism in Asia, Australasia, Africa, and Latin America represents the most massive, systematic violation of human rights ever known in history" (Muzaffar 1999: 26). Muzaffar's critique of the West's more recent record on human rights holds Western governments and international institutions such as the IMF and World Bank, the Western media, and some Western NGOs responsible for a variety of human rights abuses. This awareness of liberal complicity brings to the fore the racially and culturally inflected arguments in conventional Western scholarship and popular discourse about the Third World, the non-West, or the South. It also forces us to acknowledge the contingent and constructed nature of all knowledge, the relationship between imperialism and the postcolonial experience, and the complicated and mutually constitutive nature of identity and difference.

Recognizing the significance of race and gender in colonial discourse has produced a rethinking of both conventional European historiography and

Marxian formulations and interpretations of imperialism in postcolonial studies. The gendering of colonial discourse, how it enables colonial power, and how it defines and feminizes difference and resistance are also relevant to an understanding of human rights and IR. For instance, postcolonial scholars show how Western knowledge production about the racialized and gendered other was linked intimately to science, to the professionalization of academic disciplines, and even to the unintended intrusiveness of those who were protective of the "native." Situating this critique in reference to human rights, Manisha Desai draws attention to the conflicts and tensions evident in the development of the international women's human rights movement during the UN International Women's Decade (1975–85). She writes that at these conferences women from Third World countries challenged

> First World feminists' claims, especially those from the United States, that women were universally oppressed due to their gender and "sisterhood was global." They countered that for women in the Third World, class, race/ethnicity, nationality, and religion were as important as and woven together with gender in both oppressing them and providing the space for liberation.
>
> (Desai 1999: 186)

Similarly, Chandra Talpade Mohanty has written about how feminism itself has been contested and feminist movements challenged "on the grounds of cultural imperialism, and of shortsightedness in defining the meaning of gender in terms of middle-class, white experience, and in terms of internal racism, classism and homophobia" (Mohanty 1991a: 7). A postcolonial approach reveals the erasures of Western feminism and the challenge from Third World feminists particularly as it hones in on the question of racism and cultural oppression as a central human rights issue, and the implications of these relations.[9] It further underscores, as feminist IR scholars like Cynthia Enloe (1990, 1993) have shown, the gendered practices of big and powerful states such as the United States, and the functioning of a neoliberal global political and economic order.[10]

In sum, a postcolonial rereading of human rights discourse allows us to rethink the relationship between class, race, and gender, situates power and cultural representation, and shows how human rights abuses are shaped by both contemporaneous and historical conditions. It is clear that a postcolonial rereading must decisively move beyond the parameters of the current debate, which is shaped by the liberal and relativist positions, and dislodge these key reference points in human rights discourses. The salience of human rights in postcolonial contexts neither stems from the international diffusion of norms as presented in mainstream IR, nor is easy to fathom within the oppositional constructs of universalism versus relativism. Indeed, one may even accept that the relativist position makes universal claims, as charged by

Cheah who notes that the "Asian governmental position about the cultural limits of human rights of the Western vision of human rights is invariably linked to an argument about the need to subordinate political and civil rights to the right to development" (1999: 12). Shifting the debate away from the well-worn opposition between liberalism and relativism is critical because it forces us to reconsider how gender, culture, race and class are refracted in both positions.[11]

This chapter's analysis of the human rights movement on Burma provides an opportunity to render the multiple contradictions, locations, and mediations involved in the articulation of human rights concerns by situating them in a postcolonial critique. To this end, the chapter pays close attention to the limitations of Western, liberal dispensations on human rights, and highlights its erasures and complications, while also being aware of how such a critique may be appropriated in defense of relativism. Authoritarian rulers have a vested interest in the relativist position, and an alternative, postcolonial interrogation will necessarily involve an inquiry into how regimes of power enable and produce certain kinds of human rights practices and abuses. As Shashi Tharoor points out:

> Authoritarian regimes who appeal to their own cultural traditions are cheerfully willing to crush culture domestically when it suits them to do so. Also, the 'traditional culture' that is sometimes advanced to justify the nonobservance of human rights :... no longer exists in a pure form at the national level anywhere.
>
> (1999–2000: 4)

It is also important to consider how struggles around human rights issues have generated not only transnational solidarities comprising non-governmental organizations, activists, and ordinary people, but also a different kind of politics, from both the relativism espoused by East Asian elites, and the universalism disseminated by Western elites and institutions.

Constructing Burma's human rights problem

As alluded to earlier, the liberal discourse on rights is mostly silent on the subject of colonialism and imperialism and therefore cannot account for the relationship between colonial rule and human rights practices in the post-colonial state. Curiously, this silence contradicts the historical evidence and neglects analyses showing the imbrication of colonial discourse with power and human rights practices. Mainstream IR scholarship is not ignorant of these matters, particularly given that neo-Marxian writers have called attention to the social and economic injustices brought about by colonial rule, making it all the more problematic that these silences remain in the dominant liberal formulation of human rights. This chapter's critique begins by exploring the significance of colonialism and imperialism for Burma's emergence in the Western imagination as a physical and cultural space of repression and human rights violations.[12]

Colonialism and nationalism

British colonial rule in Burma began with the arrival of the first male officers of the imperial bureaucracy in 1825 and lasted effectively until 1942 with the onset of war in the Pacific, and the ensuing Japanese occupation. The British in Burma, as elsewhere, saw the colonial state as "a benevolent but impartial umpire" that "liberated the individual from the fetters of custom and the extortion of an exploitative ruling class" (Taylor 1987: 66). Robert Taylor has suggested that

> as the ultimate arbiters and guides of Burma, the British civil servants saw no contradiction between their powers to rule an alien land and their preachments about creating self-government in that country. Recognizing no form of self-government upon their arrival, but only an outdated form of oriental despotism, they saw themselves as the *midwives* of the modern world in backward Asia.
>
> (1987: 66, emphasis added)

The "oriental despotism" the British encountered was one that actually provided for a certain degree of autonomy and class mobility, as Burma scholars like Josef Silverstein (1977) have shown. These paternalistic and racist constructions of the other, which rationalized and ultimately underpinned colonial rule, would radically shape the contours of nationalist politics and the postcolonial state.

Colonial rule was clearly inconsistent not only with Enlightenment values of freedom, democracy, and human rights, but also with the Burmese experience and its cultural politics. British policy challenged the fluidity of ethnic identity and politics in the precolonial state, and instead solidified "racial," "tribal," and "ethnic" differences along socio-economic lines. This was true not only of indigenous minority communities but also of immigrant groups such as the Chinese and Indians. Silverstein points out that "British encouragement and protection of minorities at the expense of the dominant Burmans, plus large-scale immigration of Indians as laborers and financiers, gave rise to new social problems that exploded into violent communal riots during the 1930s" (1977: 12). The treatment of indigenous minorities as needing British protection from the "dominant" Burman community also reveals the gendering of colonial policy, and its masculinist assumptions. In this case it was not so much about white men "saving brown women from brown men" as Gayatri Spivak (1988: 296) put it, but of white men saving some brown women and men from other brown women and men. The racialized, and patriarchal, treatment of some colonized groups as needing the protection or benefaction of the colonial authority against other colonized groups was a characteristic feature of colonial practices of control and domination.

In Burma the social hierarchies introduced by a shift in the dominant mode of agriculture from subsistence to commercial were also obvious by the end of the nineteenth century. It transformed traditional social institutions and cultural practices, entrenched British legalisms and conventions about property rights, and produced a powerful landlord class and a displaced peasantry. Silverstein (1996) points out that the British "had no intention of making Burmans into Englishmen and assimilating them," and yet at the same time it was clear that notions of freedom and democracy developed in European social thought were available for consumption in the colonies and showed up the basic contradictions of imperial rule. Moreover, these notions were not necessarily antithetical to "traditional" understandings of the duties and responsibilities of rulers and the allegiance of the ruled. Yet the emergence of anticolonial protest and ideologies circulated around the meanings invested during colonial rule in the opposition between so-called tradition and modernity. Thus, modern (read European) ideas about freedom, democracy, and self-determination became rallying cries for opposition to colonial rule that were usefully deployed in the nationalist struggle against British rule. The formation of the Anti-Fascist People's Freedom League (AFPFL) and several other parties including the Burma Communist Party (BCP) shaped a nationalist movement that paved the way for independence from Britain in 1947. The AFPFL, led by Aung San Suu Kyi's father, Aung San, who was prime minister-elect in 1947, was a nationalist organization whose membership was open to all regardless of their ethnic or religious affiliation and political beliefs (Silverstein 1977: 17). His assassination and the accompanying conflict led to a state of civil war in Burma between 1948 and 1952. Civilian rule was interrupted by a military caretaker government between 1958 and 1960 and effectively ended with the 1962 military coup that overthrew the civilian government of U Nu and brought General Ne Win to power. With the collapse of civilian rule, the army ruled first through the creation of a Revolutionary Council and later through the establishment in 1974 of the Burma Socialist Program Party (BSPP).

The dynamics of post-independence politics in Burma emerged out of a historical conjuncture in which colonialism critically shaped nationalist imaginings and elite desires. And yet these nationalist desires could not be sustained in the absence of a discursive break with the past and in the face of colonial policies of divide and rule that challenged precolonial power-sharing arrangements, and interethnic relations and ties among the Burmese (see Silverstein 1980 for a discussion). The breakdown of civilian rule and the emergence of the army as a powerful political force that severely repressed political opposition are also products of the colonial encounter, notwithstanding the particular dynamics and contradictions of Burmese politics that unfolded shortly after independence. The repressive stance of the Burmese state mirrored the colonial regime's practices referred to earlier, and is reflective as well of the amalgamated or hybrid postcolonial state in other parts of Southeast Asia. For example, Benedict Anderson shows how the postcolonial Indonesian state was an "amalgam" in which the colonial inheritance and the nationalist struggle for independence were both manifested (Anderson 1990). The military regime's subsequent self-imposed isolation from other states in international relations reflected a curious admixture of reactionary and radical politics that cannot be fully appreciated without considering its colonial history.[13] The state embarked on a program called "The Burmese Way to Socialism," which involved the nationalization of the economy and an inward-looking strategy for national self-renewal. By 1988 this policy was in shambles, students protested, and Ne Win promised a political referendum. Despite his subsequent resignation, a mass protest movement against the BSPP and the military took to the streets of Rangoon. In the ensuing confrontation between the armed forces and the unarmed demonstrators, hundreds of civilians were gunned down by the army in what became known as the "8–8–88 massacre." The army's crackdown was a key turning point in Burmese politics, and was critical to the development of the democracy movement inside Burma and a transnational campaign on human rights abuses and political repression in that country.

The self-representation by the military that it is the only able mediator and provider of peace and stability in postcolonial Burma is underscored by superficial changes in such things as the name of the regime. After the August crackdown of 1988, the military government called itself the State Law and Order Restoration Council, or SLORC. It also announced that it would hold elections in 1990, which gave impetus to democracy activists like Suu Kyi and her associates who quickly formed the National League for Democracy (NLD). In addition, the SLORC's announcement led to the registration of nearly 200 parties who planned to contest the elections (Clements 1997: 15–17). The general election of May 1990 was a resounding victory for the NLD which won 392 of the 485 seats it contested, while the SLORC's National Unity Party garnered only 3 per cent of the vote (Guyon 1992: 418). The SLORC refused to honor the results and instead began arresting hundreds of NLD members and their supporters including many of the newly elected legislators. Suu Kyi was by this time under house arrest.

Burma's emergence in the human rights discourse can thus be located at this turning point in its postcolonial politics. The discursive interventions by a range of participants including the US Congress, the US State Department, and human rights organizations that have shaped postcolonial Burma's emergence in the human rights imaginary can be discerned from the hearings, documents, and statements disseminated by these entities. The next section explores how these discursive interventions have shaped the international campaign on Burma's human rights record. It also inquires into the struggle inside Burma led by Aung San Suu Kyi and the ways in which the figure of this female nationalist icon inscribes the democracy discourse both within and outside Burma.

Producing human rights

The representational power and authority of those who perpetrate human rights abuses and the sources of their power are challenged by counter-discursive strategies of human rights and democracy activists and groups. The transnational human rights discourse on Burma first arose in response to the events of 1988, but it was also galvanized by Suu Kyi's arrest in 1989 and the mass arrests of NLD members after the 1990 elections. It gathered momentum as the SLORC, since 1997 by its new name, the State Peace and Development Council (SPDC), was accused of a range of human rights abuses including forced labor, killings, arbitrary arrest, political detentions, intimidation, and torture. The transnational movement involves a national-level nonviolent movement for democracy in Burma led by Suu Kyi and the NLD, non-governmental national, regional, and international human rights organizations, and lastly major powers such as the United States, and inter-state organizations such as the United Nations. Political repression in Burma has marginalized the Burmese pro-democracy movement, and has resulted in a prolonged and repressive military offensive against separatist struggles such as those of the minority Karens, leaving in its wake a wave of refugees who have flooded into Thailand. The latter's precarious survival on the borderlands between Thailand and Burma raises important questions about the re-territorialization and construction of national identities in the Burmese state.[14] However, given the main objectives of this chapter, these issues are addressed only tangentially, and only insofar as they relate to the construction of the human rights discourse on Burma. I turn first to an analysis of US foreign policy on Burma as a way of addressing how Burma gets talked about or represented in policy circles and the broader implications of these constructions in sustaining the liberal discourse on human rights.

At a hearing before the House Subcommittee on Asian and Pacific Affairs in October 1991, Kenneth Quinn, the Deputy Assistant Secretary for East Asian and Pacific Affairs, made the following declaration, in words that construct the stereotypical authoritarian Third World state in the eyes of the United States:

> There is no freedom of speech or press in Burma. The country's only newspaper is a government mouthpiece. Several individuals were arrested for publishing an "unauthorized" report of a public press

conference ... At least three political prisoners have died in Burmese prisons this year. We estimate that 2,000 political prisoners
remain in jail, many held without charges. Large numbers of
refugees have fled to Thailand and Bangladesh.

(Quinn 1991: 793)

Quinn further submitted that "torture, disappearances, arbitrary arrests
and detentions, unfair trials, and compulsory labor, such as forced portering
for the military, persisted" (1991: 793). Quinn's testimony listing several of
the major human rights abuses in Burma was generally consistent with
those of several others, including exiled Burmese opposition leader Sein
Win, and James Ross, the Asia Program director for the Lawyers Committee
for Human Rights (House Committee on Foreign Affairs 1993). Among the
main allegations against the Burmese government was its failure to honor
the elections of 1990, the continuing imprisonment of Aung San Suu Kyi,
the harassment of the Burmese political opposition, and the general moral
turpitude of the military regime.

The hearings, however, also reveal a simultaneous cultural construction of
the United States. In opening remarks, the Guam representative, Ben Blaz,
conveyed his sentiments on the US position on human rights this way:

Aside from the fact that the question of human rights and how we
feel about it was answered by Irving Berlin with a song called God
Bless America during the war, I also wanted to point out that if any
country anywhere at any time wants to understand America, wants
to break the code, wants to know us more, they will have to know it
through the question of human rights; the key is human rights.

(House Committee on Foreign Affairs 1993: 3)

Blaz's formulation of the US commitment to freedom, democracy, and
human rights is certainly not new and can be found in doctrinal and policy
statements of presidents and key officials throughout the post World War II
era. However, the sharp contrast between expressions of concern about
human rights in countries like Burma, and the primacy of security and
national interest considerations over, and often at the expense of, human
rights, has been highlighted by critics of US foreign policy like Noam
Chomsky (1999). These contradictions are manifested in the official position
on Burma, which calls for "not hurting Americans and American businesses," while at the same time Burmese dissidents are encouraged by US
support (House Committee on Foreign Affairs 1993: 33).

Quinn's testimony, for instance, underscored the ambivalences in the
Bush administration's New World Order objectives which promised to
deliver the world from cold war tyrannies. In the case of Burma these contradictions are spelt out in the discourse of human rights, the "war" on drugs,

and a national interest that militates against military interventionism or economic sanctions in some countries but not in others considered more "vital" or "strategic" to the United States (House Committee on Foreign Affairs 1993: 32–3).[15] In fact, as Andrew Deutz points out, it was not until the 8–8–88 massacre that the US government paid attention to the human rights situation in Burma despite strong evidence of serious human rights violations. In sharp contrast, US foreign policy until 1988 was focused on "narcotics interdiction and eradication" to the tune of $80 million in assistance to the regime (Deutz 1991: 169). The official position in 1991 as outlined by Quinn was that the United States had no plans to impose a trade embargo on Burma despite calls by some policymakers and human rights groups in the United States. The following exchange between Quinn and Stephen Solarz, chair of the House Subcommittee, illustrates the selective use of economic instruments of coercion in US foreign policy and underscores the opportunism of the US human rights position when confronted with what are deemed more pressing national interest considerations:

Mr Solarz: Now we have, as I understand it, imposed total embargoes on Nicaragua, Panama, Cuba, and Vietnam and Cambodia, both of which are in the region.

           Why don't we do the same with Burma, particularly as it is among the worst human rights violators in the world?

Mr Quinn: I am not expert on this particular part of our law, but generally when we have taken steps to do those types of embargoes, they have been matters related to our national security.

           But when you look at that [an embargo], you say, is it going to be effective if we do this? I have to say the honest answer that we have come up with is no, we don't think that it will be.

Mr Solarz: Effective in terms of bringing about democracy?

Mr Quinn: In bringing about a change in the policy.

Mr Solarz: But with all due respect, if that was the measure of our embargo against North Korea, or even Cuba, or Panama –

Mr Quinn: As I said, those are related to national security issues to the United States. But if I could, to go beyond the question of whether it would be effective or not, secondly is, would it be GATT-illegal to do that, because we are now – have many strong policies and statements that we make to other countries that it is important to abide by the rules. And we believe that we should do the same.

Mr Solarz: Well, I – that is not an unreasonable argument. But my trouble with it is that we apparently violated GATT when we imposed full-scale sanctions against Vietnam, Cambodia, Cuba, Nicaragua, Panama.

(House Committee on Foreign Affairs 1993: 32–3)

The above exchange reveals also that the liberal human rights discourse has been shaped in important ways by the hegemony of the United States in the global economy. In fact, the policy contradictions US hegemony have engendered are seldom taken up in conventional analyses of human rights in IR, which instead assume the naturalness of this ideological formation. The special cultural identity of the United States is repeatedly asserted in official human rights discourse, and in the popular belief that the superpower is the keeper of democracy's flame and protector of human rights around the world. Solarz's question, however, exposes the political and economic considerations and narrow self-interest when applying trade sanctions or embargoes and holding states accountable for human rights violations.

The policy contradictions are revealing also in the case of humanitarian assistance to dissidents. Deutz writes that shortly after the 1988 crackdown, thousands of dissident students fled to the Burma–Thailand border, but many were repatriated by the Thai authorities until March of 1989, when political pressure halted the practice. Those who were not captured by the Burmese military remained in the border regions and faced serious hardship including the lack of food and medicine. Deutz notes that the official US position nearly a year into this situation, apparently reflecting concerns about "Thai sensitivities," was that the State Department was still exploring ways to assist the students. This despite the precedent set by an international relief effort organized by several non-governmental organizations (Deutz 1991: 174). In these ways, concerns about sovereignty override human rights considerations, despite the overt interventionism sometimes employed in other situations where national security or national interest appears more clearly at stake in US foreign policy discourse. Cold war fears – but now manifested in claims of China's growing influence in the region – and domino theories are also revisited in discussions of US policy toward Burma as some proponents call for a more economically interventionist US role in the liberalization of the Burmese economy (House Committee on International Relations 1996: 32). Chairman of the House International Relations Committee, Benjamin Gilman, suggested in 1995 that "illicit drug production" was the highest on the priority list of US concerns about Burma, but it is interesting that he also linked the drug trade to human rights abuses in the country. Gilman asserted that the Clinton administration had failed to "understand that the drug production problem is a human rights problem." He suggested that human rights of ethnic minorities in Burma were threatened and that these groups resorted to opium production due to economic necessity and protection against the military (House Committee on International Relations 1996: 35). Under the Clinton administration, battling the drug trade and calling on the Burmese state to support human rights raised policy contradictions (Human Rights Watch/Asia 1995: 7). In a statement to the House Subcommittee on Asia and the Pacific in 1995, Holly Burkhalter, director of the Washington office of Human Rights Watch, drew attention to continued US investment in Burma and US assistance to the regime in combating drug production and trafficking, arguing that the

> symbolic significance of providing police assistance to a police state is quite overwhelming, and I am afraid that it has the potential to overwhelm the positive signals that the US government is saying with the other side of its mouth, if you pardon my bluntness.
> (House Committee on International Relations 1996: 19)

The hearings before Congress suggest that the liberal discourse on Burma, far from being a monolithic one, has been shaped and inflected by a range of different concerns such as security, free trade, democracy, and human rights, and it is important that we are attentive to those differences. However, despite these concerns, contributors to this discourse in US policy-making circles agree that the protection of democracy and human rights in Burma remains an important objective, and should serve the long-term national interest of the United States. The inability among policy elites to also clearly specify and assert the relationship between liberal democracy and human rights suggests US ambivalence about the ability of Third World states like Burma to be more fully democratic, and therefore more like "us," even if human rights are recognized as foundational rights for all peoples.[16] This disarticulation between democracy and human rights must be seen against the corresponding orientalized and racialized construction of Burma, whose emergence in the transnational human rights discourse is inscribed by a political and cultural transgression – the denial of a democratic election. A central difficulty then with the dominant liberal discourse of human rights is that it does not allow us to contemplate how these representations figure in the *production* of Burma as a space where political, civil, cultural, and social rights are consistently violated. Instead it reproduces an orientalized other whose repressive ways are traced to a traditional and despotic politics, and whose transformation may ultimately be accomplished through proper guidance by the United States and other major powers.[17] Ultimately, it fails to disclose the racialized representations implicit in this discourse of Burmese human rights and democracy, and situates both Burma and the United States in ways that reproduce global power hierarchies and a late twentieth-century, new cold war orientalist sensibility.

The political economy of repression

The documentation and lobbying work of NGOs has intensified international attention to the human rights situation in Burma, particularly in Europe and North America, and raised awareness of the implications of foreign aid to, and investment in, Burma. This is especially critical in light of Burma's shift toward a more market-oriented strategy, which has attracted investment from neighboring Southeast Asian neighbors like Singapore and Malaysia, and Japan and the United States. One result of the confused and isolationist economic policies of the former BSPP government was a crippling and increasingly desperate economic situation for the majority of Burmese by the latter part of the 1980s. Faced with a lack of domestic capital, the government undertook liberalization initiatives in the 1990s. International human rights organizations have argued that foreign investment and aid feed the regime's repression. Asia Watch states in its 1990 report, *Human Rights in Burma (Myanmar)*, that it believed "no US government assistance of any kind should be reinstated until the Burmese government ceases its systematic repression of basic human rights" (p. 55). The position of Asia Watch, coming in the wake of the military crackdown of 1988, is consistent with Aung San Suu Kyi's arguments that investment and foreign aid will only bolster state repression, instead of addressing widespread poverty in the country.

Human rights organizations have long called for a ban on tourism to Burma, arguing that it only serves to enhance the longevity of the governing order and its repressive powers. However, in a sign that the campaign to keep tourists away from Burma might be a losing battle, Lonely Planet Publications released in 2000 an updated edition of its guide to Burma with a foreword concluding that "it was better to visit the country despite a four-year-old tourism boycott" (Tanko and Lintner 2001: 64). In response, the London-based Tourism Concern and Burma Campaign UK called for a boycott of Lonely Planet's publications in an effort to force the withdrawal of the book (Tanko and Lintner 2001: 64). The storm over the new Burma guidebook revisited questions about whether tourism would hurt or help the Burmese government, and the double standards that ostensibly apply in tourism boycotts, specifically why some states with weak human rights records get targeted by human rights groups but not others. The answer to this is unclear but a response by the director of the UK Burma Campaign suggests that Suu Kyi's dismissals of claims made by the tourist industry are an important factor, including her call that tourists, like foreign investors, should simply stay away (see Tanko and Lintner 2001: 64–5). The advocacy of human rights in Burma by transnational human rights groups consistently comes up against the claims of states, both in the region and elsewhere, that in some cases different strategies are necessary for progress on human rights.

An example of this stance is the support of the Association of Southeast Asian Nations (ASEAN) for the notion of constructive engagement with Burma, presumably so that the organization can assist in the normalization of the country's role in the region, and contribute to the dismantling of authoritarianism. Yet, as critics have pointed out, acceptance of Burma into the ASEAN in 1997 signaled that the organization and its member states were not interested in pressuring Burma on its human rights record. On the contrary, repression had been rewarded by granting Burma membership in ASEAN.[18] However, as Peter Carey notes, ASEAN's position in 1997 did not accord with earlier sentiments expressed by member states like Malaysia over Burma's treatment of Burmese Muslims (the Rohingyas) in the early 1990s (1997: 13). He suggests that these concerns were largely set aside by 1996 although little had changed in Burma, and ASEAN's welcome coincided with sizeable investment flows into Burma from Malaysia and Singapore. Malaysian and Singaporean funds to the tune of $230 million and $600 million respectively were invested in various projects mainly in the tourist industry, and $1.5 billion in Singapore–Burma trade was projected by 1996, a year before Burma's admission into ASEAN (Carey 1997: 14–15). Burma attracts investment from the region despite the negative international publicity and the campaigns of human rights organizations.

The United States' policies at an official level have involved suspension of its aid program and the imposition of some economic sanctions.[19] Despite these restrictions, US companies may still do business in Burma and until 1995 constituted, according to one source, the fourth largest source of investment in that country.[20] US oil companies Amoco and Unocal have been involved in oil drilling operations in Burma since 1991 (Guyon 1992: 457). Presently, Unocal is involved with the French company, Total, to construct a natural gas pipeline from Burma's Gulf of Martaban to Thailand, which the Burmese government hopes will be a strong revenue earner (Guyot 1998: 190).[21] Known as the Yadana pipeline project, this initiative has been roundly condemned by human rights groups, who have been pushing for sanctions that would limit such forms of economic cooperation. EarthRights International (ERI) and the Southeast Asian Information Network (SAIN) in a joint report, *Total Denial: A Report on the Yadana Pipeline Project*, link the project to the SLORC's "egregious human rights abuses occurring in the pipeline region" (ERI and SAIN 1996: 1). According to the report, the abuses fall into two categories. In the first category are "abuses committed by troops in the pipeline region in order for SLORC to honor the security guarantees it provided to the companies as an integral part of their investment deal." These abuses include, according to *Total Denial*, extrajudicial killings, torture, and rape. The second category involves "human rights violations committed by the SLORC in furtherance of the pipeline project itself," including portering and forced labor (ERI and SAIN 1996: 2).

A report by Human Rights Watch lists at least 60 US companies doing business in Burma as of 1995. Among them are corporate entities such as American Express, Caterpillar, Coca-Cola, General Electric, PepsiCo, and Sears Roebuck. Interestingly, the majority of these companies entered Burma, according to the Human Rights Watch report listing, after the 1988 massacre, and mainly in 1991 and 1992 (Human Rights Watch/Asia 1995).

However, human rights activism has had some effect in recent years as several US companies have pulled their investments from Burma, including soft drinks maker PepsiCo and clothing retailers Eddie Bauer and Liz Claiborne. At the same time, US corporations have responded to state and local laws enacted to prevent trade and business with Burma and sanctions prohibiting new corporate investments in that country by going to court.[22] In some instances, the interests of the corporate world and human rights organizations may actually intersect, and a mutually beneficial campaign can be worked out, one that promotes both a softer, more people-focused corporate image of the business entity and the tactical goals of the human rights organizations. For example, the skin-care and cosmetics giant, the Body Shop, joined forces with Amnesty International to "inspire shoppers to take action for human rights defenders around the world," including on behalf of two Burmese comedians sentenced to seven years' imprisonment (Amnesty International 1998). Yet such arrangements can also make less visible the often cynical appropriation of social and political causes and messages by corporations – the joint campaign between the Body Shop and Amnesty International may be an exception – who use these causes to sell a product. It is not unusual to find leading designer advertisements that utilize the human rights flavor of the moment or romanticize long-existing struggles such as Tibet to sell a line of clothing or fragrance in glossy Western magazines. Such orientalist fantasies about the other that are implicated in the images sold by advertisers may make for feel-good business, but the human struggles behind those images are never really understood or appreciated by the average consumer.

Ultimately, the discursive and symbolic challenge presented by the Burmese democracy movement and the transnational human rights network on Burma is bound up with the material realities and everyday struggles of the Burmese. Here, Burma's peripheral location in a globalized capitalist political economy is used strategically to exact compliance with international human rights norms by both the democracy movement and the transnational campaign. However, attention to the deeper implications of the political economy of violence and the material conditions of life in Burma have been somewhat overshadowed abroad by the emphasis on securing political democracy, and civil and political rights claims. A cornerstone of the democracy movement's critique has been its call for economic sanctions against the state, and skepticism of the market opening which it sees as benefiting only the "small, privileged elite in power" (Suu Kyi 1997: 163). However, this has been an increasingly difficult position to sustain as even some supporters of the NLD and Suu Kyi question the wisdom of economic sanctions. For instance, international NGOs operating inside Burma have walked a fine line between balancing their organizational objectives, which means cooperating with the state, and throwing their support behind the NLD cause (Purcell 1999). A few humanitarian and relief agencies, ostensibly prompted by the intervention of UN bodies such as UNICEF, entered Burma after 1989 (Purcell 1999: 76). The "human needs" approach of organizations such as World Vision Australia and the International Council of Voluntary Agencies (ICVA) conflicts with the arguments made by Suu Kyi and other members of her party that economic sanctions – including aid sanctions – against Burma were necessary to isolate the regime and bring about political change. The ICVA, for instance, argued against "punishing the poor," following up on UNICEF's 1992 report on "appalling social indices of underdevelopment in Burma" (Purcell 1999: 76, 78).

Despite more than a decade of transnational human rights organization on Burma that supports the key goals of the country's democracy movement, little has changed in the politics of Burma and the use of the state's repressive machinery. One plausible reason for this is that economic interests, sovereignty, and national security claims by both Burma and powerful states like the United States intervene in ways that make it difficult to seriously address human rights violations in the current global conjuncture. As for human rights activists and NGOs who would like to see an immediate and just solution to human rights abuses, their methods, including the invocation of international human rights law, have not produced the desired results in human rights practices. Another plausible reason is that transnational organization on human rights has generally borrowed much from the liberal discourse and contributed to its production, and thus found it very difficult to construct an alternative critique of human rights abuses, one that is sensitive to the enactment of different regimes of power in international relations and their implications. The possibilities exist for a transformatory politics by transnational human rights movements, but it is also the case that the boundaries between the transnational and national are neither easily negotiated nor subverted through the articulation of international norms or principles. In other words, sovereignty continues to be a powerful source of states' claims against transnational calls for observance of human rights. At the same time, non-governmental organizations, particularly Northern-based ones, are also complicit in producing a transnational liberal discourse on human rights, a discourse that generally ignores the production of power relations and social hierarchies on a global scale. And in part because of this complicity they are unable to also intervene in and address these configurations, which ultimately impact human rights in Burma. The next section explores the significance of Suu Kyi for an analysis of human rights in that country, and explores the construction of her identity in the liberal discourse, and in turn how she locates herself.

Gendering resistance in Burma

Postcolonial feminist writings suggest that "if the nation is an imagined community, that imagining is profoundly gendered" (Loomba 1998: 215). Loomba writes that across the colonial spectrum, the nation-state or its guiding principles are often imagined literally *as* a woman. The figures of Britannia and Mother India, for example, have been continually circulated as symbols of different versions of the national temper.

(Loomba 1998: 215)

The Third World woman may be constructed alternatively as a symbol of backwardness or modernity. In these ways, she is oppressively appropriated and repositioned in liberal discourses on human rights. This discourse, as suggested earlier, is grounded in Enlightenment social theory and political thought and remains firmly anchored to distinctive Western social, political, and cultural imaginaries. The irony is that despite its situatedness, liberal discourse is shot through and ultimately undone by its own universalist presumptions. First World or Western feminists have mostly recognized and critiqued liberal hegemony as patriarchal and exclusionary, and drawn attention to how its discourse is gendered and makes invisible women's oppression.[23] However, Western feminist discourse[24] has not satisfactorily addressed or worked through the complex intersections that map gender inequalities onto race and class divides on a global scale. Even when it speaks to so-called cultural differences it does so from a distinctively First World position and voice that can be disconcertingly universalizing, simplifying, and patronizing in reference to Third World women's struggles.

Aung San Suu Kyi: lady in waiting

The struggle for democracy in postcolonial Burma demonstrates the need to interrogate both the liberal understanding of human rights and a Western feminist discourse in which the category of Third World woman is continually reproduced,[25] and consider how and why, to use Loomba's words, "resistance itself is feminized" (Loomba 1998: 215). The visibility of Aung San Suu Kyi in the transnational human rights campaign discloses the necessity for a better understanding of the feminization of resistance, and its racialized and cultural dimensions. As leader of the opposition, Suu Kyi has come to embody for a range of participants, from US policy elites to ordinary Burmese, a fearless but feminized figure of resistance, although with different implications in each instance. She is also the chief protagonist in the narrative about Burmese repression outside Burma. Vaclav Havel, who nominated her for the Nobel Peace Prize, would later write in a foreword to *Freedom from Fear*, a collection of her political and other writings, that "Aung San Suu Kyi cannot be silenced because she speaks the truth and because her words reflect basic Burmese and universal concepts" (in Suu Kyi 1991: xiii). Adding to her international celebrity are Suu Kyi's defiance and self-sacrifices in the face of repression, and her decision to fight on despite the personal costs incurred including long separations from her children and late husband.[26] Her iconic status among Burma watchers, foreign governments, and human rights activists is the product not only of her own writings and politics, but also of representations about her in the transnational Burma human rights discourse. The relationship between these representations and her own beliefs and practices as they play out in Burma is explored in the rest of this section. This section attempts to show how Suu Kyi is constituted as a feminized and exoticized figure of resistance, even as she constitutes her own identity and politics in distinctive ways. In the enactment of her politics we find a complication of the boundaries between public and private, domestic and international, and tradition and modernity, evident in liberal thought. At the same time, she may also be complicit in reproducing a Hollywood image of herself in the Western popular imagination, which feeds on her femininity and qualities typically associated with it.[27]

When Aung San Suu Kyi is spoken of in US policy circles it tends to be mostly by white male policy elites who take for granted that they understand and identify with her politics. Yet the feminization of her political struggle by both the Burmese regime and US policymakers, and the fantasized, orientalized figure of the Burmese dissident evident in US policy documents, have come to shape popular understandings of the Burmese opposition movement. Hearings by the House Foreign Affairs Committee in 1991, which were also an opportunity for US lawmakers and officials to congratulate Suu Kyi on her receipt of the Nobel Peace Prize, produced a gendered discourse of the Burmese dissident that is also inflected by a cultural production of the other, in this case the Burmese state. Suu Kyi is glowingly inscribed in the text of the proceedings as "the leader and the symbol of the struggle of the Burmese people for freedom" with all the requisite qualities of leadership (House Committee on Foreign Affairs 1993). She is simultaneously mother of the nation, its savior, and the victim of a brutal and despotic regime that is culturally, morally, and politically the opposite of everything the United States believes in and stands for.

The practical policy implications of this discursive construction of Suu Kyi are significant for what they reveal about US foreign policy. At another hearing in 1995, again coinciding with a major event surrounding Suu Kyi – her release from house arrest – lawmakers treated her as the de facto leader of a future Burmese democratic state, and one whose freedom and security may best be safeguarded through their interventionist policies (House Committee on International Relations 1996). Aung San Suu Kyi's resistance is seen to embody liberal ideals of democracy and human rights, and hence the sympathetic treatment she receives in the West. At the same time, and what gets lost in the representation of Suu Kyi, is her commitment to Burmese spiritual and cultural resources that inflect her political thought in interesting and sometimes contradictory ways. Silverstein suggests that both the Western and Burmese traditions on democracy have merged in Burmese political history and shape Suu Kyi's political philosophy. Her writings reflect in this sense a concern for "indigenizing" her political struggle and locating it within a Burmese cultural and spiritual milieu. She has been known to turn to Buddhist teachings for support of her criticisms of the Burmese regime, maintaining that

the Burmese could find answers to the terrible political and socio-economic conditions in Burma by turning to the words of the Buddha on the four causes of decline and decay; failure to recover that which has been lost, omission to repair that which has been damaged, disregard for the need of a reasonable economy and the elevation to leadership of men without morality or learning.

(Silverstein 1996)

While still under house arrest, Suu Kyi's essay, "Freedom from fear," was released by her husband to commemorate her receipt of the European Parliament's 1990 Sakharov Prize for Freedom of Thought (Suu Kyi 1991: 180). In a passage from that essay, a formative moment in elaborating her political thought, she writes the following:

Within a system which denies the existence of basic human rights, fear tends to be the order of the day. Fear of imprisonment, fear of torture, fear of death, fear of losing friends, family, property or means of livelihood, fear of poverty, fear of isolation, fear of failure. A most insidious form of fear is that which masquerades as common sense or even wisdom, condemning as foolish, reckless, insignificant or futile the small, daily acts of courage which help to preserve man's self-respect and inherent human dignity. It is not easy for a people conditioned by fear under the iron rule of the principle that might is right to free themselves from enervating miasma of fear. Yet even under the most crushing state machinery courage rises up again and again, for fear is not the natural state of civilized man.

(Suu Kyi 1991: 184)

The fear experienced on a day-to-day basis by those under systems of rule that are repressive and predictable in their capacity for violence has informed the politics of nonviolent resistance characteristic of Suu Kyi and her democracy movement, a politics that appears informed by her devout adherence to Buddhism. The oppressiveness experienced under the Burmese regime and its normalization must therefore be countered according to Suu Kyi by ordinary acts of defiance.

At the same time, her speeches and statements reveal political beliefs grounded in liberal democratic thought. The combination of both a Buddhist-inspired set of beliefs and liberal ideology in Suu Kyi's writings constructs a cultural and political narrative of Burma different from the one that emerges from the pages of Congressional hearings in the United States, disclosing the production of a dissident political culture inside Burma, one whose core principle as articulated by Suu Kyi and the NLD is nonviolent resistance.[28] Yet it is important to note that this dissident culture is not monolithic. Suu Kyi's steadfast opposition to an armed struggle has disenchanted some of her supporters. Further, her refusal to countenance an armed movement also sits at odds with the struggles of some ethnic minorities. That impatience is being seen particularly among youth activists camped out along the Thailand–Burma border, who believe that years of nonviolent struggle have done little to advance their cause.[29] Members of her own party have also shown frustration with her leadership and failure to engage in a dialogue with the Burmese regime. She has been accused by some party members of sustaining the impasse between the regime and the NLD by her failure to engage in a dialogue, and for pulling the NLD out of the national convention set up by the regime to draft a new Burmese constitution (Mitton 1999: 28–9).

The emergence of this popular female figure, often respectfully addressed as "The Lady," in the opposition movement in Burma may not have been possible if it were not also for the fact that the Western-educated Suu Kyi is the daughter of Aung San, the venerated male nationalist leader whose image is stamped across currency notes and replicated in monuments. Her presence in Burma prior to the crackdown by the military regime in 1988 was critical to the formation of the NLD and a dissident discourse, but it is important to recall that the struggle in Burma predated Suu Kyi's arrival. Yet Suu Kyi emerges in the aftermath of 1988 as the "natural" leader of the Burmese opposition. This may have been in part due to Suu Kyi's political lineage and her relationship to Aung San, whom she has invoked in interviews, speeches, and writings. The Burmese regime's crisis of legitimacy contrasts with that of Suu Kyi, whose familial connection to the "father of independent Burma"[30] has mostly enhanced her role, political legitimacy, and credibility, and she has led the opposition NLD with apparent fearlessness about the consequences to her own well-being (Clements 1997: 3). That she is the daughter of Aung San may also insulate her from the harsher punishments meted out to other NLD leaders and members. The regime's persecution of fellow NLD members and her house arrest have only buoyed her status among Burmese and in the international community. In a nation where there are few political heroes to celebrate, she is viewed in almost reverent terms by her admirers as the one person most likely to deliver the nation from the grip of the junta.[31] Predictably, the government has characterized her as a "puppet" manipulated by neocolonialist forces and makes allusions to how her marriage to an Englishman compromises her Burmese credentials (Husarska 1999: 1–6).

Interviews with Suu Kyi in the media and her own writings constitute some of the main texts through which the cultural politics of the pro-democracy struggle can be discerned. Thus far, this chapter has elaborated aspects of the orientalized cultural production that underlies the liberal discourse of human rights. Reconsidering the Burma human rights narrative with a postcolonial rereading necessitates the appreciation of the power and nuances of this cultural politics. To this end, Alvarez *et al.* (1998) offer a helpful formulation of cultural politics as

> the process enacted when sets of social actors shaped by, and embodying, different cultural meanings and practices come into conflict with each other ... Culture is political because meanings are constitutive of processes that, implicitly or explicitly, seek to redefine social power.
>
> (Alvarez *et al.* 1998: 7)

Given this formulation, the oppositional momentum of the discourses and practices of the Burmese democracy movement may be rendered and understood more fully. More precisely, the movement's cultural project – which is simultaneously social and political – may be articulated, brought to the fore, and its significance in the face of the Western or Northern liberal discourse better understood.

A sense of the cultural order of things or culture as a "signifying system" through which "a social order is communicated, reproduced, experienced and explored" (Raymond Williams in Alvarez *et al.* 1998: 3) may be discerned in the NLD leader's commentaries on matters ranging from the overtly political to the value of friends, poetry, and traditional festivals addressed in her *Letters from Burma* (1997) which appeared in a Japanese newspaper between 1995 and 1996. In this volume, Suu Kyi eloquently describes traditional festivals and ceremonies, and draws out the deeper impact of cultural meanings associated with Buddhism and Burmese history for politics. It is also in reconstituting the cultural symbolism of her movement for democracy in Burma around popular beliefs and practices, the "common sense" of everyday life, that Suu Kyi manages to retrieve a distinctively Burmese national past and contradict the dominant representations of her in the West.

Suu Kyi's inscription as a female nationalist icon has also been reproduced in international gatherings of women who have rallied behind her and her cause. While it does not appear to be systematized in her political thought, Suu Kyi has addressed the question of women's participation in public. The relationship between gender and political leadership in her own thinking is sometimes couched in biologically essentialist terms as she claims for women innate qualities of compassion that can be translated into the political realm. For example, in a videotaped message to the Global Forum of Women Political Leaders in Manila last January she states: "I would like to think that there's built-in compassion in women because we are the ones who have to nurture the children, we are the ones who will have to look to the next generations" (In "Asian women leaders exhort ..." 2000). She also calls them "happiness makers," but at the same time reveals that she hopes for a time when there will no longer be a distinction between men and women's understandings of the world (in "Asian women leaders exhort ..." 2000). Suu Kyi's political thought has never clearly distinguished between different forms of oppression nor conceptualized the relationship between gender and oppression, but it is clear from her writings that she believes in some form of radical and universal humanism that transcends difference, but that is also grounded in specific cultural and political struggles. In these ways she also complicates dominant assumptions underlying the liberal human rights discourse.

The discourse of resistance and its appropriation

While democracy, freedom, justice, human rights, and nationalism among others are key concepts in Aung San Suu Kyi's and the NLD's resistance to the military regime, they have also been appropriated by the Burmese state to signify something quite different and repressive. The different meanings attached to concepts such as "democracy" by dissidents and the state, and the discursive closure implied on both sides, have been critical to the ongoing struggle between the military and democratizing forces in Burma. Consequently, fixing the meanings of these terms has not only been critical for consolidating the movement for democracy and human rights in Burma, but has also led to their deployment in popular discourse. For example, the government refers to its practices as "disciplined democracy."[32] Its move to *discipline* democracy clearly involves a different context and use of these concepts, as public statements and speeches by key officials indicate, than the meanings that resonate with Suu Kyi and other dissidents. This quote from Senior General Than Shwe, head of the SPDC, illustrates nicely how a patriarchal nationalism rationalizes the Burmese state's practices and responses to calls for democracy:

> [B]asic rights and democracy must be in harmony with the nature of the country and the people ... Thus we are giving priority to create [a] firm infrastructure of basic rights, such as food, clothing and shelter needs. As long as the infrastructure is firm, a superstructure of human rights can be built stage by stage.
> (Human Rights Watch/Asia 1995: 13)

In the discourse of state officials, notions of order, sovereignty, and security overlap with the way democracy is understood by the military junta, but also instructively reflect the key preoccupations of Northern policy elites. In an interview with the news magazine, *Asiaweek*, in 1999, the SPDC's

Secretary-1, Khin Nyunt, outlined the justification for the 1988 massacre, which he suggested had brought Burma back from the brink of "disintegration." For example, order implies restoration of peace and stability, and the rule of law in the face of anarchy and chaos. These views express a Hobbesian preoccupation with order and anarchy evident in realist IR, although it is utilized by Khin Nyunt to distinguish the political project of the state from that of the democracy movement.[33] The views of Khin Nyunt and Than Shwe are also not too different from the relativist position adopted by some Southeast Asian leaders like Malaysia's Mahathir Mohamad and Singapore's Lee Kuan Yew on the distinctiveness of Asian values. The allusion to so-called Asian traditions confronts the liberal or universalist discourse with its contrary, a moral relativism that is supposedly grounded in "indigenous cultural" resources. The normalization of the latter in the discourses of nationalist elites also obscures the ways in which these conventions or traditions, never uniform in themselves, have been unsettled over time. When the Burmese regime claims to subscribe to a "culturally sensitive" human rights approach, it simply glosses over its repressive implications. The historical dynamics and diversity of such traditions reveal the falsity of political elites' claims of a fixed and immutable Asian values logic.

Conclusion

This chapter attempts to illuminate the contradictions of a liberal, transnational human rights discourse on Burma and its silences and erasures; the parameters and politics of this discourse; and its relationship to the figurative, nationalist and gendered dimensions of postcolonial politics in Burma. By challenging the representation of Burma as a space of violence and repression in international relations, I am certainly not contending that human rights violations do not actually occur in that country. Rather, I am arguing that such a representation needs to be explored, situated, and not merely taken for granted, and related to global and national power relations and hierarchies. This chapter thus attempts to show how the human rights debate may be advanced by a postcolonial critique, one that interrogates, unsettles, and moves beyond both universalist and relativist claims.

I develop such a critique by first showing how Burma's colonial history is implicated in its postcolonial human rights practices. The chapter subsequently explores how Burmese repression and resistance get talked about in human rights discourses of political elites in the United States, to better situate the "Burmese problem," and the inadequacy of existing discursive and practical strategies for addressing human rights abuses. The chapter also notes how Western and regional economic interests were, and remain, supporters of the Burmese state even as the human rights campaign on Burma gains more ground. A key conclusion drawn from this account is that the liberal discourse on human rights in Burma, as elsewhere, has been underwritten by the power of those who speak authoritatively about human rights violations, and who often claim to do so from a higher moral plane. Yet the liberal discourse appears to have had little meaningful impact on securing democracy or the protection of basic human rights in Burma. The problem of realizing an effective democratic alternative in Burma suggests that sovereignty claims and narrow economic interests prevail in the face of pressures for reform, enabling the state, in this case Burma, to fend off critics of its human rights record. This may be an easy defense when directed at US policymakers who may have been complicitous in producing or supporting human rights violations committed by the United States in other countries.

Resistance to repression entails a strategic positioning on the part of dissidents, such as Aung San Suu Kyi and the NLD, against both the erasures of liberalism and the political spin of ruling elites. Recalling Edward Said's articulation of a politics that defines a "space of activism,"[34] it is clear that postcolonial human rights and democracy movements have to position themselves against global hegemonic interests even as they more directly oppose and struggle against the repressive powers of the state. This entails, as Said suggests,

> the political necessity of taking a stand, of "strategically essential-izing" a position from the perspective of those who were and are victimized and continue to suffer in various ways from an unequal, capitalist, patriarchal and neocolonial world order.
>
> (Krishna 1993: 389)

Following Said, I conclude that it is only by developing a transnational politics around human rights, one that also interrogates the liberal silences and relativist mystifications which accompany global hierarchies of race, class, culture, and gender, that a deeper understanding of the human rights situation in countries like Burma may be obtained. In fact it is precisely because of the ways in which the state's repressive power is sustained that a rereading of the Burma human rights narrative is all the more imperative and compelling.

Acknowledgements

I thank Geeta Chowdhry, Sumit Mandal, Randy Persaud, and other contributors to this volume for their comments on the chapter, and Jessica Urban for research assistance.

Notes

1   The decision by the military government to change the country's name from Burma to Myanmar has led ironically to the usage of the colonial name by the

opposition and resistance inside and outside the country. Cognizant of the implications of naming for a *postcolonial* national identity I use Burma throughout this chapter except when directly quoting or paraphrasing information where Myanmar is used.

2 In November 1999 the UN Human Rights Commission's special rapporteur accused the Burmese government of "practicing forced labor, summary executions, abuses of ethnic minorities and repression of civil and political rights" (Burton 1999: 32)

3 U Win Aung is the Burmese foreign minister.

4 For a more detailed discussion of these themes see Nair (2000).

5 Cheah also suggests that NGOs in the South must balance between the different forces of transnational and national capitals and interests, and are thus "always a part of the linkages of global capital as they invest state formations and are only effective by virtue of being so" (1999: 18).

6 See, for example, Chatterjee (1990) for a critique of the liberal discourse on civil society, which calls into question its operative definitions in Western political thought and claims to universality.

7 Some of the exceptions include Peterson (1992a); however, even here "race" is not properly addressed.

8 As previewed in the introduction to this volume; among the works in IR that explicitly address its racialized dimensions are Hunt (1987), Doty (1996b), Manzo (1996), Persaud (1997), and Pettman (1996).

9 Desai writes that at the 1975 Mexico City women's conference, most of the Third World women "refused to identify themselves as feminists" and "argued that racism was a women's issue while the First World feminists were reluctant to focus on such issues" (Desai 1999: 186).

10 Much has been written on the exploitation of female labor in the South and how poor Third World women have been incorporated into an international sexual division of labor. By paying attention to feminist writings, we better understand, for example, how the body of the female Malaysian electronics factory worker, whose poverty, youth, physical "dexterity," and political disempowerment make her desirable to Western multinationals, becomes a site for the reproduction of global capital and resistance to it. For example, Ong shows how the phenomenon of hysteria among Malay factory workers constitutes a form of resistance against the forces of transnational capital (Ong 1987).

11 Cheah (1999) makes a good case for why we must move beyond this binary.

12 I thank fellow contributors and discussants at the International Studies Association (ISA) sponsored workshop on Power in a Postcolonial World in March 2000, who drew my attention to this point.

13 Clearly, it would be impossible to do justice to this history given space constraints and the main aims of this chapter, but it is hoped that some of the key points referenced here will give the reader a sense of the relevance of colonizing practices for a discussion of human rights in Burma.

14 See for example, Karen Human Rights Group Report (April 1998).

15 Also see Quinn (1991: 794).

16 During the hearings to the House Subcommittee, Congressman Blaz noted: "I don't agree necessarily [that] the American form of democracy is the best for everybody, but I do agree very strongly that human rights is good for everybody" (House Committee on Foreign Affairs 1993: 80).

17 In a rather confused statement, the director of the Indochina–Burma Program at Harvard University, Thomas Vallely, suggested to the Congressional subcommittee that the

constitutional process [in Burma] needs to have some sort of multinational agreement with Japan, United States, ASEAN. An agreement where we say we want the constitution to look like X, and the Burmese themselves have to figure out what X is, but we have enough ability to have dialog among the parties in Burma to know what in general terms we might want, and then to use the multilateral mechanism to try to encourage the forces in the NLD and other places and the forces inside the Burmese Army that want that change.

(House Committee on International Relations 1996: 33)

18 The rewards of being an ASEAN member for Burma appeared plentiful particularly in light of the spectacular economic growth witnessed by the region up until 1997 when the Asian currency crisis hit. Regional human rights groups organized vigorously in opposition to Burma's application for membership in ASEAN, citing its human rights record (Jayasankaran 1996).

19 In testimony before the House Committee on International Relations, deputy assistant secretary of state for East Asian and Pacific Affairs, Kent Wiedemann, revealed that the United States had also urged donor countries like Japan to strictly limit development assistance to Burma. He states:

We do not provide GSP trade preferences and have decertified Burma as a narcotics cooperating country, which requires us by law to vote against assistance to Burma by international financial institutions. This and our influence with other countries have in practice prevented most assistance to Burma from the IMF, the World Bank and the Asia Development Bank. Neither Eximbank nor the Overseas Private Investment Corporation provide loans or insurance for American companies selling to or investing in Burma.

(House Committee on International Relations 1996: 5)

20 See Committee on International Relations (1996: 19); "Senate passes foreign aid bill after dispute over Myanmar" (1996); Human Rights Watch (1998b).

21 At the Seattle round of the World Trade Organization talks, leaflets were distributed calling attention to Unocal's involvement in Burma. (Los Angeles Burma Forum, "Unocal + Burma's military dictatorship = human rights abuses and environmental devastation," Seattle, WA, 1999).

22 Individual states like Massachusetts have been thwarted in their efforts to impose a penalty on any company doing business with Burma. A US court ruled in June 1999 that the Massachusetts law infringes on the right of the federal government to conduct foreign affairs and regulate commerce (Crispin 1999: 22). Also see Stumberg and Waren (1999).

23 See Desai (1999) and Peterson (1992b).

24 As Chandra Mohanty has explained, the reference to Western feminism is not meant to cast all of Western feminism(s) in a single mold but rather to draw attention to the implicitly self-referential gaze of dominant analytic variants of Western feminism that objectify the other. She also points out that this critique is applicable also to "third world scholars writing about their own cultures, which employ identical analytic strategies" (in Mohanty et al. 1991: 52).

25 For an extended discussion of the theoretical implications of the relationship between Western feminist discourse and scholarship on Third World women see Mohanty et al. (1991).

26 The Burmese regime denied Aris a visa to see Suu Kyi in Burma when he was terminally ill with cancer, but declared that Suu Kyi was free to leave to visit Aris. She refused, fearing that she would not be allowed back into Burma.

27 In the 1995 Hollywood film, *Beyond Rangoon*, Suu Kyi is represented in goddess-like fashion among throngs of desperate Burmese looking to her for guidance.

28 See Alan Clements's interview with Suu Kyi (Clements 1997) in which the NLD leader outlines her views on nonviolence and its merits.

29 See Sheridan and Phung (1999). See also Bachoe (1999).

30 This reference is contained in a statement presented by Sein Wein, prime minister of the National Coalition of the Union of Burma to the House Committee on Foreign Affairs on 18 October 1991 (House Committee on Foreign Affairs 1993: 39).

31 The ordinary risks many Burmese take to approach her, attend her rallies prior to her house arrest, and give their open support to her movement suggest more than a willingness to take chances with the ubiquitous military and police forces who monitor her movements. Although released from house arrest in 1995 she remains restricted to the capital city, but continues to cut a courageous figure to her admirers (Keane in Suu Kyi 1997: Introduction).

32 The report refers to "disciplined democracy" as the "SPDC's euphemism for continued authoritarian control" (Human Rights Watch 1999).

33 "We restored order", *Asiaweek*, December 17, 1999.

34 See Krishna (1993) for an explanation of this point in Said's thought.

BIBLIOGRAPHY

Abu-Lughod, L. (1986) *Veiled Sentiments: Honor and Poetry in a Bedouin Society*, Berkeley: University of California Press.

Adams, V. (1996) "Karaoke as modern Lhasa, Tibet: western encounters with cultural politics," *Cultural Anthropology* 11, 4: 510–46.

——(1998) "Suffering the winds of Lhasa: politicized bodies, human rights, cultural difference, and humanism in Tibet," *Medical Anthropology* 12, 1: 74–102.

Adamson, A.H. (1972) *Sugar Without Slaves: The Political Economy of British Guiana 1838–1904*, New Haven: Yale University Press.

Adlan, N. (1998) "APEC and Asia's crisis," *Far Eastern Economic Review*. 161, 22: 35.

Agathangelou, A.M. and Ling, L.H.M. (1997) "Post-colonial dissident IR: transforming master narratives of sovereignty in Greco-Turkish Cyprus," *Studies of Political Economy* 54: 7–38.

Agnew, J.A. (1994) "Timeless space and state centrism: the geographical assumptions of international relations theory," in S.J. Rosow, N. Inayatullah and M. Rupert (eds) *The Global Economy as Political Space*, Boulder, CO: Lynne Rienner.

Ahmad, A. (1992) *In Theory, Classes, Nations, Literatures*, London: Verso.

Ahmed, L. (1992) *Women and Gender in Islam: Historical Roots of a Modern Debate*, New Haven: Yale University Press.

AICMA (1986) *Silver Jubilee Special, Carpet-e-World*, Bhadohi, India: All India Carpet Manufacturer's Association.

Aidoo, A.A. (1991) *Changes*, London: Women's Press.

Albers, P.C. (1993) "Symbiosis, merger, and war: contrasting forms of intertribal relationship among historic Plains Indians," in J.H. Moore (ed.) *The Political Economy of North American Indians*, Norman: University of Oklahoma Press.

Alexander J. (1997) "Erotic autonomy as a politics of decolonization: an anatomy of feminist and state practice in the Bahamas tourist economy," in J. Alexander and C. Mohanty (eds) *Feminist Genealogies, Colonial Legacies and Democratic Futures*, London: Routledge.

——(1998) "Imperial desire/sexual utopias: white gay capital and transnational tourism," in E. Shohat (ed.) *Talking Visions: Multicultural Feminism in a Transnational Age*, Cambridge: MIT Press.

Alexander, J. and Mohanty, C.T. (1997) *Feminist Genealogies, Colonial Legacies, and Democratic Futures*, New York and London: Routledge.

Altink, S. (1995) *Stolen Lives: Trading Women into Sex and Slavery*, London: Scarlet Press.

Alva, J.J.K. (1995) "The postcolonization of the (Latin) American experience, a reconsideration of 'colonialism,' 'postcolonialism' and 'mestizaje,'" in G. Prakash (ed.) *After Colonialism, Imperial Histories and Postcolonial Displacements*, Princeton, NJ: Princeton University Press.

Alvarez, S., Dagnino, E. and Escobar, A. (eds) (1998) *Culture of Politics and Politics of Cultures: Re-Visioning Latin American Social Movements*, Boulder, CO: Westview Press.

Amin, S. (1974) *Accumulation on a World Scale*, New York: Monthly Review Press.

Amnesty International (1998) "The Body Shop and Amnesty International join forces to free human rights defenders around the world." Online. Available http://www.amnesty.it/news/1998/212may98.htm (5 May 2001).

——(1999) *Republic of Korea (South Korea) Workers' Rights at a Time of Economic Crisis*. Online. Available http://www.amnesty.org (25 February 1999).

Amott, T. and Matthaei, J. (1996) *Race, Gender, and Work: A Multi-Cultural Economic History of Women in the United States*, Boston, MA: South End Press.

Anand, D. (2000) "(Re)imagining nationalism: identity and representation in the Tibetan diaspora of South Asia," *Contemporary South Asia* 9, 3: 271–88.

Anderson, B. (1990) *Language and Power: Exploring Political Cultures in Indonesia*, New York: Cornell University Press.

——(1998) *The Spectre of Comparisons: Nationalism, Southeast Asia and the World*, London: Verso.

Appadurai, A. (1991) "Global ethnoscapes: notes and queries for a transnational anthropology," in R. Fox (ed.) *Recapturing Anthropology: Working in the Present*, Santa Fe: School of American Research Press.

Appignanesi, L. and Maitland, S. (1990) *The Rushdie File*, New York: Syracuse University Press.

Arblaster, A. (1984) *The Rise and Decline of Western Liberalism*, Oxford: Blackwell.

Argyris, C. (1992) *On Organizational Learning*, London: Blackwell.

Argyris, C. and Schon, D.A. (1978) *Organizational Learning: A Theory of Action Perspective*, Reading, MA: Addison-Wesley.

Asad, T. (1992) "Religion and politics: an introduction," *Social Research* 59: 3.

——(1993) "Multiculturalism and the British identity in the wake of the Rushdie affair," in T. Asad (ed.) *Genealogies of Religion: Discipline and Reasons of Power in Christianity and Islam*, Baltimore: Johns Hopkins University Press.

——(1997) "On torture, or cruel, inhuman and degrading treatment," in R. Wilson (ed.) *Human Rights, Culture and Context: Anthropological Perspectives*, London: Pluto Press.

Ashcroft, B. and Ahluwalia, P. (1999) *Edward Said: The Paradox of Identity*, London and New York: Routledge.

Ashley, R. (1989) "Living on border lines: man, post-structuralism, and war," in J. Der Derian and M. Shapiro (eds) *International/Intertextual Relations: Postmodern Readings of World Politics*, Lexington, MA: Lexington Books.

Ashley, R.K. and Walker, R.B.J. (1990a) "Speaking the language of exile: dissident thought in international studies," *International Studies Quarterly* 34: 259–68.

——(1990b) "Reading dissidence and writing the discipline: crisis and the question of sovereignty," *International Studies Quarterly* 34: 367–416.

Asia Watch (1990) *Human Rights in Burma (Myanmar)*, New York: Human Rights Watch.

Asian Development Bank (2001) *Asia Recovery Report*. Online. Available http://aric.adb.org (March 2001).

"Asian women leaders exhort more women to join politics" (2000) Deutsche Presse-Agentur, 17 January.

Associated Press (1998) "N.J. guards convicted in Jain beatings: immigrants abused after 1995 rioting," 7 March.

Bachoe, R. (1999) "We support Suu Kyi, say fighters," *Bangkok Post* 11 December.

Bamforth, D.B. (1994) "Indigenous people, indigenous violence: precontact warfare on the North American Great Plains," *MAN* 29, 1: 95–115.

Banuri, T. (1990) "Modernisation and its discontents: a cultural perspective on the theories of development," in F.A. Marglin and S.A. Marglin (eds) *Dominating Knowledge*, Oxford: Clarendon Press.

Baran, P. (1957) *The Political Economy of Growth*, New York: Monthly Review Press.

Barnett, R. and Akiner, S. (eds) (1996) *Resistance and Reform in Tibet*, Delhi: Motilal Banarsidass.

Barnett, R. and Lehman, S. (1998) *The Tibetans: Struggle to Survive*, New York: Umbrage.

Barro, R.J. (1998) "Malaysia could do worse than this economic plan," *Business Week* 2 November: 26.

Barry, K. (1995) *The Prostitution of Sexuality*, New York: New York University Press.

Bataille, G. (1992) "Lamaism: the unarmed society," *Lungta* 6: 33–40.

Becker, J.J. (1998) *Histoire politique de la France depuis 1945*, Paris: Armand Colin.

Bedford, D. and Workman, T. (1997) "The great law of peace: alternative internation(al) practices and the Iroquoian confederacy," *Alternatives* 22, 1: 87–111.

Beier, J.M. (1998) *Blackened Faces and Ticker-Tape Parades: Situating the Leviathan in Lakota and Euroamerican Conceptions of War*, YCISS Occasional Paper 54, Toronto: Centre for International and Security Studies.

Bellah, R.N. (1992) *The Broken Covenant: American Civil Religion in Time of Trial*, 2nd edn, Chicago: University of Chicago Press.

Bello, W. (1998a) "East Asia: on the eve of the great transformation?" *Review of International Political Economy* 5, 3: 424–44.

——(1998b) *Testimony of Walden Bello before Banking Oversight Subcommittee, Banking and Financial Services Committee, US House of Representatives*. Online. Available http://www.citizen.org/pctrade/IMF/bellow.htm.

Berger, M. (1996) "Yellow mythologies: the East Asian miracle and post-cold war capitalism," *positions: east asia cultures critique* 4, 1: 90–126.

Berger, M. and Beeson, M. (1998) "Lineages of liberalism and miracles of modernisation: the World Bank, the East Asian trajectory and the international development debate," *Third World Quarterly* 19, 3: 487–504.

Berger, P. (1967) *The Sacred Canopy: Elements of a Sociological Theory of Religion*, New York: Doubleday.

——(1996–7) *The National Interest* 46: 3–12.

Berkhofer, R.F., Jr. (1978) *The White Man's Indian: Images of the American Indian from Columbus to the Present*, New York: Vintage Books.

Berlau, J. (1997) "The paradox of child-labor reform," *Insight on the News* 13, 43 (24 November): 20–1.

Beverly, J. (1999) *Subalternity and Representation: Arguments in Cultural Theory*, Durham, NC, and London: Duke University Press.

Beyer, P. (1994) *Religion and Globalization*, London: Sage.

Bhabha, H.K. (1985) "Signs taken for wonders: questions of ambivalence and authority under a tree outside Delhi, May 1817," in H.L. Gates, Jr. (ed.) *"Race," Writing, and Difference*, Chicago: University of Chicago Press.

——(1990) "DissemiNation: time, narrative, and the margins of the modern nation," in H.K. Bhabha (ed.) *Nation and Narration*, London: Routledge.

——(1994) *The Location of Culture*, London: Routledge.

——(1995) "Signs taken for wonders," in B. Ashcroft, G. Griffiths and H. Tiffen (eds) *The Postcolonial Studies Reader*, London and New York: Routledge.

Bhagwati, J. (1997) "Interview," *Times of India*, 31 December.

Biolsi, T. (1984) "Ecological and cultural factors in Plains Indian warfare," in R.B. Ferguson (ed.) *Warfare, Culture, and Environment*, Orlando: Academic Press.

——(1985) "The IRA and the politics of acculturation: the Sioux case," *American Anthropologist* 87, 3: 656–9.

Biondi, J.P. and Morin, G. (1992) *Les Anticolonialistes (1882–1962)*, Paris: Robert Laffont.

Bishop, P. (1989) *The Myth of Shangri-la Tibet, Travel Writing and the Western Creation of a Sacred Landscape*, Berkeley: University of California Press.

——(1993) *Dreams of Power: Tibetan Buddhism and the Western Imagination*, London: Athlone.

——(1997) "A landscape for dying: the *bardo thodol* and Western fantasy," in F.J. Korom (ed.) *Constructing Tibetan Culture: Contemporary Perspectives*, Quebec: World Heritage Press.

Blackwood, E. (1995) "Senior women, model mothers, and dutiful wives: managing gender contradictions in a Minangkabau village," in A. Ong and M.G. Peletz (eds) *Bewitching Women, Pious Men: Gender and Body Politics in Southeast Asia*, Berkeley: University of California Press.

Blick, J.P. (1988) "Genocidal warfare in tribal societies as a result of European-induced culture conflict," *MAN* 23, 4: 654–70.

Booth, K. (1999) "Three tyrannies," in T. Dunne and N.J. Wheeler (eds) *Human Rights in Global Politics*, Cambridge: Cambridge University Press.

Boukhari, S. (1999) "Child labour: a lesser evil?" *Unesco Courier*, May. Online. Available http://Web5.infotrac.galegroup.com (February 2000).

Branigin, W. (1997) "Immigration panel calls for 'Americanization' effort," *Washington Post*, 1 October.

Braudel, F. (1980) *On History*, Chicago: University of Chicago Press.

Brewer, A. (1989) *Marxist Theories of Imperialism: A Critical Survey*, New York: Routledge.

Bullard, N., Bello, W. and Mallhotra, K. (1998) "Taming the tigers: the IMF and the Asian crisis," *Third World Quarterly* 19, 3: 505–55.

Bunge, R. (1984) *An American Urphilosophie: An American Philosophy BP (Before Pragmatism)*, Lanham, MD: University Press of America.

Bureau of Democracy, Human Rights and Labor, Department of State (1999a) *Human Rights Practices for 1998: Cyprus Country Report*. Online. Available http://www.usemb.se/human/human1998/cyprus.html7 (February 1999).

——(1999b) *Human Rights Practices for 1998: Turkey Country Report*. Online. Available http://www.usemb.se/human/human1998/turkey.html (February 1999).

——(1999c)*Human Rights Practices for 1998: Greece Country Report*. Online. Available http://www.usemb.se/human/human1998/greece.html (February 1999).

Burton, J. (2000) "Companies & finance: ASIA–Pacific: Kepco privatization plan favours foreign investors," *Financial Times*, 24 May. Online. Available http://news.ft.com/home/us/ (24 May 2000).

Burton, S. (1999) "Signs of hope?" *Time Australia* 22: 32.

Business Week (1998) "Asia's social backlash," *Business Week Special Report* 3591: 46–51.

Butterflies (1998) *The Convention on the Rights of the Child: The Alternate Report*, New Delhi, India: Rainbow Publishers.

Buzan, B. (1991) *People, States and Fear*, Boulder, CO: Lynne Rienner.

Campbell, D. (1992) *Writing Security: United States Foreign Policy and the Politics of Identity*, Minneapolis: University of Minnesota Press.

——(1994) "Foreign policy and identity: Japanese 'other'/American 'self,' " in S. Rosow, N. Inayatullah and M. Rupert (eds) *The Global Economy as Political Space*, Boulder, CO: Lynne Rienner.

——(1998) *National Deconstruction: Violence, Identity, and Justice in Bosnia*, Minneapolis: University of Minnesota Press.

Carey, P. (ed.) (1997) *Burma: The Challenge of Change in a Divided Society*, New York: St Martin's Press.

Casanova, J. (1984) "The politics of the religious revival," *Telos* 59: 3–33.
——(1992) "Private and public religions," *Social Research* 59, 1: 17–18.
Chagnon, N.A. (1968) *Y,anomamö, the Fierce People*, New York: Holt, Rinehart and Winston.
——(1988) "Life histories, blood revenge, and warfare in a tribal population," *Science* 239: 985–92.
Chakrabarty, D. (1992) "Postcoloniality and the artifice of history, who speaks for 'Indian' pasts?" *Representations* 37: 1–24.
Chancy, M.J.A. (1997) *Framing Silence: Revolutionary Novels by Haitian Women*, New Brunswick, NJ: Princeton University Press.
Chang, K. (1998) "When the economic growth machine derails: compressed capitalist development and social sustainability crisis in South Korea," paper presented at the International Conference on the Economic Crisis in East Asia and the Impact on the Local Population, 29–30 October, Roskilde University, Roskilde, Denmark.
Chang, K. and Ling, L.H.M. (1996) "Globalization and its intimate other: Filipina domestic workers in Hong Kong," paper presented at the International Studies Association, 16–21 April, San Diego, CA.
——(2000) "Globalization and its intimate other: Filipina domestic workers in Hong Kong," in M. Marchand and A.S. Runyan (eds) *Gender and Global Restructuring: Sightings, Sites and Resistances*, London and New York: Routledge.
Chatterjee, P. (1986) *Nationalist Thought and the Colonial World: A Derivative Discourse*, Minneapolis: University of Minnesota Press.
——(1990) "A response to Taylor's modes of civil society," *Public Culture* 3, 1: 119–32.
——(1993) *The Nation and its Fragments: Colonial and Postcolonial Histories*, Princeton, NJ: Princeton University Press.
——(1995) "Religious minorities and the secular state: reflections on an Indian impasse," *Public Culture* 8, 1: 11–39.
Chaves, M. (1994) "Secularization as declining religious authority," *Social Forces* 72, 3: 749–74.
Cheah, P. (1999) "Posit(ion)ing human rights in the current global conjuncture," in S. Geok-Lin Lim, W. Dissanayake and L. Smith (eds) *Transnational Asia Pacific: Gender, Culture and the Public Sphere*, Urbana and Chicago: University of Illinois Press.
Cheru, F. (1995) "The silent revolution and the weapons of the weak: transformation and innovation from below," in S. Gill and J. Mittelman (eds) *Innovation and Transformation in International Studies*, Cambridge: Cambridge University Press.
Chilcote, R.H. (1974) "Dependency: a critical synthesis of the literature," *Latin American Perspectives* 1: 4–29.
——(ed.) (1999) *The Political Economy of Imperialism: Critical Appraisals*, Boston, Dordrecht and London: Kluwer Academic Publishers.
Chin, C.B.N. (1998) *In Service and Servitude: Foreign Female Domestic Workers and the Malaysian "Modernity" Project*, New York: Columbia University Press.
Chin, J. (1997) "Malaysia in 1996: Mahathir–Anwar bouts, UMNO election, and Sarawak surprise," *Asian Survey* 37, 2: 181–7.
Chomsky, N. (1999) "Why Americans should care about East Timor," *Mother Jones*. Online. Available http://www.motherjones.com/east_timor/comment/chomsky.html (September 1999).
Chow, R. (1993) *Writing Diaspora: Tactics of Intervention in Contemporary Cultural Studies*, Bloomington: Indiana University Press.

Chowdhry, G. and Beeman, M. (2001) "Challenging child labor: transnational activism and India's carpet industry," *Annals of the American Academy of Political and Social Science* 575: 158–73.

Churchill, W. and LaDuke, W. (1992) "Native North America: the political economy of radioactive colonialism," in M.A. Jaimes (ed.) *The State of Native America: Genocide, Colonization, and Resistance*, Boston: South End Press.

Cisneros, L.-J. (1999) "Peru's child workers stake their claims," *Unesco Courier*, May. Online. Available http://Web5.infotrac.galegroup.com (February 2000).

Clements, A. (1997) "We are still prisoners in our own country: an interview with Aung San Suu Kyi," *The Humanist* 57, 6: 15–21.

Commission for a New Asia (1994) *Towards a New Asia: A Report of the Commission for a New Asia*, Tokyo: Sakasawa Foundation.

Connell, R.W. (1987) *Gender and Power: Society, the Person and Sexual Politics*, Cambridge: Polity Press.

——(1995) *Masculinities*, Cambridge: Polity Press.

Connolly, W.E. (1999) *Why I Am Not a Secularist*, Minneapolis: University of Minnesota Press.

Cooper, F. and Stoler, A.L. (eds) (1997) *Tensions of Empire: Colonial Cultures in a Bourgeois World*, Berkeley: University of California Press.

Cornelius, W.A., Martin, P.L. and Hollifield, J.F. (eds) (1994) *Controlling Immigration: A Global Perspective*, Stanford, CA: Stanford University Press.

Cornell, S. (1988) "The transformations of tribe: organization and self-concept in Native American ethnicities," *Ethnic and Racial Studies* 11, 1: 27–47.

Cottle, S. (1991) "Reporting the Rushdie affair: a case study in the orchestration of public opinion," *Race and Class* 32, 4: 45–64.

Cox, K.E. (1999) "The inevitability of nimble fingers? Law, development and child labor," *Vanderbilt Journal of International Law* 32, 1: 115.

Cox, R. (1983) "Gramsci, hegemony and international relations: an essay in method," *Millennium* 12: 162–75.

——(1987) *Production, Power, and World-Order*, New York: Columbia University Press.

——(1992) "Towards a post-hegemonic conceptualization of world order: reflections on the relevancy of Ibn Khaldun," in J. Rosenau and E. Czempiel (eds) *Governance Without Government: Order and Change in World Politics*, Cambridge: Cambridge University Press.

——(1993) "Structural issues of global governance: implications for Europe," in S. Gill (ed.) *Gramsci, Historical Materialism and International Relations*, Cambridge, MA: Cambridge University Press.

——(1995) *International Political Economy: Understanding Global Disorder*, Atlantic Highlands, NJ: Zed Books.

Crawford, N.C. (1994) "A security regime among democracies: cooperation among Iroquois nations," *International Organization* 48, 3: 345–85.

Cricinfo Match Report (1994) *CricInfo*. Online. Available http://www-usa.cricket.org/link_to_data...94/ENG_WI_T2_17–22MAR1994_MR.

Crispin, S. (1999) "Business decision: US court strikes down Burma-boycott law," *Far Eastern Economic Review*. Online. Available http://www.feer.com/1999/990708-/tw.html (10 July 1999).

Cumings, B. (1998) "The Korean crisis and the end of 'late' development," *New Left Review* 231: 43–72.

Daedalus (1991) Special Issue on Religion and Politics, 120, 3: v–viii.

Darby, P. (1997a) "Postcolonialism," in P. Darby (ed.) *At the Edge of International Relations: Postcolonialism, Gender, and Dependency*, London and New York: Pinter.

——(ed.) (1997b) *At the Edge of International Relations: Postcolonialism, Gender and Dependency*, London and New York: Pinter.

——(1998) *The Fiction of Imperialism: Reading between International Relations and Post-colonialism*, London and Washington, DC: Cassell.

Darby, P. and Paolini, A.J. (1994) "Bridging international relations and postcolonialism," *Alternatives* 19, 3: 371–97.

DeConde, A. (1992) *Ethnicity, Race, and American Foreign Policy: A History*, Boston: Northeastern University Press.

Deepak, L. (1985) "The misconceptions of 'development economics,' " in S. Corbridge (ed.) *Development Studies*, London: Arnold.

Deloria, V., Jr. (1992) "Is religion possible? An evaluation of present efforts to revive traditional tribal religions," *Wicazo Sa Review* 8, 1: 35–9.

DeMallie, R.J. (ed.) (1984) *The Sixth Grandfather: Black Elk's Teachings Given to John G. Neihardt*, Lincoln: University of Nebraska Press.

——(1987) "Lakota belief and ritual in the nineteenth century," in R.J. DeMallie and D.R. Parks (eds) *Sioux Indian Religion: Tradition and Innovation*, Norman: University of Oklahoma Press.

Department of Information and International Relations (1997) *International Resolutions and Recognitions on Tibet (1959 to 1997)*, Dharamsala: Central Tibetan Administration.

Der Derian, J. (1989) "The boundaries of knowledge and power in international relations," in J. Der Derian and M.J. Shapiro (eds) *International/Intertextual Relations: Postmodern Readings of World Politics*, Lexington, MA: Lexington Books.

Der Derian, J. and Shapiro, M.J. (1989) (eds) *International/Intertextual Relations: Postmodern Readings of World Politics*, Lexington, MA: Lexington Books.

Desai, M. (1999) "From Vienna to Beijing: women's human rights activism and the human rights community," in P.V. Ness (ed.) *Debating Human Rights: Critical Essays from the United States and Asia*, New York: Routledge.

Detwiler, F. (1992) " 'All my relatives': persons in Oglala religion," *Religion* 22, 3: 235–46.

Deutz, A.M. (1991) "United States human rights policy towards Burma, 1988–91," *Contemporary Southeast Asia* 13, 2: 164–87.

Devine, C. (1993) *Determination: Tibetan Women and the Struggle for an Independent Tibet*, Toronto: Vauve Press.

Dicken, P. (1992) *Global Shift: The Internationalization of Economic Activity*, 2nd edn, New York: Guilford Press.

Dillon, M. (1996) *Politics of Security: Towards a Political Philosophy of Continental Thought*, New York: Routledge.

Dirlik, A. (1997) "The postcolonial aura: third world criticism in the age of global capitalism," in A. McClintock, A. Mufti and E. Shohat (eds) *Dangerous Liaisons: Gender, Nation and Postcolonial Perspectives*, Boulder, CO: Westview Press.

Doezema, J. (1998) "Forced to choose: beyond the voluntary v. forced prostitution dichotomy," in K. Kempadoo and J. Doezema (eds) *Global Sex Workers: Rights, Resistance and Redefinition*, New York: Routledge.

Donnelly, J. (1998) *International Human Rights*, Boulder, CO: Westview Press.

–(1999) "The social construction of international human rights," in T. Dunne and N.J. Wheeler (eds) *Human Rights in Global Politics*, Cambridge: Cambridge University Press.

Dorris, M. (1987) "Indians on the shelf," in Calvin Martin (ed.) *The American Indian and the Problem of History*, New York: Oxford University Press.

Doty, R.L. (1993) "The bounds of 'race' in international relations," *Millennium* 22, 3: 443–61.

——(1996a) "Immigration and national identity: constructing the nation," *Review of International Studies* 22: 235–55.

——(1996b) *Imperial Encounters: The Politics of Representation in North–South Relations*, Minneapolis: University of Minnesota Press.

Douglas, M. (1987) *How Institutions Think*, London: Routledge and Kegan Paul.

Dower, J. (1986) *War without Mercy: Race and Power in the Pacific War*, New York: Pantheon Books.

Drinnon, R. (1997) *Facing West: The Metaphysics of Indian Hating and Empire Building*, London: University of Oklahoma Press.

Duffy, M. (1998) "The Rubin rescue," *Time* 151, 1: 46–9.

Dunaway, W.A. (1996) "Incorporation as an interactive process: Cherokee resistance to expansion of the capitalist-world system, 1560–1763," *Sociological Inquiry* 66, 4: 455–70.

Dutt, E. (1995) "Rug firms with no child labor need help," *India Abroad*, 3 February: 16.

Dworkin, R. (1977) *Taking Rights Seriously*, London: Duckworth.

Dyson, A. (1990) "Looking below the surface," in D. Cohn-Sherbok (ed.) *The Salman Rushdie Controversy in Interreligious Perspective*, New York: Edwin Mellon Press.

Eade, J. (1993) "The political articulation of community and the Islamisation of space in London," in R. Barot (ed.) *Religion and Ethnicity: Minorities and Social Change in the Metropolis*, Netherlands: Kok Pharos Publishing House.

EarthRights International (ERI) and Southeast Asian Information Network (SAIN) (1996) *Total Denial: A Report on the Yadana Pipeline Project*, Washington DC: EarthRights International.

Ebert, T.L. (1995) "Subalternity and feminism in the moment of the (post)modern: the materialist return," in K. Myrsiades and J. McGuire (eds) *Order Partialities: Theory, Pedagogy and the "Postcolonial"*, Albany NY: SUNY Press.

Economist (1994a) "Child miners: no simple way out," *The Economist* 330, 7852: 46.

——(1994b) "Islam and the West," *The Economist* 332, 7875: 44–61.

——(1995a) "Consciences and consequences: Western companies oppose overseas suppliers using child labor" (editorial), *The Economist* 335, 7917: 13–14.

——(1995b) "Living with Islam," *The Economist* 334, 7906: 13–14.

——(2000) "A survey of South-East Asia: the tigers that changed their stripes," *The Economist*, 12–18 February: 3–19.

Elshtain, J.B. (1987) *Women and War*, New York: Basic Books.

——(1999) "Exporting feminism," in T. Lim (ed.) *Global Issues*, Bellevue: Coursewise.

Enloe, C. (1990) *Bananas, Beaches and Bases: Making Feminist Sense of International Politics*, Berkeley: University of California Press.

——(1993) *The Morning After: Sexual Politics at the End of the Cold War*, Berkeley: University of California Press.

Epp, R. (2000) "At the wood's edge: towards a theoretical clearing for indigenous diplomacies in international relations," in D. Jarvis and R. Crawford (eds.) *International Relations: Still an American Social Science?*, Albany: SUNY Press.

Escobar, A. (1995) *Encountering Development*, Princeton: Princeton University Press.

Esposito, J. L., (1992) *The Islamic Threat: Myth or Reality?*, New York: Oxford University Press.

Eviota, E.U. (1992) *The Political Economy of Gender: Women and the Sexual Division of Labor in the Philippines*, London: Zed Books.

Ewers, J.C. (1975) "Intertribal warfare as the precursor of Indian-White warfare on the Northern Great Plains," *Western Historical Quarterly* 6: 397–410.

Fabian, J. (1990) "Presence and representation: the other and anthropological writing," *Critical Inquiry* 16, 4: 753–72.

Fairclough, G. (1996) "It isn't black and white," *Far Eastern Economic Review*, March: 54–8.

Falk, R. (1992) "Cultural foundations for the international protection of human rights," in A.A. An-Na'im (ed.) *Human Rights in Cross Cultural Perspective: A Quest for Consensus*, Philadelphia: University of Pennsylvania Press.

——(1999) "The challenge of genocide and genocidal politics in an era of globalisation," in T. Dunne and N.J. Wheeler (eds) *Human Rights in Global Politics*, Cambridge: Cambridge University Press.

Fanon, F. (1965) *The Wretched of the Earth*, trans. by Constance Farrington, New York: Grove Press.

——(1967) *Black Skin, White Masks*, trans. by C.L. Markmann, New York: Grove Press.

Feagin, J.R. (1997) "Old poison in new bottles: the deep roots of modern nativism," in J.F. Perea (ed.) *Immigrants Out! The New Nativism and the Anti-Immigrant Impulse in the United States*, New York: New York University Press.

Ferguson, R.B. (1990) "Blood of the leviathan: western contact and warfare in Amazonia," *American Ethnologist* 17, 2: 237–57.

——(1992) "Tribal warfare," *Scientific American* 266, 1: 108–13.

Ferguson, R.B. and Whitehead, N.L. (1992) "The violent edge of empire," in R.B. Ferguson and N.L. Whitehead (eds) *War in the Tribal Zone: Expanding States and Indigenous Warfare*, Santa Fe: School of American Research Press.

Foreign Office (1920) *Tibet (Number 70)*, London: HM Stationery Office.

Forum of Indian Leftists (1996) *Those That Be in Bondage: Child Labor and IMF Strategy in India*, FOIL Pamphlet 1. Online. Available http://www.proxsa.org/economy/labor/chldlbr.html (20 May 2000).

Foucault, M. (1972) *The Archaeology of Knowledge*, New York: Dorset Press and Pantheon Books.

——(1980) *Power/Knowledge*, ed. by Colin Gordon, New York: Pantheon Books.

Frank, A.G. (1967) *Capitalism and Underdevelopment in Latin America: Historical Studies of Chile and Brazil*, New York: Monthly Review Press.

Frankenberg R. and Mani, L. (1993) "Crosscurrents, crosstalk: race 'postcoloniality' and the politics of location," *Cultural Studies* 7, 2: 292–310.

Franklin, M.I. (forthcoming) "Sewing up the globe: ICTs and (re)materialised gender–power relations," in B. Saunders and M. Foblets (eds) *Changing Genders in Intercultural Perspective*, Brussels: Leuven University Press.

Fukuyama, F. (1989) "The end of history?" *The National Interest* 5 (summer): 3–18.

——(1992) *The End of History and the Last Man*, New York: Avon Books.

Gandhi, L. (1998) *Postcolonial Theory: A Critical Introduction*, New York: Columbia University Press.

Gardiner, R.K. (1968) "Race and color in international relations," in J.H. Franklin (ed.) *Color and Race*, Boston: Houghton Mifflin.

Gellner, E. (1982) "Relativism and universals," in M. Hollis and S. Lukes (eds) *Rationality and Relativism*, Oxford: Blackwell.

George, J. (1989) "International relations theory and the search for thinking space: another view of the Third Debate," *International Studies Quarterly* 33: 269–79.

Gerard, C.G. (1988) "Interview with Professor Semi Bi-Zan," 21 January (unpublished).

Ghosh, J., Sen, A. and Chandrasekhar, C.P. (1998) "East Asian dilemma: is there a way out?" *Economic and Political Weekly* 24: 143–6.

Gibney, F. (1997) "Stumbling giants," *Time* 150, 22: 74–5.

——(1998) "Ending the culture of deceit," *Time* 151, 3: 54.

Gill, S. (ed.) (1993) *Gramsci, Historical Materialism and International Relations*, Cambridge and New York: Cambridge University Press.

——(1995a) "Globalisation, market civilisation and disciplinary neoliberalism," *Millennium* 24, 3: 399–424.

——(1995b) "The global panopticon? The neoliberal state, economic life, and democratic surveillance," *Alternatives* 20, 1: 1–49.

——(1997) "Globalization, democratization, and difference," in J.H. Mittelman (ed.) *Globalization: Critical Reflections*, Boulder, CO: Lynne Rienner.

Gilpin, R. (1975) *US Power and the Multinational Corporation: The Political Economy of Foreign Direct Investment*, New York: Basic Books.

——(1981) *War and Change in World Politics*, New York: Cambridge University Press.

Gilroy, P. (1993) *The Black Atlantic: Modernity and Double Consciousness*, Cambridge, MA: Harvard University Press.

Glasgow, R.A. (1970) *Guyana: Race and Politics among Africans and East Indians*, The Hague: Martinus Nijhoff.

Goad, P. (2000) "Asian Monetary Fund reborn," *Far Eastern Economic Review*. 20.

Goldstein, M.C. (with the help of Gelek Rimpoche) (1989) *A History of Modern Tibet, 1913–1951: The Demise of the Lamaist State*, Berkeley: University of California Press.

——(1997) *The Snow Lion and the Dragon: China, Tibet, and the Dalai Lama*, Berkeley: University of California Press.

Goldstein, M.C. and Kapstein, M.T. (eds) (1998) *Buddhism in Contemporary Tibet*, Berkeley: University of California Press.

Goldstein, M.C., Siebenschuh, W. and Tsering, T. (1997) *The Struggle for Modern Tibet: The Autobiography of Tashi Tsering*, New York and London: M.E. Sharpe.

Gore, C. (2000) "The rise and fall of the Washington Consensus as a paradigm for developing countries," *World Development* 28, 5: 789–804.

Gould, S.J. (1981) *The Mismeasure of Man*, New York: Norton.

Grant, R. and Newland, K. (eds) (1991) *Gender and International Relations*, Bloomington: Indiana University Press.

Greely, A.M. (1972) *Unsecular Man: The Persistence of Religion*, New York: Schoken Books.

Grewal, I. (1994) "Autobiographic subjects and diasporic locations: meatless days and borderlands," in I. Grewal and C. Kaplan (eds) *Scattered Hegemonies*, Minneapolis: University of Minnesota Press.

——(1998) "On the new global feminism and the family of nations: dilemmas of transnational feminist practice," in E. Shohat (ed.) *Talking Visions: Multicultural Feminism in a Transnational Age*, New York: New Museum of Contemporary Art.

——(1999) "'Women's rights as human rights': feminist practices, global feminism, and human rights regimes in transnationality," *Citizenship Studies* 3, 4 (1 November): 337–54.

Grewal, I. and Kaplan, C. (eds) (1994) *Scattered Hegemonies. Postmodernity and Transnational Feminist Practices*, Minneapolis: University of Minnesota Press.

Grovogui, S. (1996) *Sovereigns, Quasi-Sovereigns, and Africans: Race and Self-Determination in International Law*, Minneapolis: University of Minnesota Press.

Grunfeld, T.A. (1987) *The Making of Modern Tibet*, London: Zed Books.

Guha, R. (1982) "On some aspects of the historiography of colonial India," in R. Guha (ed.) *Subaltern Studies*, vol. 1, New Delhi: Oxford University Press.

Gupta, A. and Ferguson, J. (1992) "Beyond 'culture': space, identity, and the politics of difference," *Cultural Anthropology* 7, 1: 6–79.

Guyon, R. (1992) "Violent repression in Burma: human rights and the global response," *Pacific Basin Law Journal* 10: 409–59.

Guyot, J. (1998) "Burma in 1997: from empire to ASEAN," *Asian Survey* 38, 2: 190.

Hadden, J.K. and Shupe, A. (eds) (1989) *Secularization and Fundamentalism Reconsidered*, New York: Paragon House.

Haggard, S. (1999) "Governance and growth: lessons from the Asian economic crisis," *Asia–Pacific Economic Literature* 13, 2: 30–42.

Hall, S. (1977) "Pluralism, race and class in Caribbean society," in UNESCO (ed.) *Race and Class in Post-Colonial Society: A Study of Ethnic Group Relations in the English-Speaking Caribbean, Bolivia, Chile, and Mexico*, Paris: UNESCO.

——(1986) "Gramsci's relevance for the study of race and ethnicity," *Journal of Communication Inquiry* 21: 5–27.

——(1992) "The West and the Rest: discourse and power," in S. Hall and B. Gieben (eds) *Formations of Modernity*, Cambridge: Polity Press.

——(1996) "When was 'the post-colonial'? Thinking at the limit," in I. Chambers and L. Curti, *The Post-Colonial Question: Common Skies, Divided Horizons*, London and New York: Routledge.

——(ed.) (1997) *Representation: Cultural Representations and Signifying Practices*, London: Sage.

Hallencreutz, C.F. and Westerlund, D. (1996) "Introduction: anti-secularist policies of religion," in D. Westerlund (ed.) *Questioning the Secular State*, New York: St Martin's Press.

Hamamoto, D.Y. and Torres, R.D. (eds) (1997) *New American Destinies: A Reader in Contemporary Asian and Latino Immigration*, New York: Routledge.

Han, J. and Ling, L.H.M. (1998) "Authoritarianism in the hypermasculinized state: hybridity, patriarchy, and capitalism in Korea," *International Studies Quarterly* 42, 1: 53–78.

Hannerz, U. (1990) "Cosmopolitans and locals in world culture," *Theory, Culture & Society* 7, 2–3: 237–51.

Hannum, H. (1990) *Autonomy, Sovereignty, and Self-Determination: The Accommodation of Conflicting Rights*, revised edn, Philadelphia: University of Pennsylvania Press.

Harkin, T. (1996) "Put an end to the exploitation of child labor," *USA Today Magazine* 124, 2608: 73–5.

Harris, C. (1999) *In the Image of Tibet: Tibetan Painting after 1959*, London: Reaktion Books.

Harrod, H.L. (1995) *Becoming and Remaining a People: Native American Religions on the Northern Plains*, Tucson: University of Arizona Press.

Harvey, P.J. (1995) "Iqbal's death," *The Christian Century* 112, 18: 557(2). Online. Available http://web2.searchbank.com/infotrac/session/854/687/2018324wl/41lxrn1&bkm (14 July 1998).

Hatzikosta, A. (1998) "Foreign workers and employment in Cyprus," paper presented at the 5th Mediterranean Conference, Hilton, Nicosia, Cyprus.

Havnevik, H. (1989) *Tibetan Buddhist Nuns: History, Cultural Norms and Social Reality*, Oslo: Norwegian University Press.

Heidegger, M. (1988) *Being and Time*, Oxford: Blackwell.

Heng, G. and Devan, J. (1992) "State fatherhood: the politics of nationalism, sexuality, and race in Singapore," in A. Parker, M. Russo, D. Sommer and P. Yaeger (eds) *Nationalisms and Sexualities*, New York: Routledge.

Herman, E.S. and Chomsky, N. (1988) *Manufacturing Consent: The Political Economy of Mass Media*, New York: Pantheon Books.

Hexter, J.H. (1979) *On Historians: Reappraisals of Some of the Masters of Modern History*, Cambridge: Harvard University Press.

Higgott, R. (1998) "The Asian economic crisis: a study in the politics of resentment," *New Political Economy* 3, 3: 333–56.

Ho, K.L. (1994) "Malaysia: the emergence of a new generation of UMNO leadership," *Southeast Asian Affairs*: 179–93.

Hobbes, T. (1968) *Leviathan*, New York: Penguin Books.

Hong, D. (2000) "Industrial relations management gains increasing importance," *Korea Herald*, 6 September. Online. Available http://www.koreaherald.co.kr (6 September 2000).

Hoodfar, H. (1997) *Between Marriage and the Market: Intimate Politics and Survival in Cairo*, Berkeley: University of California Press.

hooks, b. (1995) *Killing Rage: Ending Racism*, New York: H. Holt.

Hooper, C. (2000) "Masculinities in transition: the case of globalization," in M. Marchand and A. Sisson Runyan (eds) *Gender and Global Restructuring*, London: Routledge.

Holm, T. (1997) "The militarization of Native America: historical process and cultural perception," *Social Science Journal* 34, 4: 461–74.

Hopkins, A.G. (1997) *The Future of the Imperial Past*, Cambridge: Cambridge University Press.

Horsman, R. (1981) *Race and Manifest Destiny: The Origins of American Racial Anglo-Saxonism*, Cambridge: Harvard University Press.

Houphouët-Boigny, F. (1952) "Réponse à d'Arboussier," *Afrique Noire* 27: 50–2.

House Committee on Foreign Affairs (1993) (Joint Hearing before Subcommittees on Human Rights and International Organizations), *Human Rights and Democratization in Burma and Markup of H. Res. 262*, Washington, DC: US Government Printing Office.

House Committee on International Relations (1996) *Recent Developments in Burma: Hearing Before the Subcommittee on Asia and the Pacific, Committee on International Relations, House of Representatives*, Washington, DC: US Government Printing Office.

Hughes, D.M. (2000) "The 'Natasha' trade – the transnational shadow market of trafficking in women," *Journal of International Affairs* 53, 2: 625–51, New York: Columbia University. Online. Available http://www.uri.edu/artsci/wms/hughes /natasha.htm (spring 2000).

Hulme, P. and Jordanova, L. (1990) "Introduction," in P. Hulme and L. Jordanova (eds) *The Enlightenment and its Shadows*, London: Routledge.

Human Rights Watch (1998a) "The damaging debate on rapes of ethnic Chinese women," *Human Rights Watch* 10, 5: 5.

——(1998b) *Human Rights Watch World Report 1998*, New York: Human Rights Watch.

——(1999) "Burma: Human Rights Watch Development," *Human Rights Watch World Report 1999*. Online. Available http://www.org/worldreport99/asia

Human Rights Watch/Asia (1995) *Burma: Entrenchment or Reform? Human Rights Developments and the Need for Continued Pressure* 7, 10: 1–39.

Hunt, M. (1987) *Ideology and US Foreign Policy*, New Haven: Yale University Press.

Huntington, S. (1993) "Discussion," *Foreign Affairs* 72, 3: 186–94.

——(1996) *The Clash of Civilizations and the Remaking of World Order*, New York: Simon and Schuster.

Husarska, A. (1999) "Burma dispatch: lady in waiting," *New Republic* 220, 15: 16.

Husbands, C. (1994) "The political context of Muslim communities' participation in British society," in B. Lewis and D. Schnapper (eds) *Muslims in Europe*, London: Pinter.

ICFTU (1997) "Women workers the worst victims of global restructuring." Online. Available http://www.hartford-hwp.com/archives/26/136.html (13 June).

Ignatiev, N. (1995) *How the Irish Became White*, New York: Routledge.

Illiah, K. (1996) *Why I Am Not a Hindu. A Sudra Critique of Hindutva Philosophy, Culture and Political Economy*, Calcutta: Samya.

Inden, R. (1990) *Imagining India*, Oxford: Blackwell.

International Labour Organization (1996) *Child Labor: Targeting the Intolerable (Press Clippings)*, Geneva: International Labour Office.

——(1998) *Report of the High-Level Meeting on Social Responses to the Financial Crisis in East and South-East Asian Countries* (22–4 April, Bangkok), Geneva: International Labour Office.

——(2000–2) *Statistical Information and Monitoring Programme on Child Labour (SIMPOC): Overview and Strategic Plan 2000–2002*. Online. Available http://www.ilo.org/public/english/standards/ipec/publ/simpocoo/page2.htm#2 (May 2001).

Issacs, H. (1969) "Color in world affairs," *Foreign Affairs* 47, 2: 235–51.

Jabri, V. and O'Gorman, E. (eds) (1999) *Women, Culture, and International Relations*, London: Lynne Rienner.

Jacobson, M.F. (1998) *Whiteness of a Different Color: European Immigrants and the Alchemy of Race*, Cambridge: Harvard University Press.

Jayasankaran, S. (1996) "Seeing red: lobby groups protest over Burmese visit," *Far Eastern Economic Review* 159, 35: 18.

Jenkins, T. (1994) "Fieldwork and the perception of everyday life," *MAN* 29, 2: 433–55.

Jingsheng, W. (1998) "A letter to Deng Xiaoping," in C. Chang-Ching and J.D. Seymour (eds) *Tibet through Dissident Chinese Eyes: Essays on Self-Determination*, New York: M.E. Sharpe.

Johnson, C. (1998) "Cold war economics melt Asia," *The Nation* 266, 6: 16–19.

Joly, D. (1995) *Britannia's Crescent: Making Place for Muslims in British Society*, Aldershot: Avebury.

JoongAng Ilbo (1999) "Korea to propose 'Far Eastern Economic Community,'" *JoongAng Ilbo*, 11 February.

Juergensmeyer, M. (1996) *The New Cold War? Religious Nationalism Confronts the Secular State*, Berkeley: University of California Press.

Jumilla, L.T. (1993) "The 'Brunei beauties' scandal," *Sun–Star Daily*, 26 August, Cebu City, Philippines.

Juyal, B.N. (1993) *Child Labour in the Carpet Industry in Mirzapur–Bhadohi*, New Delhi: International Labour Organization.

Kabeer, N. (1996) *Reversed Realities: Gender Hierarchies in Development Thought*, New Delhi: Kali for Women.

Karabell, Z. (1996) "Fundamental misconceptions: Islamic foreign policy," *Foreign Policy* 105: 76–90.

Karen Human Rights Group Report (1998) *Wholesale Destruction: The SLORC/SPDC Campaign to Obliterate All Hill Villages in Papun and Eastern Nyaunglebin Districts*, Chiangmai, Thailand: Nopburee Press.

Kasee, C.R. (1995) "Identity, recovery, and religious imperialism: Native American women and the New Age," *Women & Therapy* 16, 2–3: 83–93.

Kaul, N. (2000) "The anxious identities we inhabit: postisms and economic understandings," paper presented at the International Association for Feminist Economics 2000 Conference, 15–17 August, Istanbul.

Kebebew, A. (1998) "Statistics on working children and hazardous child labor in brief," International Labour Organization. Online. Available http://www.ilo.org-/public/english /standards/ipec/publ/clrep96.htm (April 2001).

Keck, M.E. and Sikkink, K. (1998) *Activists Beyond Borders: Advocacy Networks in International Politics*, Ithaca, NY: Cornell University Press.

Keegan, John (1996) "Warfare on the plains," *The Yale Review* 84, 1: 1–48.

Keeley, L.H. (1996) *War Before Civilization*, New York: Oxford University Press.

Kempadoo, K. (1995) "Regulating prostitution in the Dutch Caribbean," paper presented at the 20th Annual Conference of the Caribbean Studies Association, Curaçao, Netherlands Antilles, May 1995.

——(ed.) (1999) *Sun, Sex, and Gold: Tourism and Sex Work in the Caribbean*, New York: Roman and Littlefield.

Kempadoo, K. and Doezema, J. (1998) *Global Sex Workers: Rights, Resistance, and Redefinition*, New York: Routledge.

Kent, G. (1995) *Children in the International Political Economy*, New York: St Martin's Press.

Keohane, R.O. (1984) *After Hegemony: Cooperation and Discord in the World Political Economy*, Princeton, NJ: Princeton University Press.

——(1993) "Theory of world politics: structural realism and beyond," in P. Viotti and M.V. Kauppi, *International Relations Theory: Realism, Pluralism, Globalism*, New York: Macmillan.

Keohane, R.O. and Nye, J.S. (eds) (1989) *Power and Interdependence: World Politics in Transition*, 2nd edn, Reading, MA: Addison-Wesley.

Kepel, G. (1997) *Allah in the West: Islamic Movements in America and Europe*, trans. by Susan Milner, Stanford: Stanford University Press.

Kesteloot, L. (1991) *Black Writers in French*, trans. by E. Conroy Kennedy, Washington, DC: Howard University Press.

Kikhang, Y. (1997) "Women face cultural genocide on the roof of the world," in R. Lentin (ed.) *Gender and Catastrophe*, London: Zed Books.

Kim, M. (2000) "Labor–management disputes rise along with economic recovery," *Korea Herald*, 8 August. Online. Available http:www.koreaherald.co.kr (8 August 2000).

King, T. (1990) "Godzilla vs. post-colonial," *World Literature Written in English* 30, 2: 10–16.

Klein, B. (1994) *Strategic Studies and World Order*, Cambridge: Cambridge University Press.

Klieger, P.C. (1994) *Tibetan Nationalism: The Role of Patronage in the Accomplishment of a National Identity*, Meerut: Archana.

Knaus, J.K. (1999) *Orphans of the Cold War: America and the Tibetan Struggle for Survival*, New York: Public Affairs.

Kolas, A. (1996) "Tibetan nationalism: the politics of religion," *Journal of Peace Research* 33, 1: 51–66.

——(1998) "Chinese media discourses on Tibet: the language of inequality," *Tibet Journal* XXIII, 3: 69–77.

Korea Herald (2000) "More than 5,000 bank employees likely to lose jobs in restructuring this year," *Korea Herald*, 29 September.

Korom, F.J. (ed.) (1997a) *Tibetan Culture in Diaspora: Papers Presented at a Panel of the 7th Seminar of the International Association for Tibetan Studies, Graz 1995*, Wien: Osterreichischen Akademie Der Wissenschaften.

——(ed.) (1997b) *Constructing Tibetan Culture: Contemporary Perspectives*, Quebec: Heritage Press.

Krasner, S.D. (1978) *Defending the National Interest: Raw Materials Investments and US Foreign Policy*, Princeton, NJ: Princeton University Press.

Krishna, S. (1993) "The importance of being ironic: a postcolonial view on critical international relations theory," *Alternatives* 18, 3: 385–417.

——(1994) "Inscribing the nation: Nehru and the politics of identity in India," in S.J. Rosow, N. Inayatullah and M. Rupert (eds) *The Global Economy as Political Space*, Boulder, CO: Lynne Rienner.

——(1999) *Postcolonial Insecurities: India, Sri Lanka, and the Question of Nationhood*, Minneapolis: University of Minnesota Press.

Kristof, N.D. (1998) "With Asia's economies shrinking, women are being squeezed out," *New York Times* 147, 51185 (11 June): A12.

Kuiper, E. and Sap, J. (1995) *Out of the Margin: Feminist Perspectives on Economics*, London and New York: Routledge.

Lacayo, R. (1997) "IMF to the rescue," *Time*, 8 December: 36.

Laclau, E. and Mouffe, C. (1985) *Hegemony and Socialist Strategy: Towards a Radical Democratic Politics*, London: Verso.

Lakatos, I. (1970) "Falsification and the methodology of scientific research programmes," in I. Lakatos and A. Musgrave (eds) *Criticism and the Growth of Knowledge*, Cambridge: Cambridge University Press.

Lauren, P.G. (1996) *Power and Prejudice: The Politics and Diplomacy of Racial Discrimination*, Boulder, CO: Westview Press.

——(1998) *The Evolution of International Human Rights: Visions Seen*, Philadelphia: University of Pennsylvania Press.

Laurence, K.O. (1994) *A Question of Labor: Indentured Immigration into Trinidad and British Guiana, 1875–1917*, New York: St Martins Press.

Layla, S. (1998) "Interview with Tom Harkin," *The Minaret* 20, 5 (1 May): 31–3.

Lazarus, N. (1994) "National consciousness and intellectualism," in F. Barker, P. Hulme and M. Iversen (eds) *Colonial Discourse/Postcolonial Theory*, Manchester: University of Manchester Press.

——(1999) *Nationalism and Cultural Practice in the Postcolonial World*, Cambridge, England and New York: Cambridge University Press.

Lazreg, M. (1979) "Human rights, state and ideology: an historical perspective," in A. Pollis and J. Schwab (eds) *Human Rights: Cultural and Ideological Perspectives*, New York: Praeger.

Lee, C.S. (1999) "Volvo overcomes suspicions fuelled by the IMF bailout and helps South Koreans learn to love takeovers," *Far Eastern Economic Review* 162, 17: 58–60.

Leheny, D. (1995) "A political economy of Asian sex tourism," *Annals of Tourism Research* 22, 2: 367–84.

Lewis, P. (1994) *Islamic Britain: Religion, Politics and Identity among British Muslims*, London: I.B. Tauris.

Lim, L.L. (1992) "International labour movements: a perspective on economic exchanges and flows," in M.M. Kritz, L.L. Lim and H. Zlotnik (eds) *International Migration Systems: A Global Approach*, Oxford: Clarendon Press.

Ling, L.H.M. (1996) "Democratization under internationalization: media reconstructions of gender identity in Shanghai," *Democratization* 3, 2: 140–57.

——(1999) "Sex machine: global hypermasculinity and images of the Asian woman in modernity," *positions: east asia cultures critique* 72, 2: 1–30.

——(2001a) *Postcolonial International Relations: Conquest and Desire Between Asia and the West*, London: Palgrave.

——(2001b) "Hypermasculinity," in S. Rai (ed.) *Routledge Encyclopedia of International Women's Studies*, London: Routledge.

Ling, L.H.M. and Shih, C. (1998) "Confucianism with a liberal face: the meaning of democratic politics in contemporary Taiwan," *Review of Politics* 60, 1: 55–82.

Lipschutz, R.D. and Mayer, J. (1996) *Global Civil Society and Global Environmental Governance: The Politics of Nature from Place to Planet*, Albany: SUNY Press.

Lipsitz, G. (1998) *The Possessive Investment in Whiteness: How White People Profit from Identity Politics*, Philadelphia: Temple University Press.

Lizot, J. (1994) "On warfare: an answer to N.A. Chagnon," *American Ethnologist* 21, 4: 845–62.

Lonowski, D. (1994) "A return to tradition: proportional representation in tribal government," *American Indian Culture and Research Journal* 18, 1: 147–63.

Loomba, A. (1998) *Colonialism/Postcolonialism*, London and New York: Routledge.

Lopez, D.S., Jr. (1998) *Prisoners of Shangri-la: Tibetan Buddhism and the West*, Chicago: University of Chicago Press.

Lopez, J. (2000a) "Sogo bankruptcy may signal new era in Japanese finances," *World Socialist Web Site*. Online. Available http://www.wsws.org/articles/2000/jul2000/sogo-j27.shtml (27 July 2000).

——(2000b) "McKinsey report on Japan demands 'open door' for international capital," *World Socialist Web Site*. Online. Available http://www.wsws.org/articles/2000/sept2000/jap-s13.shtml (13 September 2000).

——(2000c) "Economic instability dominates South East Asia," *World Socialist Web Site*. Online. Available http://www.wsws.org/articles/2000/sept2000/asia-s29.shtml (29 September 2000).

McClintock, A. (1992) "The angel of progress: pitfalls of the term 'post-colonialism,' " *Social Text* 31/2: 84–98.

——(1995) *Imperial Leather: Race, Gender, and Sexuality in the Colonial Contest*, New York: Routledge.

McDonald, H. (1992) "Boys of bondage: child labour, though banned, is rampant," *Far Eastern Economic Review* (July): 18–19.

MacDonald, M. (1995) "The empirical challenges of feminist economics: the example of economic restructuring," in E. Kuiper and J. Sap (eds) *Out of the Margin: Feminist Perspectives on Economics*, London and New York: Routledge.

McGinnis, A. (1990) *Counting Coup and Cutting Horses: Intertribal Warfare on the Northern Plains, 1738–1889*, Evergreen, CO: Cordillera Press.

McKay, A. (1997) *Tibet and the British Raj: The Frontier Cadre 1907–1947*, Richmond, Surrey, UK: Curzon Press.

McLagan, M. (1997) "Mystical visions in Manhattan: deploying culture in the year of Tibet," in F.J. Korom (ed.) *Tibetan Culture in Diaspora: Papers Presented at a Panel of the 7th Seminar of the International Association for Tibetan Studies, Graz 1995*, Wien: Osterreichischen Akademie Der Wissenschaften.

McNally, D. (1998) "Globalization on trial: crisis and class struggle in East Asia," *Monthly Review* 50, 4: 1–14.

Madan, T.N. (1993) "Whither Indian secularism," *Modern Asian Studies* 27, 3: 667–97.

Mahathir, M. (1999) "Malaysia: bouncing back from the brink," speech delivered to the World Economic Forum Working Lunch, 29 January, Davos, Switzerland.

Makley, C.E. (1997) "The meaning of liberation: representations of Tibetan women," *Tibet Journal* 22, 2: 4–29.

——(1999) "Embodying the sacred: gender and monastic revitalization in China's Tibet," unpublished PhD dissertation, University of Michigan.

Malik, K. (1996) *The Meaning of Race: Race, History and Culture in Western Society*, New York: New York University Press.

Malkki, L. (1994) "Citizens of humanity: internationalism and the imagined community of nations," *Diaspora* 3, 1: 41–68.

Mani, L. (1989) "Contentious traditions: the debate on Sati in colonial India," in K. Sangari and S. Vaid (eds) *Recasting Women*, New Delhi: Kali for Women.

Manzo, K. (1991) "Modernist discourse and the crisis of development theory," *Studies in Comparative International Development*, 26, 2–3: 3–36.

——(1996) *Creating Boundaries: The Politics of Race and Nation*, Boulder, CO: Lynne Rienner.

March, J.G. and Olsen, J.P. (1984) "The new institutionalism: organizational factors in political life," *American Political Science Review* 78: 734–49.

Markham, C.R. (1876) *Narratives of the Mission of George Bogle to Tibet and of the Journey of Thomas Manning to Lhasa*, London: Trubner.

Martin, D. (1991) "The secularization issue: prospect and retrospect," *British Journal of Sociology* 42, 3: 465–74.

Marty, E.M. and Appleby, R.S. (eds) (1991) *Fundamentalisms Observed* (vol. 1), Chicago: University of Chicago Press.

——(1993a) *Fundamentalisms and Society: Reclaiming the Sciences, the Family, and Education* (vol. 2). Chicago: University of Chicago Press.

——(1993b) *Fundamentalisms and the State: Remaking Polities, Economies, and Militance* (vol. 3), Chicago: University of Chicago Press.

——(1994) *Accounting for Fundamentalisms: The Dynamic Character of Movements* (vol. 4), Chicago: University of Chicago Press.

——(1995) *Fundamentalisms Comprehended* (vol. 5), Chicago: University of Chicago Press.

——(1997) *Religion, Ethnicity and Self-Identity: Nations in Turmoil*, Hanover, NH: United Press of New England.

Marx, K. (1972) "On imperialism in India," in R.C. Tucker (ed.) *The Marx–Engels Reader*, 2nd edn, New York: Norton.

——(1978) "On imperialism in India," in R.C. Tucker (ed.) *The Marx–Engels Reader*, 3rd edn, New York and London: Norton.

Mayo, K. (1927) *Mother India*, New York: Blue Ribbon Books.

Mehta, P.S. (1994) "Cashing in on child labor," *Multinational Monitor* 15, 4: 24–5.

Memmi, A. (1965) *The Colonizer and the Colonized*, Boston: Beacon Press.

——(1968) *Dominated Man: Notes Toward a Portrait*, London: Orion Press.

Mies, M. (1986) *Patriarchy and Accumulation on a World Scale: Women in the International Division of Labour*, London: Zed Books.

Mies, M., Bennholdt-Thomsen, V. and von Werlhof, C. (1988) *Women: The Last Colony*, London and Atlantic Highlands, NJ : Zed Books.

Mignolo, W.D. (1995) *The Darker Side of the Renaissance*, Ann Arbor: University of Michigan Press.

Miller, J. (1996) *God Has Ninety-Nine Names: Reporting from a Militant Middle East*, New York: Simon and Schuster.

Mills, C.W. (1959) *The Sociological Imagination*, New York: Oxford University Press.

Misra, S.D. (1999) "Indian carpet industry *vis-à-vis* the problem of child labour in India," position paper, Carpet Export Promotion Council, 26 December.

Mitton, R. (1999) "How things look inside the NLD," *Asiaweek* 16 July: 28–9.

Mo, J. and Moon, C. (1999) "Korea after the crash," *Journal of Democracy* 10, 4: 150–64.

Mohamed Jawhar, bin Hasan (1996) "Malaysia in 1995: high growth, big deficit, stable politics," *Asian Survey* 36, 2: 123–9.

Mohanty, C. (1991a) "Cartographies of struggle: third world women and the politics of feminism," in C. Mohanty, A. Russo and L. Torres (eds) *Third World Women and the Politics of Feminism*, Bloomington: Indiana University Press.

——(1991b) "Under Western eyes: feminist scholarship and colonial discourses," in C. Mohanty, A. Russo and L. Torres (eds) *Third World Women and the Politics of Feminism*, Bloomington: Indiana University Press.

——(1997) "Women workers and capitalist scripts: ideologies of domination, common interests, and the politics of solidarity," in J. Alexander and C.T. Mohanty (eds) *Feminist Genealogies, Colonial Legacies, Democratic Futures*, New York: Routledge.

Mohanty, C.T., Russo, A. and Torres. L. (eds.) (1991) *Third World Women and the Politics of Feminism*, Bloomington: Indiana University Press.

Montgomery, L. (2001) "Albanians sell Kosovo women into prostitution," *Miami Herald*, 29 May.

Moon, K.H.S. (1997) *Sex Among Allies: Military Prostitution in US–Korea Relations*, New York: Columbia University Press.

Moore-Gilbert, B. (1997) *Postcolonial Theory: Contexts, Practices, Politics*, London and New York: Verso.

Moran, J. (1997) "Child labor and the crusade of Iqbal Masih," presented to the 105th Congress, 1st Session, 143, 46, Congressional Record H 1692.

Morgenthau, H. (1950) *Politics Among Nations*, New York: Alfred A. Knopf.

Motohashi, T. (1999) "The discourse of cannibalism in early modern travel writing," in Steve Clark (ed.) *Travel Writing and Empire: Postcolonial Theory in Transit*, London: Zed Books.

Mudimbe, V.Y. (1988) *The Invention of Africa: Gnosis, Philosophy, and the Order of Knowledge*, Bloomington: Indiana University Press.

——(ed.) (1992) *The Surreptitious Speech*, Paris: Présence Africaine.

Muftuler-Bac (1993) "Northern Cyprus' security," in E. Solsten (ed.) *Cyprus, a Country Study*, 4th edn, Washington, DC: Federal Research Division, Library of Congress, US Government Printing Office.

Mukherjee, A.P. (1990) "Whose post-colonialism and whose postmodernism?" *World Literature Written in English* 30, 2: 1–9.

Muppidi, H. (1999) "Postcoloniality and the production of international insecurity: the persistent puzzle of US–Indian relations," in J. Weldes, M. Laffey, H. Gusterson and R. Duvall (eds) *Cultures of Insecurity: States, Communities, and the Production of Danger*, Minneapolis: University of Minnesota Press.

Murphy, B. (1998) "Greek police being squeezed by vice crackdown," *Athens Daily News*. Online. Available http://www.onlineathens.com/ (20 November 1998).

Murphy, C.N. and de Ferro, R.C. (1995) "The power of representation in international political economy," *Review of International Political Economy* 2: 63–183.

Muzaffar C. (1999) "From human rights to human dignity," in P. Van Ness (ed.) *Debating Human Rights*, London and New York: Routledge.

Nair, S. (2000) "Human rights, sovereignty, and the East Timor 'question,'" *Global Society* 14, 1: 101–26.

Nam, C.H. (1995) "South Korea's big business clientelism in democratic reform," *Asian Survey* 35, 4: 357–66.

Nandy, A. (1983) *The Intimate Enemy: Loss and Recovery of Self Under Colonialism*, New Delhi: Oxford University Press.

——(1996) "Themes of exile: the uprooted in South Asian politics," *The Times of India*, 19 September.

Narayan, U. (1997) *Dislocating Cultures: Identities, Traditions, and Third World Feminism*, New York: Routledge.

Neilson, B. (2000) "Inside Shangri-la/outside globalisation: remapping orientalist visions of Tibet," *Communal/Plural* 8, 1: 95–112.

Neilson J. (1989) "Islamic communities in Britain," in P. Badham (ed.) *Religion, State and Society in Modern Britain*, New York: E. Mellon.

New York Times (2000) "From the editors: *The Times* and Wen Ho Lee", *New York Times*, 26 September: A2.

Niva, S. (1999) "Contested sovereignties and postcolonial insecurities in the Middle East" in J. Weldes, M. Laffey, H. Gusterson and R. Duvall (eds) *Cultures of Insecurity: States, Communities, and the Production of Danger*, Minneapolis: University of Minnesota Press.

Norbu, D. (1990) "The Europeanization of Sino-Tibetan relations, 1775–1907: the genesis of Chinese 'suzerainty' and Tibetan 'autonomy,'" *Tibet Journal* XV, 4: 28–74.

Obiora, A.L. (1997) "Bridges and barricades: rethinking polemics and intransigence in the campaign against female circumcision," *Case Western Law Review* 47: 275–378.

O'Brien, M. (1987) "Hegemony and superstructure: a feminist critique of neo-marxism," in R. Hamilton and M. Barrett (eds) *The Politics of Diversity: Feminism, Marxism and Nationalism*, London: Verso.

O'Connell, D.J. and Taylor, J.S. (1998) "Fantasy islands: exploring the demand for sex tourism," in K. Kempadoo (ed.) *Sun, Sex, and Gold: Tourism and Sex Work in the Caribbean*, New York: Roman and Littlefield.

Olson, M. (1993) "Dictatorship, democracy, and development," *American Political Science Review* 87, 3: 567–76.

Ong, A. (1987) *Spirits of Resistance and Capitalist Discipline*, New York: SUNY Press.

Onuf, N. (1989) *World of Our Making*, Columbia: University of South Carolina Press.

Overbeek, H. and van der Pijl, K. (1993) "Restructuring capital and restructuring hegemony," in H. Overbeek (ed.) *Restructuring Hegemony in the Global Political Economy*, London: Routledge.

Oxfam International (1998) *Economic Growth with Equity: Lessons from East Asia*, Oxford: Oxfam International.

Oxford English Dictionary (1971) New York: Oxford University Press.

Panitch, L. (1994) "Globalisation and the state," in R. Miliband and L. Panitch *Between Globalism and Nationalism: Socialist Register 1994*, London: Merlin Press.

Pannikar, R. (1992) "Is the notion of human rights a Western concept?" in P. Sack and J. Aleck (eds) *Law and Anthropology*, Aldershot: Dartmouth.

Paolini, A.J. (1999) *Navigating Modernity: Postcolonialism, Identity and International Relations*, London: Lynne Rienner.

Parekh, B. (1990) "The Rushdie affair and the British press," in D. Cohn-Sherbok (ed.) *The Salman Rushdie Controversy in Interreligious Perspective*, New York: Edwin Mellon.

Parry, B. (1994) "Resistance theory/theorising resistance or two cheers for nativism," in F. Barker, P. Hulme and M. Iversen (eds) *Colonial Discourse/Postcolonial Theory*, Manchester: Manchester University Press.

Pasha, M.K. and Samatar, A.I. (1997) "The resurgence of Islam," in J.H. Mittelman (ed.) *Globalization: Critical Reflections*, Boulder, CO: Lynne Rienner.

Pei, M. (1994) "The puzzle of East Asian exceptionalism," *Journal of Democracy* 5, 4: 90–103.

Perea, J.F. (ed.) (1997) *Immigrants Out! The New Nativism and the Anti-Immigrant Impulse in the United States*, New York: New York University Press.

Perry, M.J. (1997) "Are human rights universal? The relativist challenge and related matters," *Human Rights Quarterly* 19, 3: 466–71.

Persaud, R.B. (1997) "Frantz Fanon, race and world order," in S.R. Gill and J.H. Mittelman (eds) *Innovation and Transformation in International Studies*, Cambridge: Cambridge University Press.

——(2001) *Counter-Hegemony and Foreign Policy: The Dialectics of Marginalized and Global Forces in Jamaica*, Albany: SUNY Press.

Peterson, V.S. (ed.) (1992a) *Gendered States: Feminist (Re)visions of International Relations Theory*, Boulder and London: Lynne Rienner.

——(1992b) "Security and sovereign states: what is at stake in taking feminism seriously?" in V.S. Peterson (ed.) *Gendered States: Feminist (Re)Visions of International Relations Theory*, Boulder, CO: Lynne Rienner.

——(1996) "Shifting ground(s): epistemological and territorial remapping in the context of globalization(s)," in E. Kofman and G. Youngs (eds) *Globalization: Theory and Practice*, London: Pinter.

Peterson, V.S. and Runyan, A.S. (1993) *Global Gender Issues: Dilemmas in World Politics*, Boulder, CO: Westview Press.

Pettman, J.J. (1996) *Worlding Women: A Feminist International Politics*, London and New York: Routledge.

Pieterse, J.N. (1997) "Sociology of humanitarian intervention: Bosnia, Rwanda and Somalia compared," *International Political Science Review* 18, 1: 71–93.

Piscatori, J.P. (1986) *Islam in a World of Nation States*, Cambridge: Cambridge University Press.

Porter, M.E. and Takeuchi, H. (1999) "Fixing what really ails Japan," *Foreign Affairs* 78, 3: 66–81.

Powers, W.K. (1975) *Oglala Religion*, Lincoln: University of Nebraska Press.

Prakash, G. (1992) "Postcolonial criticism and Indian historiography," *Social Text* 31/2: 8–19.

——(1994) "Subaltern studies as postcolonial criticism," *American Historical Review* 99, 5: 1475–90.

——(1997) "Postcolonial criticism and Indian historiography," in A. McClintock, A. Mufti and E. Shohat (eds) *Dangerous Liaisons: Gender, Nation and Postcolonial Perspectives*, Boulder, CO: Westview Press.

Prashad, V. (1999) "Calloused consciences: the limited challenge to child labor," *Dollars and Sense* (September). Online. Available http://web5.infotrac.galegroup .com...rn_33_0_A56027400?sw_aep (February 2000).

Pratt, M.L. (1992) *Imperial Eyes: Travel Writing and Transculturation*, London and New York: Routledge.

Preiswerk, A.R. (1970) "Race and color in international relations," in G.W. Keeton and G. Schwarzenberger (eds) *The Year Book of World Affairs*, London: Stevens.

Price, B.B. (1993) " 'Cutting for sign': museums and Western revisionism," *Western Historical Quarterly* 24, 2: 229–34.

Price, C. (1994) "Lakotas and Euroamericans: contrasted concepts of 'chieftainship' and decision-making authority," *Ethnohistory* 41, 3: 447–63.

Purcell, M. (1999) " 'Axe handles or willing minions?' International NGOs in Burma," in Burma Center Netherlands (BCN) and Transnational Institute (TNI) (eds) *Strengthening Civil Society in Burma*, Chiang Mai, Thailand: Silkworm Books.

Quinn, K.M. (1991) "Burma: democracy and human rights: statement before the Subcommittee on Asian and Pacific Affairs of the House Committee on Foreign Affairs," *US Department of State Dispatch* 2: 793–4.

Radelet, S. and Sachs, J. (1997) "Asia's reemergence," *Foreign Affairs* 76, 6: 44–59.

Ranchod-Nilsson, S. and Tetreault, M.A. (eds) (2000) *Women, States and Nationalism: At Home in the Nation?*, London and New York: Routledge.

Rao, V.V.B. (1998) "East Asian economies: the crisis of 1997–98," *Economic and Political Weekly*, 6 June: 1397–416.

Rentlen, A.D. (1988) "Relativism and the search for human rights," *American Anthropologist* 90: 64.

——(1990) *International Human Rights: Universalism versus Relativism*, London: Sage.

Repak, T. (1995) *Waiting on Washington: Central American Workers in the Nation's Capital*, Philadelphia: Temple University Press.

République Française (1949a) *Annales de l'Assemblée de l'Union Française (AAUF) 21*, 11 March.

——(1949b) *Journal Officiel (JO) 85*, 27 July.

République Française, Centre des archives d'Outre-mer (1944) *Affaires Politiques*, Dossier no. 2201/6.

——(1949) *Affaires Politiques*, Dossier no. 1164.

Rice, J. (1991) *Black Elk's Story: Distinguishing its Lakota Purpose*, Albuquerque: University of New Mexico Press.

Risse, T., Ropp, S.C. and Sikkink, K. (1999) *The Power of Human Rights: International Norms and Domestic Change*, Cambridge: Cambridge University Press.

Risse-Kappen, T. (1995) *Bringing Transnational Relations Back In: Non-State Actors, Domestic Structures, and International Institutions*, Cambridge: Cambridge University Press.

Robbins, R.L. (1992) "Self-determination and subordination: the past, present, and future of American Indian governance," in M.A. Jaimes (ed.) *The State of Native America: Genocide, Colonization, and Resistance*, Boston: South End Press.

Roberts, D. (1997) "Who may give birth to citizens? Reproduction, eugenics, and immigration," in J. Perea (ed.) *Immigrants Out! The New Nativism and the Anti-Immigrant Impulse in the United States*, New York: New York University Press.

Robertson, R. (1987a) "Church–state relations and the world system," in T. Robbins and R. Robertson (eds) *Church–State Relations: Tensions and Transitions*, New Brunswick: Transaction.

——(1987b) "General considerations in the study of contemporary church–state relationships," in T. Robbins and R. Robertson (eds) *Church–State Relations: Tensions and Transitions*, New Brunswick: Transaction.

——(1992) *Globalization: Social Theory and Global Culture*, London: Sage.

——(1995) "Glocalization: time–space and homogeneity–heterogeneity," in M. Featherstone, S. Lash and R. Robertson (eds) *Global Modernities*, London: Sage.

Roebuck, P. (1994) "Chanderpaul is king," *Sportstar* 17, 16 (April): 456.

Rojas, A. (1996) "Bay residents feel heat of hate crime," *San Francisco Chronicle*, 6 August: A13.

Roos, P.D., Smith, D.H., Langley, S. and McDonald, J. (1980) "The impact of the American Indian movement on the Pine Ridge Reservation," *Phylon* 41, 1: 89–99.

Rorty, R. (1993) "Human rights, rationality and sentimentality," in S. Shute and S. Hurley (eds) *On Human Rights*, New York: Basic Books.

Rosca, N. (1995) "The Philippines' shameful export," *Nation*, 17 April: 522–7.

Rosenberg, J. (1994) "The international imagination: IR theory and 'classic social analysis,'" *Millenium* 23, 1: 85–108.

Rosenau, J.N. (1993) *Global Voices: Dialogues in International Relations*, Boulder, CO: Westview Press.

Rousseau, G.S. and Porter, R. (eds) (1990) *Exoticism in the Enlightenment*, Manchester and New York: Manchester University Press.

Rubinstein, A.Z. (1994) "Radical Islam may threaten Muslim world, but not West," *Insight on the News* 10, 47: 37–8.

Ruggie, J.G. (1998) *Constructing the World Polity*, London: Routledge.

Rupert, M. (1995) *Producing Hegemony: The Politics of Mass Production and American Global Power*, New York: Cambridge University Press.

SACCS (2000) Press clippings from *The Times of India*, 22 January 1999, made available to the author during interview with Kailash Satyarthi (summer 2000).

Safranski, R. (1998) *Martin Heidegger: Between Good and Evil*, trans. by E. Osers, Cambridge: Harvard University Press.

Sahliyeh, E. (1990) "Religious resurgence and political modernization," in E. Sahliyeh (ed.) *Religious Resurgence and Politics in the Contemporary World*, Albany: SUNY Press.

Said, E. (1978) *Orientalism*, New York: Pantheon Books.

——(1979) *Orientalism*, New York: Vintage Books.

——(1993) *Culture and Imperialism*, New York: Vintage Books.

——(1994) *Culture and Imperialism*, New York: Knopf.

——(1997) *Covering Islam: How the Media and the Experts Determine How We See the Rest of the World*, New York: Vintage Books.

Saito, K. (1999) Speech to the Foreign Correspondents' Club in Washington, DC, 16 March.

Sakamoto, Y. (1991) "Introduction: the global context of democratization," *Alternatives* 16, 2: 119–27.

San Diego Union Tribune (1997) "US charges 7 in attack on migrant camp," 20 December: A1.

Sanchez, R. (1999) "Gunman wounds 5 at summer camp," *Washington Post*, 11 August: A1.

Sandoval, C. (1991) "US Third World feminism: the theory and method of oppositional consciousness in the postmodern world," *Genders* 10: 1–24.

Sanger, D.E. (2000) "Economic engine for foreign policy," *New York Times*, 150, 51616 (28 December): A1.

Saraf, D.N. (1986) "Indian carpets," in AICMA *Silver Jubilee Special*, Bhadohi, India: All India Carpet Manufacturers' Association.

Satyarthi, K. (1992) "Welcome address," South Asian Consultation on Child Labour in the Carpet Industry, 11–13 July, New Delhi, India.

——(1994) "The tragedy of child labor," *Multinational Monitor* 15, 10: 24.

Scheer, R. (2000) "No defense: how the *New York Times* convicted Wen Ho Lee," *Nation*, 23 October: 11–20.

Schell, O. (2000) *Virtual Tibet: Searching for Shangri-la from the Himalayas to Hollywood*, New York: Metropolitan Books.

Schoenberger, K. (2000) *Levi's Children: Coming to Terms with Human Rights in the Global Marketplace*, New York: Atlantic Monthly Press.

Scholte, J.A. (2000) *Globalization: A Critical Introduction*, London: Macmillan.

Schwartz, R.D. (1996) *Circle of Protest: Political Ritual in the Tibetan Uprising*, Delhi: Motilal Banarsidass.

Scott, D. (1999) *Refashioning Futures: Criticism After Postcoloniality*, Princeton: Princeton University Press.

Scott, J. (1995) "Sexual and national boundaries in tourism," *Annals of Tourism Research* 22: 385–403.

Scott, J.B. (ed.) (1918) *President Wilson's Foreign Policy: Messages, Addresses, Papers*, New York: Oxford University Press.

Scott, J.C. (1985) *Weapons of the Weak: Everyday Forms of Peasant Resistance*, New Haven: Yale University Press.

Secoy, F.R. (1966) *Changing Military Patterns on the Great Plains: 17th Century through Early 19th Century*, Seattle: University of Washington Press.

Sen, A. (1997) "The subject of human rights has ended up being a veritable battleground," *Chronicle of Higher Education* 43, 40 (13 June): B11.

"Senate passes Foreign Aid Bill after dispute over Myanmar" (1996) *Congressional Quarterly* 27: 2131.

Shakya, T. (1991) "The myth of Shangri-la," *Lungta* April: 21–8.

——(1999) *The Dragon in the Land of Snows: A History of Modern Tibet Since 1947*, London: Pimlico.

Shameen, A. (2000) "Business: the Daewoo blues," *AsiaWeek.com*. Online. Available http://www.asiaweek.com/asiaweek/business/2000/10/17/ (17 October 2000).

Shapiro, M.J. (1988) *The Politics of Representation: Writing Practices in Biography, Photography, and Policy Analysis*, Madison: University of Wisconsin Press.

——(1989) "Textualizing global politics," in J. Der Derian and M.J. Shapiro (eds) *International/Intertextual Relations: Postmodern Readings of World Politics*, Lexington, MA: Lexington Books.

Shepherd, G.W., Jr. and LeMelle, T.J. (eds) (1970) *Race among Nations: A Conceptual Approach*, Lexington, MA: Heath Lexington Books.

Sheridan, M. and Phung, S. (1999) "Exiles train for civil war in Burma," *Sunday Times*, 31 October.

Shohat, E. (1992) "Notes on the post-colonial," *Social Text* 31/2: 99–113.

Shome, R. (1998) "Caught in the term 'postcolonial': why the 'postcolonial' still matters," *Critical Studies in Mass Communication* 15, 2: 203.

Shrage, L. (1994) *Moral Dilemmas of Feminism*, London: Routledge.

Sikkink, K. (1991) *Ideas and Institutions: Developmentalism in Brazil and Argentina*, Ithaca, NY: Cornell University Press.

——(1993) "Human rights, principled issue-networks, and sovereignty in Latin America," *International Organization* 47, 3: 411–41.

Silverstein, J. (1977) *Burma: Military Rule and the Politics of Stagnation*, Ithaca, NY: Cornell University Press.

——(1980) *Burmese Politics: The Dilemma of National Unity*, New Jersey: Rutgers University Press.

——(1996) "The idea of freedom in Burma and the political thought of Daw Aung San Suu Kyi," *Pacific Affairs* 69, 2: 211–29. Accessed online from Infotrac http://Web5.infotrac.galegroup.com (24 May 2001).

Simmons, H.G. (1996) *The French National Front: The Extremist Challenge to Democracy*, Boulder, CO: Westview Press.

Singh, A. and Weisse, B.A. (1999) "The Asian model: a crisis foretold?" *International Social Science Journal* 51, 2: 203–16.

Smith, D.E. (1970) *Religion and Political Development*, Boston: Little, Brown.

——(1990) "The limits of religious resurgence," in E. Sahliyeh (ed.) *Religious Resurgence and Politics in the Contemporary World*, Albany: SUNY Press.

Smithsonian Institution (1991) "Showdown at 'The West as America' exhibition," *American Art* 5, 3: 2–11.

Smolin, D. (1999) "Conflict and ideology in the International Campaign Against Child Labor," *Hofstra Labor and Employment Law Journal* 383 (spring): 1–63.

Sowell, T. (1994) *Race and Culture: A World View*, New York: Basic Books.

Spivak, G. (1985) "Three women's texts and a critique of imperialism," *Critical Inquiry* 12, 1: 243.

——(1986) "Three women's texts and a critique of imperialism," in H.L. Gates, Jr. (ed.) *"Race," Writing and Difference*, Chicago: University of Chicago Press.

——(1987) *In Other Worlds: Essays in Cultural Politics*, New York and London: Routledge.

——(1988) "Can the subaltern speak?," in C. Nelson and L. Grossberg (eds) *Marxism and Interpretation of Culture*, Urbana: University of Illinois Press.

Spurr, D. (1993) *Rhetoric of Empire: Colonial Discourse in Journalism, Travel Writing, and Imperial Administration*, London: Duke University Press.

Standing Bear, L. (1978) *Land of the Spotted Eagle*, Lincoln: University of Nebraska Press.

Stiglitz, J. (2000) "The insider: what I learned at the World Economic Crisis," *New Republic*, 6 April: 56–60.

Stocking, G.W., Jr. (1995) "Delimiting anthropology: historical reflections on the boundaries of a boundless discipline," *Social Research* 62, 4: 933–66.

Strang, D. (1996) "Contested sovereignty: the social construction of colonial imperialism," in T.J. Biersteker and C. Weber (eds) *State Sovereignty As Social Construct*, Cambridge: Cambridge University Press.

Straubhaar, T. (1992) "Migration pressure," *International Migration* 31: 5–31.

Stumberg, R. and Waren, W. (1999) "The Boston Tea Party revisited: Massachusetts," *State Legislature* 25, 5: 26–8.

Sunday Business Group (2000) "Motor industry shake-up: Ford gets to grips with Daewoo." Online. Available http://web.lexis-nexis.com (2 July 2000).

Sundstrom, L. (1997) "Smallpox used them up: references to epidemic disease in Northern Plains winter counts, 1714–1920," *Ethnohistory* 44, 2: 303–43.

Suu Kyi, Aung San (1991) *Freedom From Fear and Other Writings*, London: Penguin Books.

——(1997) *Letters from Burma*, New York: Penguin Books.

Suyin, H. (1977) *Lhasa the Open City: A Journey to Tibet*, New York: G.P. Putnam's.

Sylvester, C. (1994) *Feminist Theory and International Relations in a Postmodern Era*, Cambridge: Cambridge University Press.

Symonds, P. (1999) "No end to the social crisis in Asia in sight," *World Socialist Web Site*. Online. Available http://www.wsws.org/articles/1999/jun1999/asia-s24.shtml (24 June 1999).

Takaki, R. (1993) *A Different Mirror: A History of Multicultural America*, Boston: Little, Brown.

Tanko, K. and Lintner, B. (2001) "Wish you were here?" *Far Eastern Economic Review*, 17 May: 64–5.

Tatalovich, R. (1997) "Official English as nativist backlash," in J. Perea (ed.) *Immigrants Out! The New Nativism and the Anti-Immigrant Impulse in the United States*, New York: New York University Press.

Taylor, R.H. (1987) *The State in Burma*, Honolulu: University of Hawaii Press.

Tharoor, S. (1999–2000) "Are human rights universal?" *World Policy*, xvi, 4, New York: World Policy Institute. Online. Available http://www.worldpolicy.org (May 2001).

Thiele, L.P. (1993) "Making democracy safe for the world: social movements and global politics," *Alternatives* 18: 273–305.

Thomadakis, S.B. (1995) "The economy," in G.E. Curtis (ed.) *Greece, a Country Study*, 4th edn, Washington, DC: Federal Research Division, Library of Congress, US Government Printing Office.

Tibet Online (2001) *About Tibet Online*. Online. Available http://www.tibet.org (24 March 2001).

Tibetan Women's Association (2001) Online. Available http://www.tibetanwomen.org (24 March 2001).

Tickner, J.A. (1988) "Hans Morgenthau's principles of political realism: a feminist reformulation," *Millennium* 17, 3: 429–40.

——(1992) *Gender in International Relations: Feminist Perspectives on Achieving Global Security*, New York: Columbia University Press.

Tierney, P. (2000) *Darkness in El Dorado: How Scientists and Journalists Devastated the Amazon*, New York: Norton.

Tinker, H. (1977) *Race, Conflict and the International Order: From Empire to the United Nations*, London: Macmillan.

Tobin, J. and Ranis, G. (1998) "Flawed fund: the IMF's misplaced priorities," *New Republic*, 9 March: 16–17.

Todorov, T. (1984) *The Conquest of America: The Question of the Other*, New York: Harper and Row.

——(1993) *On Human Diversity: Nationalism, Racism, and Exoticism in French Thought*, trans. by C. Porter, Cambridge, MA: Harvard University Press.

——(1999) *The Conquest of America*, 2nd edn, Norman: University of Oklahoma Press.

Tsui, A. (1998) "Benefits and pitfalls of financial liberalisation," ABD–OECD Forum on Asian Perspectives, 3 June, Paris.

Tucker, L. (1997) "Child slaves in modern India: the bonded labor problem," *Human Rights Quarterly* 19: 572–629.

Tucker, L. and Ganesan, A. (1997) "The small hands of slavery: India's bonded child laborers and the World Bank," *Multinational Monitor* 8, 1: 17.

U Win Aung (1998) "Peaceful, modern, developed and democratic Myanmar," *Presidents and Prime Ministers* 8: 1–6.

UNICEF (1997) *The State of the World's Children*, New York: UNICEF. Online. Available http://www.unicef.org/sowc97/ (May 2001).

United Nations (1948) *Universal Declaration of Human Rights*, adopted and proclaimed by General Assembly Resolution 217 A (III), Paris, 10 December. Online. Available http://www.un.org/Overview/rights.html (May 2001).

US Government Immigration Commission (1911) *Report of the Immigration Commission: Statements and Recommendations Submitted by Societies and Organizations Interested in the Subject of Immigration*, Document No. 764, Washington, DC: US Government Printing Office.

Van Der Dennen, J. and Falger, V. (1990) "Introduction," in J. Van Der Dennen and V. Falger (eds) *Sociobiology and Conflict: Evolutionary Perspectives on Competition, Cooperation, Violence and Warfare*, London: Chapman and Hall.

Van Praag, M.C. van W. (1987) *The Status of Tibet: History, Rights, and Prospects in International Law*, London: Wisdom Publications.

Venturino, S. (1997) "Reading negotiations in the Tibetan diaspora," in F.J. Korom (ed.) *Constructing Tibetan Culture: Contemporary Perspectives*, Quebec: Heritage Press.

Volunteer for Humanity (13 July 1998) Early Documentation (3).

Wade, R. (1996) "The World Bank and the art of paradigm maintenance: the East Asian miracle in political perspective," *New Left Review* 217: 3–36.

Wade, R. and Veneroso, F. (1998) "The Asian crisis: the high debt model versus the Wall Street–Treasury–IMF complex," *New Left Review* 228: 3–24.

Wald, K.D. (1991) "Social change and political response: the silent religious cleavage in North America," in G. Moyser (ed.) *Politics and Religion in the Modern World*, London: Routledge.

Walker, J.R. (1917) "The Sun Dance and other ceremonies of the Oglala division of the Teton Dakota," *Anthropological Papers* 16: 51–221.

Walker, R.B.J. (1989) "The prince and 'the pauper': tradition, modernity, and practice in the theory of international relations," in J. Der Derian and M. Shapiro (eds) *International/Intertextual Relations: Postmodern Readings of World Politics*, Lexington, MA: Lexington Books.

——(1992) "Gender and critique in the theory of international relations," in V.S. Peterson, *Gendered States: Feminist (Re)Visions of International Relations Theory*, Boulder, CO: Lynne Rienner.

——(1993) *Inside/Outside: International Relations as Political Theory*, Cambridge: Cambridge University Press.

——(1997) "The subject of security," in K. Krause and M.C. Williams (eds) *Critical Security Studies: Concepts and Cases*, Minneapolis: University of Minnesota Press.

Wallerstein, I. (1976) *The Modern World System: Capitalist Agriculture and the Origins of the European World Economy in the Sixteenth Century*, New York: Academic Press.

——(1991) "The construction of peoplehood: racism, nationalism, ethnicity," in E. Balibar and I. Wallerstein (eds) *Race, Nation, Class: Ambiguous Identities*, London and New York: Verso.

Walsh, E. (1999) "Racial slayer killed himself in struggle," *Washington Post*, 6 July: A1.

Waltz, K.N. (1959) *Man, the State, and War: A Theoretical Analysis*, New York: Columbia University Press.

——(1979) *Theory of International Politics*, Reading, MA: Addison-Wesley.

Ware, V. (1996) "Defining forces: 'race,' gender and memories of empire," in I. Chambers and L. Curti (eds) *The Post-Colonial Question: Common Skies, Divided Horizons*, London and New York: Routledge.

Waring, M. (1988) *If Women Counted; A New Feminist Economics*, New York: Harper and Row.

Washburn, W.E. (1987) "Cultural relativism, human rights and the AAA," *American Anthropologist* 89: 939.

Waziri, A.A. (1986) "A brief history of carpet weaving in Bhadohi–Mirzapur belt," in AICMA *Silver Jubilee Special*, Bhadohi: All India Carpet Manufacturers' Association.

Weiner, M. (1996). *The Child and the State in India. Child Labor and Education Policy in Comparative Perspective*, Princeton: Princeton University Press.

Weldes, J. (1999) *Constructing National Interests: The United States and the Cuban Missile Crisis*, Minneapolis: University of Minnesota Press.

Weldes, J., Laffey, M., Gusterson, H. and Duvall, R. (eds) (1999) *Cultures of Insecurity: States, Communities, and the Production of Danger*, Minneapolis: University of Minnesota Press.

Wendt, A.E. (1987) "The agent–structure problem in international relations theory," *International Organization* 41, 3: 335–70.

Westerlund, D. (ed.) (1996) *Questioning the Secular State: The Worldwide Resurgence of Religion in Politics*, New York: St Martin's Press.

Whitt, L.A. (1995) "Indigenous peoples and the cultural politics of knowledge," in M.K. Green (ed.) *Issues in Native American Cultural Identity*, New York: Peter Lang.

Whitworth, S. (1989) "Gender in the inter-paradigm debate," *Millennium* 18, 2: 265–72.

WIDER (2001) *Governing Globalization: Don't Wait for Crisis Before Reforming Key Institutions, Experts Warn: News Release*. Online. Available http://www.wider.unu.edu/publications/ (2 May 2001).

Willey, P. and Emerson, T.E. (1993) "The osteology and archaeology of the Crow Creek massacre," *Plains Anthropologist* 38, 145: 227–69.

Williams, B. (1991) *Stains on My Name, War in My Veins: Guyana and the Politics of Cultural Struggle*, Durham, NC: Duke University Press.

Williams, P. and Chrisman, L. (eds) (1993) *Colonial Discourse and Post-Colonial Theory: A Reader*, Hertfordshire: Harvester Wheatsheaf.

Willis, J.D. (ed.) (1987) *Feminine Ground: Essays on Women and Tibet*, Ithaca NY: Snow Lion Publications.

Wilmer, F. (1993) *The Indigenous Voice in World Politics: Since Time Immemorial*, Newbury Park, CA: Sage.

——(1996) "Indigenous peoples, marginal sites and the changing context of world politics," in F.A. Beer and R. Hariman (eds) *Post-Realism: The Rhetorical Turn in International Relations*, East Lansing, MI: Michigan State University Press.

Wilson, R.A. (ed.) (1997) *Human Rights, Culture and Context: Anthropological Perspectives*, London: Pluto Press.

Wolf, E.R. (1997) *Europe and the People Without History*, Berkeley: University of California Press.

Wood, C.H. (1982) *International Migration and International Trade: World Bank Discussion Papers 160*, Washington, DC: World Bank.

Woodiwiss, A. (1998) *Globalization, Human Rights and Labour Law in Pacific Asia*, Cambridge: Cambridge University Press.

World Bank (1993) *The East Asian Miracle*, New York: Oxford University Press.

World Socialist Web Site (1999) "The Indonesia elections and the struggle for democracy." Online. Available http://www.wsws.org/articles-/1999/may1999/indo-m21.shtml (May 1999).

Wuthnow, R. (1986) "Religion as 'sacred canopy' in the modern world," in J.D. Hunter and S.C. Ainlay (eds) *Making Sense of Modern Times: Peter L. Berger and the Vision of Interpretive Sociology*, London: Routledge and Kegan Paul.

——(1991) "Understanding religion and politics," *Daedalus* 120, 3: 1–20.

Xu, M. (2000) "Tibet question: a new cold war," paper presented at the World Congress of International Political Science Association, 5–11 August 2000, Quebec City.

Yuval-Davis, N. (1993) "Gender and nation," *Ethnic and Racial Studies* 16, 4: 621–32.

Zimmerman, L.J. and Bradley, L.E. (1993) "The Crow Creek massacre: initial coalescent warfare and speculations about the genesis of extended coalescent," *Plains Anthropologist* 38, 145: 215–26.

INDEX